The Author

Christopher McIntosh is the author of many books and articles in a variety of areas ranging from travel to biography. After a career in writing and publishing, he recently entered the academic world. His other works include *The Swan King*, a biography of Ludwig II of Bavaria, and *The American Express Pocket Guide to Washington, DC*.

Contributors

1983 edition: Susan Heller Anderson (Nightlife, Shopping); Robert Barton-Clegg (Wines in Paris); William Green (Nightlife). This edition: Nathalie Guillemot (Hotels, Restaurants, Nightlife, Shopping); Katherine McIntosh (throughout).

Acknowledgments

The author and publishers would like to thank the following for their invaluable help and advice: Dr & Mme Robert Amadou, Christine Baker, Annabel Campbell, Pamela Fiori, Pauline Hallam and Martine Williams of The French Government Tourist Office, Nicolle Roques of the Paris Tourist Office, M. & Mme Robert Jaulin, Hugh Johnson, Margaret Keith, Gisela Kirberg, Jeremy Lawrence, Barbara McIntosh, Elizabeth de Farcy.

Quotations

The author and publishers are grateful to those listed below for their kind permission to reprint the following extracts: Jonathan Cape Ltd (UK) and Charles Scribner's Sons (USA) for the quotation from *A Moveable Feast* by Ernest Hemingway (p122); André Deutsch Ltd (UK) and Harper and Row Publishers Inc. (USA) for quotations from *Quartet* by Jean Rhys (p85 and p98).

Few travel books are without errors, and no guidebook can ever be completely up to date, for telephone numbers and opening hours change without warning, and hotels and restaurants come under new management, which can affect standards. While every effort has been made to ensure that all information is accurate at the time of going to press, the publishers will be glad to receive any corrections and suggestions for improvements, which can be incorporated in the next edition, but cannot accept any consequences arising from the use of the book, or from the information contained herein. Price information in this book is accurate at the time of going to press, but prices and currency exchange rates do fluctuate. Dollar amounts relate to exchange rates in effect in mid-1988.

Series Editor David Townsend Jones
Editor (first edition 1983) Fiona Duncan
Editor (second edition 1986) Leonie Hamilton
Editor (this edition) Helen Panay
Art Editor Eric Drewery
Designer (this edition) Christopher Howson
Illustrators Jeremy Ford (David Lewis Artists), Illustra Design Ltd, Rodney Paull
Production (this edition) Stewart Bowling

Edited and designed by
Mitchell Beazley International Limited
Artists House, 14-15 Manette Street,
London W1V 5LB

Published by Prentice Hall Trade Division
A Division of Simon & Schuster, Inc.
Gulf & Western Building
One Gulf & Western Plaza
New York, New York 10023
PRENTICE HALL is a trademark of Simon & Schuster, Inc.

Library of Congress Cataloging-in-Publication Data
McIntosh, Christopher.
The American Express pocket guide to Paris.
Includes index.
1. Paris (France)—Description—1975-—Guidebooks. I. Title
DC708.M46 1989 914.4′3604838
88-24642
ISBN 0-13-025230-1

Maps in 4-color by Clyde Surveys Ltd, Maidenhead, England, based on copyrighted material of IGN-Paris 1982; authorization no. 99-0595; extracts from maps of the Institute Géographique National — France
Metro and autobus plans, property of the RATP, 53 ter, Quai des Grands-Augustins, Paris 6e
Typeset by Bookworm Typesetting, Manchester, England
Printed in Shekou, China

Contents

How to use this book

The American Express Pocket Guide to Paris is an encyclopedia of travel information, organized in the sections listed on the previous page. There is also a comprehensive **index** (pages 208-219), which is accompanied by a **gazetteer** (pages 219-224) of the most important streets that are shown in the full-color **maps** at the end of the book.

For easy reference, all major sections (*Sights and places of interest*, *Hotels*, *Restaurants*) and other sections as far as possible are arranged alphabetically. For the organization of the book as a whole, see *Contents*. For individual places with no separate entry in *Sights and places of interest*, see the *Index*.

Abbreviations

As far as possible only standard abbreviations have been used. These include days of the week and months, points of the compass (N, S, E and W), street names (Av., Bd., Pl., Sq.), Saint and Sainte (St and Ste), rooms (rms), C for century, and measurements.

Bold type

Bold type is used in running text primarily for emphasis, to draw attention to something of special interest or importance. It is also used in this way to pick out places — shops or minor museums, for example — that do not have separate descriptions of their own. In such cases it is usually followed in brackets by the address, telephone number and details of opening times printed in italics. In *Hotels* and *Restaurants*, look to see whether places mentioned in bold in one entry also have a separate entry of their own.

Cross-references

A special type has been used for cross-references. Whenever a place or section title is printed in *sans serif italics* (for example, *Arc de Triomphe* or *Basic information*) in the text, this indicates that you can turn to the appropriate heading in the book for further information.

Cross-references always refer to sections of the book — *Basic information*, *Planning and walks*, *Hotels* — or to entries in

How entries are organized

Paradis, Rue de

10e. Map 5E10. Métro Château-d'Eau, Poissonière.

Unexpectedly situated in the rather characterless hinterland between the *Grand Boulevards* and the Gare du Nord, this street is monopolized by retailers of glass and ceramic tableware. The goods displayed in these stores range from the breathtakingly vulgar to the stunningly beautiful. At no. 30 is the **Musée des Cristalleries** (Glassware Museum), run by the firm of Baccarat and containing a dazzling collection of glass objects dating from the early 19thC to the present day (*open Mon-Fri 9am-5.30pm, Sat 10am-noon, 2-4pm; closed Sun*).

Another interesting museum on the street is the **Musée de l'Affiche** (Poster Museum) at no. 18. This is one of Paris's most recently founded museums, which holds temporary exhibitions. It is housed in the former premises of a ceramics manufacturer with a superbly tiled entrance way (*open noon-6pm; closed Tues*).

Sights and places of interest, such as *St-Roch* or *Vincennes*.
For easy reference, use the running heads printed at the top of the page (e.g., **Bois de Boulogne**, p50 or **Hotels**, p124).

Floors

To conform with local usage, "first floor" is used throughout the book to refer to the floor above the ground floor, "second floor" to the floor above that, and so on.

Map references

Each of the full-color maps at the end of the book is divided into a grid of squares, identified vertically by letters (A, B, C, D, etc.) and horizontally by numbers (1, 2, 3, 4, etc.). A map reference identifies the page and square in which the street or place can be found — thus the **Arc de Triomphe** is located in Map **6**F3.

Price categories

Price categories are denoted by the symbols □ I□ II□ III and IIII which signify cheap, inexpensive, moderately priced, expensive and very expensive, respectively. In the cases of hotels and restaurants these correspond approximately with the following actual prices, which give a guideline at the time of printing. Although actual prices will inevitably increase, in most cases the relative price category — for example, expensive or cheap — is likely to remain more or less the same.

Price categories	Corresponding to approximate prices for **hotels** *double room with bath; single not much cheaper*	for **restaurants** *meal for one with service, taxes and house wine*
□ cheap	under $30	under $15
I□ inexpensive	$30-60	$15-25
II□ moderate	$60-90	$25-40
III expensive	$90-190	$40-80
IIII very expensive	over $190	over $80

Bold blue type for entry headings.

Blue italics for address, practical information and symbols. For list of symbols see page 6 or back flap of jacket.

Sans serif italics used for cross-references to other entries or sections.

Bold type used for emphasis.

Black text for description.

Entries for hotels, restaurants, shops, etc., follow the same organization, and are usually printed across a half column.

In hotels, symbols indicating special facilities appear at the end of the entry, in black.

Étoile ✿
3 Rue de l'Étoile, 75017 Paris
☎43-80-36-94 ⓣ 642028. Map 6E3 II□ 25 rms 25 AE CB DC VISA Métro Ternes.
Location: Close to the Arc de Triomphe. A small, intimate hotel where you can live like a prince, almost for a song, with color TV, minibar, direct-dial telephone, thick wall-to-wall carpets and functional modern furniture in your room, plus a bar and a mini-library in the lobby.

Key to symbols

- Telephone
- Telex
- Recommended sight
- Worth a visit
- Good value (in its class)
- Tourist information
- Parking
- Building of architectural interest
- Church or cathedral
- Free entrance
- Entrance fee payable
- Entrance expensive
- Photography forbidden
- Guided tour
- Cafeteria
- Special interest for children
- Hotel
- Simple hotel
- Luxury hotel
- Cheap
- Inexpensive
- Moderately priced
- Expensive
- Very expensive
- Rooms with private bath/shower
- Air conditioning
- Residential terms available
- American Express
- Carte Blanche
- Diners Club
- MasterCard/Eurocard
- Visa/Carte Bleue
- Secure garage
- Quiet hotel
- Elevator
- Facilities for disabled people
- TV in each room
- Telephone in each room
- Dogs not allowed
- Garden
- Good view
- Swimming pool
- Tennis
- Conference facilities
- Bar
- Restaurant
- Simple restaurant
- Luxury restaurant
- A la carte available
- Set (fixed-price) menu available
- Good wines
- Open-air dining
- Disco dancing
- Nightclub
- Live music
- Dancing
- Revue
- Members only

Introduction

To go to Paris is not just to experience a beautiful city (some would say the most beautiful of all); it is to feel the pulse of a civilization that has held the admiration of the world for centuries — the civilization of France. The Parisian regards Paris not only as the capital of a great nation but as the capital of all true culture. He can be forgiven if he feels he has no need to travel. Why should he go to the Himalayas when he can look at the Ile de la Cité reflected in the waters of the Seine? Why should he learn other languages when his own is so perfect?

All Parisians, even the most humble, are conscious of their heritage. They may seem arrogant, but they have much to be arrogant about. Think of the countless songs that have been written about Paris, the books that have been inspired by it, the millions of pilgrims who have beaten a path to the city over the centuries.

"Paris," wrote Henry James, "is the greatest temple ever built to material joys and the lust of the eyes." His words are as apt today as when they were written in the 1870s. Paris is indeed a temple, the doors of which are always open to anyone who is receptive to beauty, civilized values and delight of the senses. As a result, the visitor is almost inevitably transformed in some way by the experience. But it is not enough just to walk in and passively wait for the magic to work. You must become a little bit Parisian in the way you look at things and the way you react, understand something of the spirit of Paris and the history and traditions that have shaped it. Also you must avoid rigid preconceptions and expectations. Allow for the unexpected and elusive moments of pleasure that Paris so often gives.

People come here from all over the world and for a variety of reasons: to see the Paris of the travel brochures (the Eiffel Tower, Notre-Dame and Montmartre); to explore the great museums such as the Louvre; to enjoy the famous quality of Parisian food and wine; or to test Paris' reputation as the city of Eros. If you come for the last reason you may not find exactly what you had expected. Paris is not a particularly wicked city compared with many others in Europe despite its red-light districts and its scarlet reputation that was established half a century ago, but what it does have is a subtle sensuality that bubbles over into the whole environment, giving zest to the very air of the city. You can see it in the easy flow of intimacy between young lovers strolling by the Seine or idling on the café terraces. It is impossible not to be affected by it, however imperceptibly.

As for the inhabitants of Paris themselves, they can seem somewhat abrupt, even abrasive to the outsider, but this is usually a surface impression. Underneath you will find a good-humored courtesy and friendliness that does them credit considering the massive influx of visitors with whom they have to deal each year.

Remember that Paris is not just a vast museum for tourists. It is also a busy, thriving metropolis, and one that has coped superbly well with the problems that face all modern cities. While other capitals crumble under the strain, Paris remains one of the smoothest-running urban machines in the world.

What might be called "Greater Paris," that is the whole metropolitan area, covers 479sq.km (185sq. miles) and has a population of about 8½ million. But the part we are focusing on here is the city proper, which is surrounded by the beltway known as the Périphérique. This area, cut in half by the Seine, covers only 106sq.km (41sq. miles) and has just over 2½ million inhabitants;

although these are very tightly crammed into a small area, somehow, by a miraculous sleight of hand, Paris gives an impression of spaciousness. The Métro carries 4 million passengers a day — and does the job with the minimum of fuss and with subsidized fares at a very low cost. For the entertainment of its citizens and visitors, the city has some 10,000 restaurants, cafés and nightclubs, 80 municipal libraries, 2 city orchestras, 66 theaters, 27 café-theaters, 220 galleries/465 movie theaters, and 48 concert halls.

Paris is a veritable ocean. Throw in the plumb line and you will never know the depth of it . . .

Balzac, *Père Goriot*

In order to keep the city running smoothly, it is administered by a city council of 109 members who are elected for a 6yr term and meet in the palatial Hôtel de Ville. The council is headed by a mayor who also sits for a 6yr term. For over a century the city had no mayor and was controlled by the national government through a Prefect of Paris. This arrangement proved unsatisfactory because, as a result, the people of Paris had no direct influence over the running of their city. It was partly this state of affairs that enabled some disastrous mistakes in planning to be made during President Pompidou's era, such as the building of the Tour Montparnasse and the construction of a highway along part of the riverside footpath. In 1977 Paris was once again given a mayor in the person of the energetic Jacques Chirac, also twice prime minister, who has done much to improve the quality of life and the environment in Paris.

Those who knew Paris 30yrs ago, in the days before President de Gaulle came to power, will remember a city that seemed to be a symphony in shades of gray, the prevailing atmosphere one of picture-postcard scruffiness and exquisitely faded charm. The water was hazardous, plumbing was often antediluvian and the franc was a precarious currency. Today all this has changed. Although there is still a great deal of poverty in evidence, Paris, along with the whole of France, has become much more buoyant. A massive cleaning program has transformed the city center, so that the boulevards and squares now gleam with pristine tones of cream and gold. Most houses now have modern plumbing, and old buildings are being restored district by district with grants from the city. The fall in the population, one of the great problems of recent years, is being stemmed by housing subsidies and by an attempt to attract light industries back into the city instead of pushing them out in accordance with the mistaken policy exercised before 1977. The recent prosperity of Paris, and of France, and its desire to keep pace with modernization, is well illustrated by the construction of La Défense, the huge, gleaming "Manhattan-sur-Seine" complex of skyscrapers lying just outside the city limits — but not far enough for those who find it a bleak and inhospitable environment.

Inevitably there has been a price to pay for progress. Many charming old districts, such as Montparnasse and the Belleville/Ménilmontant area, have been violated; fine buildings, such as the former Halles market, have been pulled down; and brash new ones, such as the Tour Montparnasse, have been erected, marring the fine-grained visual quality of the city. But the scars are few compared with many other great cities; and at the end of the day, Paris remains essentially the same glorious temple that it was in Henry James' time.

Before you go

Documents required

For all visitors to Paris except citizens of EEC countries and Switzerland a visa is required for entry; for citizens of the EEC a passport or identity card will suffice. Vaccination certificates are not normally required unless traveling from some eastern, South American or African countries. For stays of longer than three months you will need to apply for a *carte de séjour*, which can be obtained from: Préfecture de Police, Service des Étrangers, 163 Rue Charenton, 12e ☎43-41-81-49.

If arriving by car, you need a valid driver's license (not provisional) and must be 18 or over. An international driver's license is not required. You also need the vehicle registration certificate (logbook), a national identity plate or sticker at the rear of the vehicle, and a certificate of insurance or international green card proving that you have third-party insurance.

Travel and medical insurance

It is advisable to travel with an insurance policy which covers loss of deposits paid to airlines, hotels, tour operators, etc., the cost of dealing with emergency requirements, such as special tickets home and extra nights in a hotel, as well as a medical insurance policy. Contact your local travel agent before departure.

The IAMAT (International Association for Medical Assistance to Travelers) has a list of English-speaking doctors who will call for a fee, as well as having member hospitals and clinics in France. Membership of IAMAT is free. For information and a directory of doctors and hospitals, write to: IAMAT, 736 Center St., Lewiston, NY 14092.

There is an American hospital in Paris at 63 Bd. Victor-Hugo, Neuilly-sur-Seine ☎47-47-53-00, which accepts Blue Cross and Blue Shield medical insurance. It has a 24hr emergency department. There is also a British Hospital at 3 Rue Barbès, Levallois-Perret ☎47-58-13-12.

Money

The unit of currency is the franc (f), which consists of 100 centimes (c). There are coins for 5c, 10c, 20c and ½f, 1f, 2f, 5f and 10f, and notes for the following amounts: 20f, 50f, 100f, and 500f. There is no limit to the amount of currency you can bring into France, but you can take out no more than 12,000f when you leave, unless large sums are declared on entry. On days preceding public holidays banks are open only in the morning, though exchange bureaux are open longer.

Travelers cheques issued by American Express, Thomas Cook, Barclays and Citibank are widely recognized; make sure you read the instructions included with your travelers cheques. It is important to note separately the serial numbers of your cheques and the telephone number to call in case of loss. Specialist travelers cheque companies such as American Express provide extensive local refund facilities for lost cheques through their own offices or agents.

Major international credit cards such as American Express, Diners Club, Eurocard (MasterCard) and Carte Bleue (Visa) are widely accepted — but do not assume that your card will always be accepted. Carte Blanche is less widely accepted. American citizens who also bank in Europe can make use of the Eurocheque Encashment scheme whereby they can cash personal checks with a Eurocheque Encashment card.

Customs

If you are visiting France for less than six months, you are entitled to bring, free of duty and tax, all personal effects, except tobacco goods, alcoholic drinks and perfume, which you intend to take with you when you leave. Make sure that you are carrying dated receipts for the most valuable items such as cameras and watches, or you may be charged duty.

In the following list of duty-free allowances, the figures in brackets show the increased allowances for goods obtained duty and tax paid in the EEC. All limits apply to travelers over 17 years of age.

Tobacco If you live in an EEC country, you are allowed 300 cigarettes *or* 150 cigarillos *or* 75 cigars *or* 400g tobacco. If you live outside Europe, you are allowed 400 cigarettes *or* 200 cigarillos *or* 100 cigars *or* 500g tobacco; however, if you live in a non-EEC European country you are allowed half this amount.

Alcoholic drinks 1(1.5) liters spirits (over 22% alcohol by volume) *or* 2(3) liters of alcoholic drinks of 22% alcohol or less; *plus* 2(5) liters still wines.

Perfume 50g/60cc/2fl oz(75g/90cc/3fl oz).

Other goods Commodities and articles to the value of 300f (2,400f); 150f (620f) for travelers under 15.

Certain prohibited and restricted goods cannot be imported, such as narcotics, gold and weapons. A more detailed list can be obtained from the French Government Tourist Office. Visitors are exempt from the Value Added Tax system above a certain limit, although it should be remembered that the business of filling in the necessary forms can be complicated and time-consuming.

Getting there

By air: There are daily flights to Paris from many parts of the world, including many cities in the USA, and an almost hourly shuttle service from London (Heathrow) run by British Airways and Air France.

Paris has two airports, both are within easy reach: Orly, south of the city, and the ultra-modern Roissy/Charles de Gaulle, north of the city.

Cities in the USA that are connected by direct nonstop flights to France's capital include New York, Washington, Boston, Chicago, Miami and Houston. In Canada there are flights from Montreal and Toronto. Flying time from the East Coast is approximately 6½hrs by subsonic jet, 3½hrs by Concorde. Airlines that fly direct include the following:

From New York: Air France, Pan Am and TWA fly daily; Pakistan International fly several times weekly. Air France fly Concorde daily to Roissy/Charles de Gaulle.

From Washington: TWA have a daily service and Air France fly three times a week.

From Boston: TWA fly daily to Charles de Gaulle.

From Chicago: TWA fly daily and Air France fly three times a week.

From Miami: Aeromexico fly three times a week.

From Montreal and Toronto: Air France and Air Canada fly daily.

Getting there from Britain

For those who are traveling to the Continent from Britain there are several options available. Regular flights leave from London's Heathrow, Gatwick and City airports as well as from Manchester, Dublin and some other British cities. There is also a regular train-and-ferry service from London's Victoria station to Paris (Gare du Nord), and a faster but more expensive train-and-hovercraft service from Charing Cross and Victoria stations. There are several different routes across the Channel using ferry or hovercraft for both car and foot passengers; the fastest route by ferry is from Dover to Calais, although hovercraft, from Dover to Calais or Boulogne, is even quicker (about 35mins to Calais in good weather). The cheapest, though not the most luxurious, means of getting to Paris from England is by bus. Inquire at a travel agent for all further travel details. It is wise to reserve in advance, especially during the summer.

Climate

In Aug the majority of Parisians evacuate the city as Paris can be unpleasantly and surprisingly hot—temperatures average 23°C (75°F) and you might think you were much farther south. Fall is often warm; spring brings clear blue skies, but can be chilly; and in winter it can be uncomfortably cold and damp.

Clothes

The famous Parisian *chic* is evident wherever you go; both men and women are beautifully turned out, rarely casually or scruffily dressed. The French are, however, tolerant of informality: you don't normally need to wear a tie to a smart restaurant, and women can wear pants on virtually any occasion. Pack one warm garment even for spring, a light raincoat and an umbrella.

General delivery (poste restante)

The central post office in Paris, at 52 Rue du Louvre, 75001 Paris ☎40-28-20-00, will keep all mail marked *poste restante* unless specifically addressed to another Parisian post office. The addressee's name should be written clearly on the envelope. You will need identification when you collect your mail and may be charged a small fee. If the letter is addressed to two people, e.g., Mr and Mrs, addressees must collect the letter together. Travel companies such as American Express will also hold mail.

Getting around

From the airports to the city

Trains run every 15mins between 5.30am-11.30pm to the Gare du Nord from Roissy/Charles de Gaulle (☎48-62-22-80); the journey takes 35mins. Buses take 1hr and leave every 15mins, between 6am-11pm, for the Porte Maillot terminal (☎42-99-20-18). The public buses are slow and relatively expensive.

From Orly Airport (☎48-84-32-10), south of Paris, trains take approximately 40mins and leave every 15mins for the Gare d'Austerlitz, Gare St-Michel or Gare d'Orsay. The bus goes to Les Invalides air terminal (☎43-23-97-10) every 15mins between 5.45am-11pm; the journey takes 40mins. The public buses (nos. 215, 285 and 183a) are slow.

There are taxis at each airport, but a taxi ride to your destination will certainly be expensive and will not necessarily be any quicker. From Roissy/Charles de Gaulle Airport allow at least 45mins or more in rush hour. From Orly Airport is a cheaper, shorter trip and should take only half an hour.

Public transportation

Paris has one of the best public transportation systems in the world, run by the RATP (*Réseau Autonome du Transport Parisien*) 53bis Quai des Grands Augustins, 6e. Bus and Métro tickets are interchangeable, and are cheaper if you buy a book (*carnet*) of ten, obtainable from bus or Métro stations, *tabacs* and, increasingly, from slot machines in the street. *Billets de tourisme* (tourist tickets) are also obtainable. Best value for a short stay is the *coupon jaune*, giving you unlimited travel on buses, Métro and RER for a week. To go with it you will be given a *carte orange* for which you need a passport-size photograph of yourself.

Métro

Unlike some subway systems, the Paris Métro is very clean, efficient and quite easy to understand. The lines are designated by numbers and by the names of the end stations. There are two classes, and smoking is prohibited. Inside Paris one ticket is valid no matter how far you go or how many changes you make and you must retain your ticket until you reach your destination. The Métro runs between 5.30am-1.15pm. Métro stations are a popular haunt of musicians; there are also beggars and pickpockets, so it is advisable to be vigilant.

RER (Réseau Express Régional)

This is a fast suburban service which consists of three lines. Line A goes from St-Germain-en-Laye to Boissy-St-Léger; line B goes from Robinson St-Rémy-les-Chevreuse to Roissy and Mitry-Claye and line C connects Versailles and St-Quentin-en-Yvelines to Dourdan. Within Paris there is a flat fare, which is only slightly more expensive than the Métro. I you want to change from RER to Métro, or vice versa, you must buy a *billet combiné* (combined ticket).

Buses

On the buses, one ticket is valid for up to two *sections* (fare stages) and two tickets for three stages or more within the city boundary. When you enter the bus you have to *composter* (punch) your ticket by inserting it into the machine behind the driver. On most routes the buses run from 7am-9pm.

Taxis

At the last count there were 14,300 taxis in the city. They can be ordered by telephone (☎42-02-42-02; you can pay with an American Express card), or hailed in the street. Cabs have two lights on the roof: both lit means free, one lit means occupied, both off means the driver is on his way home. All registered cabs are equipped with meters. There is a surcharge on Sun and between 10pm-6.30am. You will also pay more if you are carrying a lot of heavy or bulky objects or if you are picked up at a station — you can avoid the latter charge (and the lines) by walking 50m (50yds) away from the station.

Taxis will theoretically hold up to four passengers, but most drivers nowadays will only take three unless you offer them financial inducement in advance. This can be awkward for families or groups of four. Under normal circumstances the driver expects a tip of 12-15%.

Beware of pirate drivers who offer to take you for a "first-class" fare which will be about five times the normal one.

Getting around by car

If you value your bumpers it is wise to avoid driving in Paris — the Parisian drives as if he were in a bumper car at a fairground, and parks as though he were shoving a book into a tight shelf. The parking problem is severe, and meters are ubiquitous — they run from 9am-7pm, watched over by once purple-, now blue-uniformed ladies popularly known as *aubergines*. There are also several underground, multistory parking garages. In *zones bleues*, identified by a circular blue sign posted on the curbside, a *disque de contrôle* (parking disc) must be displayed; it is obtainable from hotels, garages and tourist offices.

Speed limits are 60kph (37mph) in the city and in built-up areas, 80kph (50mph) on the Périphérique 90kph (56mph) on country roads, 130kph (80mph) on toll autoroutes and 110kmp (68mph) on free autoroutes and four-lane highways. It is good to be aware of the following laws: cars coming from the right have the right of way unless otherwise indicated; seat-belts are compulsory; and children under ten years of age are forbidden travel in the front seat.

For further information contact the *Automobile Club de France*, 6 Pl. de la Concorde, 8e ☎42-65-34-70, or the *Touring Club de France*, 8 Rue Lucien-Sampaix, 10e ☎42-40-76-09. Automobile clubs such as the AAA, AA and RAC are affiliated with these clubs.

Renting a car

It is worth renting a car for trips out to the suburbs or out of the city, though within the center rentals are expensive and garages are scarce.

Most international car rental companies have offices in Paris and there are also many reliable and often cheaper Paris firms. Payment by credit card avoids the need for a large cash deposit. A current driver's license is required, and the minimum age is usually 21, although some companies have raised it to 25. Make sure the car is fully insured, even if it means making separate arrangements for insurance against damage to other vehicles and injury to your passengers.

Many companies are represented at the airports, and it is possible to make fly-drive arrangements before you leave your home country.

Getting around on foot

Paris is a city built on a human scale and is therefore easy and pleasant to walk in. If you are not in a hurry, this is the most enjoyable way of getting about. A combination of walking and use of the excellent public transportation system is ideal for exploring Paris. Crossing busy roads, however, can be hazardous, even at *passages cloutés* (pedestrian crossings), where drivers are supposed to give way but often don't. It is safer still to walk in one of the traffic-free zones. There is one around Les Halles and another to the E of the Pl. St-Michel.

Railroad services

France's railroad services are run by the SNCF (*Societé Nationale de Chemins de Fer*). When traveling by train, you must validate any ticket purchased in France by stamping it at the machine at the entrance to the platform. If you fail to do this you will be treated as if you are traveling without a ticket and will have to pay a surcharge.

The rail stations listed below are terminals for specific areas of France.

Gare d'Austerlitz (southwest)
Gare de L'Est (east)
Gare de Lyon (southeast)
Gare Montparnasse (west)
Gare du Nord (north)
Gare St-Lazare (northwest)

For general information ☎45-82-50-50.

Domestic airlines

Air Inter is France's major internal airline. The central office is at 12 Rue Castiglione, 1er ☎45-39-25-25.

Other transportation

If you are prepared to brave the traffic, bicycling in Paris can be an excellent way of exploring the city. Bicycles can be rented from the following:

La Maison du Vélo 8 Rue de Belzunce, 10e ☎42-81-24-72
Paris-Vélo 4 Rue du Fer-à-Moulin, 5e ☎43-37-59-22
Vélocipèderie de la Grande Gerbe 92210 Saint-Cloude ☎47-71-64-29

Montgolfier first flew his balloon over Paris in the 18thC and it has been possible to fly over the city ever since. Today, a series of tours over the city and as far afield as the Loire Valley is offered by Paris-Hélicoptère, Héliport de Paris, 15e ☎45-54-04-44.

On-the-spot information

Public holidays

New Year's Day, Jan 1; Easter Monday; Labor Day, May 1; VE Day, May 8; Ascension Day (sixth Thurs after Easter); Whit Monday (second Mon after Ascension); Bastille Day, July 14; Assumption, Aug 15; All Saints' Day, Nov 1; Remembrance Day, Nov 11; Dec 25. Most museums close but many shops and restaurants remain open.

Time zones

Like most Western European countries, France is 1hr ahead of GMT in the winter and 2hrs ahead in summer, i.e., 6hrs ahead of the eastern USA most of the year.

Banks and currency exchange

In general, banks are open Mon-Fri 9am-4.30pm, but there are no standardized banking hours. They all close in the afternoon before a public holiday. *Bureaux de change* at airports and in most stations stay open late and are often open at weekends. The American Express Office, 11 Rue Scribe, 9e ☎42-66-09-99, is open Mon-Fri 9am-5pm.

Money can also be exchanged in larger hotels, but the rate will not be as good as in banks. It is advisable to ask about exchange rates and commission as they vary from place to place. Remember that you need your passport when changing money. Checks backed by a Eurocheque Encashment Card can be cashed at all banks displaying the sign.

Shopping hours

Department stores usually remain open from 9.30am-6.30pm without interruption from Mon-Sat, and some are open until 8pm on Wed. Smaller boutiques though generally open from about 10am-6pm Mon-Sat, although they may close for an hour at lunch. While neighborhood shops often observe the traditional Mon closing, stores in the center stay open. And, while Aug was once the universal vacation month, most of the larger shops now stay open all summer.

Rush hours

Between 7.30-9am and 5-7pm, the Métro is packed with workers going to and from their offices. On Fri evenings the weekend traffic out of Paris is very heavy. It is also wise to avoid leaving Paris on the first and last days of Aug when schools and factories have their vacations.

Postal and telephone services

Post offices are marked with a blue swallow on a white disc or by the letters *PTT*, and are open Mon-Fri 8am-7pm, Sat 8am-noon. The main post office is at 52 Rue du Louvre, 1er (see *Useful addresses* p17 for other post offices). Stamps can be bought in *tabacs*, hotels and newsstands, and in coin-operated vending machines, painted yellow. Mailboxes are also yellow and marked *boîte aux lettres*. Allow 7-10 days for mail to reach France and for your letters to reach home. Addresses in Paris must all include the post code, which combines 750- with the numbers of the *arrondissements*. Thus the post code in the 1er is 75001, and so on, to the 20e where the post code is 75020. Conversely, the post code shows at once the *arrondissement* in which any address is to be found.

Telegrams can be sent from any post office or over the telephone. For telegrams in English ☎42-33-21-11; in French ☎42-33-44-11. For a small extra charge, letters sent by the *pneumatique* (fast-letter service) will be delivered within 3hrs. This applies only within the Paris area.

Public telephones are found in post offices and cafés as well as on the street. Most telephones take 50c, 1f and 5f coins. The ringing signal is a shrill intermittent tone, while the engaged signal is less shrill and more rapid. For international calls, look in the telephone code book to see if the place can be dialed direct. Otherwise dial 19, wait for the second tone, then dial 33 for the international operator.

In difficulties ask the operator (12 for inquiries, 13 for connections).

Public rest rooms

Those who knew Paris before modernization started in earnest will remember the abundance of quaint, perforated-iron kiosks known as *vespasiennes*. Now there are only about 100 of these urinals left. However, modern public rest rooms are scattered around the city and, on the whole, are clean and well looked after. You will find them in many Métro stations and public parks and you can use the facilities of nearly every café. Often you will find a lady presiding who will charge a nominal sum; otherwise in cafés leave a small tip in the saucer at the bar before you leave.

Electric current

The electric current is 220V (50 cycles AC). Plugs are two-pin round, standard European. Adapters (*transformateurs*) can be bought at any good electrical shop or at large department stores in Paris, or before you leave home.

Laws and regulations

There are no particularly surprising laws in France; laws against drug abuse are as strongly enforced as elsewhere, with greater penalties for the buying and selling of drugs. Hitchhiking is forbidden on *autoroutes* although it is tolerated on other roads. Smoking in public places such as post offices and banks is forbidden and incurs a fine.

Customs and etiquette

The French are among the most manner-conscious of all nations, and observe a rather rigid code of behavior in personal relationships which is, however, just beginning to be broken down by the younger generation. This consciousness is exemplified by the *vous* and *tu* forms of address; the former applying to everyone except relations, close friends and children. Hand-shaking is common when greeting or saying goodbye among friends, as well as between acquaintances and strangers, and close friends kiss each other energetically on alternate cheeks at least twice and often three times. It is customary when addressing someone to say "Madame" or "Monsieur" without using a surname.

Tipping

Tipping is still widely practiced in France, although most bars, restaurants and hotels include 15% service and taxes in their prices (*service compris*). If a meal or the service has been particularly good, show your appreciation by leaving a small tip. For *service non compris*, a tip of between 12 and 18% is advisable.

Small tips of up to a few francs should be given to cloakroom attendants, tour guides, doormen, hairdressers and movie-theater usherettes. Airport and railway porters have a fixed charge per item, while taxi drivers expect about 10-15%.

Disabled travelers

Special facilities for the disabled are becoming more and more usual in France and the French Government Tourist Office has some useful leaflets describing them. The leaflets also indicate which hotels cater to wheelchairs. The *Comité National Français de Liaison pour la Réadaptation des Handicapés* (38 Bd. Raspail, 75007 Paris ☎45-48-90-13) will give general advice and guidance to the handicapped person traveling in France. In their series *Touristes quand même*, they publish an excellent booklet containing invaluable information for the handicapped visitor to Paris. For further information, US visitors should send off for the International Directory of Access Guides, Travel Survey-Rehabilitation International, USA, TL Department, 1123 Broadway, New York, NY 10010.

Recently the Paris transportation authority, the RATP, has taken the imaginative step of instituting a free escort service for handicapped people called *Voyages accompagnés*. For information ☎40-02-37-25.

If you are traveling by train, it is worth finding out the facilities available before you leave, as over 300 railroad stations have wheelchairs and mobile steps.

Local publications

Useful publications giving full details of current events, movies, theaters, shows, sports, etc., are the weekly *Pariscope* and *Officiel des Spectacles* (the latter has a useful day-by-day section listing lectures and guided tours of the city), the monthly *Ville de Paris*, and *Passion*, an English-language magazine that appears about every six weeks. These can all be bought at most newsstands.

Major English bookshops include:

Attica 34 Rue des Écoles, 5^e
Brentano's 37 Av. de l'Opéra, 2e
Galignani 224 Rue de Rivoli, 1er
Le Nouveau Quartier Latin 78 Bd. St-Michel, 6e
Shakespeare and Co. 37 Rue de la Bûcherie, 5e
W.H. Smith and Son 248 Rue de Rivoli, 1er
The Village Voice 6 Rue Princesse, 6e. Not just a bookshop but also a snug little café.

Useful addresses

Tourist information

The *Office du Tourisme* (tourist office) has several branches throughout Paris. Major branches can give hotel information and make reservations for you. The central office is at: 127 Av. des Champs-Élysées, 8e ☎47-23-61-72. Open 9am-10pm in season, 9am-6pm off season, Sun and hols.

American Express Travel Service 11 Rue Scribe, 9e ☎42-66-09-99 is a valuable source of information for any traveler in need of help, advice or emergency services.

Telephone services

Tourist events in English ☎47-20-88-98
Speaking clock ☎36-99
Traffic report ☎48-58-33-33
Weather ☎36-69-00-00

Post offices

Central post offices (open 24hrs):
52 Rue du Louvre, 1er ☎40-28-20-00
71 Av. des Champs-Élysées, 8e ☎43-59-55-18

Tour operators

The following companies run bus tours around Paris:
American Express 11 Rue Scribe, 9e ☎42-66-09-99
Cityrama 4 Pl. des Pyramides, 1er ☎42-60-30-14
Paris-Vision (France-Tourisme) 214 Rue de Rivoli, 1er ☎42-60-31-25

River trips

Bateaux Mouches Port de la Conférence, 8e ☎42-25-22-55
Vedettes de Paris Quai Montebello, 5e ☎43-26-92-55
Vedettes de Paris Ile-de-France Port de Suffren, 7e ☎47-05-71-29
Vedettes Parisiens Tour Eiffel Port de la Bourdonnais, 7e ☎47-05-50-00
Vedettes du Pont Neuf 1er ☎46-33-98-38

Airlines

Air France 119 Av. des Champs-Elysées, 8e ☎45-35-61-61
Air Inter 12 Rue de Castiglione, 1er ☎42-60-36-46
British Airways 91 Av. des Champs-Élysées, 8e ☎47-78-14-14
Pan Am 1 Rue Scribe, 9e ☎42-66-45-45

Places of worship

For information contact the *Centre d'information et documentation réligieux* at Notre-Dame cathedral ☎46-33-01-01
American Cathedral 25 Av. George V, 8e ☎47-20-17-92
American Church 65 Quai d'Orsay, 7e ☎47-05-07-99
St George's (Anglican) 7 Rue Auguste-Vacquerie, 16e ☎47-20-22-51
St Joseph's English-speaking Catholic Church 50 Av. Hoche, 8e ☎42-27-28-56
St Michael's English Church (Anglican) 5 Rue d'Aguesseau, 8e ☎47-42-70-88
Synagogue 44 Rue de la Victoire, 9e ☎42-85-71-09
Union Liberale Israelite Synagogue (English Rabbi) 24 Rue Copernic, 16e ☎47-04-37-27

Major libraries

American Library 10 Rue du Général-Camou, 7e ☎45-51-46-82

Bibliothèque du Centre National d'Art et de Culture Georges-Pompidou Pl. Georges-Pompidou et Rue Beaubourg, 4e ☎42-77- ☎42-77-12-33
Bibliothèque Nationale 58 Rue de Richelieu, 2e ☎47-03-81-26
British Council Library 11 Rue Constantine, 7e ☎45-55-95-95

Embassies and consulates

Australia 4 Rue Jean-Rey, 15e ☎40-59-33-00
Austria 6 Rue Fabert, 7e ☎45-55-95-66
Belgium 9 Rue de Tilsitt, 17e ☎43-80-61-00
Canada 35 Av. Montaigne, 8^{e} ☎47-23-01-01
Denmark 77 Av. Marceau, 16^{e} ☎47-20-32-66
Finland 39 Quai d'Orsay, 7e ☎47-05-35-45
Germany, West 13/15 Av. F.D. Roosevelt, 8e ☎42-99-78-00
Greece 17 Rue Auguste-Vacquerie, 16e ☎47-23-72-28
Ireland 12 Av. Foch, 16e ☎45-00-20-87
Italy 47 Rue de Varenne, 7e ☎45-44-38-90
Japan 7 Av. Hoche, 8e ☎47-66-02-22
Netherlands 7 Rue Eblé, 7e ☎43-06-61-88
New Zealand 7/ter Rue Léonard-de-Vinci, 16e ☎45-00-24-11
Norway 28 Rue Bayard, 8e ☎47-23-72-78
South Africa 59 Quai d'Orsay, 7e ☎45-55-92-37
Spain 13 Av. George V, 8e ☎47-23-61-83
Sweden 17 Rue Barbet-de-Jouy, 7e ☎45-55-92-15
Switzerland 142 Rue de Grenelle, 7e ☎45-50-34-46
United Kingdom 35 Rue de Faubourg-St-Honoré, 8e ☎42-66-91-42
United States 2 Av. Gabriel, 8e ☎42-96-12-02

Conversion tables

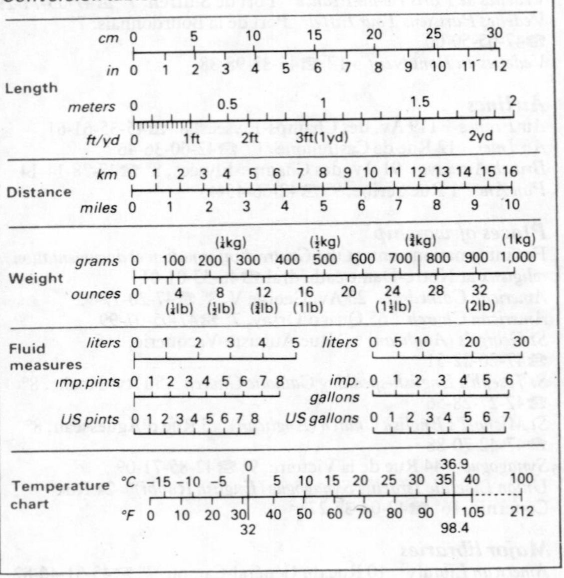

Emergency information

Emergency services

Police ☎17
Ambulance ☎43-78-26-26
Fire (*Sapeurs pompiers*) ☎18

There is no unified ambulance service — the operator will offer you the numbers of several companies.

Hospitals

For information on hospitals ☎40-27-30-00

Medical emergencies

For Paris' 24hr service ☎45-67-50-50 or ☎47-07-77-77 or ☎43-37-77-77 for *SOS Médecin*, also 24hrs.

All-night pharmacy

To find out the nearest *pharmacie de garde* (all-night pharmacy), call the *mairie* of the arrondissement where you are staying.

Help lines

English Samaritan services 3-11pm ☎47-23-80-80

Automobile accidents

—Do not admit liability or incriminate yourself.
—Ask any witness(es) to stay and give a statement.
—Contact the police.
—Exchange names, addresses, car details and insurance company details with any other drivers involved.
—In serious accidents, ask the police to contact the sheriff's clerk (*huissier*) to make out a legally acceptable account of the incident. In a dispute his report will be authoritative.

Car breakdowns

—Put on flashing hazard warning lights, and place a portable warning triangle 50m (55yds) behind the car.
—Telephone police or call the *Touring Club de France* if you are a member of an automobile club affiliated with this association. If in a rented car, call the number you have been given.

Lost passport

Contact the local police and your consulate immediately.

Lost travelers cheques

Notify the local police immediately, then follow the instructions provided with your travelers cheques, or contact the issuing company. Contact your consulate or American Express if you are stranded with no money.

Lost property

If you have lost something on the street or on public transportation, go to the *Bureau des Objets Trouvés*, 36 Rue des Morillons, 15e ☎48-28-36-36 or ☎45-31-14-80. Report all losses to the police.

Emergency phrases

Help! *Au secours!*
There has been an accident. *Il y a eu un accident*
Where is the nearest telephone/hospital? *Où se trouve le téléphone/l'hôpital le plus proche?*
Call a doctor/ambulance! *Appelez un médecin/une ambulance!*
Call the police! *Appelez la police!*

Time chart

The Gallic origins

3rdC BC The Parisii, a Gallic tribe, made the Ile de la Cité their fortified capital. They prospered from fishing and the river trade, supplemented by hunting and gathering.

The Roman era

52BC-c.AD486 In 52BC Julius Caesar's Roman legions conquered the island, which they called Lutetia, and in due course it became an important Roman center, with the governor's palace erected on the island, and the forum and arena on the Left Bank.

As early as the 2nd or 3rd decade AD, a society of mercantile watermen had established itself in Paris, and these boatmen were to play an important role in the history of the city. The symbol of Paris is a ship, and her motto is *fluctuat nec murgitur* (she is tossed but does not sink).

In AD250 St Denis came to Paris with two companions, introducing Christianity and becoming the city's first bishop. But Rome was still officially pagan, and St Denis was decapitated by an angry mob.

Several Roman emperors stayed at Lutetia, notably Constantius Chlorus, who made it his headquarters in AD292. His son, Constantine the Great (c.274-337), who made Christianity the official religion of the empire, also stayed there for a time, as did Julian the Apostate, who was proclaimed Emperor of Rome at the city in 360. In that year Lutetia was named Paris.

Early Middle Ages

5thC AD In the vacuum left by the departure of the Romans, Paris stood in danger of being engulfed by barbarians, but the morale of the city was restored by a religious young woman from Nanterre, named Geneviève, who, in 451, correctly assured the Parisians that Attila the Hun and his hordes would not attack the city. Ten years later, when the city was besieged by the Franks, she helped relieve the famine. She later became Paris' patron saint.

The Merovingians

508-752 In 508 the Christianized King Clovis of the Frankish Merovingian line made Paris his capital, and it remained in Merovingian hands until 752, when the last of the dynasty, Childeric, was finally ousted by Pepin the Short, father of Charlemagne.

The Carolingians

752-987 This was an uneasy period for Paris, with frequent raids by Norman pirates, culminating in a great siege in 885-86 which ended in defeat of the Normans by Count Eudes, who was elected King of France in 887.

The Capetians

987-996 Hugues Capet elected King of France at Senlis; his territories were not extensive, however. His descendants reigned from father to son until 1328, establishing the principle of monarchy in France.

996-1108 The reigns of Robert the Pious, Henri I and Philippe I. The building of Notre-Dame cathedral was begun in Philippe's reign.

1108-37 Louis VI the Fat. During his reign the mercantile waterman's guild was established.

1137-80 Louis VII the Young, husband of Eleanor of Aquitaine. Having been divorced by Louis, Eleanor married, in 1152, Henri Plantagenet, subsequently Henry II of England, who ruled both NW France and Aquitaine, far more land than the French king.

1180-1223 Philippe Auguste erected the fortress of the Louvre and constructed a great defensive wall around the city: the Philippe-Auguste girdle. His reign also laid the foundation of the University of Paris.

1223-85 The reigns of Louis VIII, Louis IX, who was canonized, and Philippe III. In the reign of Louis IX the Sorbonne was established. Pierre de Montreuil built Sainte Chapelle to house relics of the true cross which Louis IX had bought for a vast sum, and he worked on the St-Denis basilica, prototype of the Gothic style. In 1260 the guild of mercantile watermen officially took over the city administration, with their provost acting as mayor.

1285-1314 Philippe IV the Fair. Fair only in looks, Philippe was a cruel and vicious king who crushed the Templars, persecuted the Jews and caused misery and poverty among the Parisians through high taxation, forced labor and debasement of the currency. It was he who built the Conciergerie.

1314-28 The reigns of Louis X the Quarrelsome, Jean I (a few months only), Philippe V the Tall, and Charles IV the Fair, the last of the Capetians.

The Valois

1328-50 Philippe VI, first of the Valois kings, whose reign marked the start of a chaotic period for France; the country weakened by war with England.

1350-64 Jean II. During his reign, Étienne Marcel, provost of the merchants and mayor of the city, led a popular uprising (1358).

1364-80 Charles V the Wise, who restored order to France, built the Bastille and erected a wall on the Right Bank beyond the Philippe-Auguste wall.

1380-1422 Charles VI the Well-Beloved. A weak king, under whose reign the English invaders, and with them chaos, returned. In 1420 Paris was captured by Henry V of England.

1422-61 Charles VII the Victorious. In 1429 Joan of Arc relieved Orléans, but tried in vain to recapture Paris, which remained in English hands until 1436, when Charles VII recaptured it. In 1431 Henry VI of England had himself crowned at Notre-Dame. In 1453 the English withdrew from all of France apart from Calais.

1461-83 Louis XI. A cunning, authoritarian, but enlightened king. Under his reign Paris prospered. The city's first school of medicine was opened and its first printing press was set up, at the Sorbonne, by the German Ulrich Gering.

1483-1515 The reigns of Charles VIII and Louis XII, each of whom married Anne of Brittany; her lands were ceded to France after her death in 1514.

1515-47 François I, great patron of the arts, who was with Leonardo da Vinci when he died near Amboise. François helped to introduce the Italian Renaissance to France and acquired the first masterpieces for the

Louvre. He began the reconstruction of the Louvre, and under his rule many magnificent buildings grew up in Paris.

1547-59 Henry II was killed in a jousting accident. His wife, Catherine de Medici, began building the Tuileries palace.

1559-89 The reigns of Henry II and Catherine de Medici's three sons, François II, Charles IX and Henry III. During this period Paris was the scene of many bloody conflicts between the Catholics and the Protestants, culminating in the St Bartholomew's Day massacre in 1572, when 3,000 Huguenots were murdered in Paris. Henry III was then forced to flee Paris when the Catholic league turned against him in 1588. He was murdered at St-Cloud while laying siege to Paris in 1589. During his reign the construction of the Pont-Neuf was begun.

The Bourbons

1589-1610 Henry IV *Le Vert Galant* allayed for a time the religious uprisings by converting from Protestantism to Catholicism, and issuing the Edict of Nantes, allowing Protestants some freedom of worship. In Paris, he extended the Louvre and the Tuileries, created the Place des Vosges and completed the Pont-Neuf. He was assassinated by a fanatic named Ravaillac.

1610-43 Louis XIII. The l7thC was known as "Le Grand Siècle." Paris was now growing more magnificent as each year passed. The Ile St-Louis was developed, Marie de Medici built the Luxembourg palace and Cardinal Richelieu, first minister and far more powerful than the young king, built the Palais-Royal and founded the Académie Française. The arts flourished, but brutality was also much in evidence, and gruesome public executions were frequent. In 1622 Paris became a bishopric.

1643-1715 Louis XIV the "Sun King," under whom France reached its zenith of power and prestige. Versailles was built and became the royal court, and the capital acquired many splendid new buildings and institutions: Les Invalides, the Salpêtriére, Gobelins, the Louvre colonnade and the Comédie Française.

In 1648, when Louis XIV was still too young to rule, Paris had been convulsed by the Fronde uprising, a bloody protest against the centralized power of the monarchy. When Louis XIV took the reigns of power in 1661, he tightened the grip, abolishing the municipal institutions and the office of mayor so that Paris was ruled by the state. This was to remain the case until the Revolution. In 1685 the king ordered the Revocation of the Edict of Nantes, causing thousands of Protestants to flee.

1715-74 Louis XV's reign saw financial crisis, disastrous wars with England over Quebec and West Indian colonies and the growing unpopularity of the crown. But Paris was further enriched architecturally by the Panthéon, the Palais-Bourbon and the Pl. de la Concorde. Another encircling wall, known as the Farmers General Wall, was erected as a customs barrier, and further added to popular discontent.

1774-92 Louis XVI. The government was now financially, politically and morally bankrupt. Discontent among all classes was rife. Louis XVI, an ineffectual king, was unable to stem the tide of revolution.

The Revolution

1789-99 One of the great turning points in the history of France, and of the world. The Revolution began symbolically with the storming of the Bastille on July 14, 1789. In Oct of that year a mob invaded Versailles, and the king returned to Paris. At first he remained on the throne while various reforms were carried out, but by 1792 he was deposed and imprisoned, and the following year he and his queen Marie-Antoinette were executed. Extremists, including Danton, Marat and Robespierre, instituted the Reign of Terror, in which 2,800 people in Paris alone were executed, and another 14,000 in the rest of the country.

The Reign of Terror finally ended with the fall and execution of Robespierre in 1794. The Revolution itself could be said to have ended when, in 1799, Napoleon appointed himself First Consul — in effect, dictator of France.

The Consulate and First Empire

1799-1815 After a period of stagnation Paris began, under Napoleon, to enjoy a new period of expansion and prosperity. The Farmers General Wall was done away with, the office of Prefect of the Seine was created, and many of the exiled nobles returned. The foundations of large-scale industry were laid, and the arts flourished once more. On the negative side, the city was terrorized by Napoleon's police under the ruthless first Prefect of Police, Joseph Fouché.

In 1804 Napoleon had himself crowned Emperor in Notre-Dame. Under Napoleon, France was master of Europe until 1814 when Paris fell to the invading allied armies. Napoleon abdicated at Fontainebleau and was exiled to the island of Elba. In 1815 he escaped from Elba and returned to France for his final campaign, which ended in June 1815, at Waterloo. He was sent again into exile, this time to St Helena, where he died in 1821.

The Restoration

1815-48 After Napoleon's defeat, the Bourbon monarchy was restored and Louis XVIII crowned king. He was succeeded in 1824 by Charles X who himself was ousted during the short-lived July Revolution in Paris in favor of Louis-Philippe of the Orléans line.

These were years of modernization for Paris. Between 1812-15 the Ourcq, St-Denis and St-Martin canals were built, and 1837 saw the opening of the first French railroad line, from Paris to St-Germain-en-Laye. Pleasure steamers plied the Seine; gas lighting was installed; and a new wall, the Thiers fortifications, was erected around the city in 1841-45. Although this has vanished, it marks the line of the present Périphérique boundary. In 1832, 19,000 Parisians perished in a cholera epidemic.

The Second Republic and Second Empire

1848-70 Louis-Philippe was ousted in the "Year of Revolutions" which swept through Europe in 1848; a Second Republic was declared, only to give way to a Second Empire under Napoleon III (Emperor 1852-

70). This was a key period in the development of Paris. Baron Haussmann, Prefect of the Seine, drove his great boulevards through the city, which was divided into the present 20 *arrondissments*. Haussmann's idea behind the building of the boulevards was partly to create streets too wide for barricading in case of further street fighting and revolution. Among other new buildings, the Opéra and Les Halles sprang up, as well as the main stations, the sewers (*égouts*) and the Bois de Boulogne and Vincennes. In 1855 and 1867 spectacular international exhibitions were held in the capital. This gay period was ended by the Franco-Prussian War.

The Third Republic

1870-1945 The Third Republic was declared in 1870. Napoleon III surrendered at Sedan. Paris was besieged by the Prussians and fell to them in early 1871. St-Cloud château was burned down, and Napoleon III fled to England. Paris was taken over by the revolutionary government, the Commune, between Mar and May 1871, but it was finally suppressed; the city suffered terrible damage.

After Paris had recovered, a new period of expansion and prosperity set in, symbolized by the World Exhibition of 1889 and the building of the Eiffel Tower. The year 1900 saw the opening of the first Métro line in Paris, and the city then played host to another World Exhibition.

During the World War I Paris sustained little physical damage, and comparatively little during World War II, but the population suffered much under Nazi occupation. The city was liberated in 1944. General de Gaulle led the new provisional government, which held power for just over a year.

Since World War II

1946 The inauguration of the Fourth Republic. A new constitution. Government by coalition of Socialists, Communists, Radicals and Catholic Democrats.

1958 French army takes power in Algeria. Fourth Republic falls and de Gaulle forms Fifth Republic.

1959 EEC (Common Market) founded, with France included among the six members.

1962 Algeria granted independence.

1968 Student riots and demonstrations in the streets of Paris, reaching a peak in May.

1969 Electoral defeat of de Gaulle. Election of Pompidou as President. Les Halles market transferred to Rungis, in the suburbs.

1970 De Gaulle's death.

1973 Montparnasse Tower and the beltway completed.

1974 Pompidou's death. Election of Giscard d'Estaing as President.

1977 Election of Jacques Chirac as the first mayor of Paris since 1871.

1981 Electoral defeat of Giscard d'Estaing. A socialist government elected under the leadership of François Mitterrand.

1986 Appointment of a conservative prime minister, Jacques Chirac, under the continued presidency of Mitterrand.

1988 Re-election of Mitterrand and appointment of a socialist prime minister, Michel Rocard.

Architecture

Perhaps the most striking element of Paris' architecture as a whole is its visual harmony. Although there are samples of many different periods and styles, each blends with the other in such a way as to create an environment that is both diverse and unified. Only in the past two decades have any really disruptive elements been introduced, and even these have not destroyed the overall sense of unity. Most of the great architectural styles are represented in Paris, from Roman to ultramodern.

Roman *(1st-4thC AD)*
The only examples of the Roman era still visible are the Thermal Baths in the Cluny museum and the restored Arènes de Lutèce. Both are evidence of the heavy, grandiose and colossal elements typical of Roman concrete and brick architecture, with massive walls, barrel vaults and big rounded arches. France has comparatively few Gallo-Roman remains, though some traces are evident in the foundations of Paris' St-Denis basilica.

Romanesque *(11th and 12thC)*
Skillful use was made of vaulting and pillars to create a striking sense of space. The style is characterized by rounded arches and monumental simplicity, the columns smooth except perhaps for a flourish of carving at the top. There are few examples of the Romanesque in Paris, but those that there are include the bell tower and small chancel columns of St-Germain-des-Prés, the capitals in St-Pierre, Montmartre, the belfry which abuts the apse in St-Germain l'Auxerrois and part of St-Denis basilica crypt.

Early Gothic *(12th and 13thC)*
In place of the rounded arches and plainness of the Romanesque style, the Gothic builders used pointed arches and made great play with stained glass, sculptural decoration and vertical emphasis. It was pre-eminently an ecclesiastical style, with the ideal of liberating as much space as possible, creating a sense of void over solid and, by using verticals rather than horizontals, of producing a soaring, aspiring quality. The precursor of Gothic architecture in Europe was the St-Denis basilica designed by architect Abbot Suger, on the outskirts of Paris, but the outstanding example in Paris is the magnificent cathedral of Notre Dame; construction began in 1163 and was completed in 1330. In early Gothic churches, windows were small and decoration comparatively restrained.

Mid-Gothic *(13th and 14thC)*
As the Gothic builders became more skillful at distributing weight through the use of buttresses, they were able to liberate larger areas of wall for stained-glass windows. The Sainte Chapelle in Paris is one of the finest examples of this period to be found anywhere. The chapel, designed by Pierre de Montreuil, is on two stories, with the walls of the upper story completely covered in stained-glass windows. The cathedral of Notre-Dame at Chartres is one of the most renowned examples of the High Gothic architectural style, and served as the experiment which opened the way for later, yet more spectacular architectural developments.

Late or Flamboyant Gothic *(15thC)*
In the late phase of the Gothic period, builders abandoned themselves to exuberant decoration characterized by Flamboyant (literally "flame-like") window tracery and columns rising into fan-vaulting, as in the ambulatory of St-Séverin. Other buildings which illustrate this style in Paris are the Hôtel de Sens, Hôtel de Cluny, the Tour St-Jacques and the Billettes Cloister. The church of St-Maclou at Rouen is also an outstanding example of this exotic phase.

Renaissance (*16thC*)
Military campaigns in Italy led the French to a gradual understanding of the Renaissance. In architecture it was marked by a return to Greek and Roman forms and motifs: allegorical sculptures, Classical columns, balustrades, pediments and rounded arches. François I, who reigned from 1515-47, was a patron of the arts who did much to introduce Renaissance architecture to France, where one of its leading exponents was Pierre Lescot who designed part of the Cour Carrée in the Louvre. Other examples are the courtyard of the Hôtel Carnavalet, the Porte Dorée (golden gate) at Fontainebleau built by Gilles Le Breton, the Fontaine des Innocents at Les Halles and, in interior decoration, the rood-screen at St-Étienne-du-Mont.

French Baroque and Classicism (*17thC*)
In essence, the Baroque style is a more ornate version of Renaissance Classicism. Versailles is a striking instance; another is the E wing of the Louvre. In ecclesiastical architecture, Baroque includes the so-called "Jesuit" style (based on the church of Gésu in Rome). Paris has many churches of this kind: the Sorbonne church, Val-de-Grâce, St-Paul-St-Louise, all featuring the

The Thermal Baths, reminder of Paris' Roman heritage, show the typical use of brickwork and rounded arches.

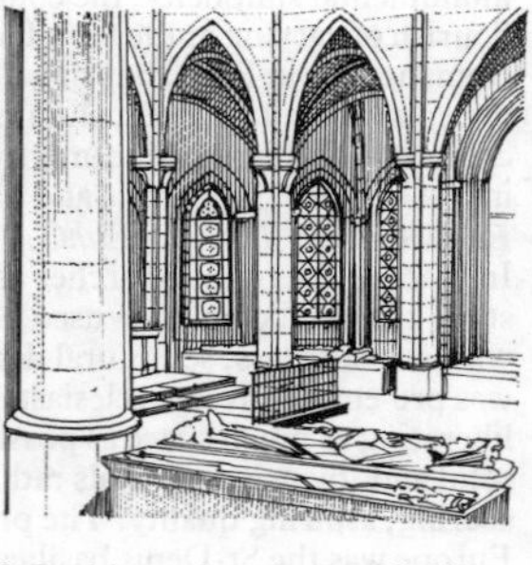

St Denis' crypt is a mixture of Gothic and Romanesque.

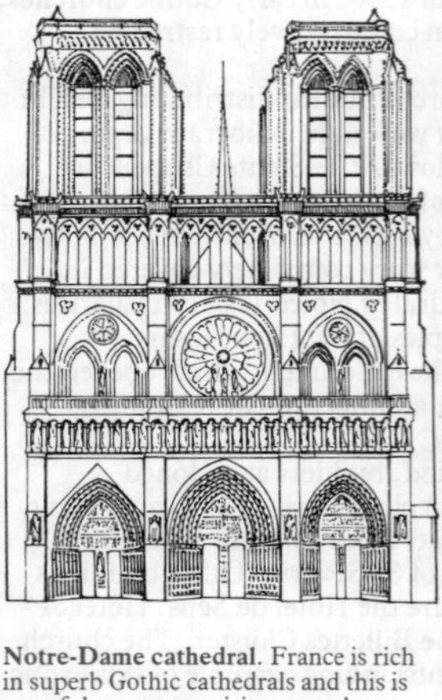

Notre-Dame cathedral. France is rich in superb Gothic cathedrals and this is one of the most exquisite examples.

Sainte Chapelle shows perfectly the Gothic architect's desire to free space for light and stained glass.

Baroque predilection for domes. One of the outstanding architects of this period was François Mansart, who also gave his name to the high-pitched "Mansard roof" as on the Val-de-Grâce cloister. His relative, Jules Hardouin-Mansart, married Baroque with the simple lines of Classicism in many superb secular buildings, notably Pl. Vendôme, and the Dôme church at Les Invalides.

***Rococo** (18thC)*

After the death of Louis XIV, and with a child king on the throne, a new, lighter style made its appearance. This was Rococo, called *Rocaille* in French and more restrained than elsewhere, and mainly a feature of interior decoration—for example, in Paris, the Oval Salon of the Hôtel de Soubise. The Hôtel Biron, now the Rodin museum, is an example of the refined elegance of the Rococo age. The 18thC Classical, monumental architecture reached its peak in Paris with such buildings as the Louvre Colonnade, the École Militaire, and the Pl. de la Concorde.

***Neo-Classicism** (late 18th-early 19thC)*

Between the 1780s and 1830s, interest in Classical antiquity was revived in contrast to the ornate Rococo style. Once again, order, balance and clarity became the keynotes. The Madeleine illustrates

The Flamboyant Gothic style of the late 15thC **Hôtel de Sens** is seen to good effect in the highly decorated turrets and battlements.

The courtyard of the **Hôtel Carnavalet**, *below left*, is a clear example of the influence of the Italian Renaissance.

The Dôme church, *below right*, is Jules Hardouin-Mansart's classically proportioned Baroque masterpiece.

the style, and Paris has the supreme examples of Neo-Classicism in the Panthéon and the chapel at Versailles.

Consulate, Empire and Restoration *(early 19thC)*
Buildings of this period are unimaginative, a heavier version of the Classical style, as in the Arc de Triomphe and Madeleine.

Second Empire and early Third Republic *(mid-19th to early 20thC)*
Uniformity went by the board and was replaced by a great mixture of styles, drawing on many periods. Advanced engineering, exemplified by the Eiffel Tower, was often combined with great extravagance of decoration, at least partly because the structural problems solved by the use of iron allowed great decorative freedom. A typical Second-Empire building is Charles Garnier's Opéra, which opened in 1875 and is one of the largest theaters in the world. The feeling of extravagant rhetoric was carried into the Third Republic period with such edifices as the Sacré-Coeur, the Grand Palais and Petit Palais, and Pont Alexandre III. The Grand Paris interior illustrates particularly well the combination of practicality and decorativeness, and its use of stylized natural forms can be seen as a precursor of the architectural experiments that characterize Art Nouveau.

The Hôtel Biron shows the refined gracefulness of the *Rocaille* period.

The Panthéon is a supreme example of Neo-Classicism.

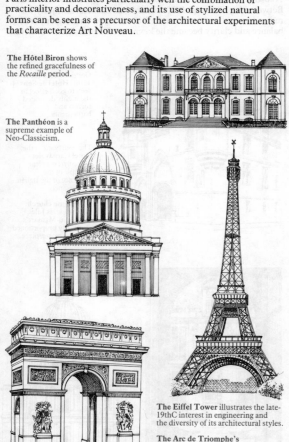

The Eiffel Tower illustrates the late-19thC interest in engineering and the diversity of its architectural styles.

The Arc de Triomphe's monumental grandeur elaborates on pure Classicism.

Art Nouveau *(late 19th to early 20thC)*
Here the mood changes markedly. Art Nouveau decorations on buildings are fluid in appearance, characterized by many elongated loops and an almost Baroque elaborateness of form. It is most obvious in the original cast-iron entrances to some Métro stations (for example at the Louvre), designed by the leading architect of Art Nouveau in Paris, Hector Guimard.

Interwar *(1918-39)*
Modernity and functionalism are the keynotes, but echoes of tradition were still retained. The combination can be seen in the Palais de Chaillot which was erected for the Paris Exhibition of 1937, and the Palais de Tokyo, where full use is made of reinforced stone and concrete.

Postwar *(1945 to present day)*
Le Corbusier was the most famous exponent of modern architecture in France, but Paris has little of his work. Bleak expanses of glass, steel and concrete can be seen particularly in the Tour Montparnasse, La Défense and the Palais de Congrès. But Paris also has some fine modern buildings such as the Pompidou Center and the Forum des Halles.

The Opéra, Charles Garnier's Second Empire extravaganza.

One of the many remaining early 20thC Art Nouveau **Métro station** entrances.

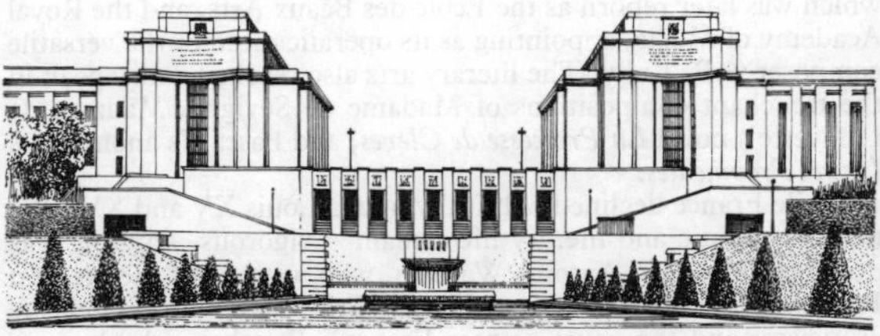

The Palais de Chaillot marries functionalism with more traditional elements of style.

Exposed tubes on its exterior characterize Rogers and Piano's exciting **Pompidou Center**.

The arts in Paris

It is hard to pinpoint the beginning of Paris' greatness as a center of art and culture. Its cultural roots can be traced back as far as the Gallo-Roman period, but in more recent times a point of origin can be seen in François Villon, widely considered to be France's (and Paris') first great poet, who combined the writing of brilliant verse with living as a thief and brigand among the maze of tiny streets and taverns of the Latin Quarter.

Villon was a forerunner of the great cultural outburst that came when Italian Renaissance art and architecture reached France under the influence of François I. François also stimulated a new interest in music, particularly songs accompanied by the lute, which were often heard in his court, and brought important Italian masterpieces — among them the *Mona Lisa* — to Paris. Literature also flourished, and it was at this time that François Rabelais (c.1494-c.1553) wrote his roistering and satirical stories of *Gargantua and Pantagruel*. The same period saw the emergence of the *Pléiade*, a group of seven poets who broke with medieval traditions, introduced Italian Renaissance forms and established the alexandrine (line of 12 syllables) as the basic meter of French verse. One of the group was Jean Antoine de Baïf, who in 1571 established an Academy of Music and Poetry in Paris.

The 17thC, known as "Le Grand Siècle", was culturally even richer. Drama was dominated by the tragedians Corneille (1606-84) and Racine (1639-99), and by Molière (1622-73), an actor and writer of sparkling comedies. The fondness at this time for strict rules of form in literature and drama found its most extreme expression in the Académie Française, founded by Cardinal Richelieu in 1635.

More stimulating and less conservative as a milieu for writers and thinkers were the *salons*, which began to flourish at about the same time, and provided a forum for philosophers and literati to exchange ideas and sharpen their wits on one another.

When Louis XIV began to rule in 1661, he proved to be the greatest patron of the arts since François I. He founded the Comédie Française, the Royal Academy of Painting and Sculpture, which was later reborn as the École des Beaux Arts, and the Royal Academy of Music, appointing as its operatic director the versatile composer G.B. Lully. The literary arts also reached a new peak in the trenchant compositions of Madame de Sévigné, Madame de Lafayette's novel *La Princesse de Clèves*, and Pascale's anonymous *Lettres Provinçales*.

While France declined politically under Louis XV and XVI, the nation's artistic and literary life remained vigorous. Painting was dominated by Jean-Antoine Watteau, who was one of the greatest Rococo artists, then later Jean-Honoré Fragonard with his delicate eroticism, and the court painter François Boucher, who became famous for his portraits of Louis XV's mistress, Madame de Pompadour. In music, operas were composed by Rameau and the German, Gluck, who had his greatest successes in Paris. And the world of letters resounded to the philosophy and wit of Voltaire, Rousseau, Montesquieu, Diderot and d'Alembert. In such company, the *salons* enjoyed their heyday under the patronge of some of the most fashionable hostesses, among them were Madame de Lambert, Madame de Deffand, Madame Geoffrin and Madame de Pompadour herself. Despite revolution and war, the early half of the 19thC saw the flowering of great artists in all fields: Eugène Delacroix in painting, Berlioz in music, Balzac and Victor Hugo in literature.

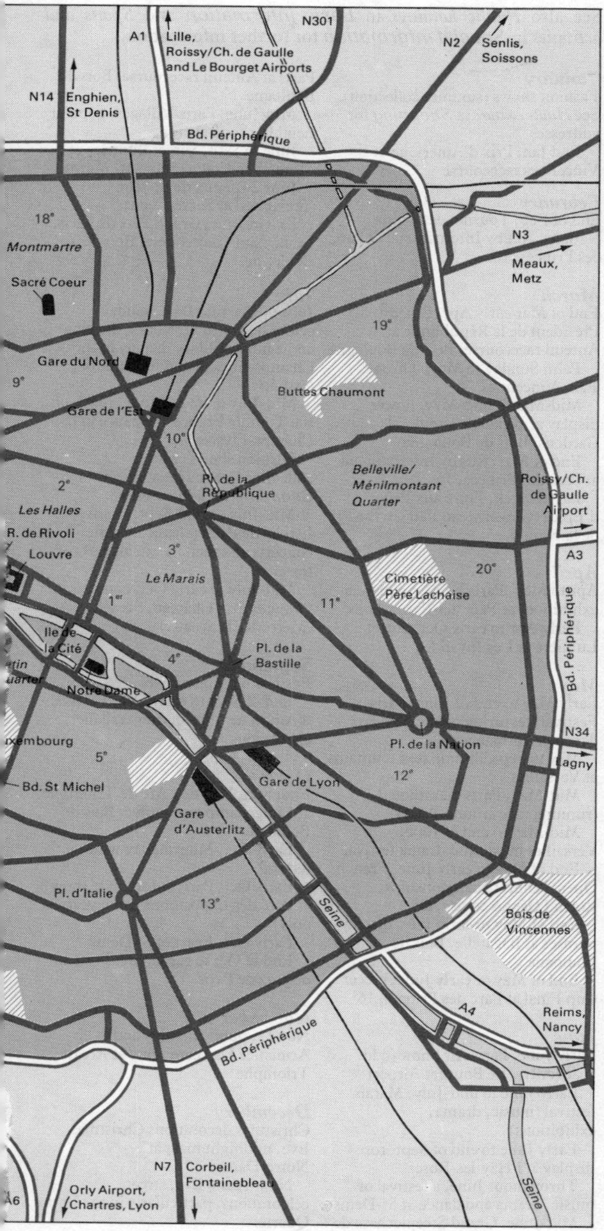

N301
A1
Lille, Roissy/Ch. de Gaulle and Le Bourget Airports
N2
Senlis, Soissons
N14
Enghien, St Denis
Bd. Périphérique
18e
Montmartre
Sacré Coeur
N3
Meaux, Metz
19e
Gare du Nord
9e
Buttes Chaumont
Gare de l'Est
10e
2e
Pl. de la République
Belleville/ Ménilmontant Quarter
Roissy/Ch. de Gaulle Airport
Les Halles
R. de Rivoli
Louvre
3e
A3
Le Marais
Cimetière Père Lachaise
20e
1er
11e
Ile de la Cité
4e
Pl. de la Bastille
Notre Dame
Bd. Périphérique
N34
Pl. de la Nation
5e
Lagny
Gare de Lyon
12e
Bd. St Michel
Gare d'Austerlitz
Pl. d'Italie
13e
Seine
Bois de Vincennes
A4
Reims, Nancy
Bd. Périphérique
N7
Corbeil, Fontainebleau
Orly Airport, Chartres, Lyon
A6
Seine

Calendar of events

See also *Public holidays* in *Basic information* and *Sports and activities* in *Special information* for further information.

January
Fashion shows (summer collection). See *Haute couture* in *Shopping* for addresses

End Jan, Prix d'Amérique at Vincennes racecourse

February
End of Feb, Tournoi des Cinqs Nations: Rugby International at Parc des Princes, 16ᵉ

March
End of Mar/early Apr, Prix du Président de la République at Auteuil racecourse, Bois de Boulogne

Palm Sunday to May, Throne Fair, Vincennes

Mid-Mar to mid-May, flower display at Bagatelle and floral Gardens, Bois de Boulogne

End of Mar, Rugby International at Parc des Princes, 16ᵉ

Easter week, Foire aux Pains d'Épice (Gingerbread Fair) in the Pl. de la Nation

April
Apr to May, Paris Fair (commercial exhibition) at Parc des Expositions

Early Apr to early Oct, Son et Lumière at Les Invalides

May
Early May to end of June, Paris Festival, featuring opera, concerts, dance performances

May to Sept, illuminated fountains at Versailles

Mid-May, Paris marathon (running race around Paris)

Mid-May to end of June, Versailles music and drama festival

End of May to early June, French Open Tennis Championships, Roland Garros courts, 16ᵉ

End of May to early July, display of roses at Bagatelle, Bois de Boulogne

End of May or early June, soccer Cup Final at Parc des Princes, 16ᵉ

June
Early June, Paris Air Show (odd years only), Le Bourget Airport

Early June to mid-July, Marais festival (music, drama, exhibitions)

Early June to end of Sept, rose display at l'Häy-les-Roses

Throughout June, a festival of music, drama and dance at St-Denis

Mid-June, Grand Steeplechase de Paris at Auteuil racecourse, Bois de Boulogne

Mid-June, Paris-Villages, popular neighborhood events

June to Sept, Son et Lumière at Moret-Sur-Loing (Seine-et- Marne)

June 24, Feux de St-Jean (fireworks) at Sacré-Coeur

End of June, Grand Prix de Paris, Longchamp racecourse, Bois de Boulogne

July
July 14, Bastille Day, holiday celebrated with fireworks, dancing and a huge military display in the Champs-Élysées and much public festivity

Mid-July or end of June, finish of the Tour de France cycle race in the Champs-Élysées

Fashion shows (winter collections). See *Haute couture* in *Shopping* for addresses

Mid-July to mid-Sept, Festival Estival de Paris (classical music concerts and recitals), in all parts of the city

Mid-July to early Oct, concerts at Orangerie du Château, Sceaux (Métro/RER Sceaux)

September
Festival de Montmartre

End of Sept to early Dec, Festival d'Automne (music, drama, ballet, exhibitions)

October
First Sun, Prix de l'Arc de Triomphe at Longchamp racecourse, Bois de Boulogne

Early Oct, Montmartre wine festival

Early Oct, Paris automobile show at Parc des Expositions (even years only)

Early Oct, Feast of St Denis

End of Oct to early Nov, Festival de Jazz de Paris

November
Nov 11, public holiday and Armistice Day ceremony at Arc de Triomphe

December
Christmas decorations Christmas Eve, midnight mass at Notre-Dame

New Year's Eve, street celebrations, particularly in the Latin Quarter.

When and where to go

The city of Paris is at its most hectic and crowded during the months of Apr and May and once again during the months of Sept and Oct. Aug is still the quietest month of the year, but no longer dead as it used to be when most Parisians went on their annual vacation and half the city closed down. Nowadays Aug is a relaxing and pleasant time to visit Paris, and only a few of the museums are closed.

Paris is a compact city bounded by a beltway, the Périphérique, and divided into 20 *arrondissements* (districts) which spiral outward from the center. Each *arrondissement* has its own style and character — say the word "*seizième*" to a Parisian, and he will conjure up an image of a certain urban ambience and lifestyle; he will even hear a special accent. Within the *arrondissements*, and often overlapping them, are *quartiers* (quarters), such as *Montparnasse*, *Montmartre* and the *Latin Quarter*.

The *Seine* divides the city into Rive Droite (Right Bank) and Rive Gauche (Left Bank) with the two islands, *Ile de la Cité and Ile St-Louis*, in the middle. The Right Bank is conspicuous by its affluence and smartness and its high concentration of imposing buildings, large shops, museums and theaters. The districts of bright lights (and red ones) are also mostly concentrated on the Right Bank. The Left Bank has its share of fine buildings and some dazzle, but on the whole its charm is more subtle, romantic and Bohemian.

From a visitor's point of view the districts of greatest interest are the 1st to the 9th, with a few pockets in outlying places. Much of this is superb walking territory. The areas outside the Périphérique do not belong to Paris proper, except for the *Bois de Boulogne* and *Vincennes*, but there are places of interest on the outskirts, such as *La Défense*, the *Flea Market* and *St-Denis* cathedral.

Area planners and visits

The following list gives a brief account of the most significant areas in the city, with their corresponding *arrondissements* (shown in French by the superior letter "e" following the number, short for *ième*). The areas are listed in an order that starts at the center of the city and works out in a spiral.

Opéra Quarter (*part of 1er, 2e and 9e; Map 8&9*). An area of grand architecture, smart shops and highbrow culture. Glossy and expensive but somewhat fraying at the edges.

Les Halles (*part of 1er; Map 10H9*). A chaotic but exhilarating mixture of old and ultra-modern, still in a state of flux.

Marais (*3e and part of 4e; Map 10&11*). An old, quiet, gracious district, with many museums, narrow rambling streets, and a strong flavor of the past.

Ile de la Cité and Ile St-Louis (*part of 1er and 4e; Map 10&11*). The former is the historic heart of Paris containing the *Conciergerie*, *Palais de Justice*, *Sainte Chapelle* and *Notre-Dame*. Busy and administrative. The Ile St-Louis, by contrast, is charming, quiet and residential.

Latin Quarter (*5e; Map 15*). This area was originally known as the *Université*, and has remained the learned quarter of Paris.

Youthful, cosmopolitan, colorful, Bohemian, with a large student population.

St-Germain (*6e and part of 7e; Map 8&9* and *14&15*). A quarter with a wide boulevard, tiny side streets, old buildings, and a thriving café life. Intellectual, artistic, elegant and fastidious.

Eiffel Tower and *Les Invalides* and environs (*remainder of 7e; Map 12&13*). Quiet, mainly residential area dominated by the axes of the *Champ-de-Mars* and *Les Invalides* complex.

Champs-Élysées and *Faubourg-St-Honoré* (*8e; Map 6&7*). Busy, expensive, grandiose.

Parc de Monceau and environs (*straddling 8e and 17e; Map 2*). Stolid and residential. The world that Marcel Proust described.

Montparnasse (*straddling 14e and 15e; Map 12*). Cosmopolitan, former Bohemian colony, torn apart by redevelopment, but retaining some of its old character.

Palais de Chaillot and environs (*16e; Map 12*). Cluster of museums set in an opulently residential *arrondissement*.

Montmartre (*18e; Map 4*). Often referred to by the locals as the "Butte." Rambling, picture-postcard quaintness, side by side with neon-lit but shabby razzle-dazzle.

Belleville/Ménilmontant (*straddling 19e and 20e; Map 11&12*) Dilapidated charm eroded by developers' bulldozers. Strong North African flavor.

On a short visit to Paris, the way to avoid frustration and cultural indigestion is to be selective. Remember that Paris has the advantage of being small and well-organized for the pedestrian, as well as having a superb Métro system, and it is a good idea to plan your sightseeing with this in mind. You may already have decided what you want to see, but if not, here are some suggested programs for a two-day and a four-day visit.

Two-day visit

Day 1 In the morning go to the *Carnavalet* museum to get a bird's-eye view of the history of Paris. Then walk through the lovely old *Marais* district to the *Pompidou Center* for a glimpse of the ultra-modern face of Paris. Go across the *Seine* through the *Ile de la Cité* and have lunch in the *Latin Quarter*. In the afternoon take a boat trip on the Seine from the *Pont-Neuf*.

Day 2 Go up the *Eiffel Tower* and perhaps have lunch in one of its restaurants. Then take the Métro from Bir-Hakeim to Charles-de-Gaulle Étoile Métro station and walk from the *Arc de Triomphe* down the *Champs-Élysées* to the *Place de la Concorde*.

Four-day visit

Day 1 Do *Walk 1/Getting to know Paris* (opposite).

Day 2 Return to the *Ile de la Cité* for a closer look at *Notre-Dame* and the *Sainte Chapelle* and perhaps the *Conciergerie* and *Crypte Archéologique*. Have lunch on the *Ile St-Louis*. In the afternoon cross to the Left Bank and explore the *Latin Quarter*.

Day 3 Take the Métro to Trocadéro and admire the magnificent view from the *Palais de Chaillot*. Cross the river and climb the *Eiffel Tower*. In the afternoon take a river trip from the Pont d'Iéna.

Day 4 In the morning visit the *Sacré-Coeur* and wander round *Montmartre*. In the afternoon walk through the *Tuileries* gardens to the *Place de la Concorde* and visit the *Jeu de Paume* museum there.

Walks in Paris

Paris is a wonderful city for walking, and the fine texture of its urban landscape is best appreciated on foot.

Walk 1/Getting to know Paris

Walks 1 and 2 can be traced on the map below.
Allow 3hrs plus, according to how many stops you make.
Maps 8,9&10. Métro Opéra (1), Louvre (13).
This walk is designed to introduce the visitor to Paris, taking a spiral route round its heart. It encompasses many well-known landmarks and contrasts the great boulevards and the rambling side streets, the Right Bank and the Left.

Begin at the Pl. de l'Opéra (**1**), dominated by the ornate *Opéra* itself and forming one of the main intersections of the city. This is the heart of the Paris of Haussmann, creator of grand townscapes, and the area is full of smart shops. Walk SW down the Bd. des Capucines and the Bd. de la Madeleine which ends at the church of the *Madeleine* itself (2), looking, as it is meant to, like a stray building from ancient Rome.

From here, go down the Rue Royale to the *Place de la Concorde* (**3**) passing between two splendid matching buildings of the Louis XV period, the one on the right housing the famous Hôtel Crillon (see *Hotels*). Cross the river by the Pont de la Concorde (**4**), which is opposite the *Assemblée Nationale*; and walk down the great artery of the Left Bank, the Bd. St-Germain (**5**), perhaps pausing for coffee at one of its host of famous cafés (see *Cafés*).

At the church of *St-Germain-des-Prés* (**6**) turn left to browse in the charming maze of old streets between the boulevard and the Seine, with their many little book and antique shops, art galleries and food stalls. Then take the Rue St-André-des-Arts and follow it E to the Pl. St-Michel (**7**), focal point of the *Latin Quarter*. This would be an ideal place to stop for lunch as the area is full of good restaurants.

From here, cross by the Pont au Double to the *Ile de la Cité* and *Notre-Dame* cathedral (**8**) and return to the Right Bank by the Pont d'Arcole (**9**), walking N with the *Hôtel de Ville* on the right and the Gothic eminence of the *Tour St-Jacques* to the left. Rues de Renard and Beaubourg lead to the E side of the *Pompidou*

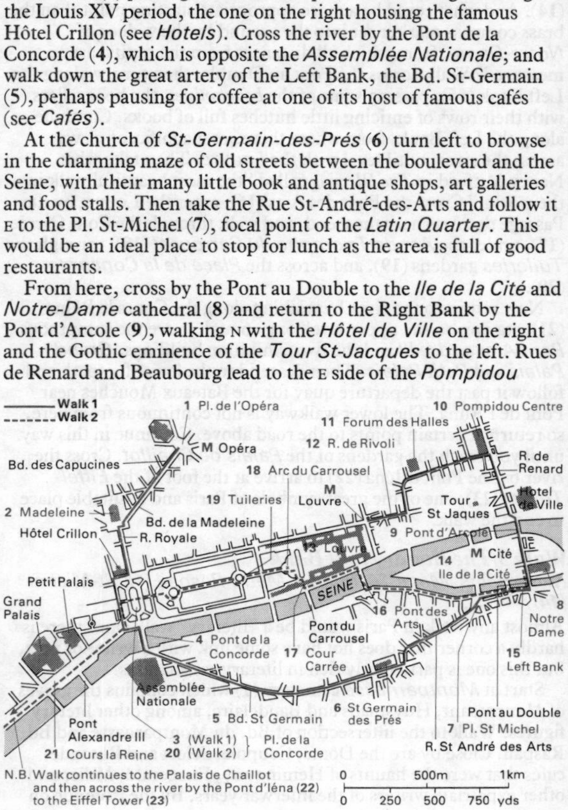

Center (**10**), Paris' most famous modern building. To reach the main entrance, walk round the lively piazza in front of the building. Having seen the Center, turn W, passing another striking modern development, the *Forum des Halles* (**11**), a shopping complex which has taken the place of the old food market. Now turn left down to the elegant *Rue de Rivoli* (**12**) with its colonnade and luxurious shops and turn right to the *Louvre* (**13**). Whether or not you visit the museum, set off for home from the Louvre Métro which, with its low reliefs and statues, is Paris' most attractive Métro station.

Walk 2/A riverside walk

Allow 2-3hrs. *Maps **9,8,7&6**. Métro Cité (**14**), Trocadéro (**23**).*

Most of the great capitals of Europe have their equivalents of the Seine, but few have as intimate a relationship with their rivers as Paris does. History and romance flow thickly in its waters, and Parisians love it tenderly. This walk, beginning and ending at Paris' two greatest landmarks, does not stay on the river banks all the time, since the main roads run along much of them, but the Seine, with its ever-changing vistas of riverscape, will never be far away.

The beginning is where Paris itself began: on the *Ile de la Cité* (**14**). And what could be a more appropriate starting point than the brass compass marker set into the ground by the W door of *Notre-Dame*, from which all distances from the capital are measured? Walk across the Pont au Double, then turn W along the Left Bank (**15**), passing some of the *bouquinistes*, the booksellers with their rows of enticing little hutches full of books. Continue along the Left Bank, from where there are magnificent views across the river, until level with the *Louvre*. Then take what Nancy Mitford in *The Blessing* called "the most beautiful walk in the world." Cross the Pont des Arts (**16**), enter the Louvre by the Passage des Arts near the E end, and walk through the Cour Carrée (**17**), under the *Arc de Triomphe du Carrousel* (**18**), through the *Tuileries* gardens (**19**), and across the *Place de la Concorde* (**20**).

Now return to the river by walking along the Cours la Reine (**21**), staying on the upper level long enough to see the sumptuous *Pont Alexandre III* and the two exhibition buildings, *Grand Palais* and *Petit Palais*. Then descend to the lower footpath and follow it past the departure quay for the Bateaux Mouches near Pont de l'Alma. The lower walkway is not continuous from here, so return at certain points to the road above. Continue in this way until you reach the gardens of the *Palais de Chaillot*. Cross the river by the Pont d'Iéna (**22**) to arrive at the foot of the *Eiffel Tower* (**23**), one of the great symbols of Paris and a suitable place to end the walk.

Walk 3/The literary Left Bank

Allow 2-3hrs. *Maps **14,15,8&9**. Métro Raspail (**1**). St-Michel (**14**).*

Almost any walk in Paris would be a "literary" walk since there is hardly a corner that does not have some link with a writer or poet, but this one is particularly rich in literary associations.

Start at *Montparnasse* cemetery (**1**) which contains the graves of Maupassant, Huysmans and Baudelaire, among other literary figures. Walk to the intersection of Bd. du Montparnasse and Bd. Raspail. Close by are the Dôme, Coupole, Select and Rotonde, cafés that were the haunts of Hemingway, Fitzgerald, Miller and other expatriate writers of the interwar years. By the Rotonde on

Bd. Raspail stands a cast of Rodin's famous *Balzac*. Turn right along the Bd. du. Montparnasse. At the corner of the Bd. and Av. de l'Observatoire is another old haunt of the American literary set, La Closerie des Lilas.

Walk down the Av. de l'Observatoire (2) into the *Luxembourg* gardens where you will find memorials to many writers including (on the E side) Murger, author of *La Bohème*, Flaubert, Stendhal, George Sand and Lecomte de L'Isle. On the W side is a particularly striking memorial to the poet Paul Verlaine. Leave the gardens on the W side by the Rue Fleurus (**3**), passing no. 27, where Gertrude Stein lived.

Turn right into the Rue d'Assas. Now follow for a while the walk taken one night by d'Artagnan, in Dumas' *Three Musketeers*, while dreaming of his beloved, as he was "passing along a lane on the spot where the Rue d'Assas is now situated." Turning into what must have been the Rue de Vaugirard, d'Artagnan made for the house of his fellow musketeer Aramis, "situated between the Rue Cassette and the Rue Servandoni" (still in existence). "The hero passed the Rue Cassette and caught sight of the door of his friend's house, shaded by a mass of sycamore and clematis, which formed a vast arch above it." This must have been somewhere near where the Rue Bonaparte begins. Walk down this street (**4**), full of antiquarian bookshops, to the Pl. St-Sulpice (**5**), described so evocatively by Henry Miller in *Tropic of Cancer*: "St-Sulpice! The fat belfries, the garish posters over the door, the candles flaming inside. The Square so beloved of Anatole France with that drone and buzz from the altar, the splash of the fountain, the pigeons cooing . . . ."

Continue down the Rue Bonaparte to Pl. *St-Germain-des-Prés* (**6**). Here is the heart of *St-Germain*, once known as the "Capitale des Lettres" thanks to the presence of poets such as Apollinaire (who lived at 202 Bd. St-Germain) and later of Jean-Paul Sartre, Simone de Beauvoir, Raymond Queneau and Albert Camus. It was in the cafés here—Les Deux Magots, for example—that the Existentialist philosophy was nurtured. Continue N on the Rue Bonaparte, then turn right into the Rue des Beaux-Arts (**7**). "I am dying beyond my means", declared Oscar Wilde, who died at no. 13 in 1900. Even so he would not recognize the contemporary luxury of l'Hôtel, as this building is now simply known (see *Hotels*).

Turn right into the Rue de Seine (**8**), where at no. 21 there is the

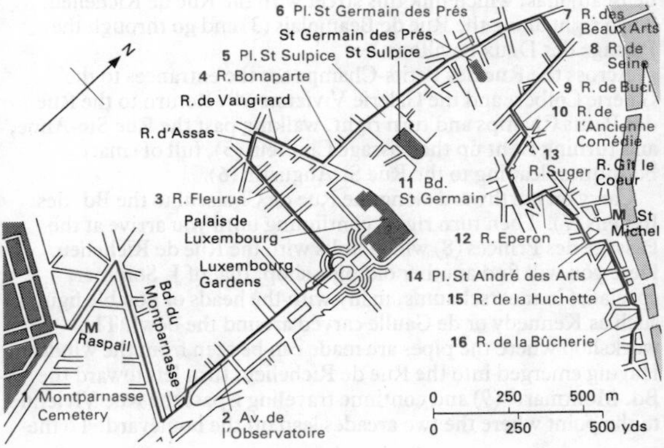

house once inhabited by George Sand. Turn left into the Rue de Buci (**9**) and right into the Rue de l'Ancienne-Comédie (**10**) and walk S to the Café Procope, no. 13, which has been a literary haunt since it was founded in 1686 (see *Cafés*). Molière and Racine came here when the *Comédie Française* was at no. 14 in the same street. Later it was patronized by Balzac, Hugo, Verlaine and many others.

Back on the Bd. St-Germain (**11**), continue your journey E past the Carrefour de l'Odéon and then turn left down the Rue Éperon (**12**) and right into the Rue Suger (**13**) where J.K. Huysmans was born at no. 11 in 1848. This road leads to the Pl. St-André-des-Arts (**14**) where there is a café called Gentilhomme, described by Jack Kerouac in his *Satori in Paris*. Just around the corner in the Rue-Git-le-Coeur is the Hôtel Vieux Paris where he, Allen Ginsburg and others of the "Beat Generation" used to stay when they were in town. From here turn left into the Bd. St-Michel and before the Seine turn right along the Rue de la Huchette (**15**) and on into the Rue de la Bûcherie (**16**), to find the famous bookshop, Shakespeare and Co., at no. 37. The shop is as full of atmosphere as it is of books, and continue the splendid literary tradition of this part of Paris in the lively poetry readings attended by young literati.

Walk 4/The arcades of Paris

Allow 3-4hrs. *Maps 9&10. Métro Palais-Royal (1&21)*.
Long before pedestrian zones came into vogue, Paris had many arcades, covered walkways and colonnades where the elegant *flaneur* could stroll or window-shop unhampered by traffic and sheltered from the rain. At the beginning of the 19thC there were about 140 arcades in Paris. The depredations of Haussmann and later developers have reduced the number to about 30, and many are rather down-at-heel, but they are gradually taking a new lease on life with the increasing pedestrianization of Paris. The first and second *arrondissements* are particularly rich in arcades and passages and by linking them up one can quite easily create a charming, off-beat walk.

Begin at the *Palais-Royal* (**1**) by entering at the SE end of the garden and going counter-clockwise round the colonnade, with its stamp and medal dealers, booksellers, and the pipe shop, À l'Oriental. Pipe shops are a notable feature of the arcades. Then double back down the Rue de Montpensier (**2**), exploring the following four covered passages, de Richelieu, Potier, Hulot and de Beaujolias, which link this street with the Rue de Richelieu. Turn right along the Rue de Beaujolais (**3**) and go through the Passage des Deux Pavillons.

Across the Rue des Petits-Champs are the entrances to the Galerie Colbert and the Galerie Vivienne (**4**). Return to the Rue des Petits Champs and turn right, walking past the Rue Ste-Anne, and turning right up the Passage Choiseul (**5**), full of smart boutiques, leading to the Rue St-Augustin (**6**).

Carry on northward along the Rue de Choiseul to the Bd. des Italiens (**7**). Then turn right, continuing until you arrive at the Passage des Princes (**8**) which links with the Rue de Richelieu. Here you will find another old pipe shop, that of J. Sommer, specialist in meerschaums, many with the heads of notable figures such as Kennedy or de Gaulle carved around the bowl. The workshop where the pipes are made can be seen from the window. Having emerged into the Rue de Richelieu, turn left toward the Bd. Montmarte (**9**) and continue traveling E past the Rue Vivienne to the point where the two arcades lead off the boulevard. To the

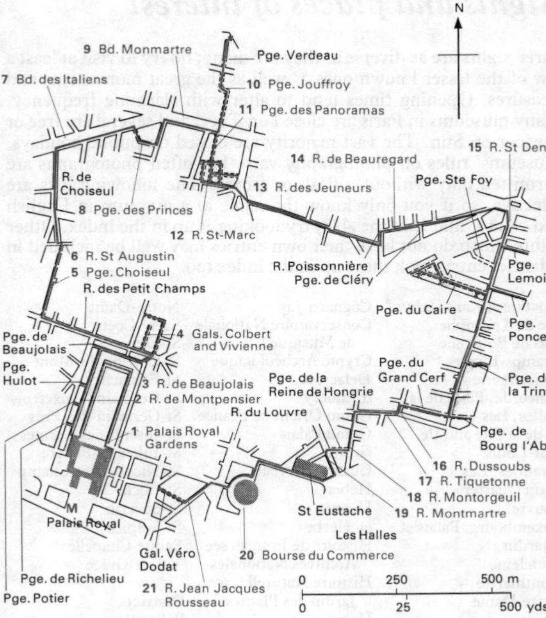

N, the Passage Jouffroy (**10**) extends into the Passage Verdeau. To the S, the Passage des Panoramas (**11**) links up with a small rabbit warren of arcades with a curious mixture of shops and restaurants.

Exit at the S side of the galleries into the Rue St-Marc (**12**), then head E, walking via the Rue des Jeuneurs (**13**), the Rue Poissonnière and the Rue de Beauregard (**14**) (off which runs the short Passage de Cléry) to the corner of the Bd. de Bonne Nouvelle and the Rue St-Denis (**15**). From here walk S down the Rue St-Denis, exploring in turn each of the seven covered passages that lead off it, to right and left: Passages Lemoine, Ste-Foy, Ponceau, du Caire, de la Trinité, de Bourg-l'Abbé and du Grand Cerf. These once fashionable walkways have come down in the world, but still possess a faded charm. The Passage du Caire has a cornice decorated with Egyptian reliefs and supported by sphinx-like heads. The Passage du Grand Cerf leads out into the Rue Dussoubs (**16**).

Turn right into Rue Tiquetonne (**17**) and left again into Rue Montorgeuil (**18**) to visit the Passage de la Reine de Hongrie, one of the few with no shops. The alley got its name when a woman who ran a stall there gave a petition to Marie-Antoinette. The queen told her that she looked very like the Queen of Hungary, and the name stuck, both to the woman and the place where she worked. Emerge into the Rue Montmartre (**19**) and skirt round the redevelopment area of *Les Halles* by the lovely *St-Eustache* church. Walk through the colonnade surrounding the *Bourse du Commerce* (**20**), then cross the Rue du Louvre and turn left down Rue Jean-Jacques Rousseau (**21**) to the lovely Galérie Véro-Dodat. This arcade, with its gracefully proportioned shop fronts and carved mahogany paneling, brings you back to near the Palais-Royal.

Sights and places of interest

Paris' sights are as diverse as they are many; do try to visit at least a few of the lesser known ones as well as the great monuments and treasures. Opening times tend to alter with alarming frequency. Many museums in Paris are closed on Tues, and several are free or cheaper on Sun. The vast majority are closed on public holidays. Museums' rules on photography vary, but often photographs are permitted only without a flash or tripod. The following lists are selective, so if you only know the name of a museum in English and cannot find it in the *A-Z*, try looking it up in the index. Other sights which do not have their own entries may well be included in a district entry; look these up in the index too.

Most important sights
Arc de Triomphe
Bois de Boulogne
Champs-Élysées
Conciergerie
Concorde, Place de la
Halles, Les
Ile de la Cité and Ile St-Louis
Invalides, Les
Latin Quarter
Louvre
Luxembourg, Palais et Jardin
Madeleine
Montmartre
Notre-Dame
Opéra
Panthéon
Place Vendôme
Place des Vosges
Pompidou Center
Sacré-Coeur
Sainte Chapelle
Tour Eiffel
Tuileries

Museums
Armée, see Les Invalides
Arménian
Art Moderne, National
Art Moderne de la Ville de Paris
Arts Africains et Océaniens
Arts Décoratifs
Arts et Métiers
Arts de la Mode, Musée des
Arts et Traditions Populaires
Balzac
Bourdelle
Bricard
Carnavalet
Cernuschi
Chasse
Cinéma
Cité des Sciences et de l'Industrie
Clemenceau
Cluny
Cognacq-Jay
Conservatoire Nationale de Musique
Crypte Archéologique
Delacroix
d'Ennery
Grand Orient de France
Grand Palais
Grévin
Gustave Moreau
Hébert
Henner
en Herbe
Histoire de France, see Archives Nationales
Histoire Naturelle, see Jardin des Plantes
Homme
Hôtel des Monnaies
Hugo, Victor
Institut Catholique
Invalides, Les
Jacquemart-André
Jeu de Paume
Le Corbusier
Légion d'Honneur
Louvre
Marine
Marmottan
Mode
Monde Arabe, Institut du
Monuments Français
Nissim de Camondo
Observatoire d'Orsay
Palais de la Découverte
Pasteur
Petit Palais
Picasso
Police
Postal
Renan-Scheffer
Zadkine
Rodin
Sculpture en Plein Air
Transports Urbains

Churches
Dôme, see Les Invalides
Madeleine
National d'Arts Asiatiques
Notre-Dame
Sacré-Coeur
St-Denis
St Étienne-du-Mont
St-Eustache
St-Germain l'Auxerrois
St-Germain-des-Prés
St-Joseph-des-Carmes
St-Julien-le-Pauvre
St-Nicolas-des-Champs
St-Roch
St-Sévérin
St-Sulpice
Sainte-Chapelle
Val-de-Grâce

Districts
Belleville/Ménilmontant Quarter
Latin Quarter
Marais
Montmartre
Montparnasse
Opéra Quarter
St-Germain Quarter

Modern buildings
Cité Universitaire
Corbusier Fondation, Le
La Défense
Forum des Halles
Mosquée
Palais de Chaillot
Palais de Congrès
Palais de Tokyo
Pompidou Center
Radio France, Maison de
Tour Montparnasse
UNESCO Building

Parks and gardens
Bois de Boulogne
Buttes Chaumont
Champ-de-Mars
Jardin des Plantes
Luxembourg
Monceau, Parc de
Montsouris, Parc de
Tuileries
La Villette, Parc de

Arc de Triomphe 🏛 ☆

*Pl. Charles-de-Gaulle, 8e ☎43-80-31-31. Map **6**F3 ▣ Open summer 10am-5.30pm, winter 10am-4.30pm. Métro Étoile.*

As much of a symbol of Paris as the *Eiffel Tower* or *Notre-Dame*, the Arc de Triomphe is the largest structure of its kind in the world — 50m (164ft) high and 45m (148ft) wide — and its massive bulk dominates the *Place Charles-de-Gaulle*, formerly the Pl. de l'Étoile. It is surely one of the biggest "white elephants" ever created. The term is curiously appropriate, because an earlier plan for the site was to erect a vast stone elephant containing an amphitheater, banqueting hall and other apartments.

The present arch was begun in 1806 on the orders of Napoleon as a monument to French military victories, but it was still unfinished at the time of his downfall. Under the restored monarchy, work on the arch continued spasmodically, and it was finally completed in 1836. Many artists worked on the decoration of the exterior, which includes four huge relief sculptures at the bases of the pillars: *The Triumph of 1810* by Cortot; *Resistance* and *Peace* by Etex; and *The Departure of the Volunteers* (commonly called "The Marseillaise") by Rude, generally considered the best of the four.

Higher up are reliefs of battles and a crowded frieze, and engraved around the top are the names of major victories won during the Revolutionary and Napoleonic periods. On the inside walls appear the names of lesser victories and of 558 generals.

Set into the ground under the arch is the **Tomb of the Unknown Soldier**, commemorating the dead of the First and Second World Wars, whose memory is kept alight by an eternal flame — a few years ago, an irreverent person cooked an omelet over it. The arch seems to invite such disrespectful gestures: in 1919 the aviator Godefroy flew under it in an airplane, defying a police ban.

Inside the cross-piece of the building is a **museum of the arch's history** which runs a continuous audiovisual program in French and English recounting the monument's great moments.

Like many other disproportionately large and grandiose monuments in Paris, the arch has merged comfortably into the townscape, settling down to an almost homey, comfortable existence, like a retired general, but no trip to Paris would be complete without a visit, and from the top there is an excellent view over the city of Paris.

Arc de Triomphe du Carrousel

*Pl. du Carrousel, 1er. Map **8**H7. Métro Palais Royal.*

This graceful arch, with its rose-colored marble columns, is linked with the greater *Arc de Triomphe* by the splendid axis formed by the *Champs-Élysées* and the *Tuileries*. Completed in 1809, it commemorates Napoleon's victories in 1805 (including Austerlitz and Ulm) which are depicted on six marble low reliefs. It was formerly surmounted by the four gilded bronze horses from St Mark's in Venice. When these were returned to Italy in 1815 they were replaced by a bronze group, representing the Restoration, riding in a chariot drawn by four horses. The arch once formed the gateway to the Tuileries Palace, burned down in 1871, and now floats in the gardens between the great jaws of the *Louvre* like a dainty morsel about to be swallowed by a whale.

Archives Nationales: Musée de l'Histoire de France

(National Archives: Historical Museum of France) 🏛 ☆

Hôtel de Soubise, 60 Rue des Francs-Bourgeois, 3e ☎42-77-

*11-30. Map **11H11** Open 2-5pm. Closed Tues. Métro Rambuteau, Hôtel-de-Ville.*
How many tumultuous events have started with an innocent-looking document? The Revocation of the Edict of Nantes by Louis XIV removed freedom of worship and drove thousands of Protestants out of France. The Revocation and the original Edict are both in the Historical Museum of France, and form part of a collection of documents belonging to the National Archives and housed in one of the great mansions of the *Marais* district, the **Hôtel de Soubise** ☆ Here also are the wills of Louis XIV and Napoleon, the Concordat of 1802 between Napoleon and the Holy See, the Declaration of the Rights of Man, letters of Joan of Arc and Voltaire — snippets of history skillfully displayed and carefully iilustrated with the use of maps, photographs and captions to create an intriguing scrapbook of the French nation. The National Archives themselves, which take up 280km (175 miles) of shelving, have been housed in the Hôtel de Soubise since 1808 and in the adjacent **Hôtel de Rohan** ☆ since 1927.

There is more to see than just the documents. The Hôtel de Soubise itself, with its elegant, colonnaded **courtyard**, is worth visiting on its own account. From 1553-1688 it was a residence of the powerful Guise family. It then became the home of the Prince and Princesse de Soubise who had it sumptuously decorated by some of the greatest artists and craftsmen of the era, including Boucher, van Loo and Lemoyne. Leaving the main room of the museum on the first floor, formerly the guard room, one passes through a series of **private apartments** ☆ Notice particularly the Princess' Oval Salon with its eight paintings of the loves of Psyche by Charles Natoire, and also her small bedroom, which now houses a permanent exhibition on the French Revolution. There are also temporary exhibitions in the apartments.

The Hôtel de Rohan (*87 Rue Vieille-du-Temple*), officially called the Hôtel de Strasbourg, as well as being part of the National Archives, is now frequently used for temporary exhibitions. It was lived in by four successive cardinals of Strasbourg who decorated their **apartments** with rlch extravagance. One of the rooms, the **Monkey Cabinet**, retains its original panels decorated with animals by Christophe Huet in 1745. The remainder of the interior is the result of skillful restoration. The courtyard has a fine relief by Robert le Lorrain, *The Horses of Apollo*.

Arènes de Lutèce

*Entrances in Rue de Navarre and Rue des Arènes, 5e. Map **16K10**. Métro Monge, Jussieu, Cardinal-Lemoine.*
Turning off the street into what seems like an ordinary Parisian park, you find yourself walking down a stone corridor and suddenly emerging into a Gallo-Roman amphitheater with terraces for spectators. It was unearthed in 1869 by accident when the Rue Monge was being constructed, and it was later restored. Now it is enjoying a second and quieter lease on life surrounded by greenery, and it makes an ideal place for playing *boules* or for simply sitting and imagining life in *Lutetia* — as Paris was known in the Roman era.

Armée, Musée de l' This museum is housed on three floors and has a collection illustrating the history of the French Army. See *Les Invalides.*

Arménian, Musée *(Armenian Museum)*

*59 Av. Foch, 16e. Map **6F1** Open Thurs, Sun only 2-6pm.*

Closed Aug. Métro Dauphine.
This small museum of works of art, documents and domestic objects provides an intriguing view of 3,000 years of Armenian history and culture. It is in the same building as the *d'Ennery* museum, housing the private collection of 19thC dramatist and librettist Adolphe d'Ennery and his wife. For location, see map on p51.

Art Moderne, Musée National d' *(National Museum of Modern Art)* 🏛 ☆

*Center Georges Pompidou, Plateau Beaubourg, 4e ☎42-77-12-33. Map **10H10** Open Mon, Wed, Thurs, Fri noon-10pm, Sat, Sun 10am-10pm. Closed Tues. Métro Hôtel-de-Ville, Rambuteau, Châtelet.*
Housed on the third and fourth floors of the *Pompidou Center*, this is the largest museum of its kind in the world, and one of the most stimulating. The third floor is devoted to frequently changing exhibitions of contemporary works, that is from about 1965 to the present, which are constantly being added to. The fourth floor houses a permanent exhibition of works from 1905 onward, starting with Fauvism (from the French word *fauve*, meaning wild beast) and progressing through Cubism, Abstract Expressionism, Dadaism, Surrealism and other movements to the present day. Under Cubism, for example, you will find a number of painters who, in their different ways, shared the same tendencies: an interest in elementary forms, such as the cube and the cylinder, and a renunciation of color in favor of light and shape. The works represented include Georges Braque's *Young Girl with a Guitar*, Picasso's *Seated Woman*, and Fernand Léger's *La Noce*, which also anticipates Futurism in its suggestion of movement through repetition of shapes in a sequence. In a similar way, Surrealism is represented by artists as diverse as Salvador Dalí, Max Ernst and Joan Miró, all of whom subsequently developed in very different directions.

Progressing through the galleries you will find that certain artists reappear as they pass through different phases. Picasso crops up at intervals as his style and subject matter change. We see him pass through a period of interest in Classical antiquity, exemplified by his *Minotaur*; then his work becomes increasingly abstract. Other painters — Kandinsky, Matisse, Braque, Léger — also manifest changing styles. Thus one perceives the dynamic way in which 20thC art has developed — schools merging, overlapping and breaking away.

The works include many sculptures as well as paintings, for example Constantin Brancusi's deliciously simple *Seal* in gray and white marble, and Raoul Haussmann's Dadaist work *The Spirit of our Times* showing a dummy-like head with a tape-measure, purse, watch and other oddments stuck to the skull.

For a proper understanding of this museum and the way the paintings are presented, it is worth joining a guided tour with one of the center's lively *animateurs*. Alternatively there is an excellent audio guide to the collection.

Art Moderne de la Ville de Paris, Musée d' *(Museum of Modern Art of the City of Paris)* 🏛 ☆

*Palais de Tokyo, 11 Av. du Président. Wilson, Paris 16e ☎47-23-61-27. Map **12G3** Open 10am-5.30pm (Wed until 8.30pm). Closed Mon. Métro Iéna, Alma-Marceau.*
This lively museum is housed in the E wing of the *Palais de Tokyo*. The whole building is a typical example of 1930s style

which, at the time, seemed so aggressively modern and now looks quaintly dated — "modernity" as an earlier generation saw it. Something of the same feeling is also present on entering the museum, helping one to see the paintings in the context of their periods: for example, Raoul Dufy's huge canvas *La Fée Electricité* (*The Good Fairy Electricity*). Other items in this very fine collection include Cubist paintings by Picasso and Braque, canvases of the Fauve school (Matisse, Derain) and works by the so-called Paris school (Modigliani, Soutine, Pascin). There are also temporary exhibitions.

In addition to the main galleries, the museum has two other sections. On the top floor is ARC (Animation, Recherche, Confrontation) devoted to off-beat contemporary exhibitions and also to concerts, lectures and other cultural events. Down on the lowest level is the **Musée des Enfants** (*entrance at 14 Av. de New York*), where children are able to participate in various creative activities from painting to dancing, under the guidance of teachers.

Arts Africains et Océaniens, Musée des *(Museum of African and Oceanic Arts)*

293 Av. Daumesnil, 12e ☎43-43-14-54. Map ***19D5*** *✗ by prior arrangement ✱ Open 9.45-noon, 1.30-5.15pm. Métro Porte-Dorée.*

This museum contains a superb collection of ethnic art: Benin bronzes, masks from New Guinea, Aborigine bark paintings and a particularly fine display of North African Islamic art. Down in the basement is one of the best tropical aquariums in Europe, complete with crocodiles.

For location, see map on p122.

Arts Asiatiques, Musée National d' See *National d'Arts Asiatiques*

Arts Décoratifs, Musée des *(Museum of Decorative Arts)* 🏛

Pavilion de Marsan, 107 Rue de Rivoli, Ier ☎42-60-32-14. Map ***8H7*** *✗ Open noon-6pm, Sun 11am-5pm. Closed Mon, Tues. Métro Palais Royal, Tuileries.*

Founded in the 1870s as part of an attempt to combat mediocrity in the applied arts, this museum presents a panorama of decorative art from the Middle Ages to the 20thC. Housed in the **Marsan pavilion** of the *Louvre*, exhibits are set out in a series of rooms furnished and decorated in the style of different eras. Here you can see medieval carvings, chests and tapestry work, Renaissance stained glass, elaborate marquetry furniture of the 17thC, Vincennes porcelain of the 18thC, and Art Nouveau woodwork of the 20thC. One of the most striking rooms is a complete **Italianate salon** of the Second Empire with richly painted and gilt wood paneling. These period rooms have lately been extended in scope, and a series of displays have been added showing furniture and household objects of recent decades. Another recent addition is the large and important **toy collection**.

Frequent temporary exhibitions on design and decoration are held. In the same building is the *Musée des Arts de la Mode*.

Arts et Métiers, Conservatoire des

292 Rue St-Martin, Paris 3e ☎40-27-20-00. Map ***10G10*** *on Sun. Open Tues-Sat 1-5.30pm, Sun 10am-5.15pm. Closed Mon. Métro Réamur-Sébastopol, Arts-et-Métiers.*

The conservatory, a college of technology and a large technical museum, is housed in the former priory of **St-Martin-des-Champs** in the NW corner of the *Marais*. The two most distinguished elements that remain from the medieval priory are the beautifully proportioned and vaulted **refectory**, now a library (visits by prior arrangement only), and the church of **St-Martin-des-Champs** which is now part of the museum. If archeologists of the future ever discover this chapel and its contents they might think that they have come upon a bizarre temple dedicated to the worship of machinery. In the Gothic ambulatory, where the shrines of saints should be, there are engine components, car and airplane motors and similar objects, some of them placed in glass cases like holy relics, suggesting perhaps the cult of "Our Ford" in Huxley's *Brave New World*.

For the technically minded, the museum is fascinating. Here you can see models and displays demonstrating the technical progress of water power, the automobile, photography, television, musical instruments and more — all examples of man's inventiveness and skill.

Arts de la Mode, Musée des
*109 Rue de Rivoli, 1er ☎42-60-32-14. Map **8H7** Open 12.30-6pm, Sun 11am-6pm. Closed Mon, Tues. Métro Palais-Royal, Tuileries.*
Not to be confused with the Musée de la Mode in the Palais Galliéra, this museum is more specifically oriented to the fashion industry and its history. Its objective is to provide a record for the industry by preserving examples of important collections and items of clothing illustrating the development of style. At present only temporary exhibitions are shown, but it is hoped that eventually there will be a permanent display.

Arts et Traditions Populaires, Musée des *(Museum of Popular Arts and Traditions)*
*6 Route du Mahatma Gandhi, 16e ☎40-67-90-00. Map **18C3** by prior arrangement ✱ Open 9.45am-5.15pm. Closed Tues. Métro Sablons.*
A cock from a church steeple, models of fishing boats, Breton peasant costumes, a blacksmith's forge, a clairvoyant's consulting room complete with crystal ball and tarot cards — these and many more curiosities are to be found in this colorful museum dealing with folk art and culture in France from the beginning of the Iron Age to the 20thC. A visit to the museum adds another element to a pleasant morning or afternoon spent in the *Bois de Boulogne* where it is situated.

For location, see map in *Bois de Boulogne*.

Assemblée Nationale: Chambre des Députés The lower house of parliament. See *Palais-Bourbon*.

Balzac, Maison de ☆
*47 Rue Raynouard, 16e ☎42-24-56-38. Map **12I1** Open 10am-5.40pm. Closed Mon. Library open 10am-6pm. Closed Sun. Métro Passy, Muette.*
This house is the only survivor of the several Paris homes lived in by the author of the great series of novels, *La Comédie Humaine*. It would no doubt appeal to Balzac's sense of irony to find it being used as a museum to his memory, for he considered it somewhat degrading. He fled there from his creditors in 1840, renting it in the name of his housekeeper to avoid their attentions, and remained in it for 7yrs. It was here that he wrote some of his last

novels, such as *La Rabouilleuse*, *Une Ténébreuse Affaire* and *La Cousine Bette*.

Whatever reservations Balzac may have had about it, to the modern visitor his house appears an idyllic place which still possesses the flavor of his era and the stamp of his personality. It is approached from a terrace lying below the level of the Rue Raynouard. Passing through a gate that seems to lead nowhere one suddenly descends some steps into a hidden garden belonging to a charming rustic-looking building with pale turquoise shutters, which appears to be a single-story cottage but is, in fact, the top floor of a large house which has another entrance on a lower street. The house is full of fascinating mementoes of Balzac, including a series of bills from tradesmen. One of them is from a glovemaker, and the caption reveals that Balzac once bought 60 pairs of gloves in a month. Personal effects on display include his coffee pot — he often drank 30 cups a day to sustain his prodigious output. There is also a library of books by and about Balzac.

Bastille, Place de la

*4ᵉ. Map **17**J12. Métro Bastille.*

Built between 1370-82, the Bastille served for four centuries as a fortress and prison — mainly for powerful people who had fallen foul of the king. On July 14, 1789 it was stormed by a Revolutionary mob and afterward demolished, an event still celebrated annually and with gusto in France. Now all that remains of the Bastille is a line of cobblestones at the W side of the square, marking out the ground plan of the once formidable building with its projecting towers.

How dear the sky has been above this place!
Small treasures of this sky that we see here
Seen weak through prison-bars from year to year.

Dante Gabriel Rossetti, *Poetical Works*

Today the Pl. de la Bastille is a huge, bustling, chaotic crossroads, bounded on the S side by the **Arsenal Basin**, now a boating marina, and surrounded by rather garish movie theaters, cafés and shops. It is dominated by the **July column**, a massive bronze edifice surmounted by an allegorical figure of *Liberty*, which commemorates the Parisians killed in the street-fighting of 1830 (the fall of Charles X) and 1848 (the fall of Louis-Philippe).

At the time of writing the SE section of the square is being redeveloped to accommodate a new opera house, the **Opéra de la Bastille**, due to be completed in 1989.

Beaubourg Familiar name for Paris' vibrant cultural center. See *Pompidou Center*.

Beaux-Arts, École des *(School of Fine Arts)* 🏛

*17 Quai Malaquais, 6ᵉ ☎42-60-34-57. Map **9**I8. Open Mon-Fri 9am-6pm (courtyards). Times of temporary exhibitions vary. Métro Pont-Neuf, Rue-du-Bac.*

In his *Paris Sketch Book*, 150yrs ago, William Thackeray wrote of this building: "With its light and elegant fabric, its pretty fountain, its archway of the Renaissance, and fragments of sculpture, you can hardly see, on a fine day, a place more *riant* and pleasing." His words apply equally well today.

Temporary exhibitions from the school's collection are held here about three times a year, but it is a pleasure simply to wander through the courtyards and mingle with the students.

Beaux-Arts de la Ville de Paris, Musée des Objects and paintings from antiquity to 20thC and excellent temporary exhibitions. See *Petit Palais*.

Belleville/Ménilmontant Quarter
19ᵉ and 20ᵉ. Map ***19C5***. *Métro Belleville. Ménilmontant.*
Located at the E end of the Rue du Faubourg-du-Temple, this is the area to go to if you want to catch a glimpse of the down-at-heel charm that used to characterize so much of Paris, captured in the film *The Red Balloon*, which was made here. Comprising the two former villages of Belleville and Ménilmontant, it is situated on a hilly site bounded roughly by the Rue des Pyrénées to the E, the *Père Lachaise* cemetery to the S, the Boulevards of Belleville and Ménilmontant to the W and the Rue de Belleville to the N.

The district has changed somewhat since Rousseau wrote in 1776: "After dinner I followed the boulevards as far as the Rue du Chemin-Vert by which I gained the heights of Ménilmontant, and from there, taking the paths through the vineyards and meadows, I made my way to Charonne, crossing the smiling countryside that separates these two villages."

Today the area presents a rather sad appearance, particularly S of the Rue de Ménilmontant, with a mixture of decay and brash new development. Fortunately, however, a restoration program has come just in time to save some fragments of this remarkable district before it is destroyed.

You will not find picture-postcard prettiness here, nor any elegant cafés or smart shops, but you will find some startling patches of a Paris that has long since vanished, shown in the little streets and alleys running N of the Rue de Ménilmontant. Off the Rue de l'Ermitage is a strange little rustic lane, the **Villa de l'Ermitage**, with dilapidated cottages and overgrown gardens. In a nearby street, the **Rue de la Mare**, is a doorway, **no. 32**, leading to a hidden street of row houses.

The streets in the angle between the Bd. and Rue de Belleville have, for the most part, held out against redevelopment, and this part of the district has become a stronghold for North African Jews, with kosher food shops much in evidence. There is also a thriving Arab population, and the two races live in total harmony. You can get excellent couscous and other North African food here at very reasonable prices.

To chart the full extent of this district, start at Ménilmontant Métro and walk in a semicircle around to Belleville Métro, or vice-versa.

Bibliothèque Nationale 🏛 ☆
58 Rue de Richelieu, 4ᵉ ☎47-03-81-26. Map ***9G8*** *Medallions and Antiques Gallery open Mon-Sat 1-5pm. Mansart Gallery open noon-6pm. Photography Gallery (in the Galerie Colbert arcade, entered from 2 Rue Vivienne) open noon-6.30pm. Métro Bourse, Palais-Royal, Quatre-Septembre, Pyramides.*
As befits one of the world's greatest collections of books, manuscripts, prints, maps, medallions and other treasures, the Bibliothèque is housed in a splendid mansion, the main entrance of which is in the Rue de Richelieu, reached via a fine courtyard. The building was created by Cardinal Mazarin in the 17thC out of two adjacent houses, the Hôtel Tubeuf and the Hôtel Chivry, and the resulting complex covers an entire block. After Mazarin's death the mansion was split between different owners. Part of it, which had come into the hands of the crown, became the repository of the

royal library, later the National Library, which ultimately took over the whole of Mazarin's mansion. Since 1537, a copy of every French book published has, by law, been kept in the library.

Accredited scholars have access to the Bibliothèque's service departments, and members of the public can view the medallion collection on the first floor, the temporary exhibitions in the ground-floor **Mansart Gallery** and the superb **Mazarin Gallery** at the top of the imposing stairway, and those in the **Photographic Gallery**. Through a glass door, the magnificent Second Empire reading room, with its domed ceiling and cast-iron columns, gives the impression of a Byzantine cathedral.

Bois de Boulogne

Map 18C3.

"I will not describe the Bois de Boulogne. It is simply a beautiful, cultivated, endless, wonderful wilderness." This was Mark Twain's reaction in *The Innocents Abroad* to the 900ha (2,224 acre) park on the western outskirts of Paris, which was once a royal hunting forest. Today he might be slightly less fulsome in his praise, for the Bois could no longer be described as a wilderness — there are too many roads. Furthermore, it is, in places, rather monotonous and much of it is haunted by libidinous characters, especially at night.

However, there are many spots of great beauty, and you must be prepared to seek these out. The most delightful of all must surely be the **Bagatelle** (*open daily 8.30am-7.30pm*). It is a relatively small park within a park where in the 18thC the Count of Artois, the future King Charles X, built himself an enchanting little villa (constructed in less than 70 days on a bet with Marie-Antoinette) surrounded by a romantic and picturesque garden with artificial waterfalls, grottoes, Gothic ruins and other follies. Later, a second building, the Trianon, was added near the villa. Today the Bagatelle (the word means trifle) is a place of potent magic with a renowned flower garden. There is also an elegant restaurant, **La Roseraie de la Bagatelle**, where you can sip afternoon tea languidly and dream.

Another appealing oasis in the Bois is the **Pré Catelan** () also a self-contained park. Its attractions include a majestic copper beech with a wider span of branches than any other tree in Paris. In addition, the Pré has a Shakespeare Garden containing plants mentioned in the master's works (*guided tours at 11am, 3pm, 4.30pm*).

If you have children with you, the spot to head for is the **Jardin d'Acclimatation** (), an amusement park on the N side of the Bois (*open daily 10.30am-6.30pm*). Here you will find, among other things, a zoo, a go-kart track, merry-go-rounds, a miniature golf course and a café, **La Ferme du Golf**, where youngsters can sit in a farmyard and eat an ice cream or pizza while goats, sheep and ducks mill around their tables. Within the Jardin d'Acclimatation is the *en Herbe* museum and just near it the *Arts et Traditions Populaires* museum.

Other attractions of the Bois include lakes (one of which, the **Lac Inférieur**, has boating facilities), two racecourses (**Auteuil** and **Longchamp**) and the **Municipal Floral Garden** of Paris.

One of the best and most enjoyable methods of travelling about in the Bois is on two wheels (bicycle rental near Pavillon Royal). There is also a bus (no. 244) which goes diagonally through the park from Porte Maillot. However, you may prefer, like the famous Englishman who broke the bank at Monte Carlo, to "walk along the Bois de Boulogne with an independent air."

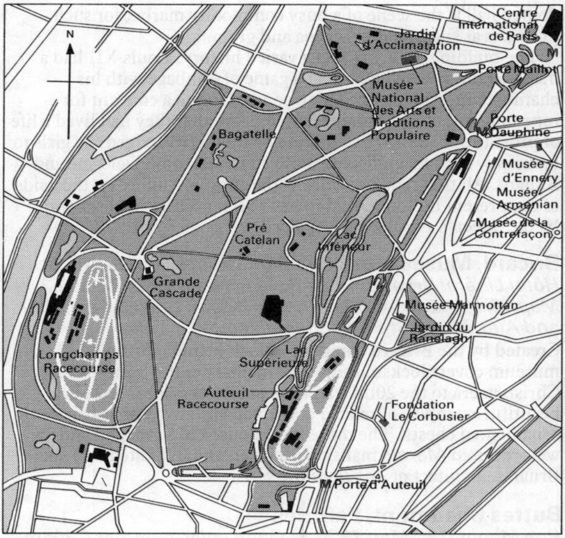

Bourdelle, Musée

16 Rue Antoine-Bourdelle, 15ᵉ ☎45-48-67-27. Map ***14K6*** *▣ ▣ on Sun. Open 10am-5.40pm. Closed Mon. Métro Falguière, Montparnasse-Bienvenue.*

This charming oasis in *Montparnasse* was for 45yrs the home and studio of Antoine Bourdelle (1861-1929), a sculptor of genius who, along with his friend Rodin, helped to give sculpture a new lease on life. Where Rodin's work has the fluidity of emotion, Bourdelle's is characterized by the thrusting, harnessed power of the will in such creations as his *Héracles Archer* and *Tête d'Apollon*. These and other works are displayed in a series of light, spacious rooms and leafy courtyards. Part of the museum is used for temporary exhibitions by other sculptors.

Bourse *(Stock Exchange)* 🏛 ☆

4 Pl. de la Bourse, 2ᵉ ☎42-61-85-90. Map ***9F8*** *▣ ▣ Open Mon-Fri 12.30-2.30pm. Métro Bourse.*

Outwardly a serene, 19thC Classical building surrounded by Corinthian columns, inwardly a scene of apparent bedlam with brokers in the main dealing room gesticulating wildly and yelling "*J'ai!*" or "*Je prends!*". To enable visitors to make sense of this puzzling spectacle, which they can witness from a gallery, they are first given a series of film shows and lectures on the workings of the Bourse and the stock market. It's all very slick and well organized — just what you would expect, in fact, from one of the bastions of French capitalism.

Bourse du Commerce *(Commercial Exchange)*

Rue de Viarmes, 1ᵉʳ. Map ***10H9****. Métro Châtelet-Les-Halles, Les Halles.*

Victor Hugo once compared this drum-shaped building to a jockey's cap without the peak. Built in the 18thC and modified in the 19th, it once served as a corn exchange. Now the majestic domed hall is the scene of a busy commodity market for such products as sugar, coffee, cocoa and grain.

The building's site has had a varied history. Louls XII had a mansion there which he lost at a game of cribbage with his chamberlain, who proceeded to convert it into a convent for repentant girls — postulants had to prove that they had lived a life of prostitution. In 1572 Catherine de Medici dislodged the girls to make way for a magnificent palace constructed by Delorme and Bullant. All that remains today is the curious column on the S side of the present building, said to have been used as an observatory by the queen's astrologer, Ruggieri.

Bricard, Musée *(Lock and Metalwork Museum)* 🏛

Hôtel Libéral Bruand, 1 Rue de la Perle, 3e ☎42-77-79-62. Map ***11****H11* *Open 10am-noon, 2-5pm. Closed Sun, Mon and Aug. Métro St-Paul, Chemin-Vert.*

Created by the Bricard company of lock manufacturers, this museum covers locksmithing and ancillary crafts from the early Christian era to the 20thC. Apart from locks galore, there are beautiful examples of related craftsmanship, from door handles to ornamented chests. The museum is housed in a graceful and well-restored *Marais* mansion designed and inhabited by Libéral Bruand, architect of *Les Invalides*.

Buttes Chaumont, Parc des

Rue Manin, 19e. Map ***19****C5* *Open daily, summer 6.30am-11pm, winter 7am-9pm Métro Buttes-Chaumont.*

This park is totally unlike any other in Paris and has a strongly romantic appeal. Brilliantly landscaped by Haussmann on a disused quarry site, it has steeply undulating wooded contours and a lake with a rocky island rising dramatically from the center, spanned by two high bridges. On the island one path leads up a flight of steps through a grotto-like tunnel to the summit which is crowned by a small Classical temple with an open colonnade. From here there is a superb view over the city to the N, E and W, with *Montmartre* and the *Sacré-Coeur* standing out against the horizon.

This is one of the few Parisian parks where one can actually sit on the grass. There are rides in a donkey cart for children, and on the W side is an inviting restaurant called the **Pavillon du Lac** (open for lunch and tea) with tables overlooking the lake.

Carnavalet, Hôtel et Musée 🏛 ☆

23 Rue de Sévigné, 3e ☎42-72-21-13. Map ***11****I11* *on Sun* *Open 10am-5.40pm. Closed Mon. Cabinet of drawings, etc, open Mon-Fri 2-5pm, Sat 10am-noon. Métro St-Paul, Chemin-Vert.*

If you visited no other building in Paris but this one you would still come away with a good understanding of the spirit of the city. Here, every phase of Parisian history, from the early Renaissance onward, is illustrated, in painting, sculpture, models, furniture and decoration — all on view in a series of splendid rooms. One of the most pleasing displays is of old tradesmen's signs, including the entire front of a druggist's shop. Another section deals with the Revolution, and here you will find models of the guillotines, portraits of Revolutionary leaders, placards, pictures of the royal family in captivity, and other mementoes.

The building itself, situated at the heart of the *Marais*, tells its own part of the story. Built in the 1540s and later modified by Mansart, it possesses a gracious entrance courtyard with allegorical reliefs of the four seasons and a contemporary statue of *Louis XIV* by Coysevox; anachronistically dressed as a Roman general wearing a wig. From 1677-96 the house was occupied by Mme de Sévigné, who immortalized herself by a series of lively and witty letters and who played hostess to distinguished writers and thinkers of her time. Her apartments are preserved as part of the museum, and she still casts her benign spell over the building.

Catacombs

*1 Pl. Denfert-Rochereau, 14e ☎43-22-47-63. Map **14M7** Open Tues-Fri 2-4pm, Sat, Sun 9-11am, 2-4pm. Métro Denfert-Rochereau.*

Here is a creepy experience: a walk of three-quarters of an hour through a subterranean necropolis. These are not ancient catacombs like the ones in Rome but former stone quarries which were filled with the bones cleared from many Parisian cemeteries during the 18th and 19thCs. They have been open to the public since 1874. The tunnels leading to the ossuary pass a representation of a fort, carved out of the rock by an 18thC tunnel worker in his leisure time. Then a chamber with black and white painted pillars leads off to a doorway over which are the words: "*Arrête! C'est ici l'empire de la mort.*" ("Stop! This is the empire of death.") Beyond it stretches tunnel after tunnel, lined on each side with neatly-piled bones interspersed with rows of grinning skulls and enlivened by plaques bearing inscriptions of death. There are between five and six million skeletons here. The whole place is a *memento mori* of the most dramatic kind, a veritable temple of death.

The visitor sees only a small part of the 300km (187 miles) of tunnels created by stone-quarrying.

Cernuschi, Musée

*7 Av. Velasquez, 8e ☎45-63-52-75. Map **2D5** on Sun. Open 10am-5.40pm. Closed Mon. Métro Villiers, Monceau.*

Paris possesses this interesting museum of Chinese art thanks to a colorful Milanese financier named Cernuschi. A disciple of Garibaldi, Cernuschi was once condemned to death for his Revolutionary activities but reprieved by Napoleon III, later becoming a French citizen. Before his death in 1896 he bequeathed his house and magnificent collection of Chinese objects to the city of Paris. Not as large or impressive as the collection in the *Guimet* museum, this exhibition nevertheless gives a very informative picture of the development of Chinese art from prehistoric times. It includes a selection of paintings by modern Chinese artists, but perhaps the most evocative picture is a 13thC ink-and-brush drawing of a bird on a twig which combines humor and simplicity with sophistication.

The museum is situated in a fine house just near the E gate of the *Monceau* park.

Champ-de-Mars

*7e. Map **12I3**. Métro Trocadéro, École-Militaire.*

The Champ-de-Mars is the back garden of the *Eiffel Tower*. It was originally laid out in the 1760s as a parade ground for the *École Militaire*, which is why it is named after Mars, the god of war. These days it is anything but martial — just a typically tranquil Parisian park with a symmetrical pattern of tree-lined avenues and numerous pleasant and secluded little corners in which to sit and read or contemplate the wonders of Eiffel's engineering.

Champs-Élysées, Avenue ★

*8e. Map **6&7**. Métro Étoile, George V, Franklin-D-Roosevelt, Champs-Élysées-Clemenceau, Concorde.*

If there is one Parisian street that is known throughout the world it is this one. It forms a great triumphal tree-lined sweep from the *Place de la Concorde* to the *Arc de Triomphe*. At its lower end, as far as the intersection known as the **Rond-Point**, it is bounded by strips of park. Then, along the stretch that climbs in a shallow ramp toward the Arc de Triomphe, it is lined by imposing buildings: offices, smart shops, movie theaters and numerous restaurants and sidewalk cafés.

The lower part of the avenue was laid out by Louis XIV's gardener, Le Nôtre, in 1670, and the upper part some 40yrs later. However, the road remained a muddy and insalubrious thoroughfare until it acquired an element of fashion and style in the 18thC with the bullding ofthe grand houses in the *Rue du Faubourg-St-Honoré*. From very early in its history it was trequented by ladies of pleasure. In 1778, for example, a Swiss guard apprehended a priest there in the company of a young black woman to whom he claimed to be giving religious instruction. Half a century later Balzac wrote of the "dark-eyed houris" who frequented the avenue. Their successors are still operating here today.

The street is an obvious route for processions. It was down the Champs-Élysées that the victorious German troops marched in 1940, and 4yrs later the same street witnessed the triumphant return of de Gaulle. Walk down it and you will feel a swell of exultation, but curiously, despite its many cafés, it is not the most inviting place to linger. The ghosts of all those marchers seem to hurry you on.

Charles-de-Gaulle, Place

*8e. Map **6**F3. Métro Étoile.*

The great intersection encircling the *Arc de Triomphe* was given its present name after de Gaulle's death in 1970, but most Parisians still call it by its apt former name, the Pl. de l'Étoile (star). The Arc de Triomphe was built between 1806-36, but it was not until 1854 that Haussmann was commissioned by Napoleon III to create the grand townscape that we see there today.

Twelve great avenues radiate from Étoile. They include the *Champs-Élysées*, which plunges down to the *Place de la Concorde*, the gracious, park-lined **Av. Foch** with its luxurious buildings stretching toward the *Bois de Boulogne*, and the **Av. de la Grand Armée**, which points to Neuilly and *La Défense*.

The Pl. Charles-de-Gaulle is one of the most photographed parts of Paris — especially from the air where its layout looks particularly dramatic.

Chasse, Musée de la *(Museum of Hunting)* 🏛 ☆

*Hôtel Guénégaud, 60 Rue des Archives, 3e ☎42-72-86-43. Map **11**H11 ✉ ✱ Open 10am-12.30pm, 1.30-5.30pm. Closed Tues. Métro Rambuteau, Hôtel-de-Ville.*

Everything you ever needed to know about hunting is assembled in an attractive old *Marais* mansion: hunting weapons of all kinds, stuffed animals, paintings of famous hunters and huntresses such as *Diana*, by Breughel and Rubens, and *St Eustache*, by Cranach.

The building, the **Hôtel Guénégaud**, with its well-mannered courtyard and dignified design, was built by François Mansart between 1648-51 and was in a dilapidated condition when François Sommer took it over in the early 1960s — his own big-game trophies are among those on display. Now the building stands beautifully restored to delight architectural as well as hunting enthusiasts.

Cinéma, Musée du ☆

Palais de Chaillot, Place du Trocadéro, 16e ☎45-53-74-39/ 45-53-21-86. Map 12H2 Guided visits 10am, 11am, 2pm, 3pm, 4pm. Closed Tues. Métro Trocadéro.

The modest entrance to this museum (allied to the *Cinémathèque Française)* at the bottom of a flight of steps in the *Palais de Chaillot* does not prepare the visitor for the riches within. The museum's eloquent curator, Alain Gabet, or one of his staff, takes visitors first through the early technology of cinematography, then through a series of galleries full of the trappings that have enabled moviemakers to create a world of make-believe. There are sets from famous movies like *The Cabinet of Doctor Caligari*, costumes, such as the tunic worn by Rudolph Valentino in *The Sheik*, and Garbo's robes, papier-mâché monsters, a robot from Fritz Lang's *Métropolis* . . . and much more. The conducted visit takes about an hour and a quarter.

Cinémathèque Française

Palais de Chaillot, Jardin du Trocadéro, Av. Albert-de-Mun, 16e ☎47-04-24-24. Map 12H2 Closed Mon. Métro Trocadéro.

The movie library in the *Palais de Chaillot* is a national institution for the screening of distinguished movies from all periods of cinema history. A different movie is shown at every performance, so between this and the other auditorium shortly to open in the Palais de Tokyo there is always a rich choice for the connoisseur. Subscribers pay a lower entrance fee, but the Cinémathèque is open to everyone.

Details of programs are available at the box office and in the press.

Cité Universitaire

Bd. Jourdan, 14e. Map 19D4. Métro Cité-Universitaire.

This sprawling student community on the s perimeter of Paris, with its pavilions for different nationalities, is an excellent place to study contrasting styles of architecture. Each building reflects some aspect of its country's architecture: the Greek pavilion is a Hellenic temple, and the Indo-Chinese building resembles a pagoda. Admirers of Le Corbusier will be interested in the Swiss and Brazilian halls which he designed. Inaugurated in 1925.

Clemenceau, Musée

8 Rue Franklin, 16e ☎45-20-53-41. Map 12H2 Open Tues, Thurs, Sat, Sun 2-5pm. Métro Passy, Trocadéro.

The apartment where the statesman Georges Clemenceau lived from 1895 until his death in 1929 is preserved exactly as he left it, down to the quill pen with which he wrote. The atmosphere has the stamp of an exceptionally powerful and many-faceted personality.

Cluny, Musée de ☆

6 Pl. Paul-Painlevé, 5e ☎43-25-62-00. Map 10J9 Open 9.45am-12.30pm, 2-5.15pm. Closed Tues. Métro St-Michel, Odéon.

This outstanding museum in the *Latin Quarter* is a remarkable archeological site housing a great collection of ancient and

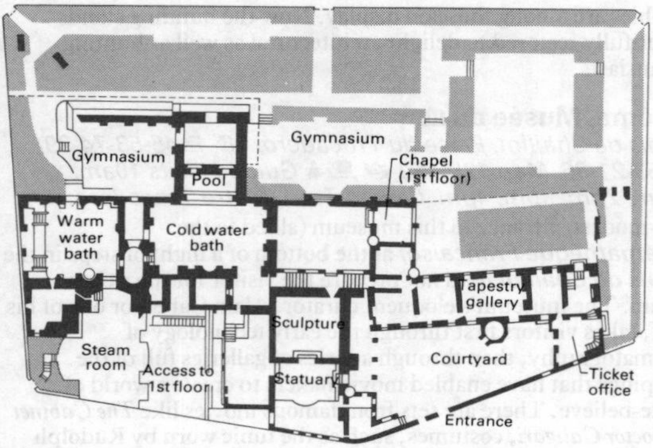

medieval objects. It comprises two buildings: the remains of the Gallo-Roman baths, the **Thermes de Lutèce** (c.200); and the medieval **Hôtel de Cluny**, constructed in the 14th and 15thC for the rich abbots of Cluny as their Parisian residence.

Everything that exists elsewhere exists in Paris.

Victor Hugo, *Les Misérables*, 1908

The museum owns one of the finest collections of medieval tapestry work in existence and its most famous exhibit is the set of six tapestries known as the *Lady with the Unicorn* ★ woven in lovely muted colors in lively detail. The tapestries were made in the late 15thC for a lawyer named Jean Le Viste. Five of the tapestries symbolically illustrate the five senses and the sixth is thought to illustrate mastery of them.

The museum's rooms contain many other treasures, including everyday objects from the Middle Ages. On the first floor is a small chapel containing some impressive Gothic tracery. Passing into the Roman building, one is overwhelmed by the vast room of the thermal baths, with its great vaulted roof, a most impressive relic from the Roman period. In this and in adjacent rooms, Roman artifacts are exhibited.

One of museum's newest galleries contains a sizeable array of very interesting early medieval ecclesiastical and votive items such as reliquary boxes, patens, chalices and candle holders, some of them crafted out of Limoges enamelwork; while another, light-filled new room contains sculpture from the Cathedral of Notre-Dame de Paris.

Cognacq-Jay, Musée

25 Bd. des Capucines, 2e ☎42-61-94-54. Map ***8F7*** *on Sun. Open 10am-5.40pm. Closed Mon. Métro Opéra, Madeleine.*

Founded in the 1920s by Ernest Cognacq, creator of the Samaritaine chain of shops, and his wife, Louise Jay, this is an elegant museum of 18thC art, housed in the premises of a former Samaritaine shop. Paradoxically, Cognacq was no art-lover — he boasted that he had never entered the Louvre — and he became a collector purely for status reasons. However, with the help of experts he succeeded in acquiring many works of the highest rank, such as Boucher's *Le Retour de Chasse de Diane*, Tiepolo's *Le Festin de Cléopatre* and Reynolds' portrait of *Lord Northington*.

Watteau, Fragonard, Rembrandt and Gainsborough are among other artists represented.

There is also a remarkable collection of porcelain ornaments, gold and silver boxes and other small objets d'art. Some of the rooms have lovely 18thC woodwork and furniture, and the entire museum is a pleasing mixture of intimacy and quiet luxury — a place of beauty and repose contrasting with the hectic hustle of the *Opéra Quarter* that surrounds it.

Collège de France

Pl. Marcellin-Berthelot, 5e. Map ***15****J9. Métro Maubert-Mutualité.*

This great institute of learning in the *Latin Quarter* was founded in 1529 by François I at the instigation of the scholar Guillaume Budé, whose statue now stands in the W courtyard. The college was founded to counteract the hidebound dogmatism of the neighboring *Sorbonne* and was for a time known as the "Three-Language College" because Hebrew, Greek and Latin were taught there. Subsequently, its syllabus expanded to include many other academic disciplines from Arabic to physics, and today it maintains a high reputation.

Smaller and less bombastic in architecture than the Sorbonne, it has something of the intimate atmosphere of a small Oxford or Cambridge college.

Comédie Française 🏛

2 Rue de Richelieu, 1er ☎40-15-00-15. Map ***9****H8 ✗ Sun 10am ▣ Métro Palais-Royal.*

After it was founded in 1680 by Louis XIV this famous company of actors moved house several times but finally settled on the present site at the end of the 18thC. The theater, which has evolved over the years into the grand colonnaded building that we see today, is set in a prime position next to the *Palais-Royal*, facing a busy intersection with attractive fountains, the **Pl. André Malraux**.

Despite its name, the company does not necessarily perform comedies. Traditionally the repertoire has emphasized classical French dramatists such as Molière, Corneille and Racine, but lately it has been widened to include modern and foreign playwrights.

Conciergerie

1 Quai de l'Horloge, Ile de la Cité, 4e ☎43-54-30-06. Map ***10****I9 ▣ Open 10am-6.pm (5pm in winter). Métro Cité.*

The Conciergerie has a gloomy atmosphere that matches its gloomy history as a place of imprisonment, death and torture. Part of the great palace which was built on the N side of the *Ile de la Cité* by King Philippe le Bel (1284-1314), it is now incorporated into the *Palais de Justice* complex. The name is derived from the title of a royal officer called the Concierge ("*Comte des Cierges*," "Count of the Candles") who was superintendent of the palace and who also had the right to administer justice in its environs. Increasingly the Conciergerie took on the functions of a prison, especially after the building became for a time the seat of parliament which was also the country's supreme court.

It was here that such malefactors as Ravaillac, assassin of Henry IV, and Damiens, who attempted to kill Louis XV, were brought and hideously tortured before being executed. However, it was during the Revolution that the Conciergerie received its real baptism of blood. Its most famous prisoner was Marie-Antoinette, who was kept here before being taken to the guillotine. Her cell is now a chapel to her memory, but her name is only one of a list of many who passed through the Conciergerie on their way to execution in a gory chain of death. The Revolutionary leader Danton condemned 22 *Girondins*, Robespierre condemned Danton, the Thermidor Convention condemned Robespierre . . . In all, nearly 2,600 prisoners were sent for execution from the Conciergerie between the winter of 1793 and summer of 1794. You can still see the grim little room where they were shaved and relieved of their possessions before being taken to the tumbrils. In 1792, 288 prisoners were murdered in the prison itself.

Despite thc unpleasant vibrations created by this history, the building does, in fact, possess some beautiful features: the **Salle des Gardes**, the first room you enter, with its elegant vaulting and carved bosses; the magnificent **Salle des Gens d'Armes** — 69m (226ft) long and 27m (88ft) wide — with its three rows of eight pillars, is sometimes used as a setting for concerts; and the **kitchen**, with its four fireplaces, each big enough to roast an entire ox, is an interesting feature; in the 14thC it provided food for 5,000 people. Also of interest is the chapel, which housed the 22 condemned *Girondin* deputies. It now contains a depressing but intriguing little collection of mementoes, including a guillotine blade, Marie-Antoinette's crucifix and two portraits of her from life.

Concorde, Place de la ★

8e. Map 8G6. Métro Concorde.

The largest square in Paris is also arguably the most striking and beautiful townscape in the world, but to appreciate the square fully you must brave the whirling blizzard of traffic and cross the road to the center.

This vantage point provides stately vistas in all directions: W up the *Champs-Élysées* to the *Arc de Triomphe*; E through the *Tuileries* to the *Louvre*, with the *Jeu de Paume* museum and the *Orangerie* on either side; S across the **Pont de la Concorde** to the *Palais-Bourbon* and N up the **Rue Royale** to the *Madeleine* between the matching colonnaded facades of the **Hôtel Crillon** (see *Hotels*) on the left and the **Hôtel de la Marine** on the right.

There once stood in the middle an equestrian statue of *Louis XV* in whose reign the square was laid out. This was removed during the Revolution and replaced briefly by an allegorical statue of *Liberty*. Now the site is occupied by the 3,300yrs-old **obelisk of Luxor**, given to King Louis-Philippe by Mohammed Ali, Viceroy of Egypt, and erected in 1836 — thus putting an end to political arguments over the question of which monument should stand there. A few yards from this spot stood the guillotine which, during the Revolution, claimed over a thousand victims including Louis XVI and Marie-Antoinette. Two **fountains** resplendent with water nymphs and sea gods stand to the N and S of the obelisk.

Marking the octagonal perimeter of the original square are eight **statues** allegorically representing the towns of Lyon, Marseille, Bordeaux, Nantes, Lille, Strasbourg, Rouen and Brest. The curious pavilions on which they rest were once let out as tiny dwelling houses with just two rooms, one above the other. Other statues of note are the **Marly horses** sculpted by Guillaume Coustou in the 1740s, which flank the E end of the Champs-Élysées, and the statues of *Fame* and *Mercury* on winged horses by Coysevox, which stand on either side of the entrance to the Tuileries.

The Place de la Concorde is the magnificent pulsating heart of

Paris, as breathtaking by day as it is by night, when floodlight transforms its buildings, obelisks, fountains and statues into a stunning *tableau vivant*.

Conservatoire National de Musique
14 Rue de Madrid, 8e ☎42-93-15-20. Map **3E6** *Open Wed-Sat 2-6pm. Métro Europe.*
For music enthusiasts, this museum has an impressive collection of instruments, including some exquisite harpsichords and spinets. Here we find Marie-Antoinette's harp, Beethoven's clavichord, Paganini's guitar, and no fewer than five Stradivarius violins. Concerts are given frequently, sometimes using instruments from the museum. At the time of writing there is a plan, not yet finalized, to move the Conservatoire and museum to the new complex at La Villette in the fall of 1989.

Corbusier Fondation, Le
8 Sq. du Docteur-Blanche, 16e ☎42-88-41-53. Map **18D3** *Open Mon-Fri 10am-12.30pm, 1.30-6pm (5pm on Fri). Closed Sat, Sun and Aug. Métro Jasmin.*
The name Le Corbusier is synonymous with modern French architecture. This foundation, the purpose of which is to present Le Corbusier's work to the public, occupies two villas designed by the master himself in the 1920s. It encompasses a library, a photographic archive and a collection of paintings and sculptures by the architect.

Temporary exhibitions are held on various aspects of his work. For location, see map on p51.

Crypte Archéologique ☆
Pl. du Parvis Notre-Dame, 4e ☎43-29-83-51. Map **10I9** *Open 10am-6pm, last admissions 5.30pm. Métro Cité.*
Opened in Aug 1980, this splendid addition to Paris' museums consists basically of an important archeological site in front of *Notre-Dame* which was roofed over following its excavation. The resulting vault is the largest structure of its kind in the world. Descending a stairway from the square, one literally steps down into the Paris of an earlier age, finding an underground chamber where Gallo-Roman ramparts jostle the cellars of medieval houses. The remains are superbly presented, with information on the early history of Paris, illustrated by detailed models of the city at various stages. An object lesson in the imaginative use of an archeological site.

La Défense
Map **18C3**.
This vast commercial and residential complex, lying beyond the river to the W of Paris, has been nicknamed "Manhattan-sur-Seine." Unfortunately it has all of the brutality and none of the style of "Manhattan-sur-Hudson." Begun in the 1960s, it dominates the western horizon of the city with its growing cluster of skyscrapers.

The main zone of La Défense focuses on a long podium running approximately W-E and descending toward the Seine in a series of terraces laid out with trees. On the S side, the bleak prospect is far from enhanced by a Joan Miró sculpture resembling two monstrous wilting pieces of fungus that are garishly and unattractively painted bright blue, red and yellow.

The forest of glass and concrete which surrounds the podium includes such buildings as the **Grande Braderie**, a vast three-cornered hall filled with small shops and stalls of every description, and the **Quatre-Temps**, the largest commercial center in Europe with a floor space twice the area of all the shops in the *Champs-Élysées*. There are also hotels, restaurants, movie theaters, a skating rink and a station for the RER railroad. The latest addition is a vast rectangular arch containing offices.

At the western end of the podium there is a view of an outlying zone of La Défense and the bizarre apartment buildings are painted in splotches of gray, blue, brown and green as though they had been camouflaged.

La Défense is a symbol of the aggressive prosperity that has overtaken France in the past 20yrs. Despite its multitude of amenities, it is a place that dwarfs and crushes the spirit, but at least in Paris modern man's desire to build such structures has been concentrated into one area well away from the center.

Delacroix, Musée

6 Pl. de Furstenberg, 6ᵉ ☎43-54-04-87. Map 9I8 ▣ Open 9.45am-5.15pm. Closed Tues. Métro St-Germain-des-Prés.

Eugène Delacroix (1798-1863) was one of the great romantic painters of the 19thC, a Wagner among artists. His vivid canvases of battle scenes, lion hunts and other stirring subjects have a controlled fire to them, like Delacroix himself, whom Baudelaire described as "a volcanic crater artistically concealed beneath bouquets of flowers."

In his last years, Delacroix lived a life of almost monastic seclusion in a charming Left Bank apartment with a studio overlooking a little garden. This apartment, in the *St-Germain Quarter*, is now preserved as a museum, full of photographs, letters, portraits and other mementoes of the artist.

Dôme church A masterpiece by Hardouin-Mansart containing the tomb of Napoleon. See *Les Invalides*.

École Militaire

Pl. Joffre, 7ᵉ. Map 13J4. Not open to public except by special arrangement. Write to: Général Direction, École Militaire, 1 Pl. Joffre, 75007. Métro École-Militaire.

Where its neighbor, *Les Invalides*, is an officer in ceremonial dress, the École Militaire is a sergeant major bawling out across the *Champ-de-Mars* to the *Eiffel Tower*. The long Classical facade has a great central-domed portico, and the vast courtyard facing the Pl. de Fontenoy is imposing. It still serves as a military academy as it did when it was built by Gabriel in the reign of Louis XV, and when Napoleon was sent there at age 15 in 1784 — when he passed out he was told he would go far given the right circumstances!

Égouts *(Sewers)*

Entrance at corner of Quai d'Orsay and Pont de l'Alma, 7ᵉ ☎47-05-10-29. Map 13H4 ▣ Open Mon, Wed, last Sat of month 2-5pm. Métro Alma-Marceau.

"Below Paris," wrote Victor Hugo in *Les Misérables*, "is another city." He was referring to the sewer network, the existence of which is vital to the gracious city above. Its tunnels would stretch from end to end as far as Istanbul, and a small section of this labyrinth has been equipped for public viewing. Visitors are shown an exhibition of documents on the history of the sewers, followed by an audiovisual display about the workings of the system. A guided tour takes visitors through dripping tunnels, past waste-collection pits and along the edge of a murky gray river. Instructive but smelly. Once you know the odor of the sewers you will catch whiffs of it occasionally from grates as you walk through the city.

Eiffel Tower See *Tour Eiffel*.

d'Ennery, Musée
*59 Av. Foch, 16ᵉ ☎45-53-57-97. Map **6**F1 ✉ ✗ Open Thurs and Sun only 2-5pm. Closed Aug. Métro Dauphine.*
Ming vases, netsuke, images of Buddha, porcelain dogs, Chinese furniture — these and other Oriental objects collected by the 19thC dramatist Adolphe d'Ennery and his wife are displayed in part of their opulent house in the Av. Foch. They bought indiscriminately, and only about one in ten of the objects are of any real value. However, the museum has a curious, musty charm. The house is also shared by the *Arménian* museum. For location, see map on p51.

Étoile See *Charles-de-Gaulle, Place*.

Faubourg-St-Honoré, Rue du See *St-Honoré, Rue du Faubourg*.

Flea Market See *Marché aux Puces*.

Forum des Halles ☆
*1ᵉʳ. Map **10**H9. Métro Châtelet-Les-Halles, Les Halles.*
Opened in 1979 as part of *Les Halles* redevelopment. This complex is a commercial counterpart of the *Pompidou Center*, but, where the latter thrusts boldly up, the Forum goes down. Built on four descending levels, it has concave glass and aluminum walls which plunge down to a sunken courtyard, frequently used by open-air performers, which displays a curiously stirring sculpture by Julio Silva entitled *Pygmalion*, consisting of a group of dream-like mythological figures.

The overall design of the center has a spare, crisp elegance and avoids the harsh, plastic colors that mar so many modern shopping precincts. The Forum has 200 shops (including clothes boutiques, jewelers, booksellers and furniture shops), 10 movie theaters and 12 restaurants, one of which has a terrace overlooking the courtyard. It also houses, on level minus-one, a branch of the *Grévin* museum (☎42-61-28-50), which contains an imaginary reconstruction of a Parisian street of 1885, and a **Museum of Holography** on level one (☎42-96-96-83). From the lowest level there is access to the Métro and RER, and there are two large underground parking lots. At the N side of the Forum is the **Pavillon des Arts**, a striking steel-and-glass building in which temporary exhibitions are held.

Gobelins (Tapestry Factories)
*42 Av. des Gobelins, 13ᵉ ☎43-37-12-60. Map **16**M10 ✉ Open Tues, Wed, Thurs 2.15-3.15pm; tour lasts 75mins. Métro Gobelins.*
If you have ever struggled with a home tapestry kit and found that it tried your patience, you should visit the Gobelins factory to find out what patience really means. Here, skilled weavers, carefully chosen and trained from the age of 16, work their way millimeter by millimeter across huge upright looms at the rate of as little as one square meter a year. Thus it often takes 3-4yrs to complete a

single tapestry with two or three people working on it full time.

The techniques used are essentially the same as when the Gobelins was founded as a royal factory under Louis XIV, but the tapestries are now worked in a far wider range of colors (14,920 of the city altogether), and the subjects are no longer scenes of royal occasions and the like but copies of modern paintings or designs.

The Gobelins is a state enterprise, and its products are never sold. They are either made use of by the government or given as gifts. The atmosphere of the factory complex in the SE of Paris is rather like an old university college, with a cobbled quadrangle, garden and apartments for the employees.

A guided tour of the factory is given, which incorporates the two other state workshops of **Savonnerie** (carpets) and **Beauvais** (tapestries made on a horizontal loom). In an era of mass-production, here is craftsmanship of the highest standard and well worth a visit.

Grand Orient de France, Musée du *(Freemasonry Museum)*

16 Rue Cadet, 9e ☎45-23-20-92. Map ***4E9*** *Open 2-6pm. Closed Sun, Métro Cadet, Richelieu-Drouot.*

What did Lafayette, Garibaldi and Franklin D. Roosevelt have in common? Answer: they were all Freemasons, as you will discover from this intriguing museum of Masonic documents, mementoes and regalia, mainly but not entirely related to French Masonry. In the same building there is a bookshop selling material of Masonic and esoteric interest.

Grand Palais, Galeries Nationales du ☆

Av. du Général Eisenhower, 8e ☎42-89-54-10. Map ***7G5*** *Open 10am-8pm, Wed 10am-10pm. Closed Tues. Métro Champs-Élysées-Clemenceau.*

The Grand Palais and the *Petit Palais*, built for the Universal Exhibition of 1900, echo each other like two thunderous fanfares across the Av. Winston-Churchill, which runs from the *Champs-Élysées* to the *Pont Alexandre III*. Some people would call them fussy and pompous, but it would be fairer to call them joyous and exuberant pieces of architectural rhetoric, though the Grand Palais oversteps the mark perhaps with its gargantuan porticoes, its frescoes and its mass of cartouches and swags of carved stonework.

The western part of the building is now given over to the *Palais de la Découverte*, a science musuem. The rest is used for temporary art exhibitions and other large-scale shows. The interior is as imposing as the exterior, particularly the main hall with its domed and vaulted roof in glass and iron. The N section of the building, fronted by a pleasing little garden with a fountain, contains a good self-service restaurant and a movie theater showing free films on subjects related to the arts.

Grands Boulevards

9e and 10e. Map ***8F7-11G11****. Métro Madeleine, Opéra, Rue Montmartre, Bonne-Nouvelle, Strasbourg-St-Denis, République.*

This is the name given to the string of boulevards extending roughly from the *Madeleine* to the Pl. de la République — Bds. Capucines, Italiens, Montmarte, Poissonière, Bonne-Nouvelle, St-Denis and St-Martin. They were constructed under Louis XIV to replace an obsolete line of fortifications, and soon became known just as "The Boulevard." In the middle of the 18thC The Boulevard became elegant and fashionable, but the main stretch from the Bd. Montmartre to the Pl. de la République has long since become rather tawdry.

The Boulevard is the source or distributive center of all the flitting fancies of France.

Richard Whiteing, *The Life of Paris*

Grévin, Musée
10 Bd. Montmartre, 9e ☎47-70-74-72. Map 9F9
Open 1-6pm. Métro Richelieu-Drouot, Rue Montmartre.
Cabinet fantastique are the words over the doorway, and fantasy is certainly what one experiences on entering this museum. As an appetizer, the visitor passes through a grotto with distorting mirrors, then through a series of ornate rooms filled with waxworks of contemporary personalities. Down in the basement are more waxworks arranged in a sequence of fascinating historical tableaux. Upstairs there is a conjuring show in a delightful little theater, followed by a *spectacle d'illusion* in a *palais de mirages*, where visitors are miraculously transported into a variety of exotic environments, including a jungle. Founded in 1882 by the caricaturist Grévin. There is another branch of the museum in the *Forum des Halles*.

Guimet, Musée Former name of the *Musée National d'Arts Asiatiques*.

Gustave Moreau, Musée
14 Rue de la Rochefoucauld, 9e ☎48-74-38-50. Map 4E8
Open 10am-12.45pm, 2-5.15pm. Closed Tues. Métro Trinité.
"His sad and scholarly works," writes the novelist Huysmans about the symbolist painter Gustave Moreau (1826-98), "breathed a strange magic, an incantatory charm which stirred you to the depths of your being."

The artist's house, which is located on the edge of *Montmartre*, where he lived a reclusive life, is now filled with a collection of his strange, dreamlike works, such as his paintings of *Salome*, "the symbolic incarnation of undying Lust, the goddess of immortal Hysteria", as Huysmans described her in his novel *À Rebours (Against Nature)*.

Halles, Les ☆
1er. Map 10H9. Métro Châtelet-Les-Halles, Les Halles.
This area of the city is bounded roughly by the Rue Étienne-Marcel and the *Rue de Rivoli* to the N and S, with the *Bourse du Commerce* and the *Pompidou Center* marking the W and E boundaries. During the 12thC it became a bustling food market (Zola called it "the belly of Paris") and remained so until 1979 when the traders all moved to a huge new site at Rungis near Orly Airport, taking the atmosphere with them and leaving the city of Paris with the problem of deciding what to do with the area.

The years since then have been a total transformation which is still far from complete. The graceful old glass-and-iron market hall, built under Napoleon III, has been torn down and replaced by a commercial complex called the *Forum des Halles*. An exciting new below-ground complex has been created beneath the new park and children's playground in front of the Bourse du Commerce. Here is located the **Vidéothèque de Paris** (*2 Grande Gallerie, Porte St-Eustache, 1er ☎40-26-34-30. Open Sun and Tues-Fri 12.30-11pm, Sat 10am-11pm. Closed Mon*), an archive of movie material of all eras relating to Paris. The Vidéothèque has three projection rooms where movies from a collection of 2,500 titles are shown, with each week devoted to a different theme. In addition there are facilities for individual viewing.

In the same complex, and about to open at the time of writing, is the Jacques Cousteau **Oceanographic Museum**, incorporating a large aquarium.

The changes have been radical, but slowly Les Halles is adjusting to a new role as a center of entertainment, shopping and culture. Parts of it have taken on a brash seediness, with sex shops much in evidence. However, some of the old buildings have been renovated, the 16thC **Fontaine des Innocents** has been restored, and much of the area has been pedestrianized.

The old market has mostly, though not completely, disappeared. There remain a few semi-wholesale food merchants and a number of restaurants and bars of character: a particularly striking example is the **Les Halles Bar** (*15 Rue Montmartre*) with its tiles depicting scenes of the market in its heyday.

When all the scars have finally healed, Les Halles promises to emerge as one of the liveliest districts in Paris.

Hébert, Musée 🏛

Hôtel Montmorency, 85 Rue du Cherche-Midi, 6e ☎42-22-23-82. Map ***14K6*** *Open 2-6pm. Closed Tues. Métro St-Placide, Sèvres-Babylone.*

Housed in a small and gracious 18thC mansion on the Left Bank, this museum is devoted mainly to temporary exhibitions of the works of society painter Ernest Hébert (1850-1900) and his contemporaries. There is also a small permanent display downstairs. Visitors hear gentle tape-recorded music, chosen to relate to the theme of the exhibition.

Henner, Musée

43 Av. de Villiers, 17e ☎47-63-42-73. Map ***2D4*** *Open 10am-noon, 2-5pm. Closed Mon. Métro Malesherbes.*

This collection contains about 700 paintings, drawings and sketches by the Alsatian artist Jean-Jacques Henner (1829-1905), one of the great individualists among painters. Following no school but inspired by the old masters, he created canvases of a delicate luminosity and haunting grace.

En Herbe, Musée

Jardin d'Acclimatation, Bois de Boulogne, 16e ☎40-67-97-66 Open Sun-Fri 10am-6pm, Sat 2-6pm. Métro Sablons.

Located on the N side of the *Bois de Boulogne* within the **Jardin d'Acclimatation**, this museum exists "to enable children to discover art while having fun." The museum mounts lively temporary exhibitions on such subjects as "Masks and Masquerades" and "The Eiffel Tower," and there is a supervised studio in which children can paint or draw impressions of what they have seen.

For location, see map in *Bois de Boulogne*.

Histoire de France, Musée de l' This museum displays important historical documents dating back to the 7thC. See *Archives Nationales*.

Histoire Naturelle, Museum d' Galleries concerning paleontology, paleobotany, mineralogy and entomology. See *Jardin des Plantes*.

Homme, Musée de l' *(Museum of Mankind)*
Palais de Chaillot, Pl. du Trocadéro 16ᵉ ☎45-53-70-60. Map 12H2 Open 9.45am-5.15pm. Closed Tues. Métro Trocadéro.

Occupying the w wing of the *Palais de Chaillot*, this museum contains one of the world's most important collections devoted to anthropology, ethnology and prehistory. The objects are, for the most part, arranged according to geographical region and include all manner of intriguing objects, from a Navajo sand painting to Japanese costumes. The excellent South American section includes a shriveled Inca mummy in a fetal position which inspired Munch's painting *The Scream*. There is an interesting room devoted to the arts and technologies of different world regions, and another labeled "Anthropology" dealing with the biology and physical characteristics of man. A recent addition to the museum is a display of musical instruments from all over the world. Performances using these instruments are given on certain Sundays.

The museum holds film shows three or four times a week and special exhibitions are staged periodically. There is an attractive restaurant, **Le Totem**, with a superb view of the *Eiffel Tower*.

Hôtel Biron 18thC mansion by Gabriel the Elder. See *Rodin, Musée*.

Hôtel des Monnaies *(Mint)* ☆
11 Quai Conti, 6ᵉ ☎40-46-56-66. Map 9I8 to workshops on Tues, Fri 2.15-3pm. Museum hours not known at time of writing. Shop open Mon-Fri 9am-5.30pm, Sat 9-11.30am. Métro Pont-Neuf, Odéon, St-Michel.

This simple but dignified mansion, which overlooks the Seine, was once the home of the Princess de Conti, but was taken over by Louis XV in the 18thC and remodeled by Jacques Denis Antoine to serve as the Royal Mint. There is a permanent **museum of coins and medallions** and equipment for making them. In addition the Hôtel des Monnaies mounts temporary exhibitions on related subjects. As the making of coins has been transferred elsewhere, the workshops in the building now concentrate on the manufacture of medallions of all kinds. There is a **sales gallery** in the building (*accessible from 2 Rue Guénegaud, 6ᵉ*) where a rich selection of these medallions are available. The medallions are not necessarily solemn objects — one has the cancan as its theme and shows a high-kicking leg. The Mint will even make you your own medallion — if you can afford it.

Hôtel de Rohan 18thC mansion built for the bishops of Strasbourg. See *Archives Nationales*.

Hôtel de Sens
2 Rue du Figuier, 4ᵉ ☎42-78-14-60. Map 11I11. Forney Library open Tues-Fri 1.30-8.30pm, Sat 10am-8.30pm. Closed Sun, Mon. Métro Pont-Marie, St-Paul.

This mansion at the s edge of the *Marais* is such a perfect specimen of medieval architecture, with its pepper-pot turrets and pointed arches, that if you came upon it without prior knowledge you might think it was 19thC imitation Gothic or perhaps a stray building from a Hollywood movie about the Middle Ages. In fact it is one of the oldest houses in Paris and was built by Tristan de Salazar, Archbishop of Sens, between 1475-1507. It was an anachronism for its day, since the archbishop, who came from a military family, could not resist adding a few touches to create the illusion of a fortified castle: a dungeon, watch-tower and watchwalk. The building was a late burst of Gothic feudalism at the dawn of the French Renaissance. It is now owned by the City of Paris and houses the Forney Library, a library of science, technology, arts and crafts. Admire the building's fine **courtyard**.

Hôtel de Soubise 18thC mansion with superb courtyard. See *Archives Nationales*.

Hôtel des Ventes 🏛
9 Rue Drouot, 9e ☎42-46-17-11. Map ***4F8*** *▣ Open Mon-Sat 11am-6pm. Closed Sun and July 25-mid Sept. Métro Richelieu-Drouot.*
The Parisian equivalent of Christie's, or Sotheby's or Parke Bernet, the Hôtel des Ventes has, like auction rooms everywhere, an atmosphere of glamor and excitement. In France, auctioneering is a more strictly regulated business than in most countries, and is controlled by the *Compagnie des Commissaires Priseurs*, the auctioneers' professional body, whose members can display gold plaques outside their doors.

The old Hôtel des Ventes, known as the Hôtel Drouot which stood on this site, was demolished in the 1970s, and the auctions moved temporarily to the Gare d'Orsay. However, in 1980 they moved back into the new Hôtel Drouot, a stylish building of steel, dark-tinted glass and concrete with traditional touches such as a high-pitched, vaulted roof and dormer windows.

Inside there are several floors of auction rooms where all kinds of objects — French tapestries, Italian drawings, autographed letters, Chinese vases — change hands under the eye of a *commissaire priseur* perched behind a high desk.

An amusing place to visit even if you are not bidding.

Hôtel de Ville *(Town Hall)* 🏛 ☆
Pl. de l'Hôtel-de-Ville, 4e ☎42-76-40-40. Map ***10I10*** *▣ to salons, Mon 10.30am. Open Mon-Fri 9am-6.30pm, Sat 9am-6pm. Closed Sun. Métro Hôtel-de-Ville.*
There has been a town hall on this site ever since 1357, the year when one of the earliest mayors of Paris, Étienne Marcel, moved the city council there. His equestrian statue now stands facing the river by the s side of the building.

The first town hall was replaced by a more imposing one in Renaissance style which was burned down by the *Communards* in 1871. The present edifice (1874-82) is a fairly convincing copy of its Renaissance predecessor, but has a ponderous 19thC touch to the ornate facade with its numerous statues of Parisian dignitaries ensconced in niches.

Before 1830, the **Pl. de l'Hôtel-de-Ville** formed part of the riverside and was called the Pl. de Grève (meaning foreshore). It was there that unemployed Parisians gathered — hence the term *faire la grève* (to strike). It was also the scene of numerous executions over the centuries.

For many years Paris had no mayor and was governed by a prefect of the city, but as recently as 1977 the office of mayor was re-established, and today the Hôtel de Ville is his headquarters. The 109 councilors meet in a spacious wood-paneled chamber which can be viewed during sessions from a public gallery.

Other rooms in the town hall can be visited by conducted tour on Mon mornings. A feast of visual extravagance, Paris must have kept an army of artists and craftsmen employed here for many years. For those interested in *fin-de-siècle* decor and painting, they are, perhaps, of particular interest.

The public relations department of the Hôtel de Ville is housed at *29 Rue de Rivoli*. Here you can find out any information relating to the municipality; interesting exhibitions on Paris are also held here.

Hugo, Victor, Musée ☆

*6 Pl. des Vosges, 4e ☎42-72-16-65. Map **11/12** on Sun. Open 10am-5.40pm. Closed Mon. Métro St-Paul, Chemin-Vert, Bastille.*

This is the house where Victor Hugo, author of *Notre-Dame de Paris* (*The Hunchback of Notre-Dame*) and other famous novels, lived from 1832-48. By the time of his death, Hugo had attained the status of national hero. He was given a spectacular public funeral and buried in the *Panthéon*. Many people do not realize that Hugo, as well as being a great writer and distinguished public figure, was also an artist of genius, and the house is full of his drawings, paintings and lithographs — mostly dream-like or surrealistic works depicting eerie landscapes with curious vegetation and somber castles. There are also many portraits, documents and other mementoes of Hugo's public and private life.

One room is devoted mainly to illustrations of *Notre-Dame de Paris* by various artists and also contains Rodin's powerful bust of *Hugo*. (Hauteville House in Guernsey, where Hugo lived in exile from 1856-70, is also run as a museum by the City of Paris.)

Ile de la Cité and Ile St-Louis ★

*1er and 4e. Map **10&11**. Métro Cité.*

The Ile de la Cité floats in the Seine like a graceful galleon carrying over 2,000yrs of history as its cargo, for it was here that Paris began when the tribe known as the *Parisii* settled on the island in the 3rdC. Trailing behind it is the smaller and less heavily laden Ile St-Louis.

A visit to the *Crypte Archéologique* in the square in front of *Notre-Dame* takes the visitor back to the Ile de la Cité's earliest times, and the different stages of settlement can be seen in layers. Another good place to begin is the little garden on a spit of land at the NW end of the Iles, approached by a stairway from the *Pont-Neuf*. On the other side of the bridge, where the island begins to widen out, is a charming little triangular square called the **Pl. Dauphine**, which André Breton describes in his novel *Nadja* as "one of the most profoundly secluded places I know." Farther on, straddling the width of the island and bounded by the Bd. du Palais, is the vast historic complex containing the *Palais de Justice*, the *Sainte Chapelle* and the *Conciergerie*. Across the Bd. du Palais is the rather forbidding Préfecture de Police, headquarters of the immortal Inspector Clouseau, which is offset by the gay **flower market** in the Pl. Louis Lépine near the entrance to the Métro station. On Sun the flower market becomes a colorful **bird market**.

The focal point of the island is the **Pl. du Parvis Notre-Dame**, crowned by Notre-Dame cathedral and bounded on the N side by the Hôtel-Dieu hospital, the foundation of which dates back to the 7thC. A riverside walk leads round the S side of the cathedral to the garden of the **Sq. de l'Ile de France**, at the E tip of the island. At the very end is the **Mémorial de la Déportation**, an underground vault commemorating the French victims of Nazi concentration camps. Its stark simplicity conveys solemnity, dignity and compassion.

Immediately to the N of the cathedral lies a cluster of streets, including the **Rue Chanoinesse**. The name of this street derives from the canons of Notre-Dame whose houses used to line the street. Only two of these, nos. 22 and 24, remain, dating from the 16thC, but there are many fine facades belonging to later periods.

Off the Rue Chanoinesse is the Rue de la Colombe where the line of the old Gallo-Roman wall is traced in the cobblestones. Continue N to the **Quai aux Fleurs**; there are no flowers here, but of interest are two **stone heads** over the doorways of nos. 9 and 11. These represent the ill-fated lovers Abelard and Héloise who lived in a house on the site in the 12thC. The Quai aux Fleurs leads E from here to the **Pont St-Louis**, linking the two islands.

The Ile St-Louis, named after Louis IX of France, has a different and quieter atmosphere from its neighbor, being more private and picturesque. Georges du Maurier in *Peter Ibbetson* writes graphically of the island "with its stately old mansions *entre cour et jardin*, behind grim stone portals and high walls, where great magistrates and lawyers dwelt in dignified seclusion — the nobles of the robe; and where once had dwelt, in days gone by, the greater nobles of the sword — crusaders, perhaps, and knight templars . . . ."

Many of these houses have remained intact. Two of the finest are the **Hôtel de Lauzun** ☆ (*17 Quai d'Anjou*) and the **Hôtel Lambert** ☆ (*1-3 Quai d'Anjou*), both designed by Louis XIV's architect Le Vau. The former can be visited by application to the Town Hall (☎*42-77-40-40*).

The island is an architectural feast and also the town's first real-estate development, built as a unit in the 17thC. All along the river front are houses with stately porticos and interesting stone carving, many of them also bearing plaques commemorating the distinguished men who lived there — aristocrats, politicians, artists, poets. No. 6, Quai d'Orleans, was, in the 19thC, a meeting place of expatriate Polish artists and writers and today is the **Adam Mickiewicz Museum**, named after the man who is considered to be the Polish Dante. It contains the mementoes of his life and of other famous Poles such as Chopin. There is also a library and a fine collection of pictures by French as well as Polish artists (🎫 *open Thurs 2-5pm; closed July 14-Sept 15*).

The spine of the island is the **Rue St-Louis-en-l'Ile**, with its **church** ☆ of the same name, built between 1664-1725 and marked by a curious pierced spire and an ornate wrought-iron clock. The street is full of little shops and restaurants, many with old and interesting frontages. At no. 35 is the travel bookshop **Librairie Ulysse**, the doorway of which is full of notices offering or asking for lifts to faraway places — India, Katmandu, Morocco, Sri Lanka. Two doors away, at no. 31, is **Berthillon**, one of the best ice-cream shops in Europe, with a constant line outside to prove it. For those who prefer a cup of tea there is the **Salon de Thé St-Louis** at no. 81 where no fewer than 54 varieties are served. Devotees of beer might be interested in the **Brasserie de l'Ile St-Louis**, beside the Pont St-Louis. It is much frequented by rugby-playing types, especially Englishmen, and has the boisterously convivial atmosphere of an Alsatian beer hall.

The Ile St-Louis is, however, mostly a peaceful place with its quiet streets, its little park, **Sq. Barye**, at the E end, and the tree-lined riverside walk which runs around most of the island.

The **quays** ☆ which line the banks of the Seine on either side of the Ile de la Cité and Ile St-Louis afford some superb views of the islands and of Notre-Dame. Particularly magnificent are the views from Pont des Arts, Sq. René Viviani, Pont de l'Archevêché, Pont de la Tournelle and the Pont de Sully on the Left Bank, and Quai Mégisserie and Quai des Celestins on the Right Bank. The parapets of many of the quays are lined with little second-hand bookstalls, *bouquinistes*, especially along the Left Bank.

Institut Catholique de Paris

*21 Rue d'Assas, 6ᵉ. Map **14**J7. Métro Rennes, St-Placide.*
This is both a Carmelite seminary and a college of high repute offering courses in a wide variety of subjects. It was here that in the years 1888-90 Edouard Branly discovered radio waves. The Institute now contains the **Branly Museum**, illustrating his work (▣ *open Mon-Fri 8.30am-noon, 1-6pm; closed Sat, Sun, Aug, Christmas and Easter university vacations*). It also houses a **Museum of the Bible and the Holy Land** (▣ *open Mon-Wed 9am-8.30pm, Thurs, Fri 9am-7.30pm, Sat 9am-12.30pm; closed Sun, Christmas, Easter and summer university vacations*) containing archeological finds from Palestine.

Institut de France

*21-25 Quai de Conti, 6ᵉ. Map **9**I8. Not open to public except cultural groups by arrangement. Métro Pont-Neuf, St-Germain-des-Prés.*
"There is no venerable forest," wrote Zola in *L'Oeuvre*, "no mountain road, no prairie or plain where the sun sets so triumphally as behind the dome of the Institut. This is Paris going to sleep in her glory."

The institute is indeed a majestic building, with a concave semi-circular facade facing the Seine. It was founded as a college and library with money bequeathed by Cardinal Mazarin, and was built by the ubiquitous architect Le Vau in 1663-4 on the site of the Nesle gate and tower, part of the medieval city wall of Philippe Auguste, no longer extant.

The college was suppressed after the Revolution and in 1805 the building became the seat of the recently created Institut de France, which it remains to this day. Of the five learned academies which make up the institute, the best known is the Académie Française comprising 40 distinguished literary figures, approved by the head of state, whose main task is to protect the interests of the French language. Alas, they are currently fighting a losing battle against the rising tide of *franglais*.

Zola, even though he wrote with such reverence of the building, was one of many famous Frenchmen, including Balzac, Maupassant, Proust and Molière, who were refused admission to the Académie Française. Most of the honored members have attained total obscurity.

Invalides, Les 🏛 ☆

*7ᵉ. Map **13**I5. Métro Invalides, Latour-Maubourg, École-Militaire, Varenne.*
When Louis XIV's architects designed this building in the 1670s as a home for his invalided soldiers, they poured into it all the architectural rhetoric of the Sun King's era. The 196m (645ft) long **facade** overlooks a wide **esplanade** stretching down to the *Seine*; the great portico is guarded by statues of *Mars* and *Minerva*; the dormer windows in the roof are framed by huge stone suits of armor; the **courtyard** with its double colonnade is worth seeing; and the **Dôme church** (opposite) dominates the whole edifice. Most of the building is the work of Libéral Bruand, but the Dôme church was designed by Jules Hardouin-Mansart and the esplanade by Robert de Cotte.

Once this building housed nearly 6,000 old soldiers. Now the number has dwindled to around 100 and Les Invalides has taken on a new role as the home of four museums and as the resting place of Napoleon Bonaparte.

Musée de l'Armée *(Army Museum)*
☎45-55-92-30 ✉ Tickets also valid for other museums on two consecutive days. Open Apr 1-Sept 30, 10am-6pm, Oct 1-Mar 31, 10am-5pm.
This collection of militaria, one of the largest in the world, is divided into two sections, one housed on the E side of the courtyard, the other on the W. The E side tells the story of the French Army, illustrated by pictures, models and military mementoes of all kinds. Two large rooms on the ground floor, the **Salle Turenne** and the **Salle Vauban**, were once refectories for the inmates of the building. Now the former contains a fine collection of flags and standards, including those from the First World War, while the latter is devoted mainly to exhibits relating to the cavalry, among them a row of lifesize dummies of dashing uniformed men on horseback.

Upstairs, on the second floor, is a series of rooms covering different periods of French military history, dealing with defeat as well as victory. Predictably, Napoleon I features prominently. His death mask is here, and a reconstruction of the room at Longwood House, St Helena, where he died on May 5, 1821.

On the third floor, where there were once craft workshops manned by the invalids, there are now exhibits relating to the Second Empire and the Franco-Prussian War.

On the W side of the courtyard are two more former refectories, the **Salle François I** and the **Salle Henri IV**, which return to the era when suits of armor were worn. Presented here are soldiers standing at attention in glass cases or mounted on dummy horses.

The two rooms at the rear are filled with offensive weapons from the 15th to the 17thC, and there are also rooms dealing with prehistoric and Oriental weaponry. Upstairs, on the first and second floors, the exhibits are from the First and Second World Wars. In addition there is a room full of model artillery guns; look out of the window into the **Cour de la Victoire** and you will see an impressive collection of the real thing.

Musée des Plans-Reliefs *(Museum of Relief Maps and Plans)*
☎47-05-11-07 ✉ Same ticket for Musée de l'Armée. Open Apr 1-Sept 30, 10am-5.45pm; Oct 1-Mar 31, 10am-4.45pm.
Housed on the fourth floor, this museum owes its origin to Louvois, Louis XIV's Secretary of State for War, who suggested to the king that scale models be made of fortified frontier and maritime towns in France. This was done, and the practice was continued by subsequent regimes up to the end of the 19thC. Here are miniature versions of Mont Saint-Michel, Neuf-Brisach, Metz, Strasbourg and numerous other towns; detail is fine.

Musée des Deux Guerres Mondiales *(Museum of Two World Wars)*
☎45-51-93-02 ✉ Same ticket as for Musée de l'Armée. Open summer 10am-6pm, winter 9am-5pm. Closed Sun, Mon.
This museum, not part of the Musée de l'Armée, has a small collection of posters, documents and relics from the First and Second World Wars and holds temporary exhibitions on related subjects. The entrance is in the NW corner of **Cour d'Honneur**.

Musée de l'Ordre de la Libération *(Museum of the Order of Liberation)*
51bis Bd. de Latour-Maubourg ☎47-05-35-15 ✉ Open 2-5pm. Closed Sun.
The Order of Liberation was created by de Gaulle to honor those

who gave outstanding service in the freeing of France. The museum, separate from the Musée de l'Armée, has photographs, documents and mementoes related to the themes of the Free French, the Resistance, the Deportation and the Liberation.

St-Louis-des-Invalides †

This church, with its cool, light, barrel-vaulted interior, was where soldiers of Les Invalides worshiped. Its main entrance faces the Cour d'Honneur. When the Dôme church was added, the two opened into one another and shared a common altar, but a glass barrier now separates them.

Berlioz's *Requiem* was played for the first time in 1837 on the superb 17thC organ.

Dôme church 🏛 † ★

Same ticket as for Musée de l'Armée.

When the rest of Les Invalides had been completed, Louis XIV decided that it needed an added touch of splendor, so he commissioned Hardouin-Mansart to add the Dôme church to the s side of the building. It was begun in 1677 and completed by Robert de Cotte after Mansart's death in 1708. With its high, slender, gilded **dome** and its **portico** with two rows of columns (Doric below, Corinthian above), it is considered one of the great masterpieces of its era.

However, the church is less visited for its architecture than for the fact that it contains one of the most prestigious tombs in the world, the **tomb of Napoleon Bonaparte**, whose body was brought here from St Helena in 1840 and entombed amid lavish funeral celebrations. The Emperor now lies encased in six coffins, one inside the other, which in turn are placed in a red porphyry sarcophagus. This rests in an open circular **crypt** surrounded by a gallery in which are reliefs commemorating his achievements. His son, the King of Rome, also lies here.

Appreciate the rest of the interior: the altar with its elaborate baldachin supported on twisted columns; the **cupola** with its vivid paintings by La Fosse; and the side chapels containing the tombs of Maréchal Foch and other military heroes.

Napoleon would have been pleased with his final resting place. "I wish my remains," he said, "to repose on the banks of the Seine among the people of France whom I have loved so much."

Jacquemart-André Musée ☆

158 Bd. Haussmann, 8e ☎45-62-39-94. Map 7E5 Open 1.30pm-5.30pm. Closed Mon, Tues. Métro St-Philippe-du-Roule, Miromesnil.

Like several other Paris museums such as the *Marmottan* and the *Nissim de Camondo*, this was originally a private house and collection. It was created by the Banker Edouard André and his wife, the portraitist Nélie Jacquemart, who continued to add to the collection after André's death in 1881 and left it in her will to the *Institut de France*, along with the grand Neo-Classical house which her husband had built in 1875. Its opulent interior forms a pleasing setting for art of the 18thC and the Italian Renaissance which the Andrés collected voraciously and with great discernment.

Among the collection of Italian art you will find sculpture by Donatello, paintings by Botticelli, Titian and Uccello — see the magnificent *St George Slaying the Dragon*. French 18thC art is represented by Watteau, Fragonard, Greuze and Boucher, and foreign schools by Rembrandt, Reynolds, Murillo and others. There are frescoes by Tiepolo, a Savonnerie carpet, four *Gobelins* tapestries depicting the seasons, and a wealth of furniture and objets d'art. Notice too, the *Boucicault Book of Hours*, which belonged to Diane de Poitiers.

Jardin des Plantes: Museum d'Histoire Naturelle

(Botanical Gardens: Natural History Museum)
*5ᵉ. Map **16K11** ▣ ☕ ✱ Open summer 9am-6pm; winter 9am-5pm. Métro Jussieu, Monge, Gare d'Orléans-Austerlitz.*

"This morning," writes Henry Miller in *Tropic of Cancer*, "having nothing better to do, I visited the Jardin des Plantes. Marvelous pelicans here from Chapultepec and peacocks with studded fans that look at you with silly eyes."

He might have added that there are llamas, bison, tigers, bears, baboons, a round animal house built under Napoleon in the shape of a Legion of Honor cross, an open-air café and more. The Jardin des Plantes, lying near the Seine to the E of the *Latin Quarter*, is much more than a park and encompasses not only a botanical garden but also a **menagerie** and a Natural History Museum. The menagerie, the oldest public zoo in the country and dating back to the Revolution, is very popular despite its rather antiquated installations.

Near the menagerie, the **botanical garden** was established in the 17thC as a medicinal herb garden and now contains a wide variety of European and tropical plants as well as a maze and a tunnel-like avenue of plane trees.

Along the SE side of the garden is a row of buildings housing four departments of the **Natural History Museum**.

Paleontology: Passing the skeleton of a mammoth you enter a room full of bones and pickled organs, human and animal. Upstairs there are more skeletons as well as casts of alarming prehistoric monsters.

Paleobotany: A small collection of plant fossils, petrified tree trunks and other such recondite objects. A museum for the specialist.

Mineralogy: Fossils, precious stones, crystalline growths, some in lurid colors.

Entomology: A tiny collection of brightly colored beetles and other interesting insects from all over the world with maps of their habitats.

The Natural History Museum also holds frequent temporary exhibitions relating to its various departments.

Jeu de Paume, Musée du

Map 8G6. This building, a Second-Empire pavilion in the *Tuileries* gardens, was for many years the home of one of the world's greatest collections of Impressionist paintings. Now the entire collection is housed in the *Musée d'Orsay*, and the Jeu de Paume is currently being turned into a gallery for contemporary art, which is due to be ready in 1990.

Latin Quarter ★

*5ᵉ. Map **15**. Métro St-Michel, Maubert-Mutualité, Cardinal-Lemoine.*

The name *Quartier Latin* carries with it the image of a way of life: colorful, vibrant, intellectual, rebellious, Bohemian and, above all, cosmopolitan. It lies at the heart of the Left Bank and comprises most of the 5ᵉ and a sliver of the 6ᵉ districts, taking in the streets immediately to the W of the **Bd. St-Michel**.

Its name derives from the presence of the *Sorbonne* university and other colleges in the district, the scholars of which formerly spoke Latin. The area is still full of students, not only from the

Sorbonne but also from the neighboring *Collège de France*, the university of Jussieu a little farther to the E and the École Normale Supérieure to the S.

There is another reason why the term "Latin Quarter" is appropriate. The area now called the **Montagne Ste-Geneviève,** around the *Panthéon*, was once the focal point of the Roman colony. Although the governor had his palace on the *Ile de la Cité*, it was here that the forum, temple and baths were built. Virtually the only Roman remains that can be seen in Paris now are the great thermal baths in the *Cluny* museum and in the *Arènes de Lutèce*.

The main artery of the Latin Quarter is the Bd. St-Michel, or **Boul'Mich** as it is known by all. This busy tree-lined thoroughfare full of bookshops and cafés rises near the Luxembourg gardens and descends southward into the Pl. St-Michel by the Seine, which is dominated by the huge St-Michel fountain.

The Boul'Mich is intersected by the other great artery of the Left Bank, the **Bd. St-Germain**. At their intersection is the *Cluny* museum, one of many architectural riches in the district. Turn up the Rue Soufflot and you will be confronted by the massive facade of the Panthéon standing on the Montagne Ste-Geneviève. Nearby are the church of *St-Étienne-du-Mont*, the **Ste-Geneviève library**, built in the mid-19thC on the site of the medieval Montaigu college, and the **Lycée Henri IV**, the buildings of which incorporate the refectory and belfry of the old abbey of Ste-Geneviève.

There are three other important churches in the area, *St-Séverin, St-Julien-le-Pauvre* and **St-Nicholas-du-Chardonnet**. The last named is the stronghold of traditional Catholics and mass is said here in Latin.

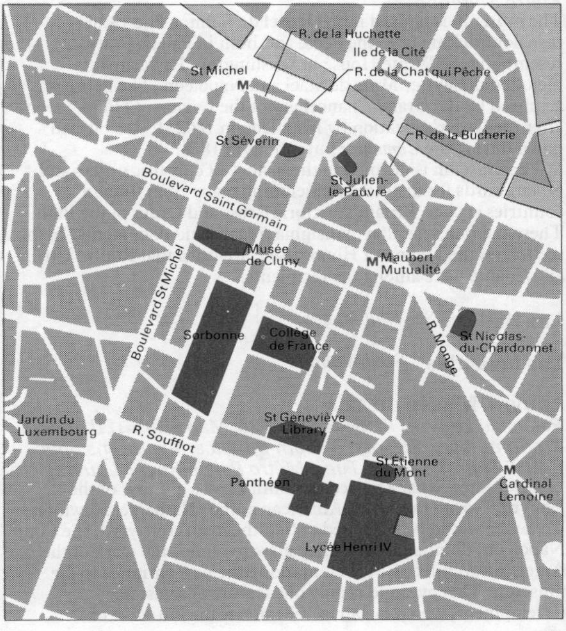

The district's main attraction, however, lies not so much in its monuments as in the tortuous side streets that twist around each other along the bank of the Seine. The strongest impression of the cosmopolitan Bohemian life is gained in the streets around St-Séverin and St-Julien-le-Pauvre. Here are restaurants of many nationalities, small bookshops, intimate little cafés, nightclubs and experimental cinemas. The pedestrian zone of the **Rue de la Huchette** and its tributaries is particularly full of color and atmosphere. Leading off the Rue de la Huchette is the amusingly named **Rue du Chat-qui-Pêche** (Street of the Fishing Cat), said to be the smallest street in Paris. A stone's throw to the E (*at 37 Rue de la Bûcherie*) is one of the most enticing bookshops in the city, **Shakespeare and Co**, which specializes in English-language material, both new and second-hand. Between the wars Sylvia Beach owned the original Shakespeare and Co at 12 Rue de l'Odéon, where it was the meeting place of expatriate literati such as Joyce, Pound, Miller and Hemingway. Eventually it was reincarnated in its present location by a genial American, George Whitman, who still runs the place with great verve and accommodates penniless writers in rent-free rooms above the shop.

In the Latin Quarter one senses fewer barriers than in many other districts; the area seems to invite anyone who goes there to participate in its life. No doubt this is because of the presence of so many nationalities and so many students; certainly the student riots of 1968, whatever harm they did, kept alive the feeling of youthfulness that characterizes this district.

Légion d'Honneur, Musée 🏛

Hôtel de Salm, 2 Rue de Bellechasse, 7ᵉ ☎45-55-95-16. Map 8H6 ✉ ✗ by prior arrangement. Open 2-5pm. Closed Mon. Métro Solférino.

The museum is housed in the **Hôtel de Salm**, a fine 18thC mansion backing onto the Seine and built in Palladian style, resembling the White House in Washington. Its occupants included the writer Mme de Staël and Napoleon. The house was acquired by the Grand Chancellery of the Legion of Honor, soon after the Order's creation by Napoleon in 1802. It was burned down during the *Commune* but rebuilt in 1878.

The museum is devoted to the history of chivalric orders and other awards for distinction, including many from foreign countries such as Britain's Victoria Cross and Order of the Bath. There is a rich selection of insignia, regalia and documents. In the section on the Legion of Honor itself, we learn that Rodin, Utrillo and Colette were among the recipients.

Les Halles See *Halles, Les*.

Les Invalides See *Invalides, Les*.

Louvre, Musée du 🏛 ★

Palais du Louvre, 1ᵉʳ ☎42-60-39-26. Map 9H8 ✉ ⊡ on Sun ✗ compulsory ☕ Open 9.45am-5pm (certain rooms open until 6.30pm). Closed Tues. Métro Palais-Royal, Louvre.

"I never knew what a palace was until I had a glimpse of the Louvre," wrote the 19thC American author Nathaniel Hawthorne. Today he would be surprised to find the main courtyard, the Cour Napoleon, dominated by a crisp glass pyramid, the work of the American architect I.M. Pei, marking the new entrance to the museum. This pyramid is only one feature of a vast new development, which began in 1981 under the initiative of

President Mitterrand and is still not complete, involving vast underground excavations to create new galleries, public reception areas and service facilities. The development also includes the conversion of the old Ministry of Finance quarters in the Pavillon Richelieu into galleries.

In the process of excavating the Cour Napoleon, some 20,000 artifacts were found, the remains of a *quartier* that was demolished in 1852. Equally impressive was the discovery of the foundations of the original 12thC fortress, built by Philippe Auguste, renovated by Charles V as a residence and then demolished by François I in the 16thC in order to create a palace that was added to piecemeal by every important French monarch up to Napoleon III.

Above these foundations is the **Cour Carrée** ★ which was designed by Pierre Lescot for François I in the Renaissance style. In the 17thC Louis XIII commissioned Le Mercier to extend the W facade of the Cour Carrée in the same style, and the remainder of the court was built by Louis XIV. Particularly noteworthy is the majestic **colonnade** ★ of 52 Corinthian columns along the outside of the court. This was the work of Claude Perrault and is one of the outstanding examples of the Classical style in Paris. From the Cour Carrée the Louvre grew haphazardly westward in two gigantic wings as successive monarchs added pavilion after pavilion until it finally linked up with the now vanished Tuilieries palace. Today the Louvre is so vast that it can only be encompassed in a single sweep of the eye if one observes it from the air or from a high vantage point.

The art collection grew in a similar piecemeal way. Begun by François I, it was built up by his successors and continued to expand after it was opened to the public in 1793. It was the fifth museum in the world to be opened in this way. The greatest leaders were the greatest collectors: François himself, then later Louis XIV and Napoleon. As the collection grew, more and more of the palace was opened up to accommodate it.

There are so many exhibits that if you were to spend half a minute in front of each one it would take three months, night and day, to see the whole collection. So clearly anyone visiting the Louvre must ration their time carefully. If possible, try to make more than one visit. A good idea for the first-time visitor is to take one of the general guided tours. Then, having obtained a bird's-eye view of the museum, return later to explore individual parts in greater detail. What follows is a brief guide to the main sections and their highlights, bearing in mind that the locations of exhibits may change, since the museum will remain in a state of flux for some time.

Reception area and underground galleries
The spacious underground reception area, which has striking views of the palace through the walls of the pyramid, contains three restaurants, a museum shop and three auditoriums and can be reached directly from the Palais-Royal Métro station. From here you can go into the museum by a choice of routes. To the N and S you can ascend into one of the main wings of the building. Alternatively, and more dramatically, you can proceed to the E through the gallery devoted to the History of the Louvre, containing some of the objects found during the excavation, then continue via the Gothic Crypt of St Louis into the huge crypt under the Cour Carrée containing the massive, cyclopean remains of the ramparts and keep of the 12thC fortress. For a startling time-warp effect, go straight from here into the Egyptian galleries where you will come face to face with an enormous sphinx.

In addition to the new underground areas, the museum has

seven sections: Greek Antiquities, Roman Antiquities, Oriental Antiquities, Egyptian Antiquities, Objets d'Art, Painting, and Drawing.

Greek and Roman Antiquities

This heading encompasses every chapter in the history of Classical art from early Hellenic times to the end of the Roman Empire. The department occupies the ground-floor galleries in a section of the S wing and also part of the Cour Carrée including the 16thC **Galérie des Caryatides**, once used as a ballroom, with its row of caryatids looking curiously like some of the exhibits. The armless *Venus de Milo* ★ was found in 1820 by a peasant on the Greek island of Milos and is one of the most prized items. Dating from the 3rd-2ndC BC, she embodies all the idealized beauty and dignity which the Greeks invested in their portrayals of the human form. Notice that her face is rather masculine, a reminder that the Greeks of that time particularly exalted male physical beauty.

Another famous exhibit in this section is the headless *Winged Victory of Samothrace* ★ dating from about 200BC and dominating the grand staircase which was built especially for her display. The statue commemorates a naval victory and stands upon the prow of a ship, symbolizing victory with far more impact than any arch of triumph.

Belonging to a much earlier period (6thC BC) is the *Hera of Samos* ☆ In this work and the other statues nearby you will notice the stiffness and frontal emphasis often found in ancient Egyptian statues — so different from the *Venus de Milo*. Hera, in her enclosed roundness, recalls statuary made from tree-trunks. To the left of Hera you will see the *Rampin Horseman* ☆ He has an archaic smile, and his beard and hair are stylized, geometrical approximations of reality. Notice also the bronze *Apollo of Piombino* ☆ with copper inlay (5thC BC).

Oriental Antiquities

Currently occupying the ground-floor rooms on the N side of the Cour Carrée, this section is, in fact, devoted mainly to the civilizations of Mesopotamia, the Far Eastern section of the collection being in the *Musée National d'Arts Asiatiques*. Among the most impressive items here are the black basalt stele bearing the *Code of Law of King Hammurabi of Babylon (1792-50BC)* ☆ (gallery 4), *Stele of the Vultures* ☆ and *Stele of Naram-Sim* ☆ (gallery 1).

Egyptian Antiquities

This is one of the finest Egyptian collections in the world, thanks to long-standing French prominence in this field. Founded in 1826, its first curator was the great Egyptologist Champollion, decipherer of the Rosetta stone, now in the British Museum in London. Situated on the ground floor in the SW corner of the Cour Carrée and in a first-floor gallery along the S side, it contains such masterpieces as the great sandstone bust of *Amenophis IV (Akhenaton)* ☆ which was presented to France by Egypt in 1972, and stands at the top of the stairs. Notice too the superb **Gebel-el-Arak knife** ☆ (gallery 236A), dating from about 3400BC, **jewels of Rameses II** ☆ (gallery 240C), and statue of *Queen Karomama* ☆ (gallery 246F).

Sculpture

Housed on the ground floor of part of the S wing, this section encompasses the whole history of French sculpture from its origins to the end of the 19thC, including works by foreign sculptors such as Michelangelo's *Captives* ☆ and Benvenuto Cellini's bronze relief of the *Nymph of Fontainebleau* ☆ The French sculptures, which are scheduled to be moved to the Pavillon Richelieu when it

LOUVRE FLOOR PLAN

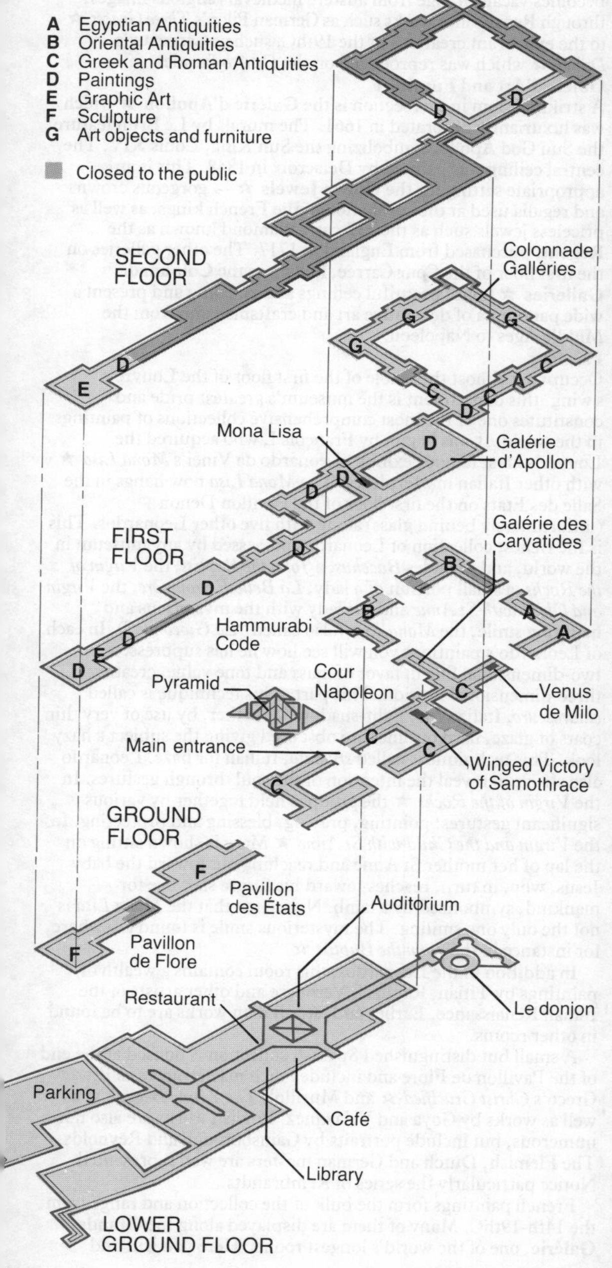
A Egyptian Antiquities
B Oriental Antiquities
C Greek and Roman Antiquities
D Paintings
E Graphic Art
F Sculpture
G Art objects and furniture
Closed to the public
SECOND FLOOR
Colonnade Galléries
FIRST FLOOR
Mona Lisa
Galérie d'Apollon
Galérie des Caryatides
Hammurabi Code
Pyramid
Cour Napoleon
Venus de Milo
Main entrance
Winged Victory of Samothrace
GROUND FLOOR
Pavillon des États
Auditorium
Pavillon de Flore
Restaurant
Le donjon
Parking
Café
Library
LOWER GROUND FLOOR

becomes vacant, range from austere medieval religious images, through Renaissance works such as German Pilon's *Three Graces* ☆ to the exuberant creations of the 19thC, such as Carpeaux's *Dance* ☆ which was reproduced on the *Opéra* facade.

Objets d'Art and Furniture

A striking room in this section is the **Galérie d'Apollon** ☆ which was luxuriantly decorated in 1661. The murals by Le Brun feature the Sun God Apollo, symbolizing the Sun King, Louis XIV. The central ceiling was painted by Delacroix in 1848. This is an appropriate setting for the **Crown Jewels** ☆ — gorgeous crowns and regalia used at the coronation of the French kings, as well as priceless jewels such as the 137-carat diamond known as the **Regent**, purchased from England in 1717. The other galleries on the first floor of the Cour Carrée, known as the **Colonnade Galleries** ☆ house beautiful ceilings and paneling and present a wide panorama of decorative art and craftsmanship from the Middle Ages to Napoleon.

Painting

Occupying almost the whole of the first floor of the Louvre's s wing, this department is the museum's greatest pride and constitutes one of the most comprehensive collections of paintings in the world. It was begun by François I, who acquired the Louvre's most famous exhibit, Leonardo da Vinci's *Mona Lisa* ★ with other Italian masterpieces. The *Mona Lisa* now hangs in the Salle des États on the first floor of the Pavillon Denon (unfortunately behind glass) along with five other Leonardos. This is the richest collection of Leonardos possessed by any museum in the world, and includes *Bacchus*, a *John the Baptist*, the *Virgin of the Rocks*, a small portrait of a lady, *La Belle Ferronnière*, the *Virgin and Child with St Anne* and the lady with the mysterious and haunting smile, the *Mona Lisa* (also called "*La Gioconda*"). In each of Leonardo's paintings you will see how he has suppressed two-dimensional line in favor of mass and tone value, creating three-dimensional illusion. This part of his technique is called *chiaroscuro*, Italian for "light-shadow." Further, by use of very thin coats of glaze, hard outlines are obscured giving the subject a hazy look. This technique is called *sfumato*, Italian for haze. Leonardo also strove to reveal the intention of the soul through gestures. In the *Virgin of the Rocks* ★ the group is held together by various significant gestures: pointing, praying, blessing and protecting. In the *Virgin and the Child with St Anne* ★ Mary is shown sitting on the lap of her mother St Anne and reaching out toward the baby Jesus, who, in turn, reaches toward his future sacrifice for mankind, symbolized by a lamb. Notice too that the *Mona Lisa* is not the only one smiling. The mysterious smile is found elsewhere, for instance in the *John the Baptist* ☆

In addition to the Leonardos, this room contains a wealth of paintings by Titian, Raphael, Veronese and other artists of the Italian Renaissance. Earlier and later Italian works are to be found in other rooms.

A small but distinguished Spanish collection is housed at the end of the Pavillon de Flore and includes such masterpieces as El Greco's *Christ Crucified* ☆ and Murillo's *The Young Beggar* ☆ as well as works by Goya and Velázquez. English works are also not numerous, but include portraits by Gainsborough and Reynolds. The Flemish, Dutch and German masters are well represented. Notice particularly the series of Rembrandts.

French paintings form the bulk of the collection and range from the 14th-19thC. Many of them are displayed along the **Grande Galérie**, one of the world's longest rooms. Here you will find

Poussin's limpid canvases of mythological and allegorical subjects, La Tour's religious paintings with their striking effects of light and shadow, and Watteau's delicate scenes of gaiety touched with a nuance of melancholy.

If it is size and splendor you want, then move round into the 19thC rooms where you will find David's vast painting *The Coronation of Napoleon* ☆ In the same section are works by other 19thC painters such as Delacroix and Corot.

Drawing

Only a small part of the drawings collection, mainly pastels, is on permanent display on the first floor of the Flore Pavilion, but other parts of the collection are brought out frequently for temporary exhibitions on specific themes.

Luxembourg, Palais et Jardin 🏛 ☆

*Map **15**J8. Métro Luxembourg.*

The Palais du Luxembourg, which houses the French Senate, used to be open for guided tours on Sunday, but these have been suspended, so the interior riches of the building are no longer visible to the public.

The palace was built 1612-24 by Marie de Medici, widow of Henry IV. Finding the Louvre boring as a place of residence, she bought the house and grounds of the Duc de Piney-Luxembourg, then standing in a semi-rural position on the s edge of the city. Besides the duke's house (now known as the **Petit Luxembourg**) she built a grandiose mansion designed by Salomon de Brosse in the style of the Pitti Palace in Florence, but keeping the traditional French layout around a grand courtyard. However, her stay was short-lived for in 1630, 5yrs after she had moved in, she was banished for life to Cologne.

During the Reign of Terror (1793-4) the palace became a prison, but after 1795 it housed the higher parliamentary assemblies, and the building underwent a series of alterations and enlargements.

The Petit Luxembourg next door is now the residence of the Senate's president.

The gardens, like the palace, are French with Italian touches such as the Baroque **Medici fountain** ☆ which stands at the end of a long pool filled with goldfish and flanked by shaded walkways. The focal point of the gardens is a large octagonal pool, surrounded by formal terraces and parterres and usually filled with a fleet of toy sailing boats. The rest is an engaging mixture of formality and intimacy, with plenty of little secret corners as well as broad, straight avenues. One of the great delights of this park is its statues. Here you will find, among others, *Delacroix*, *Paul Verlaine*, *George Sand*, *Stendhal* and *Flaubert*. In the **Av. de l'Observatoire**, which forms an extension to the gardens, is an exuberant fountain with an armillary sphere held up by female figures representing the four quarters of the globe.

The gardens also have tennis courts, donkey rides, a marionette theater (the Théâtre du Luxembourg), a school of bee-keeping and arboriculture, and an open-air café under the trees which reminds one of a Renoir painting. In fact the Luxembourg Gardens have just about all the ingredients for a good day out, except that you cannot sit on the grass.

Madeleine 🏛 † ☆

*Pl. de la Madeleine, 8e. Map **8**F6 ✗ compulsory. Open 8.30am-7pm. Métro Madeleine.*

Built to look like a Roman temple, this edifice, with its simple lines and colonnade of soaring Corinthian columns, stands at the hub of one of the most prosperous districts of Paris, confident of its architectural splendor, yet oddly uncertain of its role as a Christian church. Begun as a church in 1764, during the reign of Louis XV, it never seems to have quite thrown off the image of the bank that it nearly became in the early 19thC — other ideas included a theater, a banqueting hall, a Temple of Glory to Napoleon's army and a railroad station. After many changes of design and plans for its use, it was finally consecrated as a church in 1842.

Contrasting with the rather austere exterior, the sensual beauty of the interior comes as something of a surprise — a feast of softly colored marble, gilt Corinthian columns, rich murals and some fine sculpture, including the *Baptism of Christ* by Rude, and the *Ascension of the Magdalen* by Marochetti which dominates the high altar.

The church possesses a superb organ, played in the past by Camille Saint-Saëns, among others, and concerts are held here once a month. By the E side of the church is an attractive little flower market.

Le Marais ★

*3e and 4e. Map **10&11**. Métro Hôtel-de-Ville, St-Paul, Chemin-Vert, St-Sébastien-Froissart, Filles-du-Calvaire, Temple, Arts-et-Métiers.*

This fascinating district has a grave beauty that is haunting, powerful and peculiarly un-Parisian. The stamp of the Middle Ages is still firmly imprinted on the narrow, huddled streets, lined by venerable houses built in the 16th, 17th and 18thC.

The name means "marshland," and this is what the area was, until in the 12thC it was drained by the Knights Templar and became the site of many other religious communities which have since disappeared but bequeathed their names to certain streets: Rue des Blancs-Manteaux, Rue des Filles-du-Calvaire, Rue Ste-Croix-de-la-Bretonnerie. The Knights' fortress, the Temple, became a prison during the Revolution, and it was here that the royal family was held. Today nothing remains of the building. The site, lying at the N of the Marais, is now a charming and secluded little park, the **Square du Temple**, where somber associations are easily forgotten.

In the 15thC the Marais had begun to be a fashionable residential district for the aristocracy, and by the 17thC it had reached its heyday, abounding in gracious mansions of the kind that became the model for the traditional French *hôtel*, with a courtyard at the front and formal garden at the back. There are still more mansions left in the Marais than in any other district of Paris. By the early 18thC the nobility began to move W to the Faubourg-St-Germain. The Marais became less favored and thereby began a gradual decline which lasted until de Gaulle's Minister of Culture, André Malraux, made it a conservation area in 1962 just in time to save it from wholesale redevelopment. Since then an enthusiastic restoration program has uncovered many treasures.

Not surprisingly, the Marais possesses what is claimed to be the oldest house in Paris, **no. 3 Rue Volta**, built in about 1300, and also the second oldest, **no. 51 Rue de Montmorency**, built in 1407 as a charitable lodging house by Nicholas Flamel, who is said to have made a fortune through alchemy. The house is now a restaurant. Near the Rue Volta is the Temple Quarter which includes the *Conservatoire des Arts et Métiers* technological museum, and the church of *St-Nicolas-des-Champs*.

This northern part of the Marais also boasts, to the W, the

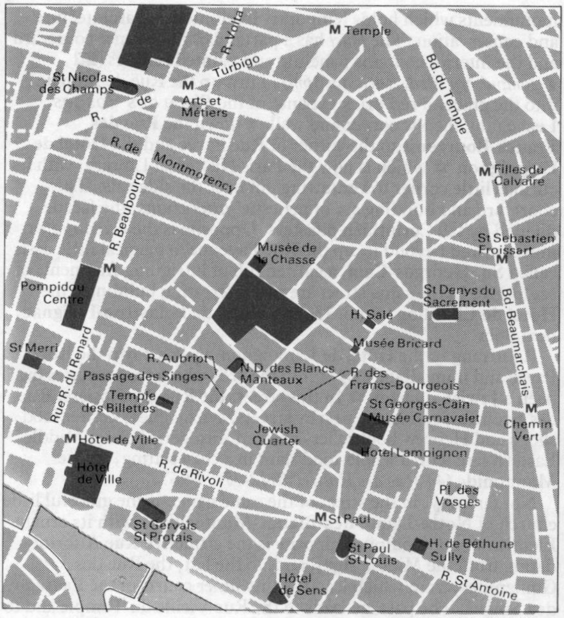

Archives Nationales, housed in the outstanding **Hôtel de Soubise** and **Hôtel Rohan**, and, to the E, the *Carnavalet* museum. Just to the N of the Archives Nationales, in the Rue des Archives, is another notable feature, the **Hôtel Guénégaud**, now housing the *Chasse* museum, a quietly harmonious Mansart building. Around the *Carnavalet* are a wealth of beautiful *hôtels*. Best known are the **Hôtel Libéral-Bruand** in the Rue de la Perle, now the *Bricard* museum, and the **Hôtel Salé** in Rue de Thorigny, the home of the *Picasso* museum. Also worth seeing in nearby Rue de Turenne are the **Hôtel de Montresor**, now a school, and the **Hôtel de Grand-Veneur**, former home of the master of the royal hunt. The facade is adorned with a boar's head and other symbols of hunting and, inside, the impressive staircase is decorated with trophies (ask the caretaker to visit). Farther along the street is **St-Denys-du-Sacrement**, built in 1835 in the Roman style, which contains a *Deposition* by Delacroix.

Beginning at the Seine, a short itinerary takes in some of the southern part of the Marais' most interesting features. Just E of the *Hôtel de Ville* is the church of **St-Gervais-St-Protais** ☆ A Gothic building with a superb Classical facade, the interior contains some fine works of art, including lovely stained glass, and, in the N transept, a Flemish *Passion* painted on wood. Walk down to the river and along to the *Hôtel de Sens*, one of the oldest mansions in the city. Continue E for a short distance, then turn up the Rue des Jardins-St-Paul, leading into the **Village St-Paul**, a charming collection of craft studios and antique stores.

Twisting N, turn left at the Rue St-Antoine to visit the church of **St-Paul-St-Louis**, built in the Jesuit style in the 17thC. Return down Rue St-Antoine to the 17thC **Hôtel de Béthune Sully** at no. 62, now the headquarters of the administration of national monuments which holds temporary exhibitions on architecture and conservation. The *hôtel* has a particularly fine inner courtyard and the interior contains paneling and painted ceilings (🎫 *✗ compulsory Wed, Sat, Sun 3pm*). Turn up the Rue de Birague into the graceful red brick expanse of the *Place des Vosges*. Leave it by the NW corner and walk W down the **Rue des Francs-Bourgeois** to the corner of Rue Pavée and the **Hôtel de Lamoignon** ☆ which is now the Paris Historical Library, with its curious little corner tower jutting out over the sidewalk. The courtyard and building are of majestic proportions, the facade divided by tall Corinthian pilasters. Opposite is the *Carnavalet* museum and beyond it, up the Rue Payenne, a magical little oasis called **Sq. Georges-Cain**, a garden full of intriguing fragments of sculpture. In the same street are two interesting buildings, the **Hôtel de Chatillon**, at no. 13, and **Hôtel de Polastron-Polignac**, next door.

Returning to the Hôtel de Lamoignon, walk S down the Rue Pavée and immediately right into the area which for centuries has been a **Jewish quarter** ☆ In this street, the Rue des Rosiers, Rue des Écouffes, and in the nearby streets, synagogues, kosher food shops and Hebrew booksellers abound. For good kosher Middle Eastern fare with a whole-food slant in a cozy setting, try **Le Maïmonide** (*44 Rue des Rosiers ☎42-77-53-96*).

Not far away, in the street of the same name, is the graceful little church of **Notre-Dame-des-Blancs-Manteaux** ☆ with its ornate Flemish wooden pulpit. Opposite is the attractive **Rue Aubriot**, dating from the Middle Ages, and, to the left, the Rue des Guillemites, from which lead the tiny inner courts of the **Passage des Singes**. The passage leads to the Rue Vieille du Temple and to the left is the **Hôtel des Ambassadeurs de Hollande** ☆ one of the finest mansions in the Marais (*not open to public*), once the home of Beaumarchais who wrote the *Marriage of Figaro* there.

The lower half of the Rue des Archives has the curious nickname of "the street where God was boiled," dating from 1290 when a money lender was said to have cut up a host (communion bread) with a knife. To his surprise the host began to bleed whereupon he threw it into boiling water which immediately turned red. The unfortunate man was apprehended and burned at the stake and soon after a church was built on the site of his house to commemorate the miracle. Around this a monastery called Carmes-Billettes grew up in the 14thC. The **Church of Billettes** was rebuilt in the 18thC and is now Lutheran, but the charming little **cloister** still survives, the only complete medieval cloister in Paris.

A little distance to the W lies another interesting church, that of **St-Merri**, completed in 1612, but anachronistically built in the Flamboyant Gothic style. It has a richly decorated W front, and the oldest bell in Paris, made in 1331.

A block to the N of this church, up the Rue St-Martin, lies the *Pompidou Center*, taking the visitor with a jolt from some of the oldest architecture in Paris to a building that points uncompromisingly to the future.

Marché aux Puces *(Flea Market)*

Map 19C4. Métro Porte-de-Clignancourt.

There were once spectacular bargains to be had at this sprawling bazaar lying in a seedy area to the N of the Périphérique. Alas, this is no longer the case, and the only cheap stalls are the ones selling tawdry modern goods. Most of the market, now more than 2000 stalls, consists of a maze of alleys lined with booths selling an intriguing but over-priced variety of antiques and bric-à-brac, from furniture to second-hand clothes. For prospective buyers it is frustrating, but for those who simply want to stroll and look it can be fun.

Marine, Musée de la *(Maritime Museum)* 🏛
Palais de Chaillot, Pl. du Trocadéro, 16e ☎45-33-31-70. Map ***12H2*** *Open 10am-5.30pm. Closed Tues. Métro Trocadéro.*
The symbol of Paris is a ship, so it is appropriate that the city should possess a fine maritime museum, sharing the SW wing of the *Palais de Chaillot* with the *de l'Homme* museum. There is hardly anything relating to the French Navy and to seafaring in general that you will not find here, from old ship's cannons and figureheads to the bridge of a modern warship, from astrolabes to radar equipment. The museum is particularly proud of its collection of model ships, which include Christopher Columbus' *Santa Maria*, and of its paintings on naval themes, among them Vernet's series on the ports of France. Another prized possession is a sumptuous barge made for Napoleon, in cream, green and gold, propelled by 28 oars.

Marmottan, Musée 🏛 ☆
2 Rue Louis-Boilly, 16e ☎42-24-07-02. Map ***18D3*** *Open 10am-5.30pm. Closed Mon. Métro Muette.*
This collection was begun by the 19thC industrialist Jules Marmottan and enlarged by his son Paul who left it, along with his imposing house, to the *Institut de France* which now administers it as a museum. Its appeal lies not so much in the value of the individual works as in the wayward charm of a private collection, comprising paintings, furniture and ornaments, displayed in a series of beautiful rooms.

Although there are works of many periods, there are three groups of items which are given pride of place: a series of rooms devoted to works of art and furniture of the Napoleonic era; a collection of medieval illuminated manuscripts; and a collection of works by Monet and his contemporaries. These include Monet's *Impression, Soleil Levant*, from which the term Impressionist is derived, and also many of his paintings of water lilies.

For location, see map on p51.

Mint Now contains a museum with a collection of stamping presses, punches, coins and medallions. See *Hôtel des Monnaies.*

Mode, Musée de la *(Fashion Museum)* 🏛
Palais Galliéra, 10 Av. Pierre 1-de-Serbie, 16e ☎47-20-85-23. Map ***6G3*** *Open 10am-5.30pm. Closed Mon. Métro Iéna, Alma-Marceau.*
To many people, Paris and fashion are synonymous. Visit this stylish museum and you are sure to learn something new about the art of dressing. The museum has no permanent collection but plays host to a continuous series of well-mounted temporary exhibitions on various aspects of clothing and its history.

Even if fashion does not interest you it is worth taking a look at the building. The **Palais Galliéra** was built in a striking Neo-Classical style by the Duchesse de Galliéra in the decade 1878-88. The S front gives onto a charming public **garden** where, on clear days, the sun splashes down onto the colonnaded facade and over the park with its fountains, statues and shaded benches, creating an impression of Italy.

Monceau, Parc de

Entrance in Bd. de Courcelles, 8ᵉ. Map 2E4. Métro Monceau.
This is an unusual and rather poetic place. The entrance is a gateway in a tall railing along the Bd. de Courcelles, revealing a picturesque garden in the English style. Beside a little lake there is a semicircular Roman colonnade, and dotted about among the chestnuts, acacias and plane trees are curious objects: a pyramid, a stone archway, some Classical columns. These are all follies remaining from the garden designed for the Duke of Orléans by the writer and painter Carmontel in the late 18thC.

Monde Arabe, Institut du

*Quai St-Bernard, 5ᵉ ☎46-34-25-25. Map **16**J10 ▣ Museum open Tues-Sun, 1-8pm. Closed Mon. Métro Cardinal-Lemoine Jussieu.*
Islamic architecture for the space age is how one might describe the intended effect of the building that houses this new institute, the result of a collaboration between France and 19 Muslim countries. The S side of the building, for example, is shielded from the sun by metal screens based on Islamic patterns, but with apertures designed to open and close like the eye of a camera. Unfortunately the overall effect of the building is rather harsh and inhospitable, with its razor-sharp edges, dull gray tones and unfriendly touches like an elevator that shrieks at you when you press the button. Don't be put off, because the museum inside contains a fine collection of art and artifacts illustrating the development of Islamic culture from its origins to the present day. Other facilities include a library, an audiovisual center and a top-floor restaurant commanding a fine view over Paris.

Montagne St-Geneviève Area of university buildings and famous colleges on the Left Bank. See *Latin Quarter*.

Montmartre ★

18ᵉ. Map 4. Métro Abbesses, Pigalle, Blanche, Anvers, Barbès-Rochechouart, Château-Rouge, Marcadet-Poissoniers, Jules-Joffrin, Lamarck-Caulaincourt.
In AD250 the martyred St Denis is said to have picked up his severed head and walked up and over a hill to the N of the city. Since then millions of people have made the journey in more conventional style up through the winding streets of what is now called Montmartre or simply the **Butte** (hillock). Montmartre is a district full of contrasts. By turn quiet, raucous, quaint, sordid and hauntingly beautiful, it is a must on the itinerary of anyone who wishes to absorb the spirit of Paris.

For centuries Montmartre was a country village, bristling with windmills that supplied flour to the city below. Then in the 19thC it became part of Paris and its picturesque charm and atmosphere and low rents attracted painters, sculptors, writers and musicians. The late 19thC was the heyday of Bohemian Montmartre, when Toulouse-Lautrec drew the cancan girls at the **Moulin Rouge** in Pl. Blanche, when Picasso, Braque and others created Cubism at the **Bateau-Lavoir** studios (burned down in 1970 but since rebuilt) in the **Pl. Emile-Goudeau**, and when artists' models hung about the Pl. Pigalle looking for work. By 1914 most of the artists had migrated to the Left Bank, and the great tourist influx had begun.

Today Montmartre has a number of different faces. The garish nightlife which Toulouse-Lautrec loved to portray has now spread all along the Bd. de Clichy and the surrounding streets. Pigalle today has become decidedly sleazy, the artists' models now

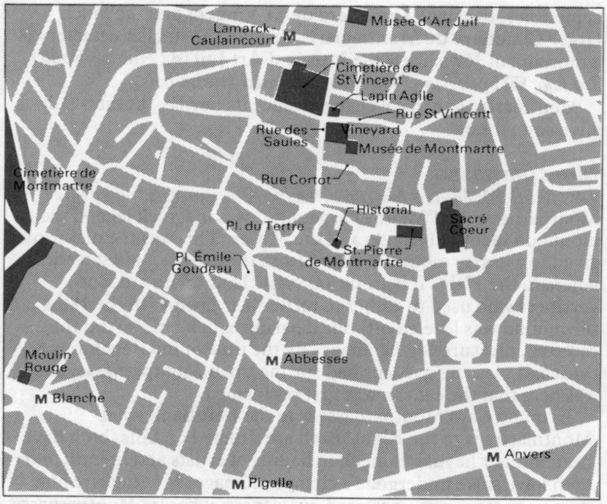

replaced by numerous members of an older profession. This is the Montmartre of neon lights, strip clubs and cheap glitter. Farther up the hill, in the area around the *Sacré-Coeur*, the ghost of the old Montmartre still lingers, but strictly for the tourists' benefit. Yet behind the facade of fake Bohemianism, Montmartre is still a village, an ordinary community with a strong sense of its own history. This aspect is most evident on the N side, an area of quiet residential streets.

One of the best ways to begin a visit to Montmartre is to take the Métro to Lamarck-Caulaincourt and go to the **Musée de Montmartre** ☆ (*17 Rue St Vincent* ▣ *open 2.30-6.30pm, Sun 11am-6pm*). A house inhabited by many artists in the past, it contains interesting mementoes of the district. This route passes another famous meeting place of the Bohemian days, the café **Lapin Agile** at the pretty, countrified intersection of the **Rue des Saules** and the **Rue St-Vincent** ☆ On the slope to the right of the terraced garden in front of the museum there is a little **vineyard**. This is the last surviving vineyard within the Parisian boundaries and every year, on the first Sat in Oct, the vintage is celebrated by festivities and a procession.

The lights winking up at a pallid moon, the slender painted ladies, the wings of the Moulin Rouge, the smell of petrol and perfume and cooking . . . . The Place Blanche, Paris, Life itself . . . .

Jean Rhys, *Quartet*, 1969

Behind the museum is the pretty **Rue Cortot**, within a short walk of the Butte's most prominent feature, the magnificent church of *Sacré-Coeur*. Beside this landmark is the church of **St-Pierre**, a remanant of the great medieval abbey of Montmartre. Downhill to the W lies the **Pl. du Tertre** with its cafés and cobbled, leafy square crammed with artists selling their pictures to the throngs of tourists. Just off the Pl. du Tertre is the **Historial** (*11 Rue Poulbot* ▣ *open 10.30am-12.30pm, 2-6pm*). A wax museum with tableaux on the history of Montmartre, it features Utrillo, Steinlen, Toulouse-Lautrec, Van Gogh, Victor Hugo and Chopin, among others. Some of these people are buried in the Butte's two cemeteries, the small **Cimetière de St-Vincent** and the much larger **Cimetière de Montmartre**. Beyond the smaller cemetery is a museum of Jewish art, the **Musée d'Art Juif** (*42 Rue des Saules, 3rd floor* ☎ *open Sun-Thurs 3-6pm; closed Jewish hols*).

Montmartre may have changed since its heyday, but it is still alive and vibrant.

Montparnasse

*14ᵉ. Map **14**. Métro Montparnasse-Bienvenue.*

Montparnasse, or "Mount Parnassus," was in Greek legend the mountain sacred to Apollo and the Muses. This was the nickname given to a grassy mound, formed from the debris of old quarries, where in the 17thC it became a favorite haunt with student versifiers who used to gather to recite their poems. In the 18thC the mound was leveled off, but the name stuck, and so did the carefree, pleasure-loving image. By the time of the Revolution, cafés and pleasure gardens had sprung up in Montparnasse, and it was here that the cancan was first performed.

In many ways Montparnasse is to the Left Bank what Montmartre is to the Right. Both are situated on hills, both have been in their heyday Bohemian haunts of artists and literati, and both have since undergone a change of image. Montmartre now thrives on its picture-postcard quaintness, whereas Montparnasse has, in recent yars, become the victim of a brutally insensitive policy of redevelopment, exemplified by the *Tour Montparnasse*, the new railroad station and the rash of new buildings around it. The opulently modern **Sheraton Hôtel** overlooks an area of condemned and boarded-up buildings; the once charming **Rue de la Gaîté**, whose little theaters are now down-at-heel, is swamped by an increasing number of sex shops.

Yet the old Montparnasse struggles valiantly to survive, and there are still glimpses of it along the Bd. Montparnasse, once the center of flourishing artistic endeavor. Among those drawn to the boulevard and its surrounding streets were artists Rousseau, Van Dongen, Modigliani, Chagall and Whistler, writers Apollinaire, Rilke, Max Jacob and Cocteau, musicians Satie and Stravinsky, and political exiles including Lenin and Trotsky. Between the wars the district was particularly popular with American expatriates, most notably Ernest Hemingway.

The crowd of artists and intellectuals thronged the new cafés of the boulevard: La Coupole, Le Sélect, Le Dôme, La Rotonde and La Closerie des Lilas, which was one of Hemingway's favorite retreats. In *A Moveable Feast* the author recalls seeing the English occultist, Aleister Crowley, at the café, "a rather gaunt man wearing a cape." Crowley was another of the eccentric and colorful characters who used to frequent the district, and he appears pseudonymously as Oliver Haddo, the villain of Somerset Maugham's novel, *The Magician*, in which a Montparnasse café scene is vividly described.

Those were the days when Montparnasse was one mad continuous party, a period that is vividly described by Michel Georges-Michel in his novel *Les Montparnos* (1924). It was this writer who coined the word "Montparno" to refer to an inhabitant of the district.

Today the sparkling café life of Montparnasse has declined. Only La Coupole, Le Sélect and Le Closerie des Lilas keep alive something of the atmosphere. The writers have dispersed, although there are still many artists' studios in the area.

Montparnasse enjoyed a brief moment of glory during the Liberation of Paris in 1944 when the **Gare Montparnasse** was used as the headquarters of General Leclerc. It was there that the German military governor signed his surrender. In 1967 it was demolished to make way for the present station complex which incorporates huge blocks of offices and apartments.

The station is the point of arrival from Brittany, so Montparnasse is traditionally a Breton area, especially the Rue Montparnasse where there are still excellent restaurants serving pancakes and Breton cider.

The streets to the NW of the station are relatively unspoiled. Here you will find the *Postal* museum in the Bd. de Vaugirard and the *Bourdelle* museum in the street named after the sculptor Antoine Bourdelle. The sculptor himself is buried in the tranquil **Montparnasse cemetery** which also contains the graves of writers such as Baudelaire and Maupassant, composers César Franck and Saint-Saëns, and other distinguished figures. One of the graves has a bronze effigy of a couple sitting up in bed — no doubt very daring for its time. Another is decorated with Brancusi's sculpture, *The Kiss*, a tender and moving piece of work.

Montsouris, Parc de

*14e. Map **19D4**. Métro Cité-Universitaire.*

The most striking feature of this appealing park, with its hills, lake and rambling paths, is a Moorish-looking building with onion domes which is a replica of the Bey of Tunis' palace, given by the Bey for the Paris Exhibition of 1867. Sadly it is now derelict.

The park also contains the Paris meteorological observatory and a tower marking the S bearing the former Paris meridian.

Monuments Français, Musée des 🏛 ☆

*Palais de Chaillot, Pl. du Trocadéro, 16e ☎47-27-35-74. Map **12H2** Open 9.45am-12.30pm, 2-5pm. Closed Tues. Métro Trocadéro.*

Try to imagine part of the facade of Chartres cathedral standing right next door to a tympanum from Reims, a pair of gargoyles from Nantes and some sculptures from Notre-Dame, and you will get some idea of what you will see when you enter this museum. You might well think for a moment that you had wandered by accident into the *Cinéma* museum, also housed in the *Palais de Chaillot*, and were looking at relics of a Hollywood movie studio's props department — except that the replicas here are better made than on any movie set. They are so well made in fact that, close up, it is hard to tell that these are not stone or wood carvings but plaster copies. The same skill is seen in the department devoted to mural painting, where you may suddenly find yourself apparently inside a 12thC Romanesque church, painted with biblical scenes in flat ochers, browns and reds.

The original idea behind the museum was to restore French sculpture to its rightful place among the arts by showing casts of distinguished works. Formerly called the Museum of Comparative Sculpture, it was given its present title in 1937 and widened to include mural paintings and a small amount of stained glass. For the student of sculpture it is a treasure house, for the lay visitor an enjoyable feast of make-believe.

Mosquée de Paris, Institut Musulman 🏛

*Pl. du Puits-de-l'Ermite, 5e ☎45-35-97-33. Map **16L10** compulsory Open 9am-noon, 2-6pm. Closed Fri. Métro Monge.*

Lending an exotic touch to a somewhat drab district of Paris near the *Jardin des Plantes* is this corner of the Middle East, built in the 1920s. It incorporates fine craftsmanship from all over the Islamic world and its most pleasing feature is a central courtyard with a traditional Moorish garden. If you tour the building with a guide, you will be given a fascinating introduction to the Muslim religion (in French). You can also refresh yourself in a traditional Arab café with divan seats and dim lights. Sipping a glass of sweet mint tea here you might imagine yourself in Cairo or Marrakesh.

Mouffetard, Rue ☆

*5e. Map **16K10**. Métro Monge.*

This "wonderful, narrow, crowded market street," as Hemingway described it, begins at the **Pl. de la Contrescarpe**, one of those little leafy village squares which bring a feeling of rusticity to so much of Paris. From here the Rue Mouffetard descends s in a haphazard fashion. It is lined with charming old houses and store fronts with interesting signs, such as at **no. 122**, which reads "At the Sign of the Clear Spring" and which has a well carved on the facade, and **no. 134** with its swirling pattern of birds, foliage and wild boar. **Nos. 101** and **104** mark the entrances to two tiny undisturbed passages, **Pge. des Patriarches** and **Pge. des Postes**. The street itself remains a bustling shopping area, the food stores bursting with mouth-watering cheeses, fruit and delicacies.

As its lower end is the little church of **St-Médard**. Here in the 1720s there grew up a curious cult in which groups of people assembled in the charnel house and took part in orgies of convulsion, hysteria and self-mortification in the hope of attaining miraculous cures or visions. These meetings of *convulsionnaires* were stopped by a royal order in 1732.

The Rue Mouffetard and its tributaries constitute one of the few authentic Parisian "villages" that survive and flourish.

National d'Arts Asiatiques, Musée *(Musée Guimet)*

*6 Pl. d'Iena, 16e ☎47-23-61-65. Map **6G3** ✉ Open 9.45am-5.15pm. Métro Iena, Boissière.*

If the East holds any appeal for you then this treasure house of Asian art is a must. Its nucleus is a collection formed by the 19thC industrialist Emile Guimet, whose intention was to gather together objects illustrating the civilizations and religions of the Orient. Since the museum became a national one, it has been greatly enriched by the addition of other Oriental collections and now houses a splendid, wide-ranging array of art works from Afganistan, Pakistan, India, Vietnam, Laos, Cambodia, China, Korea, Japan, Thailand, Tibet and Nepal. The museum is particularly renowned for its Cambodian sculptures as well as for its magnificent Tibetan *tangkas* (devotional paintings used for meditation) and ritual instruments reflecting the richly colorful and highly symbolic world of Tantric Buddhism. In the fall of 1989, the museum will unveil a new setting for its permanent collection of Chinese and Japanese religious art works, which will be traditionally arranged in ritual fashion and then sanctified by a Chinese Buddhist priest.

Scholars are welcome to visit the museum's research and study center, housing a library, a photographic archive and an auditorium.

Nissim de Camondo, Musée 🏛

*63 Rue de Monceau, 8e ☎45-63-26-32. Map **7E5** ✉ Open 10am-noon, 2-5pm. Closed Mon, Tues. Métro Villiers.*

Like the nearby *Cernuschi* museum, this consists of a private house and contents bequeathed to the nation. Its creator, Count

Moïse de Camondo, was a rich collector with a passion for 18thC decorative art. In 1910 he built a house in the style of the Petit Trianon at Versailles where he set out to re-create the atmosphere of an 18thC interior. Thanks to his discrimination and finely tuned visual sense, the effect is one of harmony combined with the highest quality. The furniture is by such master cabinet-makers as Jacob, Riesener and Saunier, and the tapestries come from the great workshops of *Gobelins*, Beauvais and Aubusson — one particularly fine set depicts the famous fables of LaFontaine.

The museum is sumptuous, though it is hard to imagine such objects ever being approached other than on tiptoe.

Notre-Dame de Paris, Cathédrale de 🏛 ✝ ★

Pl. du Parvis Notre-Dame 4e ☎43-54-22-63. Map 10J10. Church ✗ compulsory, open 8am-7pm. Treasury open 10am-6pm, Sun 2-6pm. Towers open 10am-4.30pm winter, 10am-5.30pm summer. Museum 10 Rue du Cloître Notre-Dame, open Wed, Sat, Sun, 2.30-6pm. Métro Cité.

One of the world's great architectural masterpieces, the cathedral of Notre-Dame dominates the skyline of central Paris with its lacy facade and its two solid rectangular towers. It has fascinated artists and writers over the centuries and was made the setting for Victor Hugo's famous novel, *Notre-Dame de Paris (The Hunchback of Notre-Dame)*, whose hero, the bell-ringer Quasimodo, has become a figure of legend. "A vast symphony in stone" is how Hugo described the building in the novel.

For 800yrs the history of Paris has revolved around the cathedral. Its towers have looked down upon wars, revolutions, executions, pilgrimages and, today, a virtually unceasing stream of tourists. It is one of the symbols not only of Paris but of France itself, and appropriately just in front of the main doorway is a brass plaque set into the ground marking the zero point from which all distances from Paris are measured.

The site of Notre-Dame has been a place of worship since pagan times, when a temple to Jupiter stood there. Later came two adjacent Christian churches, one to the Virgin Mary and the other to St Stephen. These were removed in the 12thC and the building of Notre-Dame was begun — a process that was to take nearly 200yrs. By 1330 the cathedral stood complete in its essential form, though in the 17th and 18thC sweeping alterations were carried out in the interior. In the Revolution most of the statues of the portals and choir chapels were destroyed, the bells were melted down, the treasures plundered, and the cathedral became a Temple of Reason. In the mid-19thC a magnificent restoration was carried out by Viollet-le-Duc, who replaced hundreds of destroyed carvings. During the *Commune* of 1871 the whole cathedral very nearly perished when the *Communards* made a bonfire of chairs in the choir. Luckily the building was saved by the lack of air and the dampness of the walls.

An unusual feature of the cathedral is that its floor is absolutely level with the street, so that it seems to welcome passers-by to enter without formality.

Before going into the building, spend a while taking in the abundant sculptures on the **facade** ★ remembering that most are skillful copies or restorations by Viollet-le-Duc and his pupils. It was he who carved the 28 kings of Israel who stand in a row, known as the **King's Gallery**, across the facade as ancestors of Jesus Christ. The heads of the originals of these are now in the *Cluny* museum. The three doorways are known as the **portals of**

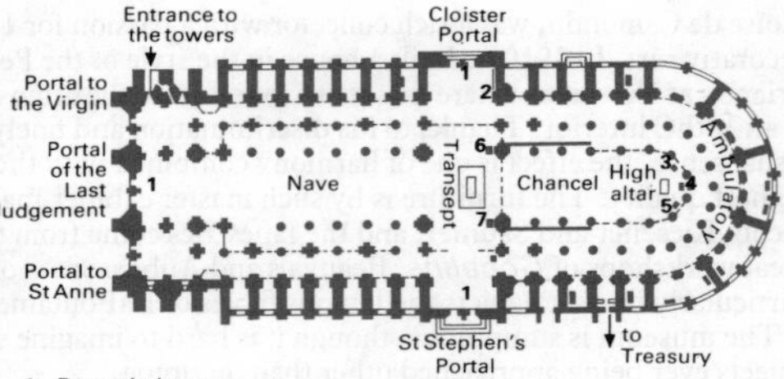

1 Rose windows
2 Virgin and Child 13thC
3 Statue of Louis XIV
4 Pièta 18thC
5 Statue of Louis XIII
6 Statue of St Denis 18thC
7 Virgin and Child 14thC

the Virgin Mary, of the Last Judgment, and **of St Anne**, and the stonework is richly carved with appropriate figures, such as Christ sitting in judgment (over the central doorway) flanked by the Virgin Mary and St John as intercessors. Notice some of the smaller carvings, such as the zodiacal signs on the left-hand portal and the curious medallions on the central one, representing virtues and vices: purity is a salamander and pride is a man being thrown from a horse — these have also been given an alchemical interpretation. The other facades also have some fine carving; the most famous sculpture of all is that of the *Virgin* ☆ by the door of the N transept, carved in the 13thC and unscathed in the Revolution, but for the loss of the Child.

I listened to Vespers and watched the sounding nave grow dusky and the yellow light turn pale in the eastern clerestory . . . .
Henry James, *Parisian Sketches*, 1875-76

Go inside the cathedral and, before looking at individual features, take in the majestic construction of the building, with its walls rising in the traditional Gothic manner, through three tiers of arches to a ribbed, vaulted ceiling that seems infinitely far away. Stand in the center of the transept and you will feel the full impact of the architecture. From here you will also get a good view of the **rose windows** ☆ — three great shimmering pools of light and color to the N, S and W. Only the N rose, made in 1270, retains most of its original glass. The S window was extensively restored in the 18thC and the W window in the 19th. It is partly hidden by the largest organ in France. Features of the transept that are worth seeing include the lovely 14thC statue of the *Virgin and the Child* ☆ against the S pillar flanking the entrance to the chancel, and the 18thC statue of *St Denis* against the opposite pillar.

Around the nave are a series of chapels containing many fine sculptures and paintings, mostly from the 17thC. In the St Peter chapel on the S side there is some beautiful woodwork of the 14thC, carved with representations of saints. In the ambulatory there are more chapels, filled with the mausoleums of various bishops of Paris.

The high altar in the chancel was made in the 19thC to a design by Viollet-le Duc. Behind it is an 18thC *Piéta*, to the right a statue of *Louis XIII* who, in 1638, consecrated his kingdom to the Virgin. To the left is a statue of *Louis XIV*.

On the S side of the ambulatory a door leads to the **treasury**, where a collection of plate and other treasures can be seen including a reliquary said to contain a fragment of the Cross.

No visit to Notre-Dame would be complete without climbing the **towers**. You ascend via the N tower, then cross over to the S one, passing a series of splendid gargoyles and carved monsters, including the **striga** (a kind of vampire) who gazes, chin resting on his hands, over the city. In the s tower you can visit, with a guide, the belfry containing the great 13-ton bell which is rung only on special occasions.

The s tower can be climbed to the top and on the descent you pass a room containing a **museum of the cathedral's history**. If you want a more detailed presentation of the building's history go across the road to the **cathedral museum**, housing a small but interesting collection of objects, pictures and documents which illustrate the life story of this remarkable building.

Observatoire 🏛

*61 Av. de l'Observatoire, 14ᵉ. Map **15M8** ✉ ✗ compulsory. Open first Sat in month. Apply in writing to Secretariat at above address. Métro Port-Royal, Denfert-Rochereau.*

This chaste building, with its two-domed octagonal towers, was built between 1667-72. No iron was used in the construction because it might have affected the instruments, and wood was also avoided for fear of fire. The s wall of the building marks the latitude of Paris.

Today, the Observatory remains a major research center for astronomy and related services. It is the headquarters of the Time and Frequences Laboratory which sets the legal time for France, and also the headquarters of the International Earth Rotation Service which contributes to setting universal time. In theory the building and its small museum can be visited by guided tour on the first Sat of every month, but there is usually a waiting list, sometimes of two or three months. However, the charming **garden** behind the Observatory, entered from the Bd. Arago, is open to all, free of charge.

Opéra 🏛 ☆

*Pl. de l'Opéra, 9ᵉ ☎47-42-57-50. Map **8F7** ✉ Foyer and amphitheater open 11am-4.30pm (except during afternoon performances), box office 11am-8pm. Closed Sun. Métro Opéra.*

When Charles Garnier, architect of the Opéra, was asked by the Empress Eugénie whether the building was to be in the Greek or Roman style, he replied indignantly, "It is neither Greek nor Roman. It is in the Napoleon III style, Madame!"

In fact, no building epitomizes more strikingly the heavy opulence of that era. During its construction between 1862-72 the builders encountered an underground lake which now lies beneath the cellars of the building, where the "Phantom of the Opéra" had his dwelling in the horror movie of that name. Above, however, all is brightness and gaiety.

The ornate facade with its multitude of columns, friezes, winged figures and busts of famous composers is the architectural equivalent of Offenbach's music: lighthearted and irresistible. Inside the building the tone changes. The richly colored marble staircase with its caryatids holding up elaborate candelabra evokes the setting for Belshazzar's Feast.

As for the auditorium, it has all the right ingredients: red velvet, gold leaf and an abundance of plaster nymphs and cherubs. The only discordant element is the domed ceiling painted by Chagall — exquisite but out of key.

During the day you can walk around the building in return for a small fee, but really the only way to see the Opéra is to attend a performance there — always a great experience.

After the opening of the new Opéra de la Bastille, scheduled for 1990, the old Opéra plans to concentrate mainly on dance and ballet, with some concerts by guest orchestras.

Opéra Quarter

9e and 2e. Map 8&9. Métro Madeleine, Opéra Havre-Caumartin, Chaussée-d'Antin, Richelieu-Drouot, Quatre-Septembre, Pyramides, Tuileries, Palais-Royal.

This distinctive area surrounding the magnificent *Opéra* falls roughly between the Bd. Haussmann and the *Rue de Rivoli* to the N and S, and the Rue de Richelieu and the *Madeleine* to the E and W. More than any other district of Paris, it bears the stamp of Baron Haussmann, Napoleon III's energetic Prefect of the Seine, who replanned much of central Paris in the years 1853-70 and whose signature was the wide boulevard and spacious townscape. It was he who carved out the **Pl. de l'Opéra**, which many considered unnecessarily large at the time, as well as the **Av. de l'Opéra**, the Rue Auber and the Rue Halévy, which clasp the ornate Opéra buildings as in a forked stick.

The **Bd. des Italiens** and its extensions were already a fashionable area for rich pleasure-seekers, but with Haussmann's developments and the Gare St-Lazare near at hand, the quarter also became a thriving commercial and financial center. This transformation was accelerated by the building of the Métro at the beginning of the century (four lines now converge at Opéra Métro station).

The district today preserves both of these aspects. Everywhere you look there seem to be palatial banks, such as the frothy pile of the Crédit Lyonnais building in the **Bd. des Italiens**, and huge stores — Trois Quartiers in the **Bd. de la Madeleine**, Printemps and Galéries Lafayette in the **Bd. Haussmann**. There are also many smaller but often more expensive stores, some bearing anglophile names like "Old England," others inimitably French, such as the couturiers in the elegant **Rue St-Honoré**, which becomes the even more elegant *Rue du Faubourg-St-Honoré*. The most luxurious street of all, however, is the **Rue de la Paix** ☆ leading from the Opéra to the *Place Vendôme* and lined with sumptuous couturiers and jewelers, including **Cartier**.

Theaters in the district, apart from the Opéra itself, include the **Olympia** auditorium in the Bd. des Capucines (mainly for pop concerts), the experimental **Opéra Studio** and the *Comédie Française*, the seat of Classical French drama (see *Nightlife*).

One of the Comédie's greatest (and funniest) dramatists, Molière (1622-73), is commemorated by the **Molière fountain**, near the site of his house in the Rue de Richelieu. The fountain is a grand affair with a bronze statue of the playwright sitting on a pedestal supported by two languid female figures — a somewhat solemn monument for so humorous a writer.

Another appealing **fountain** lies a short distance farther up the Rue de Richelieu in the **Sq. Louvois**, a small park beside the *Bibliothèque Nationale*. Podgy cherubs on dolphins support a great bowl decorated with the signs of the zodiac, surmounted by four buxom women representing four great rivers of France, the Seine, Saône, Loire and Garonne. The park, with its chestnut trees, is one of the few intimate little retreats in the district. Near the entrance is a *colonne Morris*, one of those charming onion-domed advertisement pillars which, alas, are disappearing almost as fast as the *pissotières*.

If you are looking for imposing architectural riches you need only cross the road to the *Bibliothèque Nationale* or go W to the

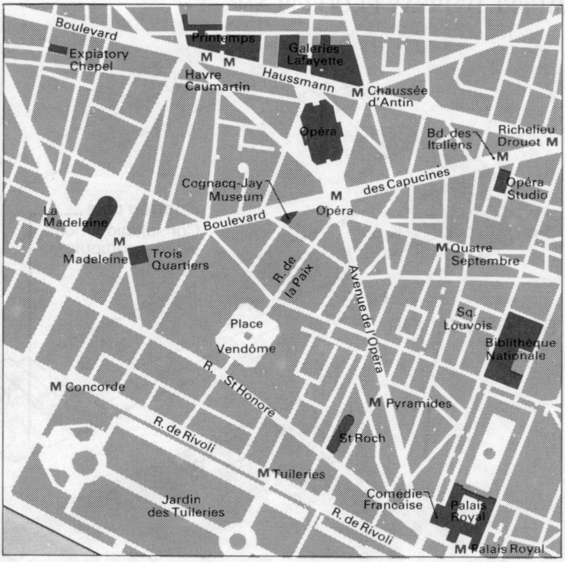

Place Vendôme and the *Madeleine*, or S to the *Palais-Royal* or the church of *St-Roch*. There are not many museums in this quarter, but the *Cognacq-Jay* museum, in the Bd. des Capucines, has a superb collection of paintings and objets d'art. which is well worth a visit.

One rather curious monument lies on the NW fringes of the quarter. This is the **Expiatory Chapel**, built by order of Louis XVIII to the memory of his brother and sister-in-law, Louis XVI and Marie-Antoinette. It stands in the **Sq. Louis XVI**, now another tranquil little garden off the Bd. Haussmann, but formerly a cemetery where lie victims of the guillotine from the Revolution. Louis XVI and Marie-Antoinette were also buried here, until Louis XVIII had their bodies removed to *St-Denis*. The chapel itself looks rather like a glorified waterworks from the outside. Inside it is a frostily Classical mausoleum, somewhat like a miniature *Panthéon*, with statues of the unfortunate couple and a gloomy little crypt below (*open 10am-noon, 2-5pm or 6pm*).

At no. 5 Rue Daunou is the famous American watering-hole, **Harry's Bar**. On the night before a US presidential election, a mock poll is held among the clientele — and more often than not predicts the winner.

Orangerie, Musée de l'

Pl. de la Concorde, 1er ☎42-97-48-16. Map ***8G6****. Open 9.45am-5pm. Closed Tues. Métro Concorde.*
Across the Tuileries from the *Jeu de Paume* is this matching pavilion housing the Walter and Guillaume collection of paintings covering the period from the end of Impressionism to 1930 and including works by Renoir, Cézanne, Soutine and Picasso. The gallery's other major possession is a collection of Monet's *Nymphéas (Waterlilies)*, rivaling those displayed in the *Marmottan* museum. In the remaining rooms of this pavilion, temporary exhibitions are frequently held.

MUSÉE D'ORSAY FLOOR PLAN

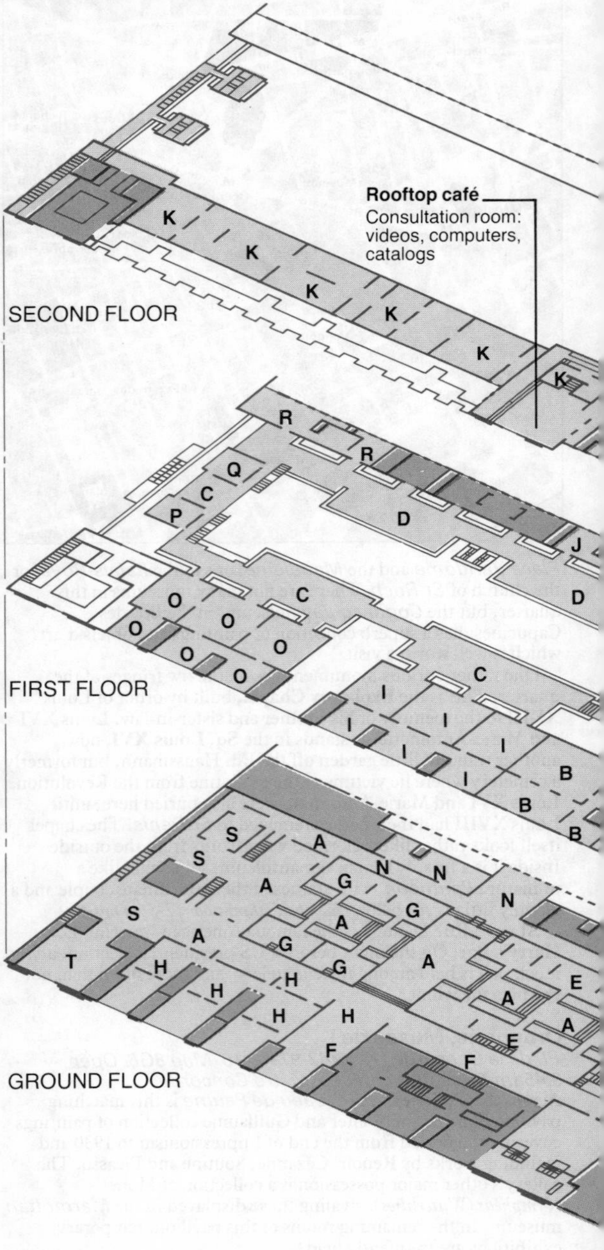

Orsay, Musée d'

62 Rue de Lille, 7e ☎40-49-48-25. Map 8H7 ✉ ♿ Open Tues, Wed, Fri, Sat 9am-6pm. Thurs 10am-9.45pm (June 20-Sept 20 opens daily 9am). Closed Mon. Métro Solférino, RER Musée d'Orsay.

What better place for a museum of the 19thC (more precisely the second half of the 19th and the early years of the 20thC) than the former Gare d'Orsay, a splendid example of fin-de-siècle grandeur.

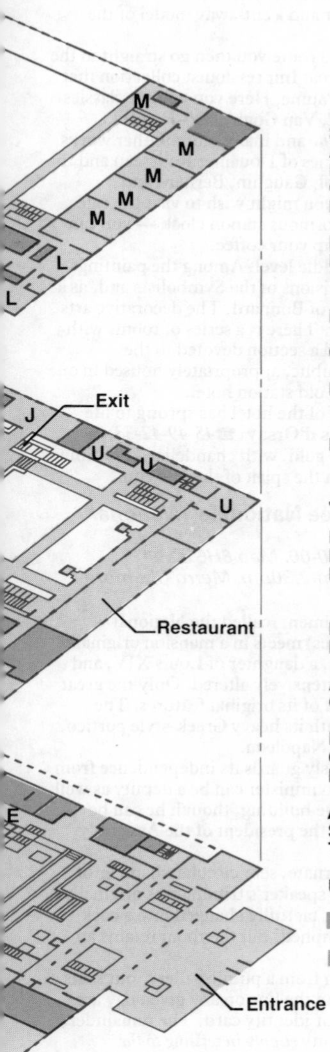

Sculpture
- **A** 1850-70
- **B** Third Republic decorative arts
- **C** Rodin et al
- **D** Rosso, Bernard et al

Painting
- **E** Ingres, "Ingrisme," Delacroix, history painting and the portrait 1850-80
- **F** Daumier, Millet, Rousseau, Corot, Realism, Courbet
- **G** de Chavannes, Moreau, Degas before 1870
- **H** Manet, Monet and Renoir before 1870, Fantin-Latour, Whistler, Realism, Orientalism
- **I** Painting at the Salon 1880-1900, Naturalism, foreign schools, Symbolism
- **J** After 1900: Bonnard, Vuillard et al
- **K** Impressionism
- **L** Neo-Impressionism
- **M** Douanier-Rousseau, the Pont-Aven School, the Nabis

Decorative arts
- **N** 1850-80

Art Nouveau
- **O** France, Belgium, Guimard, the Nancy School
- **P** Guimard
- **Q** International Art Nouveau
- **R** Vienna, Glasgow, Chicago

Architecture
- **S** The Paris Opéra
- **T** Pavillon Amont: 1850–1900

- **U** Birth of the film maker

- ■ **Temporary exhibitions**
- ■ **Closed to the public**

which has been beautifully restored and skillfully converted for museum purposes.

The museum is on three levels. You begin on the ground floor, where you encounter, among other works, the cool, formal classicism of Ingres, the fluid, romantic canvases of Delacroix, the calm, pastoral scenes of Millet and Corot, and the early work of Manet, Monet and Renoir. There are also some striking sculptures, such as François Rude's *Napoleon Awakening to Immortality*, as well as an architecture section with a model of the Opéra Quarter under a glass floor and a cut-away model of the Opéra building itself.

If you follow the recommended route you then go straight to the upper level where you find the great Impressionist collection that used to be housed in the Jeu de Paume. Here you will see classics such as Monet's *Rouen Cathedral*, Van Gogh's *Self-Portrait*, Renoir's joyful *Moulin de la Galette* and many more. Other works on this floor include the eerie scenes of Douanier Rousseau and the paintings of the Pont-Aven school: Gauguin, Bernard and Sérusier. While on the top floor you might wish to visit the café located behind the face of the enormous station clock — you can watch the hands moving as you sip your coffee.

Finally you descend to the middle level. Among the paintings exhibited here are the uncanny visions of the Symbolists and, as a total contrast, the vivid canvases of Bonnard. The decorative arts are well represented on this floor. There is a series of rooms with superb Art Nouveau objects, and a section devoted to the decorative arts of the Third Republic, appropriately housed in one of the ornate public rooms of the old station hotel.

The elegant former restaurant of the hotel has sprung to life again as the **Restaurant du palais d'Orsay** (☎*45-49-42-33*), a large, bright room, all white and gold, with chandeliers—a dining ambience wholly in keeping with the spirit of the museum.

Palais-Bourbon: Assemblée Nationale *(National Assembly)*

33 Quai d'Orsay, 7e ☎42-97-60-00. Map ***8H6*** *✗ compulsory. Open Sat 11am-2.30pm. Métro Chambre-des Députés, Invalides.*

The French lower house of parliament (called the National Assembly or Chamber of Deputies) meets in a mansion originally built by the Duchess of Bourbon, a daughter of Louis XIV, and later acquired by the state and extensively altered. Only the great courtyard facing s preserves most of its original features. The facade looking onto the Seine, with its heavy Greek-style portico, was constructed on the orders of Napoleon.

The National Assembly jealously guards its independence from the government and the state. No minister can be a deputy as well, and the president cannot enter the building, though he can be received in the adjacent house of the president of the Assembly, the **Hôtel de Lassay**.

The 577 deputies meet in an ornate, semicircular chamber of red, white and gold. The marble speaker's tribune was originally adorned with a Napoleonic eagle, tactfully changed into a cock when republicanism finally triumphed, but the room retains an aspect of imperial splendor.

During sessions you can watch from a public gallery, but seats are limited. The first ten people in the line on any given day are admitted on showing a passport or identity card. The remainder must have a pass signed by a deputy (*apply in writing to the Quaestor's Office, 126 Rue de l'Université, 75007 Paris*).

Other parts of the building which visitors are allowed to see include the **library**, a discreetly grand room with a ceiling decorated by Delacroix depicting a **history of civilization**.

The Palais-Bourbon has the atmosphere of an exclusive London club; the deputies even have their own barbershop.

Palais de Chaillot 🏛 ☆

Pl. du Trocadéro, 16e. Map **12***H2. Métro Trocadéro.*

The commanding height on the Right Bank of the Seine, known as the Chaillot, has been occupied by a series of buildings beginning with a country house built by Catherine de Medici in the 1580s. After the Restoration, Charles X wanted to build a monument to commemorate the French capture of the Trocadéro fort near Cadiz in Spain. This was never built, but the name stuck and was given to an elaborate palace created on the site for the Paris Exhibition of 1878. Its successor, built for the Exhibition of 1937, was called the Palais de Chaillot, and the name Trocadéro was kept for the square onto which the N side of the building faces. The whole complex is aligned with the *Eiffel Tower* and the *Champ-de-Mars* across the river, creating a dramatic townscape.

With its simple lines, Neo-Classical colonnades and heroic sculptures, the palace is reminiscent of the monumental Nazi and Soviet architecture of the period. But it has aged well, and its sandstone facade has a crisp elegance.

From a spacious piazza with a magnificent view of the Eiffel Tower, two curving wings reach out, embracing a garden that slopes down toward the Seine, the central axis of which is laid out in a descending series of fountains and pools.

The Palais de Chaillot is now occupied by the following museums: *Cinéma, de l'Homme, Marine* and *Monuments Français*. Also housed here are the film library of the *Cinémathèque Française* and the **Théâtre National de Chaillot** with its two auditoriums.

Palais des Congrès: Centre International de Paris

Pl. de-la-Porte-Maillot, 17e ☎46-40-27-01. Map **6***D2. Métro Porte-Maillot.*

A streamlined, multipurpose building, opened in 1974, dominates the chaotic spaghetti intersection by the NE corner of the *Bois de Boulogne*. It comprises the Palais des Congrès and a vast hotel. The palais itself is a low-rise block which houses exhibition halls, shops, restaurants, movie theaters, conference rooms, a discotheque, an air terminal and the huge and impressive **Main Conference Hall**, home of the Paris Symphony Orchestra and also used for conferences (no admittance unless attending a performance, or a participant). Beside this is the high-rise Hôtel Concorde La Fayette, with 1,000 rooms. The whole complex, known as the Centre International de Paris (CIP), is a planners' dream with every facility — except charm.

Palais de la Découverte *(Palace of Discovery)*

Av. Franklin-D-Roosevelt, 8e ☎43-59-16-65. Map **7***G5* 🎫 ☕ *in Grand Palais. Open Tues-Sun 10am-6pm. Closed Mon. Planetarium lectures four or five times a day. Métro Champs-Élysées-Clemenceau.*

The imposing W wing of the Grand Palais with its huge domed entrance hall is a place in which to wonder at the properties of the symbol Pi, the structure of the atom, the nature of laser beams or the fundamentals of genetics. These and many other branches of discovery are imaginatively presented and kept up to date. What makes the Palais de la Découverte exciting is that docents are present in every room to explain and demonstrate the exhibits.

The museum has a **planetarium** where different aspects of the universe are projected onto a hemispherical dome. There are regular temporary exhibitions, film shows and lectures.

Palais de l'Élysée

55 Rue du Faubourg-St-Honoré, 8e. Map 7F5. Métro St-Philippe-du-Roule, Champe-Élysées-Clemenceau.

Built in 1718 for the Comte d'Evreux and later lived in by Madame de Pompadour and Napoleons I (who signed his abdication here) and III, among others, this palace with its extensive garden has been since 1873 the official residence of the French president and the meeting place of the Council of Ministers. The public is not allowed in but can glimpse the elegant facade and courtyard beyond a heavily guarded gateway.

Palais Galliéra 19thC Italian Renaissance-style building. See *Mode, Musée de la.*

Palais de Justice *(Law Courts)*

Bd. du Palais, 1er ☎43-29-12-55. Map 10I9 ✉ ✗ Open Mon-Sat 10am-6pm. Closed Sun. Métro Cité.

Together with *Sainte Chapelle* and the *Conciergerie*, the Palais de Justice forms a vast complex of buildings running the whole width of the *Ile de la Cité*, with an imposing courtyard and entrance on the Bd. du Palais. There was a palace here in Roman times, and later the site was occupied by a magnificent royal residence which in the 14thC became the seat of parliament. Since the Revolution, the buildings have been occupied by civil and criminal law courts.

Shining gates, ascending flights of steps, *Liberté, Egalité, Fraternité* in golden letters, *Tribunal de Police* in black. As it were, a vision of heaven and the Judgement.

Jean Rhys, *Quartet*, 1929

The most impressive room in the complex of courts and galleries is the **Lobby** (Salle de Pas-Perdus), formerly the great hall of the palace which was twice destroyed by fire and rebuilt in its present form in the 1870s. The royal courtiers are now replaced by lawyers and litigants scurrying about the "cathedral of chicanery," as Balzac called it. If you want to see them in action you can drop into any of the courts with the exception of the juvenile court. Opening times are approximate.

Palais-Royal

Pl. du Palais-Royal, 1er. Map 9H8. Métro Palais-Royal.

Few buildings in Paris have played as many different roles as the Palais-Royal. Built by Cardinal Richelieu in the 17thC as his private palace, it later came into the hands of the Orléans family, one of whom was the dissolute regent Philippe II of Orléans who turned the palace into a scene of frenzied orgies. His descendant, the so-called "Philippe Égalité," in order to raise money built matching terraces of apartment houses around the garden, with an arcade at the group level in which there were premises for tradesmen. These buildings form the splendid quadrangle that one can enter to the N of the palace.

In the heated period before the Revolution, this quadrangle was the scene of rallies and demonstrations — the "nucleus of the

Revolution" Marat called it. Then, after the execution of Philippe Égalité, the palace, its gardens and cafés became a center of gambling and prostitution.

Returned to the Orléans family at the Restoration, the palace was sacked during the Revolution of 1848 and set on fire by the mob during the *Commune* of 1871. Soon afterward it was restored, and today it has settled down to a more tranquil existence. The palace is now occupied by administrative offices and the garden is a public park with the buildings around it given over to apartments and small shops, selling a variety of goods from stamps to handbags.

The Palais-Royal (now the office of the Council of State and closed to the public) finally seems content after its hectic past. The fountain plays drowsily in the middle of the courtyard, and the sunlight filters lazily through the trees — a fine spot for a noon siesta.

A controversial addition to the Cour d'Honneur consists of a series of black-and-white columns of unequal height created by the artist Buren.

Palais de Tokyo 🏛

13 Av. du Président Wilson, Paris 16e ☎47-23-36-53. Map 12G3 ▣ Open Mon-Fri 9.45am-5pm, Sat, Sun 9.45am-5.30pm. Closed Tues. Métro Iéna, Alma-Marceau.

Also known as the Centre de la Photographie et du Patrimonie Photographique, this museum occupies the W wing of the Tokyo complex, erected for the World Exhibition of 1937. It is used for temporary exhibitions of photographic art. The building also houses a branch of the cinémathèque film archive and a movie theater, due at the time of writing to open shortly.

Panthéon 🏛 ☆

Pl. du Panthéon, 5e ☎43-54-34-51. Map 15K9 ▣ ✗ but ✗ compulsory for crypt ▣ in crypt, fee elsewhere. Open 10am-noon, 2-5pm (5.30pm in summer). Métro Luxembourg, Cardinal-Lemoine.

For half of its life this building has led a schizophrenic existence. It was initiated by Louis XV in thanksgiving for his recovery from an illness, and was intended as a more magnificent shrine to Paris' patroness Saint Geneviève than the old abbey church of that name (later demolished). Situated in a commanding position on the Montagne St-Geneviève, it was built in the form of a Greek cross, with a **dome** at the intersection and a massive portico with Corinthian columns. Hardly had it been completed than the new Revolutionary government decided to change it from a church into a mausoleum for the bodies of great Frenchmen. For this purpose many of the windows were removed and blocked up, hence the rather bald and forbidding appearance that the building now presents. Twice it was to revert to its role as a church and then be changed back to a secular mausoleum. The last occasion was in 1885 when it was finally secularized to provide a suitable resting place for Victor Hugo. Did they consider that there was not enough room for God *and* Hugo?

When you enter the building it strikes a chill, with its pale, diluted light that filters down from the high windows and through the clerestory in the dome, seeming to freeze as it falls on the chaste stonework and the great empty expanse of floor. However, as you look around, there is much to please the eye, particularly the series of **paintings** by the 19thC symbolist Puvis de Chavannes depicting scenes from the lives of St Geneviève and St Germain d'Auxerre. His deliberately flat, pale colors harmonize well with the building. There is also a horrifying painting showing the newly decapitated St Denis reaching out to pick up his head while an astonished executioner looks on.

The **crypt**, which runs in a series of vaulted corridors beneath the whole building, holds the remains of countless illustrious Frenchmen. The tombs are housed in gloomy little rooms looking for all the world like prison cells. Hugo shares one with Zola — a curious pair of cell-mates. Rousseau's tomb is like a dog kennel, out of which reaches a hand holding a torch. Others buried here include the building's architect, Soufflot, the chemist Berthelot and the Resistance leader Jean Moulin. A distinguished assembly but one that the visitor is glad to escape from into the light of day.

Paradis, Rue de

*10e. Map **5E10**. Métro Château-d'Eau, Poissonière.*

Unexpectedly situated in the rather characterless hinterland between the *Grand Boulevards* and the Gare du Nord, this street is monopolized by retailers of glass and ceramic tableware. The goods displayed in these stores range from the breathtakingly vulgar to the stunningly beautiful. At no. 30 is the **Musée des Cristalleries** (Glassware Museum), run by the firm of Baccarat and containing a dazzling collection of glass objects dating from the early 19thC to the present day (*open Mon-Fri 9am-5.30pm, Sat 10am-noon, 2-4pm; closed Sun*).

Another interesting museum on the street is the **Musée de l'Affiche** (Poster Museum) at no. 18. This is one of Paris' most recently founded museums, which holds temporary exhibitions. It is housed in the former premises of a ceramics manufacturer with a superbly tiled entrance way (*open noon-6pm; closed Tues*).

Pasteur, Musée

*25 Rue de Docteur-Roux, 15e ☎45-68-82-82. Map **13L5** by prior arrangement. Open 2-5.30pm. Closed Sat, Sun and Aug. Métro Pasteur, Volontaires.*

The name of Louis Pasteur (1822-95) has been immortalized in the word "pasteurization." His development of immunization and other disease-controlling methods has become legendary and saved innumerable lives. Pasteur's house, now surrounded by the buildings of the Pasteur Institute, is a museum affording an interesting glimpse of both the scientific and private life of this great man. His remains rest in a magnificent tomb in the basement built in the form of a small Byzantine chapel with rich mosaics illustrating different aspects of his work.

Père Lachaise, Cimetière

*20e. Map **19D5**. Open Mon-Sat Mar 16-Nov 5, 7.30am-6pm; Nov 6-Jan 15, 8.30am-5pm; Jan 16-Mar 15, 8am-5.30pm; Sun and hols 9.30 to seasonal closing time. Métro Père-Lachaise.*

Like many old cemeteries, this one, the largest in Paris, has a powerfully romantic appeal. Named after Louis XIV's confessor, this cemetery was originally the site of a Jesuit house of retreat, and its hilly ground was laid out in 1804. The closely huddled graves encompass a wide variety of sepulchral art. It is easy to lose one's way among the twisting, tree-lined lanes, but in return for a small tip the custodian will provide a map which marks the graves of the many celebrities buried here. These include Molière, Balzac, Chopin, Rossini, Colette, Edith Piaf and Oscar Wilde. The monument to Wilde is a massive block by Jacob Epstein, adorned with a winged Egyptian figure. One of the most visited graves is that of the spiritualist Allan Kardec, whose followers can sometimes be seen communing with his spirit by passing their hands over his statue.

Petit Palais 🏛

Av. Winston-Churchill, 8e ☎42-65-12-73. Map 7G5 ☒ ☒ on Sun ✗ by prior arrangement. Open 10am-5.40pm. Closed Mon. (Hours of temporary exhibitions vary.) Métro Champs-Élysées-Clemenceau.

Completed in 1900 along with its neighbor, the *Grand Palais*, this building has rather more harmonious proportions and a less obstrusive personality. Lying a stone's throw from the *Champs-Élysées*, it houses the **Musée des Beaux Arts de la Ville de Paris** whose galleries divide into two groups.

In the galleries facing the outside of the building, you will pass from ancient Egyptian and Classical sculptures, through medieval and Renaissance art, to paintings, furniture and porcelain of the 18thC. The inner galleries are devoted to French art of the 19th and early 20thC. This is a wonderfully rich collection including works by Delacroix, Courbet, Corot, Manet, Monet, Cézanne, Pissarro, Sisley, Redon and Bonnard. Among famous individual works are Courbet's painting of two sleeping women, *Le Sommeil*, and Bonnard's vibrant *Nu dans le Bain*. Bonnard's palette is here on display as well — a riot of color like his paintings. The museum also has often superb temporary exhibitions.

These galleries are surrounded by a courtyard which, with its Roman-style colonnade, pool and garden, is a charming place in which to take a break.

Picasso, Musée

Hôtel Aubert-de-Fontenay (Hôtel Salé), 5 Rue de Thorigny, 3e ☎42-71-25-21. Map ***11H11*** *☒ Open 9.45am-5.15pm. Closed Tues. Métro St-Sébastien-Froissart.*

Picasso was rare among major artists in that all his life he kept a significant proportion of his own paintings and sculpture for his personal collection. Much of this collection passed to the French government in lieu of tax after Picasso's death, and it was decided to create a new museum to house it. The Hôtel Salé (to use its familiar name) was chosen for the purpose. The gracious 17thC *Marais* mansion both emphasizes and complements the modernity of Picasso's work.

Although many of his famous paintings are already in other museums, this collection gives a unique personal view of the whole span of Picasso's long, creative life. The works range from his astonishing childhood creations such as *Girl with Bare Feet*, painted when he was only 14, through his blue, rose and Cubist periods to the inimitable style of his later years. The joy, anguish and turbulence of his private life are brought out in these works, for Picasso was an extraordinarily self-revelatory artist.

The museum contains works by other artists from Picasso's collection, including paintings by Cézanne, Renoir, Matisse and Rousseau.

Place Charles-de-Gaulle See *Charles-de-Gaulle, Place*.

Place de la Concorde See *Concorde, Place de la*.

Place Vendôme See *Vendôme, Place*.

Police, Musée de la Préfecture de

1bis Rue des Carmes, 5e ☎43-29-21-57. Map ***10J9*** *Open Mon-Thurs 9am-5pm, Fri 9am-4.30pm. Métro Maubert-Mutualité.*

A sober but fascinating collection of documents and objects is housed in this little museum in the heart of the *Latin Quarter*. It presents a panorama of police and criminal activity in Paris from the *ancien régime* to 20thC. It includes a frightening display of criminal tools and weapons, as well as orders for the arrest of prominent figures, such as Danton and Charlotte Corday (who killed Marat in his bath) from the Revolution.

Pompidou Center *(Centre National d'Art et de Culture)* ★

Plateau Beaubourg, 4e ☎42-77-12-33. Map ***10H10*** *for museums on Sun. Day passes available. Open Mon, Wed, Thurs, Fri noon-10pm; Sat, Sun 10am-10pm. Closed Tues. Métro Hôtel-de-Ville, Rambuteau, Châtelet.*

Like the *Eiffel Tower* nearly a century ago, the Georges Pompidou Center (or **Beaubourg** as it is informally called) has aroused both shock and admiration. It is now one of the major attractions of the city and a place that pulsates with energy. Shaped like a giant matchbox on its side, brightly painted as though in a child's coloring book and enveloped in a cat's cradle of gleaming steel girders, it looks like a crazy oil refinery. Even if you are a die-hard opponent of modern architecture, it will take your breath away, especially if you come upon it at night when, confronted by its glittering expanse, you might think you had wandered onto the set of a science-fiction movie.

It is one of the most revolutionary buildings of its age. Built on the initiative of President Georges Pompidou as part of the redevelopment of *Les Halles* and opened in 1977, it was designed by the British architect Richard Rogers and the Italian Renzo Piano. The building is turned, as it were, inside-out, so that its intestines — pipes, shafts, escalators, etc — are festooned around the outside, thus liberating large areas of space within. The main escalator runs in a transparent tube up the front of the building, so that the visitor can see a changing panorama of the city while ascending the five stories.

The Beaubourg radiates a sense of celebration that spills over into the surrounding area. As a foretaste of the building itself the visitor crosses a huge sloping piazza which is the scene of perpetual "happenings." Here one may come across a poet, a juggler, a fire-eater or a group of street actors.

The function of the Beaubourg is to provide a multimedia center in which modern art and culture are made accessible to the public in a new and exciting way. Its four main departments are listed here.

Art Moderne, Musée Nationale de ☆ has the largest collection of its kind in the world, illustrating all the main schools of the 20thC.

Bibliothèque Publique d'Information (Public Information Library), which is essentially a library of the 20thC with some half a million books, planned to reach a million.

Centre de Création Industrielle (Industrial Design Center) has a gallery on the ground floor presenting exhibitions on all aspects of our planned environment.

Institut de Recherches Contemporaines Acoustiques Musicales (Institute for Contemporary Acoustic and Musical Research), the underground studios of which are closed to the public, but lectures and demonstrations are held here. On the top floor there is a large gallery for temporary exhibitions.

Other features of the Beaubourg include a **library** and supervised **play center** for children, a reconstruction of the **studio of the sculptor Brancusi**, a lively movie theater called the Salle Garance, an auditorium for lectures, concerts and theatrical performances, and a top-floor self-service restaurant with a superb view over Paris.

Pont Alexandre III ☆

*7e and 8e. Map **7H5**. Métro Champs-Élysées-Clemenceau, Invalides.*

The broadest bridge in Paris and also one of the most beautiful, it forms part of a great triumphal way leading down the Av. Winston-Churchill, past the *Grand Palais* and *Petit Palais*, across the *Seine* and down the esplanade to *Les Invalides*. It was built for the World Exhibition of 1900 and named after Tsar Alexander III of Russia (1845-94). It is flanked by two massive pillars at each end, the decorations of which represent, on the Right Bank, medieval and modern France, and, on the Left, Renaissance France and the era of Louis XIV. All along the bridge are cast-iron lamp standards with the ornate, prosperous look that characterized the *Belle Epoque*.

Pont-Neuf ☆

*1er. Map **9I8**. Métro Pont-Neuf.*

"Of all the bridges which were ever built, the whole world who have passed over the Pont-Neuf must own that it is the noblest, the finest, the grandest, the lightest, the longest, the broadest that ever conjoined land and land together upon the face of the tremendous globe."

Thus wrote the 18thC English novelist Laurence Sterne about the bridge which spans the *Seine* in two sections, divided by the w spike of the *Ile de la Cité*. He might have added that, despite its name, it is also the oldest. Completed in 1607 under Henry IV, whose equestrian statue stands at the center, it has 12 arches, all of slightly different sizes. The cornices overlooking the river are carved with a row of amusing caricatured faces of Henry IV's ministers and courtiers, and there are comic carvings of stall-holders, pick-pockets and tooth-drawers.

The bridge, the two halves of which are not quite in line, was designed by Androuet du Cerceau.

Portes St-Denis et St-Martin

*10e. Map **10F10**. Métro Strasbourg-St-Denis, St-Martin.*

These two triumphal arches, situated close to each other on the *Grands Boulevards*, were built in the 1670s to commemorate Louis XIV's military victories, and they replaced two fortified gates which had disappeared along with the old perimeter wall. Both bear reliefs glorifying the Sun King, but the Porte St-Denis is the grander and more elaborate of the two. They now overlook the seedy environment that has grown up around them, with its garish movie theaters and fast-food stalls.

Postal, Musée ☆

*34 Bd. de Vaugirard, 15e ☎43-20-15-30. Map **13L5** ✉ ✗ on request. Open 10am-5pm. Closed Sun. Métro Montparnasse-Bienvenue, Pasteur, Falguière.*

Did your know that during the Siege of Paris, in 1870, microfilm messages were carried out of the city by pigeons whose wings were stamped with a postmark? This is one of many snippets of information one gleans from a visit to the Postal Museum. Here on four floors is an imaginative display on philately and the history of postal communication — everything relating to the subject from postmen's uniforms and mailboxes to modern sorting machines and stamp-making equipment. And, of course, there are stamps galore for the philatelist. On the ground floor is a gallery showing temporary exhibitions of postage-stamp art and related work.

Quatre-Saisons, Fontaine des *(Four Seasons Fountain)*

*57-59 Rue de Grenelle, 7e. Map **8I6**. Métro Rue-du-Bac.*
When this fountain was built by Bouchardon in the 1730s to supply water to the district, Voltaire complained that such a splendid monument should not have been erected in so narrow a street. He had a point, for the facade cannot be seen properly unless you are standing right in front of it. A central portico with a seated figure representing Paris is flanked by reclining personifications of the Seine and Marne; and on either side are curved walls adorned with statues of the four seasons.

Radio France, Maison de 🏛

*116 Av. du Président Kennedy, 16e ☎42-30-21-80. Map **12I1** 🖼 📷 in museum ✗ compulsory. Open 10.30am, 11.30am, 2.30pm, 3.30pm, 4.30pm. Closed Sun. Métro Ranelagh, Passy, Mirabeau.*
This huge glass-and-aluminum edifice, shaped like a giant cylinder, is the nerve center of French radio. It is a statistician's delight — ½ km (⅓ mile) in circumference, with 3,500 personnel, 58 studios and 1,000 offices. Architecturally, it may leave the visitor cold. Its main attractions, however, are the extensive **museum of the history of radio and television** and the concerts and shows held here on a regular basis.

Renan-Scheffer, Musée

*16 Rue Chaptal, 9e ☎48-74-95-38. Map **4D8** 🖼 Open 10am-5.40pm. Closed Mon. Métro St-Georges, Pigalle.*
From 1830 this secluded house in Montmartre was the home of the painter Ary Scheffer and the scene of Friday-evening salons attended by such celebrities as Delacroix, Liszt, George Sand and Chopin. Another guest was the writer Ernest Renan, who married Scheffer's niece. Their daughter later took over the house and continued to hold salons there. It is now a branch of the *Carnavalet* Museum. The ground floor houses a permanent exhibition of portraits and memorabilia connected with George Sand. The first floor is reserved for temporary exhibitions culled from the Carnavalet collections and relating to the literary and artistic life of the 19thC.

Rivoli, Rue de ☆

*1er and 4e. Map **8,9,10&11**. Métro Hôtel-de-Ville, Châtelet, Louvre, Palais-Royal, Tuileries, Concorde.*
Like so many long Parisian thoroughfares, the Rue de Rivoli begins with one personality and ends with another. It starts at the *Place de la Concorde* and runs down beside the *Tuileries* and the *Louvre* in a long, uniform colonnade with many smart stores and an elegant café or two — a place for promenading in style. This section was laid out between 1800-35.

Beyond the Louvre, the street becomes progressively less formal as it wends its way past the *Hôtel de Ville* and on into the *Marais*.

It ends, however, not with a whimper but with a bang, with the marvelous facade of the church of **St-Paul-St-Louis**.

Rodin, Musée 🏛 ★

Hôtel Biron, 77 Rue de Varenne, 7e ☎47-05-01-34. Map 13I5 ▣ ▣ Open 10am-5.15pm (4.30pm in winter). Closed Tues. Métro Varenne.

Auguste Rodin (1840-1917) is widely considered to be the greatest sculptor of the 19thC. You will see why when you visit this museum, housed in a splendid 18thC mansion near *Les Invalides*. It is impossible not to marvel at the way in which Rodin magically transformed stone, clay or bronze into the living tissue of human emotion and experience. Take, for example, his famous work, *Le Baiser (The Kiss)*, which powerfully evokes in white marble the tenderness of love between man and woman; or his *Homme qui Marche (Walking Man)*, which embodies all the urgency and thrust of human aspiration; or *La Cathédrale*, where a pair of hands speaks of piety and contemplation.

The delightful garden surrounding the museum makes an ideal setting for many of Rodin's works. Here we find, among others, casts of his *Balzac, Le Penseur (The Thinker), La Porte de l'Enfer* and *Les Bourgeois de Calais (The Burghers of Calais)*. Temporary exhibitions of work by other artists are held in a building to the right of the entrance.

The lovely **Hôtel Biron** was built by Gabriel The Elder for a rich wig-maker in 1728 and was subsequently lived in by, among others, Marshal Biron, who was beheaded in 1793. Later the building became a convent and much of the painted and gilt paneling was ripped out by the mother superior, though some has been restored.

At the beginning of this century the building was bought by the state and made available for artists. Rodin himself occupied a ground floor studio from 1907 until his death.

Rue de Rivoli See *Rivoli, Rue de*.

Sacré-Coeur, Basilique 🏛 ✝ ☆

35 Rue du Chevalier-de-la-Barre, 18e ☎42-51-17-02. Map 4C9. Church ▣ ▣ ✗ Dome and crypt ▣ open 9.30am-noon, 2-6pm. Métro Abbesses, Lamarck-Caulaincourt.

Subject of countless travel posters and paintings, the Sacré-Coeur has acquired the status of a visual cliché. However, seen afresh, in its superb setting on *Montmartre*'s hill, the Butte, it has stunning impact and beauty, whether glimpsed from a train drawing into one of the northern stations or revealed suddenly around a corner in one of the old streets that surround it.

The church rose, like a phenix, from the ashes of the Franco-Prussian War of 1870. As a reaction to the despair aroused by France's defeat, a national vow was adopted in 1873 by parliament to erect a church in Paris as a symbol of contrition and a manifestation of hope. A competition was held and there were 78 entries. The winner was an architect named Abadie, with a Romano-Byzantine design. The first stone was laid in 1875 and the cathedral was completed by 1914, but the First World War delayed consecration until 1919. Since 1885, worshipers have kept up perpetual adoration before the high altar, continuing night and day even through the Nazi occupation.

The material used for the church was Château-Landon stone, which hardens and whitens with age — notice how much grayer the stonework of the interior is compared with the gleaming exterior. The design is not to everyone's taste, but many find the outline of its five beehive-like domes pleasing.

Approach the church by the long flight of steps from the S (you can go part of the way by funicular railroad). This way you get the full impact of the main facade with its great portico surmounted on each side by equestrian statues of *St Louis* and *Joan of Arc*. The bell tower to the N, higher than the rest of the church, contains one of the largest bells in the world, weighing over 17 tons.

The inside is light and elegantly proportioned. The eye follows the great rounded arching sweeps of stonework, up to the cupola with its clerestory and its two encircling balconies and down again to the nave, coming to rest on the natural focal point of the interior, the great mosaic in the alcove above the high altar. This **mosaic**, one of the largest in the world, depicts Christ with outstretched arms exposing a golden heart, while around him are grouped worshipers including the Virgin, St Michael and Joan of Arc.

The crypt, entered by a stairway from the W aisle, is somewhat gloomy and severe. It contains the church treasury and a number of chapels, the central one possessing a *Pièta* on the altar. By the same stairway one ascends to the dome, with dizzying views down into the church and out over Paris.

St-Denis, Basilique 🏛 ✝ ☆

Pl. de l'Hôtel-de-Ville, St-Denis ☎42-43-00-71. Map ***19B4*** *Open Apr 1-Sept 30 Mon-Sat 10am-7pm, Sun 1-7pm; Oct 1-Mar 31 Mon-Sat 10am-5pm, Sun 1pm-5pm. Métro St-Denis-Basilique.*

Visitors on their way to Paris from Charles de Gaulle Airport are often surprised to see an imposing cathedral rising out of grim industrial surroundings. It is the Basilica St-Denis, necropolis of the kings of France and precursor of Gothic architecture, which was soon to sweep over Europe.

It was in the 12thC that the learned Abbot Suger, friend of Louis VII, decided to rebuild his church dedicated to the Apostle of France, St-Denis. Having been beheaded in Montmartre by the ungrateful Gallo-Romans for trying to bring them Christianity, St-Denis walked northward with his head tucked under his arm until he fell down, on the spot where his church was later founded. The prestige of being buried near the relics of a saint made the church a natural choice for a royal necropolis for all but a handful of French kings and their queens, starting with Dagobert in the 7thC. The tombs and statuary of the kings are as good a reason for visiting St-Denis as the church itself. The tombs are empty, however — during the Revolution, 800 royal bodies were pitched into a communal grave in the crypt under the N transept. Luckily the tombs were saved from destruction: the archeologist Lenoir had the foresight to remove them to safety some time earlier.

In the late 13thC Louis IX (St Louis) ordered purely symbolic effigies to be made of all his ancestors back to the 7thC, but, from the death of Philippe The Bold in 1285, likenesses were taken from real portraits. Notice particularly the Renaissance mausoleums of François I and Henry II. Unfortunately, all the tombs are chained off and close inspection is difficult.

The beginnings of lightness, harmony and rational disposition of the elements in the church itself proclaim the spirit of a new age, and the close of the Dark Ages. Elements which had been developed separately were now combined for the first time: the Latin cross plan with radiating pilgrimage chapels, the pointed arch, the ribbed groin vault — look for these facets of Suger's original plan in the ambulatory, apse and facade. The latter has an air of dissymmetry with its pointed Gothic and rounded Romanesque arches and its missing N tower. The facade boasts the first-ever rose window, a feature which was soon to become standard.

Within the church, a further progress toward lightness was made in the next century when the architect Pierre de Montreuil gave the nave, side aisles and chancel an architectural lift that recalls his masterwork, *Sainte Chapelle*.

St-Étienne-du-Mont 🏛 † ☆

Pl. St-Geneviève, 5e ☎43-54-11-79. Map ***15**K9. Open Mon-Sat 7.30am-noon, 2.30-7pm, Sun 7.30am-noon, 4-7pm. Métro Cardinale-Lemoine.*

Built between 1492-1626, the church is a mixture of styles which defy all the rules of architectural purity. The result is rather like a crazy composite photograph, amalgamating elements from contrasting buildings. Take the main **facade** ☆ for example, with its three pediments piled one on top of the other and combining Classical motifs with a Gothic rose window stuck in the middle. The belfry is similarly eclectic, begun in the medieval style and topped with a little Renaissance dome. Nevertheless, the whole effect is pleasing.

I . . . . bent my steps to the curious church of St-Étienne-du-Mont — the church that hides its florid little Renaissance facade behind the huge Neo-Classic drum of the Panthéon . . . .

Henry James, *Parisian Sketches*, 1875-76

The interior, which preserves greater consistency of style, has some remarkable features, notably the 16thC **roodscreen** ☆ with its delicately pierced stonework and its two flanking spiral stairways. This is the only surviving roodscreen in Paris. Notice also the flamboyant vaulting over the transept, the 5.5m(18ft) hanging keystone, the splendidly ornate organ loft (1630) and the richly carved wooden pulpit (1650). At the W end of the nave is a slab indicating where the Archbishop of Paris, Mgr. Sibour, was assassinated by an unfrocked priest in 1857. Those buried in the church include Pascal and Racine, commemorated by plaques on either side of the entrance to the Lady Chapel.

There is also a chapel to St Geneviève, created in 1803 and containing the stone on which her body had rested in the former abbey church of St-Geneviève before her remains were destroyed during the Revolution. All that is left of her body is a bone or two, now preserved in an elaborate reliquary.

Although the church was badly plundered and damaged during the Revolution, it was later skillfully restored and today contains some valuable works of art. Particularly striking is the series of **stained-glass windows** in the cloister.

St-Eustache 🏛 † ☆

2 Rue du Jour, 1er ☎42-36-31-05. Map ***10**H9. Open 9am-7pm. Métro Halles.*

This lovely church, the largest in Paris after *Notre-Dame*, deserves to be better known than it is. For centuries it has stood at the focal point of Parisian history and, until recently, was the local church of the *Les Halles* market. Now it surveys the new *Forum des Halles* and the chaotic building site around it with the solid equanimity of the Middle Ages confronting the transcience of the present day. The site was originally occupied by a small 13thC chapel to St Agnes, which was later rededicated to St Eustace, the 2ndC Roman who, like St Hubert later on, is said to have seen a vision of the Cross between the antlers of a stag. The building as we see it today, with its elegant flying buttresses, took shape between 1532-1640 and is a curious mixture, the form being Gothic, the details Classical.

Many famous names crop up in the history of the church. Cardinal Richelieu, Madame de Pompadour and Molière were baptized in it, and Louis XIV celebrated his first communion here. During the Revolution the church was pillaged, then made a Temple of Agriculture. In 1844 it suffered a worse fate when it was devastated by a fire. It was completely restored by Baltard and today stands as one of the finest of Paris' architectural monuments.

The interior is thrilling, with its exhilarating vertical emphasis. Everything thrusts upward to the ceiling with its delicate network of ribbed vaulting and elaborately carved bosses. The stained glass is luxurious, and there are some important works of art here, including an early Rubens *Pilgrims at Emmaus* and a sculpture of the *Virgin* by Pigalle on the altar of the Lady Chapel.

One of the church's proudest possessions is its organ, one of the finest in the city, and concerts are held here periodically, carrying on a well-established musical tradition. It was here in 1855 that Berlioz conducted the first performance of his *Te Deum*.

St-Germain l'Auxerrois 🏛 †

2 Pl. du Louvre, 1er ☎42-60-13-96. Map ***9H9****. Open Mon-Sat 8am-12.45pm, 2-7pm, Sun 8am-12.45pm, 3-7pm. Métro Louvre, Pont-Neuf.*

Opposite the E end of the *Louvre* stands this church which embodies a fascinating resumé of medieval architecture. There has been a church on this site since the 6thC when an oratory dedicated to St Germanus was built. The present building is the fourth on the spot and is a combination of five centuries of architectural design.

12thC: the oldest part of the building is the Romanesque belfry behind the transept crossing. It played a somber role during the Wars of Religion when, in 1572, Catherine de Medici ordered the bells to ring out to signal the start of the Massacre of St Bartholomew. Three thousand Huguenots, in town to celebrate the marriage of Henri de Navarre to his cousin Marguerite de Valois, were slaughtered in their beds and thrown from the windows.

13thC: the Gothic ambulatory and chancel, the Lady Chapel on the right and the central portal were all added.

14thC: St-Germain l'Auxerrois became the royal parish church when Charles V transformed the Louvre from fortress to a medieval palace. The nave dates from this century.

15thC: the unusual and Flamboyant Gothic **porch** was built, with its lovely multi-ribbed vaulting.

16thC: the Renaissance came and left its mark on the doorway N of the choir. The late Gothic transept portals were added.

In the 17thC, Versailles was built, the court abandoned the Louvre to the court artists who made their studios there, and St-Germain became their parish church. Many artists, sculptors and poets are buried here: Chardin, Boucher, Nattier, Van Loo, Coysevox, Le Vau, de Cotte, Gabriel, Soufflot, Jodelle, Malherbe. Even today artists and show people come here on Ash Wednesday to celebrate a special mass. Royalists have not been forgotten: every year on Jan 21, the anniversary of his execution in 1793, a mass is said for Louis XVI.

St-Germain-des-Prés 🏛 †

Pl. St-Germain-des-Prés, 6e ☎43-25-41-71. Map ***9***/*8. Open 7.30am-7.30pm. Métro St-Germain-des-Prés.*

The oldest church in Paris stands passively at the hub of the lively *St-Germain Quarter*. Its origin dates back to AD542 when the Merovingian King Childebert I, sone of Clovis, brought back from Spain the tunic of St Vincent and a golden cross said to have been made by Solomon. To receive these relics he built a monastery and church which was at first called the Basilica of St-Vincent and St-Croix but later came to be named after St Germanus, the Bishop of Paris, who consecrated the church in AD558 and was buried there. As the burial place of the Merovingian kings and a seat of the great Benedictine order, it became virtually a miniature state in its own right, possessing 17,000ha (42,000 acres) of land, its buildings fortified by towers and a moat fed from the Seine. For centuries it stood in meadows called the Pré aux Clercs.

The church was destroyed twice by the Normans, and its present form dates from the 11thC. During the Revolution the abbey was dissolved and the property subjected to an orgy of vandalism in which the royal tombs and most of the buildings were destroyed, the church itself being turned into a saltpeter factory. Of the once splendid complex of building only the church, minus its transepts, and the abbot's palace on the NE side remain.

Except for a few capitals and columns, nothing that can be seen in the church is earlier than 11thC. The interior is an interesting mixture of different periods, with its Romanesque arches, Gothic vaulting and polychrome wall painting by the 19thC artist Hippolyte Flandrin. The works of art in the church include a 14thC Virgin and Child known as *Notre-Dame de Consolation*, and a number of fine tombs, including that of John Casimir, a 17thC king of Poland who became abbot of St-Germain. There are also tombs to two Scottish noblemen, William Douglas and James Douglas, courtiers of Henry IV and Louis XIII respectively.

Beside the church, facing S, is a little garden shaded by chesnut trees, a tranquil and secluded refuge from the busy Bd. St-Germain.

St-Germain Quarter

6e and 7e. Map ***8&9, 14&15****. Métro St-Germain-des-Prés, Rue-du-Bac, Solférino, Mabillon, Odéon.*

The St-Germain district is really made up of two adjacent quarters: St-Germain-des-Prés, consisting roughly of the northern half of the 6e; and the Faubourg-St-Germain, comprising the NE section of the 7e. These two areas have their own distinct personalities, complementing each other well.

The former community first grew up around the great medieval monastery and church of *St-Germain-des-Prés*, but for centuries it lay outside the Paris boundaries and remained cut off from the life of the city. Its only link with the Right Bank was a ferry (*bac*) which was reached by what is now called the Rue du Bac. This remained the case until the 17thC when Louis XIV began to extend the *Louvre*, for which purpose stone had to be brought from the quarries at Denfert-Rochereau to the S. The ferry was too slow a means of bringing it across the river, and so the **Pont-Royal** was built, ending the isolation of St-Germain and putting it firmly on the map of Paris. It was, incidentally, also Louis XIV who established the *École des Beaux Arts*, across the river from the Louvre. Later, after the Louvre had become a museum, the bridge known as the Passerelle des Arts (now **Pont des Arts**) was built so that the students could cross the river to look at the works of art.

The construction of the Pont-Royal turned St-Germain-des-Prés into a thriving community which soon became a favorite haunt of writers and intellectuals of all kinds.

The Faubourg (suburb) St-Germain is, as the name implies, of more recent origin. During the reign of Louis XIV the aristocracy had been concentrated around the court at Versailles, but under the more relaxed regime of Louis XV they felt able to take up residence in Paris again and chose the plain to the E of *Les Invalides* as the place to build their homes. The result can be seen today in the gracious houses that line such streets as the **Rue de Lille**, the **Rue de l'Université**, the **Rue de Grenelle** and the **Rue de Varenne**. Most of the larger ones have now become government buildings or embassies. The **Hôtel de Matignon** ☆ (*no. 57 Rue de Varenne*) is now the residence of the Prime Minister, while the **Hôtel de Courteilles** ☆ (*at no. 110 Rue de Grenelle*) has become the Ministry of Education. The Rue de Grenelle is also the site of the lovely *Quatre-Saisons* fountain. A few well-heeled families, however, remain in the area, and the atmosphere retains the privileged, inward-looking quality that it has always possessed, whether dominated by aristocrats or civil servants.

The buildings belong to a felicitous period when French architecture had thrown off the Italian influence and blossomed into a light but restrained elegance that was typified by the **Hôtel Biron** ★ at the western end of the Rue de Varenne, which is now the *Rodin* museum and one of the few houses in the area which the public can enter.

Edward Bulwer-Lytton described the Faubourg-St-Germain vividly in his novel, *Pelham*: "I love that *quartier*! If ever I go to Paris again I shall reside there . . . . *there*, indeed, you are among the French, the fossilized remains of the old régime — the very houses have an air of desolate, yet venerable grandeur . . . . You cross one of the numerous bridges, and you enter another time — you are inhaling the atmosphere of a past century; no flaunting *boutique*, French in its trumpery, English in its prices, stares you in the face . . . . Vast hotels, with their gloomy frontals and magnificent contempt for comfort; shops, such as shops might have been in the aristocratic days of Louis Quatorze . . . . all strike on the mind with a vague and nameless impression of antiquity; a something solemn even in gaiety, and faded in pomp, appears to linger over all you behold."

The link between these two areas is the Bd. St-Germain, a great bow-shaped thoroughfare which touches the Seine at each end. Begin a stroll down the boulevard perhaps somewhere near the secluded little Jesuit-style church of **St-Thomas d'Aquin**, which lies just off the route to the N. This is still the Faubourg-St-Germain, but, approaching the church of *St-Germain-des-Prés* itself, everything becomes busier, more colorful and more cosmopolitan. Turn right opposite the church into the **Rue des Ciseaux** and a little Italian enclave with many pizzerias. This spills over into the **Rue des Canettes** (Duckling St.) which runs up to *St-Sulpice* — notice the ducklings over the doorway of no. 18. Farther E the **Rue Grégoire de Tours** is full of Greek restaurants. This street leads into the **Rue de Buci**. Here and in the neighboring **Rue de Seine** is one of the best food markets in the city of Paris.

Nearby is the church of *St-Germain-des-Prés*, dominating the intersection of the Bd. St-Germain, the Rue de Rennes and the Rue Bonaparte. This is the heart of the district that has come to be known as the "*Capitale des Lettres*" (Literary Capital), a role which it began to take on in the 17thC when the Comédie Française

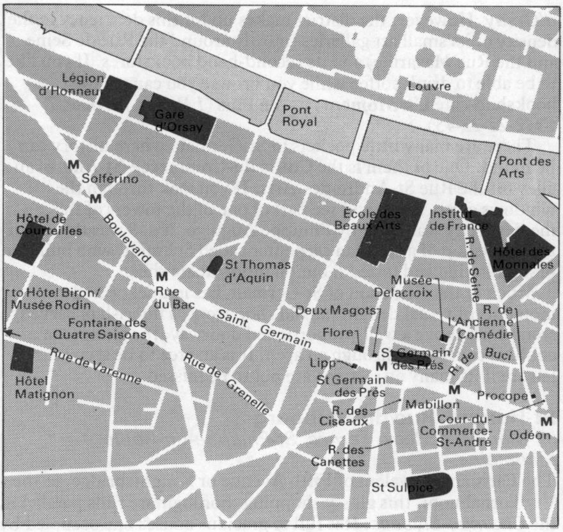

played in what is now the Rue de l'Ancienne Comédie. The café **Procope**, at no. 13, as popular now as ever, was the haunt of Molière, Corneille, Racine and, in later centuries, Voltaire, Balzac, Verlaine and Anatole France.

Between the wars the quarter was fueled by an influx of writers from *Montmartre* and *Montparnasse* who met habitually in the three great cafés in front of St-Germain-des-Prés: **Flore, Lipp** and **Deux Magots**. Publishers, booksellers, painters and art dealers also set up shop there in increasing numbers. After the Second World War, St-Germain became the headquarters of a new generation of intelligentsia, revolving around Jean-Paul Sartre and the Existentialists. In those days they crowded into jazz cellars such as the Tabou in Rue Dauphine, and small bars, such as the Bar Vert in the Rue Jacob. The atmosphere of the district has changed since then, but the "*Germanopratins*," as the inhabitants are called, remain friendly and lively, and there is always plenty to do and see, especially around the Pl. St-Germain-des-Prés by the church, where on most evenings you will find sword-swallowers, fire-eaters and other street performers at work.

A gentler atmosphere of festivity is often to be found nearby in the quaint little tree-lined Rue de Furstenberg, where the glow of the old-fashioned street lamps attracts singers, guitarists and harpists. The great 19thC artist Delacroix had his studio here (now the *Delacroix* museum) and the Romantic spirit is still strongly felt, especially at night.

Truely Paris, comprehending the suburbs, is for the material the houses are built with, and many noble and magnificant piles, one of the most gallant cyttyes in the world.

John Evelyn, *The Diary*

Apart from the Delacroix, there are few museums in this part of Paris — the handful includes the *Hôtel des Monnaies*, the *Légion d'Honneur* in the Rue de Bellechasse, and the *Musée d'Orsay*. However, the district makes up for this deficiency in the density of its small art galleries (mostly around the Rue de Seine and the Rue Mazarine) and its second-hand bookstores. If you like to be able to drink coffee while you browse you can try the bookshop-café **Un Moment.... en Plus** (*1 Rue de Verenne, 7e ☎42-22-23-45*).

There are many little pockets in St-Germain where history can be found. One of them is the **Cours du-Commerce-St-André**, an alley off the Rue St-André-des-Arts. If you look through the windows of **no. 4** you will see part of one of the towers of the medieval city wall built by Philippe Auguste. **No. 9** was the site of the workshop of a German carpenter called Schmidt, who built the first guillotine and tested it out on unfortunate sheep.

Much of the attraction of St-Germain lies in unexpected moments of visual delight: an old shop front, a flourish of carved stonework above a well-proportioned doorway, the glimpse of a cobbled courtyard through an arch. It is an area to be seen at leisure if its many attractions are not to be missed.

St-Honoré, Rue du Faubourg

*8e. Map **7&8**. Métro Ternes, St-Philippe-du-Roule, Madeleine.*

The Parisian equivalent of Fifth Avenue or Knightsbridge, or the Via Tornabuoni, this glossy shopping thoroughfare runs parallel to the *Champs-Élysées*. It is full of gracious houses one occupied by the aristocracy after the district took over from the *Marais* as the fashionable place to live. Today few people, apart from the president (see *Palais de l'Élysée*), actually live here, and the old mansions have found new uses. No. 35 houses the **British Embassy** and no. 96 the **Ministry of the Interior**. Another mansion, at no. 112, disappeared in the 1920s to make way for the discreetly opulent **Hôtel Bristol** (see *Hotels*). For the rest, the street is mostly occupied by smart stores with such famous names as Heim, Hermès, Lanvin, Yves St Laurent, Courrèges and Helena Rubinstein. Beside the window of the Hermès shop is a jet spurting clouds of perfume at the passers-by, filling the air with the aroma of high living.

St-Joseph-des-Carmes 🏛 ✝

*70 Rue de Vaugirard, 6e. Map **14**J7. Métro Rennes, St-Placide.*

This elegant little church forms part of the *Institut Catholique de Paris* complex which stands on the site once occupied by a great Carmelite monastery with vast gardens, many treasures and a priceless library. During the Revolution the monastery was closed, its treasures confiscated and the buildings turned into a prison where, in September 1792, 115 priests and three bishops were massacred. Their bones are buried in the crypt of the church which today possesses a gloomy atmosphere despite its fine works of art including, to the left of the transept, a marble *Virgin and Child* after a model by Bernini.

St-Julien-le-Pauvre 🏛 ✝ ☆

*1 Rue St-Julien-le-Pauvre, 5e ☎43-54-20-41. Map **10**J9. Open 9am-noon, 3-6pm. Métro St-Michel, Maubert-Mutualité.*

This enchanting little building, set in a charming garden, **Sq. René Viviani**, facing *Notre-Dame* from the Left Bank, is the oldest complete church in Paris, built between 1170-1240. Only parts of *St-Germain-des-Prés* are older. The beauty of the interior, with its elegantly foliated **capitals**, is all the more potent for its modesty. The **wooden screen** (iconostasis) across the choir is a reminder that this is now a church of the Melchite (Greek Catholic) rite. From the square there is also an attractive view across the Rue St-Jacques to *St-Séverin*.

St-Martin Canal

*19e and 10e. Map **5&11**. Métro Jaures, J. Bonsergent, Goncourt.*

Built in the early 19thC, the St-Martin Canal links the Seine with the Canal de l'Ourcq and runs through a tunnel for about half its length. It is a working canal, plied by many barges and lined by warehouses and depots, but it has its picturesque moments, when it shakes off the dust and stops work for a pause. Particularly romantic is the stretch between the Sq. Frédéric Lemaître and the Rue Bichat, with its tree-lined banks and hump-backed bridges. Here the atmosphere is not unlike Amsterdam. Recently the canal has undergone some improvements such as the construction of a new boating marina in the Arsenal Basin S of the Place de la Bastille. (You can take a boat trip up the canal with **Quiztour**, *19 Rue d'Athènes, 9e ☎45-26-16-59*.)

St-Michel, Boulevard Called the Boul 'Mich, this is the main artery of the Left Bank. See *Latin Quarter*.

St-Nicolas-des-Champs 🏛 †

*254 Rue St-Martin, 3e ☎42-72-92-54. Map **10**G10. Open Mon-Sat 9am-7pm, Sun 9.30am-noon. Métro Arts-et-Métiers.*

Begun in the 12thC, this church boasts distinguished features from different periods: a Flamboyant Gothic facade and belfry, a fine Renaissance **doorway** on the S side and many paintings of the 17th, 18th and 19thC. In the St-Michel chapel, a pudgy archangel steps daintily on a pitiful bald-headed devil. The high altar is curiously like a stone bath complete with lion's feet. In short, the church is a mixture of beauty and bathos.

St-Roch 🏛 † ☆

*296 Rue St-Honoré, 1er ☎42-60-81-69. Map **8**G7. Open 8am-6.30pm. Métro Pyramides, Tuileries.*

As Paris grew toward the W in the 17thC, the need arose for a new parish church in the vicinity of the *Palais-Royal*. St-Roch was created, and the author of the *Grand Siècle*, Louis XIV himself, laid the first stone in 1635. The interior is marked by some of the great creative personalities which make Louis' century alive to us today. There is the tomb of *André Le Nôtre*, a kind old man, friend to Louis XIV and the first gardener to make history, with the park of Versailles. He also created the nearby *Tuileries*. Other tombs include those of the playwright Corneille and the philosopher Diderot.

The church itself was designed by some of the most important architects of the 17thC, notably Jacques Lemercier, and work prolonged into the 18thC, making it a combination of Classical and Baroque elements, with a Jesuit-style facade designed by de Cotte in 1736.

Unlike the Gothic churches of Paris, the church is not oriented E-W but N-S because of the terrain. It is also unusually long, with one chapel following another beyond the chancel.

In the nave, one can admire the vaulting, which has penetrating arches. This part of the building was financed in 1719 by John

Law, the Scottish wheeler-dealer of the Mississippi Bubble. Notice the pulpit in the highly theatrical Baroque style by Challe, 1755. The round domed room after the chancel, the Lady Chapel, was designed by Jules Hardouin-Mansart. Its ceiling portrays the cloudscape of the *Triumph of the Virgin* by J.B. Pierre, 1750; and above the altar, with its nativity group, is a mass of clouds in gilded stucco. Behind the Lady Chapel is the small, round Holy Communion Chapel, and behind this a Calvary Chapel. The church has three organs and excellent acoustics, making it a splendid musical auditorium, and concerts are given here about once a week.

On leaving, one should pause by the facade in which bullet holes can be seen. These are a reminder of a terrible battle which took place in front of the church in 1795. The Republican Convention was under attack by royalties and anarchists, but thanks to the technical skill of the leader of the Republican forces, the Revolution was saved. The leader: a 27-year-old general, Napoleon Bonaparte.

St-Séverin 🏛 † ☆

Rue des Prêtres St-Séverin, 5e ☎43-25-96-63. Map ***10****J9. Open Mon-Sat 11am-1pm, 3-7pm, Sun 9am-1pm, 3-7.45pm. Métro St-Michel.*

Tucked away among the labyrinth of narrow streets in the *Latin Quarter* to the E of the Bd. St-Michel, St-Séverin is one of the best cherished medieval churches in the city, possessing a quiet magic all of its own. The church is named after two saints named Séverin: a hermit who once lived on the site in an oratory dedicated to St Martin, and a namesake of the same era who was Abbot of Agaune.

The present building was begun in the early 13thC and much altered and enlarged in the 15thC when it was stamped with the so-called "Flamboyant" (flame-like) style which can be seen in the shape of the stonework in the **stained-glass windows**. The double **ambulatory** ☆ with its forest of columns, one of them with twisted veins, is particularly fine.

What the church lacks in size it makes up for in the perfection of its proportions and the delicacy of its decoration. Every arch, column, piece of ribbed vaulting and lozenge of stained glass sings out in joyful harmony. Perhaps this is why it is such a wonderful place in which to listen to music — don't miss a concert here if you get the chance. The only discordant note is the ungainly Baroque touch given to the chancel in the 18thC when part of the arcade was rounded and faced with false marble — the effect is that of a nun wearing an ostrich-feather hat.

Adjoining the church to the S is a little garden shaded by trees and bordered on two sides by the arcades of the former charnel house. Standing in the garden (possible during concerts), one feels one is in a time warp, as beyond its cloistered calm stands the neon-lit front of a brash restaurant in the street outside.

St-Sulpice 🏛 † ☆

Pl. St-Sulpice, 6e ☎46-33-21-78. Map ***15****J8. Open Mon-Sat 7.30am-7.30pm. Métro St-Sulpice.*

Unlike many of the other great churches of Paris, this one does not form part of an imposing townscape. It looms unexpectedly out of the maze of narrow streets to the N of the *Luxembourg, Palace*. Starting life as a modest medieval church dedicated to St Sulpicius, the 16thC Archbishop of Bourges, it was reconstructed in a piecemeal fashion between the years 1655-1788 by six different architects, the essential Classical form being the work of the

Florentine Giovanni Servandoni. The result is not the hodge-podge that one might expect, but a grand and harmonious whole, apart from the unmatching towers over the portico with its two tiers of columns.

During the Revolutionary period the church became a Temple of Reason, then of Victory. In November 1799 it was the scene of a sumptuous banquet in honor of Napoleon Bonaparte.

Its interior houses vast recesses of space and the stillness is trapped beneath a great weight of stone. There are many interesting objects in the church, including two enormous shells serving as holy-water stoups, with rock-like bases sculpted by Pigalle. Another feature worth noticing is the bronze meridian line running from a plaque set into the floor of the S transept to a marble obelisk in the N transept. The sunlight, passing through a window in the S transept, strikes the line at different points to mark the equinoxes and solstices. The **Lady Chapel**, at the E end of the church, is heavily ornate, with a *Virgin and Child* by Pigalle floating above a cascade of plaster clouds. Don't miss the **murals** by Delacroix in the side chapel immediately to the right of the main door. The one depicting Jacob struggling with the Angel is particularly compelling. The splendid organ, with its 6,588 pipes, is one of the largest in the world, and organ recitals are given here frequently.

Sainte Chapelle 🏛 † ★

*4 Bd. du Palais, 4e ☎43-54-30-09. Map **10**I9 ✉ ✗ Open 9.30am-6.30pm. Métro Cité.*

It is hard to describe the beauty of this church without hyperbole; its interior is one of the most thrilling visual experiences that Paris affords. Formerly adjacent to a palace of the medieval kings, it now stands hidden away in a side courtyard of the *Palais de Justice* on the *Ile de la Cité*. It was built by Louis IX (St Louis) in the 1240s to house relics believed to be the Crown of Thorns and a portion of the True Cross — these cost the king more than the church itself. They were kept in a tabernacle on a platform over the high altar, and on feast days St Louis would take out the Crown of Thorns and hold it up before his courtiers and the public. The relics are now kept in *Notre-Dame*. When the Revolution came, the church suffered the indignity of being turned into a flour shop, then a club and finally a storage place for archives. Under the *Commune* in 1871 it narrowly escaped destruction by fire.

The building has an unusual "double-decker" construction with two chapels, one above the other. The upper one, dedicated to the Holy Crown and the Holy Cross, was intended only for the king and his retinue. The lower one, dedicated to the Virgin Mary, was for the staff of the chapel and certain officials of the court.

Enter by the rather dark **lower chapel**, its low ceiling supported by columns painted in the 19thC. From here mount a spiral staircase to the **upper chapel** ★ and emerge into a soaring chamber where one is dazzled by the jeweled light that pours through the enormous **stained-glass windows** ★ on every side. The remarkable effect of lightness was achieved by the then revolutionary technique of supporting the roof on buttresses.

The window to the left of the entrance depicts scenes from Genesis. The remainder, taken clockwise, show more Old Testament events as well as the story of Christ. The next-to-last window is devoted to St Helena and the True Cross, together with St Louis and the relics of the Crucifixion. The rose window on the W shows scenes from the Apocalypse.

Sainte Chapelle and its neighbor, the *Conciergerie*, present a striking contrast. The latter represents the baseness and cruelty of the Middle Ages; the former embodies all that was God-seeking in the medieval world.

Salpêtrière, Hôpital

Bd. de l'Hôpital, 13e. Map ***16L11***. *Métro St-Marcel.*
Les Invalides with a gentler voice could be the description of this sprawling hospital in SE Paris. It stands on the site of a former factory for gunpowder — which is 75 percent saltpeter, hence the name. Built by Louis XIV to a design by Le Vau as a refuge for beggars, it became a hospital, an asylum for the insane, a house of correction for prostitutes, and a prison. The inmates were often treated brutally, but toward the end of the 18thC the Salpêtrière pioneered a more humane treatment of the insane, and today it has a justifiably distinguished reputation in the field of neurology and neuro-psychiatry, and as a general hospital. The main **facade**, with its central domed **St-Louis chapel** which was designed by Libéral Bruand, is one of the most majestic in Paris.

Sciences et de l'Industrie, Cité des *(City of Science and Industry)*

See *La Villette*.

Sculpture, Musée en Plein Air *(Open Air Sculpture Museum)*

Quai St-Bernard, 5e. Map ***16K11*** ⊡ *Open daily. Métro Jussieu, Gare d'Orléans-Austerlitz.*
If you are tired of the *Venus de Milo* and want to see modern sculpture, you will find it at this open-air museum, which is situated in a riverside park near the *Jardin de Plantes*. There is a permanent display, and temporary exhibitions are also held here.

Seine

Lovers, painters and songwriters have for so long made the Seine their own that it is easy to forget the vital role that the river has played in Paris' history as an artery of trade and a strategic route since Roman times. In fact, without the Seine there would be no Paris. It is not for nothing that the badge of Paris depicts a boat, for the men who operated the river trade were for centuries the leading citizens of the town, and it was their corporation that formed the municipal administration in the Middle Ages.

Parisians often measure the river's waterlevel by looking at the statue of the *Zouave* (an Algerian soldier of the Second Empire) which stands at the E side of the Pont de l'Alma. When the Zouave has his feet in the water it is a sign that the river is getting dangerously high. In the notorious floods of 1910 the water reached his chin.

The Seine provides some of the most beautiful riverscapes in the world. To get to know the river at close hand, walk along the riverside path (see *Planning and walks*) or take a trip on one of the famous Bateaux-Mouches which leaves regularly from the Pont de l'Alma.

Sewers

See *Égouts*.

Sorbonne

Rue Sorbonne, 5e. Map ***15J9***. *Métro Maubert-Mutualité, Luxembourg.*
The imposing buildings of the Sorbonne, which dominate the center of the *Latin Quarter*, testify to the long and distinguished

history of this world-famous university. Founded in 1253 by Louis IX's (St Louis) confessor Robert de Sorbon, it started life as a college for 16 poor theological students but rapidly grew into a powerful body which had its own government, laws and jurisdiction — virtually a state within a state. In the 17thC its chancellor, Cardinal Richelieu, commissioned the architect Jacques Lemercier to reconstruct the college buildings and added the magnificent domed Jesuit-style **church**, the interior of which can, unfortunately, be seen only during temporary exhibitions.

The university was closed during the Revolution and then re-opened by Napoleon as the premier university of France. Alas, it no longer exists as a university in its own right. After the student riots of 1968, in which it played a key role, the Sorbonne became merely part of the University of Paris with its multitude of buildings scattered over the city.

However, the glory of the past still clings to the buildings: the great courtyard with its **superb sundial** surmounted by a relief of Apollo in his chariot; the Baroque library possessing over 1.5 million volumes; and the ornate lecture rooms with their numerous murals.

It is amusing to walk around and rub shoulders with the students. They no longer talk Latin, as they did in the days when the name "Latin Quarter" was born, but they are heirs to an illustrious tradition.

Tour Eiffel *(Eiffel Tower)* ★

*7e ☎45-50-34-56. Map **12H3** stages 1 and 2 stages 3 to top for groups Open Oct to before Easter daily 10am-11pm; Easter to Sept daily 9.30am-11pm (except Fri, Sat and hols Apr-Jun 9.30am-midnight and Jul-Aug daily 9.30am-midnight).*

The controversy which once raged over this world-famous tower has long since died down, and it has become universally accepted as the unofficial symbol of Paris. The reason why it was built has been almost forgotten: to commemorate the centenary of the French Revolution in 1889. Those who think that Gustave Eiffel's design is bad enough should remember that it was one of 700 submitted for a competition in which rival proposals included a gigantic lighthouse capable of illuminating the entire city, and a tower shaped like a guillotine to honor the victims of the Reign of Terror. Fortunately Gustave Eiffel's design was unanimously accepted, and the iron tower was completed in time for the centenary and the World Exhibition of the same year. It rose 300m (984ft) and was a miracle of engineering, comprising 9,700 tons of material. Today its height, including aerials, is 320.75m (1,052ft).

Whenever we think of the city, we do well to remember Mirabeau: "Paris is a sphinx; I will drag her secret from her," but in this neither he nor any man has succeeded.

Hilaire Belloc, *Paris*

At first is was widely reviled. The writer Huysmans scornfully called it a "hollow candlestick," and a group of distinguished Parisians published a manifesto declaring it a "dishonor to Paris." Many advocated its demolition, but it was saved by the First World War when it became an important military radio and telegraphic center. In 1964 it was classified as a national monument.

The journey to the summit is made in three stages. The first and second platforms of the tower, which can be reached by elevator or stairs, support restaurants and souvenir shops. The third and top platform, which can be reached only by elevator, has a bar, souvenir shops and the office in which Eiffel worked, recently restored. The superb **panorama** ★ over the city can be viewed from behind glass or from a balcony.

The tower has witnessed some strange scenes in its history. One man died trying to fly from it with artificial wings; in 1923 a daredevil journalist succeeded in riding a bicycle down from the first floor; and in 1954 it was scaled by a mountaineer. However, most people climb it for the view or simply to be able to say that they have been to the top of the famous Eiffel Tower.

Tour Montparnasse *(Montparnasse Tower)*

Centre Maine-Montparnasse, 37 Av. de Maine, 14e ☎45-83-52-56. Map ***14L6*** *Open 1 Apr-30 Sept 9.30am-11.30pm; 1 Oct-31 Mar 10am-10pm. Métro Montparnasse-Bienvenue.*

Opened in 1973, this 200m (656ft) high tower, with its adjacent shopping center dominates the whole quarter. It is regarded as one of the worst atrocities ever inflicted on Paris, a sad relic of Georges Pompidou's misguided attempts to "modernize" the French capital.

It rises like a vast black tombstone from the center of *Montparnasse*, dominating the skyline from almost every part of the city and creating a discordant element in the otherwise human scale of central Paris. Fortunately the law has now been changed to prohibit buildings of this and similar height in the city.

It must be admitted, however, that the view from the top of the tower is spectacular and interestingly different from the one afforded by the *Eiffel Tower*. The fifty-sixth floor has a viewing gallery with a bar and a good restaurant. You can also go right up on to the flat roof of the building.

The adjacent **Maine-Montparnasse** shopping center is a multi-level complex containing shops, restaurants and squash courts. It is linked to the tower by a vast bleak podium, which makes a good place for roller-skaters.

Tour St-Jacques *(St Jacques Tower)*

Sq. St-Jacques, 4e. Map ***10I9****. Métro Châtelet.*

This curiously haunting edifice, rising out of a little park off the *Rue de Rivoli*, is all that remains of the medieval church of St-Jacques-la-Boucherie, once a starting point for pilgrims setting out for the shrine of St James of Compostella in Spain. The church was demolished in 1802, but the bell-tower was spared to be used for dropping globules of molten lead in the manufacture of shot. It was later bought by the City of Paris and restored and now serves as a meteorological station. At the base sits a statue of *Blaise Pascal* who, in 1647, carried out the first meteorological experiment with a barometer at the summit.

Transports Urbains, Musée des *(Urban Transport Museum)*

60 Av. de Sainte-Marie, 94160 St Mandé ☎43-28-37-12. Map ***19D5*** *for groups. Open Sat, Sun, Apr 15-Oct 31, 2.30-6pm. Closed weekdays. Métro Porte-Dorée.*

What are a Glasgow corporation tram and a London trolley bus doing in a Paris suburb? Answer: they are part of an intriguing museum devoted to urban public transportation vehicles from horse-drawn buses to Métro carriages, housed in a former RATP bus depot and run entirely by an amateur association. Its members are very willing to share their enthusiasm with any visitor. Your will find plenty here to stir nostalgia.

For location, see map on p122.

Tuileries ☆

1er. Map 8H7. Métro Tuileries.

If you want to see French formal gardening at its most elegant, you need go no farther than the Jardin des Tuileries, laid out by Louis XIV's gardener, Le Nôtre, and occupying a splendid site bounded by the *Louvre*, the *Place de la Concorde* and the *Rue de Rivoli*, with the *Jeu de Paume* and *Orangerie* museums on raised terraces at the western end. The central avenue, with its two ponds, is dramatically aligned with the *Champs-Élysées* and the Louvre.

There seem to be almost as many statues in the gardens as there are trees: ancient gods and goddesses, allegorical figures of rivers and the seasons, and a bust of Le Nôtre himself. There are many modern sculptures, forming a sort of extension of the reorganized Louvre.

However, contrasted with the gaiety of the gardens is the tragic specter of the vanished Tuileries palace, which once ran N-S between the two projecting western pavilions of the Louvre, with the *Arc de Triomphe du Carrousel* forming the entrance to its courtyard. Queen Catherine de Medici built the palace in the 16thC but never lived there because her astrologer warned her not to, and subsequently an evil spell seemed to afflict the building. It witnessed violent and dramatic events, such as the escape of Louis XIV and his family across the gardens in 1792, the massacre of the Swiss Guards at the same time, and the riots which led to the departure of Charles X in 1830 and of Louis-Philippe in 1848. Finally, it was sacked and burned by the *Communards* in 1871.

At Paris I took an upper apartment for a few days in one of the hotels on the Rue de Rivoli: my front windows looking into the garden of the Tuileries (where the principal difference between nursemaids and the flowers seemed to be that the former were locomotive and the latter not).

Charles Dickens, *The Uncommercial Traveller*, 1861

UNESCO Building 🏛

7 Pl. de Fontenoy, 7e ☎45-68-10-00. Map 13J4 for exhibitions for performances for groups by prior arrangement Closed Sat, Sun. Métro Ségur.

This Y-shaped structure must have seemed daringly modern when it was opened in 1958, but now it has a rather old-fashioned look. In the grounds the black metal Alexander Calder mobile and Henry Moore's *Figure in Repose* add to the period flavor, as does the rather unattractive Picasso mural in the interior. They are security-conscious here, so one cannot just walk in and look without being organized, but there are regular exhibitions which the public can attend, and the main assembly chamber is used for spectacles ranging from circuses to piano recitals. The atmosphere is lively and international.

Val-de-Grâce 🏛 † ☆

1 Pl. Alphonse-Laveran, 5e ☎43-29-12-31. Map 15L9. Church open 8am-6pm. Métro Port-Royal.

One of the great architectural treasures of Paris, the Val-de-Grâce hides its light under a bushel, tucked away as it is down the Rue

St-Jacques. Anne of Austria, wife of Louis XIII, installed a Benedictine convent here in 1622 which she used as a retreat. The buildings still remain, including the superbly proportioned **cloister**. Later she added the church in thanksgiving for the birth of a son in 1638, the future Louis XIV, after 23 childless years of marriage; the young king himself laid the first stone of the building in 1645.

The church, in the Jesuit style, has many beautiful features including a **cupola** ☆ painted with frescoes by Mignand, an unusual six-columned baldachin over the altar, and an attractive sculpted ceiling, the pattern of which is reproduced in the floor tiles.

In the Revolution the convent was turned into a military hospital, which it remains to this day. It incorporates a museum relating to the history of military medicine which, at the time of writing, is closed for an indefinite period because of alterations. The Val-de-Grâce stands in an area devoted to medicine, with its large hospital and various medical institutions.

Vendôme, Place 🏛 ★

1er. Map 8G7. Métro Tuileries.

Few squares in the world convey such an impression of effortless opulence and wealth as this one. Built under Louis XIV to a design by Jules Hardouin-Mansard (1645–1708), it presents a uniform facade of the utmost beauty of proportion: an arcade at ground level, then Corinthian pilasters rising through two stories, topped by a roof with dormer windows. The keystones over the arches are carved with Bacchanalian faces, each one bearing a different expression like a ring of revelers at some expensive feast. This jolly throng has witnessed many dramatic events in the square. The statue of Louis XIV, which stood in the center, was destroyed during the Revolution and later replaced by a bronze column constructed by Denon, Gondouin, and Lepère in 1806–10, commemorating Napoleon's victories in Germany and modeled on Trajan's column in Rome. This monument was pulled down during the *Commune* but later re-erected. It is surmounted by a statue of Napoleon.

Besides numerous financiers and aristocrats, the square housed such colorful characters as the Austrian F.A. Mesmer, inventor of mesmerism, who held sessions of "animal magnetism" at **no. 16**, and Chopin, who died at **no. 12**.

Today the square is occupied mainly by offices and expensive stores. The **Ministry of Justice** is at nos. 11 and 13, and the luxurious **Ritz** (see *Hotels*) at no. 15. You will also find here banks, jewelers and art dealers. Like a beautiful woman grown used to riches, the Place Vendôme has an aloofness that does not invite closer acquaintance — unless you happen to be very well-heeled.

Victor Hugo Museum

See *Hugo, Victor, Musée*.

La Villette, Parc de

19e. Map 19C5 ☎42-78-70-00 (recorded information). Métro Porte de la Villette.

This is one of Paris's most exciting recent developments. La Villette is a former cattle market and abattoir district at the intersection of the Canal de l'Ourcq and the Canal St-Denis at the extreme NE corner of Paris, which has undergone a vast redevelopment program and has now emerged as a futuristic park and museum complex covering 55ha (136 acres).

Among its main features is the **Cité des Sciences et de l'Industrie**, one of the largest and most imaginative scientific and technical centers in the world (*☎40-05-70-00 or, for recorded information, ☎42-46-13-13 ▣ Closed Wed morning and Mon*). It incorporates a permanent series of displays called *Explora* covering such themes as the nature of the earth and the universe, organic life, scientific laws, language and communication, conveyed by means of a brilliantly conceived series of installations, such as computers that the visitor can operate, videos, lasers and mathematical games. Other sections of the City include the Médiatheque documentation center, a current events room, a movie theater, a planetarium and large area for temporary exhibitions on scientific, technical and industrial themes.

Near the City of Science and Industry is **La Géode** (*☎40-05-70-00 or ☎40-05-06-07 for recorded information ▣ closed Mon*), a gleaming sphere of stainless steel housing an auditorium in which films are projected on to a huge hemispherical screen that gives spectators the impression of being enveloped in the image.

Across the Canal de l'Ourcq is the **Grande Halle** (*☎42-49-77-22*), a converted cattle market which is now used for a variety of large-scale events such as cultural exhibitions, trade fairs and concerts.

Still under construction at the time of writing, and scheduled to open in the fall of 1990, is the **Cité de la Musique** (City of Music), which is planned to include the relocated *Conservatoire National de Musique* and its museum of instruments as well as a concert hall.

Other buildings in the park include a pop and rock music auditorium called the Zenith, a gallery devoted to electronic games (due to open at the end of 1989), a center for the study of local history known as the **Maison de la Villette**, and the **Théatre Paris-Villette**, a neighborhood theater.

In between these buildings and flanking the canals is a large area of attractively landscaped park with plenty of trees and grassy areas. There are also apartments, bars, restaurants and stores. For scientifically minded adults and children, La Villette is an absorbing place for a day's outing.

Vincennes

*Map **19D5** ▣ ✗ compulsory for both keep and chapel. Open 10-11.15am, 1.30-5.15pm, 4.30pm in winter. Closed Tues. Métro Château-de-Vincennes, RER Vincennes.*

The Château de Vincennes is made up of a series of rectangular buildings of different periods, parts of which have served at various times as royal residence, prison, porcelain factory and arsenal. The main entrance is approached across a vast moat, now overgrown with grass, and the whole place has a rather forbidding aspect which mirrors its grim history. Henry V of England died of dysentery here in 1422, and in 1944 it was the scene of the execution of 26 members of the Resistance by the Nazis who blew up part of the castle and set one of the pavilions on fire. The **keep** ☆ or *donjon* is the only medieval one in the environs of Paris and houses the **museum of the Château**.

Opposite the keep is a Gothic chapel, the **Sainte Chapelle**, which was founded by Charles V in 1379, and modeled on the one of the same name on the *Ile de la Cité*. It has some fine stonework and magnificent **stained-glass windows**. Both chapel and keep can only be seen with a guide. To the s of the keep and chapel are two 17thC **pavilions** facing each other across a courtyard. Louis XIV spent his honeymoon in one of these buildings in 1660.

The restoration of the château was begun on the order of Napoleon III and continued spasmodically for a century. It is now complete.

Bois de Vincennes ★

This great open space of woodlands lies to the SE of Paris at the opposite pole to the Bois de Boulogne. Flanking the city like lungs, these two great parks have provided generations of Parisians with easy access to greenery, open air and a variety of recreations.

Enclosed by Philippe Auguste in the 12thC as a royal hunting ground, it was made into a park for the citizens of Paris by Louis XV and was given to the town by Napoleon in 1860. Since then, many inroads have been made into it, and much of the greenery has been lost. In recent years, however, the municipality has started to reclaim some of the lost parkland; thousands of trees have been planted and new avenues laid out.

If you are lucky enough to have lived in Paris as a young man, then wherever you go for the rest of your life, it stays with you, for Paris is a moveable feast.

Ernest Hemingway to a friend, 1950

Though not as fashionable or well-known as the *Bois de Boulogne*, this park contains just as many features of beauty and interest. Starting at the château and traveling clockwise, you come first to the **floral garden** (*open 9.30am-6 or 7.30pm*), an attractively laid out garden, which is planted with an interesting variety of flora and includes a small lake, riding stables, a children's play area and restaurant. Flower shows are held in the Bois de Vincennes regularly.

The park was formerly the home of the university of Paris VIII, one of the more progressive of French universities, which has unfortunately been moved to a less scenic location in a different part of the city.

Nearby are the **Minimes Lake** with three islands, a restaurant and boating facilities, and the garden of the **School of Tropical Agronomy**, with its Oriental touches and its **temple** commemorating the Indo-Chinese killed in the First World War.

Turning S you come to the **Breuil School of Horticulture**, with more lovely gardens and an arboretum, and beside it the Vincennes **trotting and cycling tracks**.

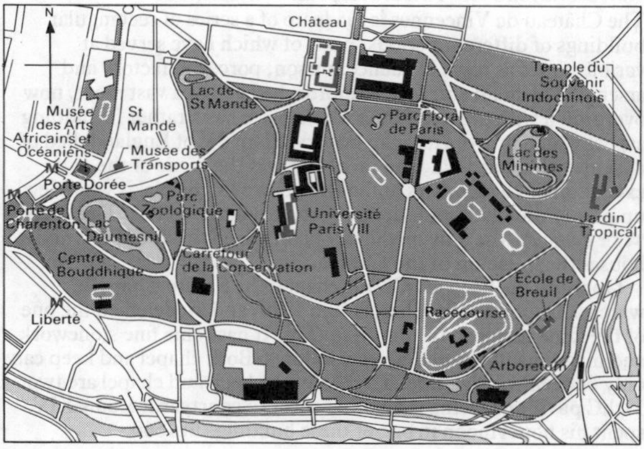

A walk E through the woods will bring you to the **Daumesnil Lake**, a popular boating place with a plush café-restaurant on one of its two islands. Near the lakes is the **Buddhist Center,** the temple of which contains the largest effigy of Buddha in Europe, made of glass fiber and covered with gold leaf.

On the opposite side of the lake is the **zoological park,** the largest of the Paris zoos (*open 9am-5.30 or 7pm*). Here you can see elephants, bison, kangaroos, peacocks and many other animals and birds roaming in natural-looking surroundings. There are two cafés and a huge artificial rock from the top of which you have an excellent view over the Bois to the E and Paris to the W.

See also the *Arts Africains et Océaniens* and *Transports Urbains* museums, all of which are close by and merit a diversion.

Vosges, Place des 🏛 ★

4e. Map 11I11. Métro St-Paul, Chemin-Vert.

The oldest square in Paris is also arguably the most beautiful. It was built on the orders of Henry IV who wished to create a square suitable for fêtes and ceremonial occasions, but was not finished until 1612, 2yrs after his death. Planned as a single unit of matching facades, it was begun with the **King's Pavilion** on the S side, which is counterbalanced to the N by the **Queen's Pavilion**. The buildings are constructed of red brick and pale gold stone, with an arcade at ground level in which are a number of stores and cafés — try **Ma Bourgogne** at the NW corner.

My Paris is a land where twilight days
Merge into violet nights of black and gold;
Where, it may be, the flower of dawn is cold:
Ah, but the gold nights, and the scented ways!

Arthur Symons, *Poems*

The Place des Vosges, like the rest of the *Marais* in which it is situated, is rather uncharacteristic of the city of Paris in its solid, quiet elegance. The poet Gérard de Nerval left behind him a vivid description of the houses in the square at sunset:

"When you see their high windows and brick facades, interspersed and framed with stone, at the moment when they are lit up by the splendid rays of the setting sun, you feel the same veneration as you do before a parliamentary court, assembled in red robes trimmed with ermine."

The square had many distinguished residents. Mme de Sevigné was born at **no. 1bis**, Richelieu lived at **no. 21,** and Victor Hugo at **no. 6,** now a museum (see *Hugo, Victor, Musée*).

In the garden enclosed by the square, where summer fêtes and duels once took place, children now play together and lovers stroll. Fashionable Paris has long since moved westward, but the Place des Vosges retains an aristocratic patina.

Zadkine, Musée

*100bis Rue d'Assas, 6e ☎43-26-91-90. Map **14K8** Open 10am-5.40pm. Closed Mon. Métro Vavin, Notre-Dame-des-Champs.*

Here is a collection of works by the Russian-born painter Ossip Zadkine, assembled in the home where he lived and worked from 1928 until his death in 1967. The house, studio and garden are all crammed with Zadkin's creations, which display a remarkable range of styles from his early primitive and Cubist sculptures to the monumental work of his later years.

Where to stay

Hotel life in Paris can be a mixed delight: like any other city it has its hazards, but on the whole it is full of pleasant surprises. Few cities have such a rich and varied choice of hotels, and many of them preserve an old-fashioned style of management that is rapidly dying out elsewhere, as well as cleanliness, courtesy, a high ratio of staff to guests, and often a quintessentially French atmosphere. On the debit side, however, Paris has its share of sleazy hotels, and smallness of rooms is a common characteristic, so it is wise to choose carefully and reserve well in advance.

Reservations

Though Paris boasts some 1,300 hotels from the French grade of one star and up, the problems of getting a room on short notice are manifold: it is best to reserve at least a month in advance (see *Sample reservation letter* in *Words and phrases*). If last-minute reservation is unavoidable, you can use the services of the tourist offices found at Orly and Roissy-Charles-de-Gaulle airports, the Gare du Nord, Gare d'Austerlitz, Gare de Lyon and Gare de l'Est; and at the main Tourist Office at 127 Av. des Champs-Élysées, 8e. July and Aug, by the way, are two of the least heavily reserved months.

Price

The price categories quoted for each hotel in this book are a rough guide to what you can expect to pay. There are five of these: cheap, inexpensive, moderate, expensive and very expensive (See *How to use this book* for the approximate prices these correspond to.) In Paris, "very expensive" means some of the best hotels in the world, whereas "cheap" signifies the bare essentials; in the latter, cleanliness, relative comfort and atmosphere are what count. Prices in the intervening categories are dependent on the lavishness of the fittings and amenities, the size of the room and the quality and quantity of the service. Nearly all the hotels listed here have the standard amenities of toilet, bath and/or shower, and bidet. In France, two people occupying one room will pay little more than one.

Tipping

Hotel prices now always include all service and taxes, and sometimes breakfast. If you are particularly pleased with the service you can slip a few more francs into the palm of the chambermaid and/or receptionist.

Meals

French hotel breakfasts are the one blot on the nation's gastronomic copybook: too often individually packed portions of butter and jam, and cardboard croissants are served up, except in topnotch establishments, which charge a fortune for good breakfasts. A breakfast is not usually included in the price, and unless you give priority to breakfasting in bed, you'll probably find better value around the corner from the hotel at a nearby café or *salon de thé*.

Choosing

Apart from price, a convenient location is usually the most important factor in choosing a hotel, so it is best to decide on where you want to stay first and then to pick the most suitable hotel in the area (see list of hotels by *arrondissement*).

In Paris, the two most popular areas are St-Germain and the Champs-Élysées/Rue St-Honoré district. Both are central, and the former is one of the liveliest, yet most historic parts of the city, whereas the latter is the most sophisticated and business-oriented. Becoming increasingly popular since renovation was begun in the 1960s is the *Marais* — the lovely old town houses make ideal small hotels. *Montparnasse*, once Bohemian, has attracted giant luxury hotels such as the **Meridien Montparnasse** since the redevelopment began.

If you are reserving at the last minute through the Tourist Office's reservation service, do not be too put off if all you are offered is hotels in one of the less central of Paris' 20 *arrondissements* — the capital is small and compact (it can be easily walked across in about 1½hrs), and has an excellent Métro and bus system.

The selection in this book has been made not only to give a wide choice of price and area, but also with other various priorities in mind: atmosphere, relative quiet and space. Addresses, telephone numbers (telex where appropriate), and nearest Métro stations are given, as well as symbols showing which hotels are particularly luxurious or simple and which represent good value. Other symbols show price categories, and give a resumé of the facilities that are available. See *How to use this book* for the full list of symbols. You can deduce the *arrondissement* in which the hotel is located from the last two numbers of the postcode. When hotels and restaurants are described elsewhere in the book, they appear in bold type.

Hotels classified by arrondissement

1er
Ducs d'Anjou to
Family Hôtel to
France et Choiseul
Inter-Continental
Lotti
Meurice
Montana-Tuileries
Ritz
St-James et Albany to
Tuileries to

4e
de la Bretonnerie to
Deux Iles
Fauconnier
Maubuisson
Vieux Marais

6e
L'Abbaye St-Germain to
L'Hôtel to
Marronniers to
Pas-de-Calais
Perreyve
Relais Christine to
St-André-des-Arts
de Seine

7e
Lenox to
Montalembert
Pont Royal to
Quai Voltaire to
St-Simon
Sofitel-Paris-Invalides
Solférino to
Suède to
Université to

8e
Bradford
Bristol
Crillon
George V
Lancaster
Plaza-Athénée
Résidence Lord Byron to
Royal Monceau

9e
Chopin
Grand Hôtel

10e
Terminus Nord to

14e
Meridien Montparnasse

15e
Hilton
Nikko to

16e
Raphael to
Résidence Foch to

17e
Étoile
Regent's Garden to
Splendid Étoile

18e
Résidence Charles-Dullin to
Terrass'

L'Abbaye St-Germain
10 Rue Cassette, 75006 Paris ☎45-44-38-11. Map ***14J7*** *to 45 rms 45 Métro St-Sulpice.*
Location: In a short, quiet street close to St-Germain-des-Prés and the Luxembourg Gardens. This magnificent and extraordinary converted 17thC convent shows just what results can be obtained when the ancient and modern are skillfully combined. Contemporary sofas are surrounded by 18thC antiques in the downstairs lobby, while the rooms themselves, some of which have original beams and alcoves, are tastefully decorated with successfully unusual color schemes and fabrics. Furthermore, the courtesy and helpfulness of the staff are exemplary. With so much to recommend it, however, it is hardly surprising that it can be extremely difficult to find a room here in peak periods, so be sure to make a reservation well in advance.

Bradford
10 Rue St-Philippe-du-Roule, 75008 Paris ☎43-59-24-20. Map ***7F4*** *48 rms 48. Métro St-Philippe-du-Roule.*
Location: Next to the Rue du Faubourg-St-Honoré, with the Champs-Élysées nearby. Friendliness is one of the best features of this unassuming hotel. The rooms are large and pleasantly furnished, the bathrooms brand new. Also most welcome in an area blighted by heavy traffic is the almost total quiet and seclusion of the little Rue St-Philippe-du-Roule.

de la Bretonnerie
22 Rue Ste-Coix-de-la-Bretonnerie, 75004 Paris ☎48-87-77-63 305551. Map ***10I10*** *to 31 rms 31. Métro Hôtel-de-Ville.*
Location: Almost at the heart of Paris, in the fascinating Marais district, between the Jewish Quarter and Pompidou Center. This quiet hotel, housed in a 17thC building, has a cozy atmosphere. It combines modern comfort with good use of the building's traditional features, such as rough stone walls and exposed wooden beams. Furnishings and decoration are suitably harmonious in their surroundings.

Bristol
112 Rue du Faubourg-St-Honoré, 75008 Paris ☎42-66-91-45 280961. Map ***7F6*** *200 rms 200 AE CB VISA Métro Champs-Élysées-Clemenceau.*
Location: In a prime part of one of the most exclusive and expensive streets in Paris. Heads of government and high-flying diplomats who have an appointment with the President at the Élysée Palace generally like to stay at the Bristol, which is very conveniently located just down the road. It is also one of Paris' finest hotels—both traditional and luxurious, it is richly decorated with original oil paintings, antiques and Oriental carpets. Bathrooms are sumptuous and several are in the Art Deco style. There is a hairdressing salon and massage parlor, conference room, and an excellent restaurant. The private parking lot and swimming pool are marks of distinction shared with few Paris hotels.

Chopin
46 Passage Jouffroy, 75009 Paris ☎47-70-58-10. Map ***9F9*** *38 rms 38 CB VISA Métro Rue Montmartre.*
Location: In one of Paris' distinctive arcades, close to the Opéra Quarter. It must have occurred to anyone who has wandered through the area of delightful arcades, which branch unobtrusively off the noisy Grands Boulevards, that this would be an ideally traffic-free place to stay in Paris (or live in, for that matter). The charming mid-19thC Hôtel Chopin, in the Passage Jouffroy, fills the bill perfectly, even if the majority of its rooms are small. The Chopin is a relaxing and soothing place to stay.

Crillon
10 Pl. de la Concorde, 75008 Paris ☎42-65-24-24 290204. Map ***8G6*** *201 rms 201 AE CB VISA Métro Concorde.*
Location: Overlooking one of the most famous townscapes in the world, at the hub of the Right Bank. The Crillon has long been established as one of the great classic hotels of the world. Its air of quiet excellence is symbolized by the fact that it displays no ostentatious signs, only its name in discreet letters over the entrance to its magnificent 18thC premises in one of the best positions of any hotel in Paris. Formerly an aristocratic mansion, it was turned into a hotel in 1907, and the sumptuous decor and formal inner courtyard were preserved. Here you

will find the last word in elegance and controlled good taste along with a good restaurant, a famous bar and a clientele that includes official guests of the French government and the occasional movie star shunning the company of other movie stars. The only drawback is that traffic noise, albeit muffled, from Pl. de la Concorde creeps insidiously into many of the bedrooms.

Deux Iles
*59 Rue St-Louis-en-l'Ile, 75004 Paris ☎43-26-13-35. Map **10J10** 17 rms 17. Métro Cité.*
Location: On the Ile St-Louis, the smaller and quieter of the Seine's two islands, in the heart of Paris. The Hôtel des Deux Iles occupies a 17thC building in the quiet street that runs the length of the Ile St-Louis. The rooms could not by any stretch of the imagination be described as large, but they do have delightfully tiled bathrooms; the bar in the cellar, with its open fire and comfy sofas, is the ideal place for a *rendezvous galant* on a cold winter's evening.

Ducs d'Anjou
*1 Rue Ste-Opportune, 75001 Paris ☎42-36-92-24. Map **10H9** to 38 rms 33 AE CB Visa Métro Les Halles.*
Location: In the Halles/Beaubourg area. This hotel is a pleasant if unremarkable base from which to explore the vicinity, which includes the Forum des Halles, that curious cross between a mega-shopping center and a meeting place for people of every description. The rooms are very quiet, if somewhat dark, and the hotel is located on the very pretty Pl. Ste-Opportune.

Étoile
*3 Rue de l'Étoile, 75017 Paris ☎43-80-36-94 Telex 642028. Map **6E3** 25 rms 25 AE Visa Métro Ternes.*
Location: Close to the Arc de Triomphe. A small, intimate hotel where you can live like a prince, almost for a song, with color TV, minibar, direct-dial telephone, thick wall-to-wall carpets and functional modern furniture in your room, plus a bar and a mini-library in the lobby.

Family Hôtel
*35 Rue Cambon, 75001 Paris ☎42-61-54-84. Map **8G7** to 25 rms 10 Visa Métro Madeleine.*
Location: In the fashionable area between the Rue St-Honoré and La Madeleine. Surprisingly for such a luxurious area, this hotel is just what its Anglified name suggests — a *hôtel familial*. Run by a friendly and courteous husband and wife, it has a tranquil air and simply furnished but attractive bedrooms. If you want a room with a bathroom, reserve well in advance.

Fauconnier
*11 Rue du Fauconnier, 75004 Paris ☎42-74-23-45. Map **11I11** 100 beds. Métro St-Paul.*
Location: In a small street by the Seine, opposite the Ile St-Louis. Like the nearby **Maubuisson**, this is a government-subsidized hotel-hostel, in theory for young people, in a superb 17thC former private house, with beams, original floor tiles, stone flagging and antique furniture. Rooms have anything from two to six beds in them, and although there used to be an upper age limit of 30, anyone willing to share a room with a stranger — or strangers — of the same sex is now welcome. Spotless, friendly, and of course very cheap.

France et Choiseul
*239 Rue St-Honoré, 75001 Paris ☎42-61-54-60 Telex 680959. Map **8G7** 120 rms 120 AE CB Visa Métro Tuileries.*
Location: In the smart, fashionable area of the Rue St-Honoré and Pl. Vendôme. An unhurried, timeless air and a courtly, old-fashioned style of management mark out this traditional Paris hotel with its upright Louis XV-style furniture. The rooms are small, but have been carefully modernized, each with its own up-to-date bathroom. There's a pretty patio at the rear.

George V
*31 Av. George V, 75008 Paris ☎47-23-54-00 Telex 290776. Map **7F4** 301 rms 301 AE CB Visa Métro George V.*
Location: Just off the Champs-Élysées, in the city's principal business area. Unlike the equally luxurious **Crillon**, with its discreet elegance, the George V is grand and unashamedly lavish. Flemish tapestries, sculptures, ormolu clocks and original paintings (including Renoir's *Le Vase des Roses*) complement the gracious 18thC-style furniture. The hotel has a delightful bar and a lovely inner courtyard, where in summer meals

are served amid red umbrellas and masses of potted plants as part of the excellent restaurant, **Les Princes**.

Grand Hôtel
2 Rue Scribe, 75009 Paris 42-68-12-13 220875. Map 8F7 492 rms 492 Métro Opéra.

Location: On Pl. de l'Opéra. Paris' largest old hotel was designed by Charles Garnier, architect of the Paris Opera House which dominates the view from the front windows. It was recently refurbished, along with the celebrated Café de la Paix adjoining it. The hotel is too vast to have a sharply defined clientele, though because of its location it is naturally a favorite with visiting musicians and singers who are performing at the Opéra. As well as a delightful, centrally placed winter garden, the establishment has well-appointed rooms, a sauna, a sun lounge, a gymnasium, and 17 air-conditioned conference rooms.

Hilton
18 Av. de Suffren, 75015 Paris 42-73-92-00 200955. Map 12I3 456 rms 456 Métro Champ-de-Mars.

Location: Close to the Seine and the Eiffel Tower. The Paris Hilton, considerably more luxurious and expensive than many others in the Hilton chain, was the first modern hotel built in Paris after the war. By the late 1970s it seemed to be dated, and redecoration was carried out. No expense is spared to provide home comforts for Americans in Paris, for instance movies on closed-circuit color TV.

L'Hôtel
13 Rue des Beaux-Arts, 75006 Paris 43-25-27-22 270870. Map 9I8 to 27 rms 27 Métro St-Germain-des-Prés.

Location: In the heart of the St-Germain-des-Prés Quarter. The ornate style of this hotel is not to everyone's taste — there are antiques everywhere, pink Venetian marble in the bathrooms, and velvet on virtually every surface, from the elevator to the uniforms. The facilities include a winter garden with restaurant and resident pianist, and an intimate cellar bar. You may be given the room containing Mistinguett's own Art Deco furniture, the bedroom (and bed) that Oscar Wilde died in, or one of the two top-floor suites with flower-decked balconies and a view over the church of St-Germain-des-Prés. Fellow guests may include Mick Jagger, Julie Christie or any number of personalities (both real and aspiring) from showbiz, fashion or advertising. This extravaganza is the brainchild of Guy-Louis Duboucheron, who converted it in 1967 from the cheap, sleazy hotel that Oscar Wilde knew. Although he has been accused of charging inflated prices, it is, perhaps, fairer to say that he has merely a shrewd understanding of what his assets are worth.

Inter-Continental
3 Rue Castiglione, 75001 Paris 42-60-37-80 220114. Map 8G7 500 rms 500 Métro Tuileries.

Location: Close to Pl. Vendôme. The hotel was built in 1878 by Charles Garnier, architect of the Paris Opera House, and also of the **Grand Hôtel**. Several of its amazingly ornate *salons* are now listed as historic monuments. It was completely and intelligently renovated about 10yrs ago and, while keeping its original atmosphere almost intact, it now has all the trappings of a modern luxury hotel: air conditioning throughout, color TV in all rooms, 24hr room service, a bar, a discotheque and conference rooms complete with secretaries and interpreters. The Inter-Continental also has a beautiful patio, which is a highly fashionable spot for outdoor eating when the **Rôtisserie Rivoli** serves its meals there in summer. The top-floor rooms afford a majestic view over the Tuileries Gardens.

Lancaster
7 Rue de Berri, 75008 Paris 43-59-90-43. 640991. Map 7E4 67 rms 67 Métro St-Philippe-du-Roule.

Location: In a fairly quiet street just off the Champs-Élysées. This haunt of American movie stars and big-time journalists looks and feels more like a smart private house than a hotel. Most of its rooms overlook a charming, flower-filled, statue-studded courtyard. The less fortunate ones on the street side have double-glazing, so a good night's sleep is guaranteed despite the proximity of the 24hr traffic on the Champs-Élysées.

Lenox
9 Rue de l'Université, 75007 Paris ☎42-96-10-95 260745. Map 8I7 to 34 rms 25 Métro Rue-du-Bac.
Location: Three minutes' walk from the Bd. St-Germain and the Seine. One of those rare hotels that stands out, not only in its class, but by any standards, because of a special thoroughbred quality. All the bedrooms and the reception area have been furnished and decorated with excellent taste, and the whole atmosphere has a warm elegance. What's more, the staff are extremely friendly, and the service is willing. Light meals will be provided in your room at any time of the day.

Lotti
7 Rue Castiglione, 75001 Paris ☎42-60-37-34 240066. Map 8G7 133 rms 133 Métro Tuileries.
Location: Only moments from the Pl. Vendôme and Rue St-Honoré. A luxury hotel of manageable proportions with a subdued, but regal air, the Lotti caters to the high society of many countries, but particularly Britain, Italy and France. The decor is traditional and extremely tasteful, with no two bedrooms the same. The service is quick, efficient and unobtrusive, and an air of calm and sophistication pervades the whole establishment.

Marronniers
21 Rue Jacob, 75006 Paris ☎43-25-30-60. Map 9I8 to 37 rms 37. Métro St-Germain-des-Prés.
Location: In the heart of the St-Germain-des-Prés Quarter, on the Left Bank. Mother Nature has a strong hold on this tall hotel, from the profusion of leaves, flowers and birds on the wallpaper and carpets, the fruit on the crockery, and the flower-filled vases, to the delightful little garden at the back, with its veranda, white garden furniture, and horse-chestnut trees (which give the hotel its name). There are two cozy lounges in the very old vaulted cellars. To top it all, the prices are as soothing as the service.

Maubuisson
12 Rue des Barres, 75004 Paris ☎42-72-72-09. Map 10I10 92 beds Métro Hôtel-de-Ville.
Location: In a tiny street behind St-Gervais-St-Protais church by the Hôtel-de-Ville. This hotel-hostel with dormitories is, in every respect, like the **Fauconnier** (a couple of minutes' walk away), from the 17thC building, original flooring and quiet location to the rock-bottom prices.

Meridien Montparnasse
19 Rue Cdt-Mouchotte, 75014 Paris ☎43-20-15-51 200135. Map 14L6 950 rms 950 Métro Montparnasse-Bienvenue.
Location: In the center of Montparnasse. Formerly a member of the worldwide Sheraton chain, this hotel was built as part of the Montparnasse redevelopment scheme, dominated by the controversial Maine-Montparnasse Tower. The building itself, by Pierre Dufau, who also designed part of *La Défense*, is an elegant white giant, rising 35 stories and contrasting strongly with its unlovely surroundings. With the benefit of the Gare Montparnasse and Métro at its side, the hotel caters with renowned efficiency for its guests, including tour groups and executives who appreciate its many facilities, among them conference rooms and three restaurants. This hotel has recently changed ownership and is now part of the Air France chain.

Meurice
228 Rue de Rivoli, 75001 Paris ☎42-60-38-60 230673. Map 8G7 187 rms 187 Métro Tuileries.
Location: Opposite the Tuileries Gardens. Opened in 1816, the Meurice used to receive almost all the crowned heads of Europe. During the German occupation, the governor of Paris, General Von Choltitz, set up his headquarters here. More recently the hotel has been patronized by Salvador Dalí, Gulf State Arabs, and other wealthy members of the international set. Recent renovation spared the gilded paneling, tapestries and huge chandeliers, but installed beautiful pink marble bathrooms and air conditioning in every room.

Montalembert
3 Rue Montalembert, 75007 Paris ☎45-48-68-11 200132. Map 8I7 61 rms 60 Métro Rue-du-Bac.

Location: On the Left Bank, between the Seine and the Bd. St-Germain. A slightly less expensive alternative to the **Pont Royal** in the same street, the Montalembert is an old school house, converted to make a large, somewhat soulless hotel in the heart of the literary Left Bank. The literary crowd who used to patronize it have, however, de-camped in recent years to the **Pont Royal** and other nearby hotels, but it remains a reasonably priced, functional base from which to explore the area. All the rooms have been modernized and have well-equipped bathrooms.

Montana-Tuileries
12 Rue St-Roch, 75001 Paris ☎42-60-35-10 Ⓣ 210311. Map 8G7 25 rms 23 AE VISA Métro Pyramides.
Location: Just off the Rue de Rivoli and Rue St-Honoré. If you feel like giving yourself a treat but can't afford the luxury hotels that line the Rue de Rivoli (**Meurice, St-James et Albany, Inter-Continental**), take a few steps down a side-street and try this small but spacious hotel. It has almost all the facilities of its more illustrious neighbors, from TV and direct-dial telephone to mini-bar in each room, but it won't cost the earth.

Nikko
61 Quai de Grenelle, 75015 Paris ☎45-75-62-62 Ⓣ 260012. Map 12J1 to 779 rms 779 AE VISA Métro Bir-Hakeim.
Location: On the quais overlooking the Seine, opposite Maison de Radio France. With admirable efficiency, the Japanese moved into the Paris hotel scene and within a mere 4yrs the Nikko's restaurant, **Les Célébrités**, had earned a much-coveted reputation for its excellent foods. The hotel itself offers all the amenities of a smoothly run international hotel from streamlined accommodations (with Japanese or western decor), to a clutch of bars, a sauna and a swimming pool. There is also a good Japanese restaurant, the **Benkay**.

Pas-de-Calais
59 Rue des Sts-Pères, 75006 Paris ☎45-48-78-74 Ⓣ 270476. Map 8I7 41 rms 41 VISA Métro St-Germain-des-Prés.
Location: On the Left Bank, just off Bd. St-Germain. This labyrinthine hotel was recently given a face-lift, but much of the downstairs furniture, though modern, looks amusingly passé. The best of the rooms (which are more stylishly decorated) overlooks a small courtyard notable for its trelliswork.

Perreyve
63 Rue Madame, 75006 Paris ☎45-48-35-01 Ⓣ 205080. Map 14J7 30 rms 30 AE VISA Métro Rennes.
Location: A quiet street near the Luxembourg Gardens. The Jardin du Luxembourg, a pocket of relaxing greenery in the hurly-burly of the Left Bank, is just round the corner from this charming hotel, which was recently renovated with admirable good taste. The rooms are comfortable and the bathrooms, though small and rather cramped, are sparkling clean.

Plaza-Athénée
25 Av. Montaigne, 75008 Paris ☎47-23-78-33 Ⓣ 650092. Map 7G4 220 rms 220 AE CB VISA Métro Franklin-D-Roosevelt.
Location: Near the Seine and the Champs-Élysées, but away from the noise and bustle. Perhaps the most glamorous and elegant hotel of all in Paris, attracting a galaxy of stars, and a particular favorite of wealthy South Americans and Greeks. Afternoon tea can be taken in the elegant long gallery, and there is a beautiful inner patio. Gorgeous period-style suites and attractive bedrooms, superb service (albeit slightly cool toward mere mortals), two celebrity-studded bars and an excellent restaurant, the **Régence-Plaza**.

Pont Royal
7 Rue Montalembert, 75007 Paris ☎45-44-38-27 Ⓣ 270113. Map 8I7 to 80 rms 80 AE VISA Métro Rue-du-Bac.
Location: In a small street between the river and the Bd. St-Germain. Close to the famous literary publishing house of Gallimard and conveniently located for the restaurants and charms of the Left Bank, yet only a short walk to the river, Notre-Dame and the Louvre, this hotel — named after the nearby bridge — provides a consistent standard of comfort for visiting publishers and a good base for the tourist who wants a genuinely middle-of-the-road hotel. The rooms, if a little small, are pleasantly

furnished and comfortable, each with TV, mini-bar and even a safe; the bathrooms reflect the style and standard of the typical chain (Mapotel) hotel. Service prompt and straightforward, and reflects the general style. The restaurant, **Les Antiquaires**, is a safe bet for a business lunch, though there is plenty of more interesting competition nearby. There is an underground parking garage close to the front of the hotel.

Quai Voltaire
19 Quai Voltaire, 75007 Paris ☎42-61-50-91. Map 8H7 to 32 rms 25 Métro Solférino.
Location: On the Left Bank overlooking the Seine, opposite the Tuileries Gardens. Twenty-nine of the rooms in this light, bright and unfortunately rather noisy little hotel afford a superb view over the Seine — a view enhanced by the tall French windows. The establishment has a literary past — it was patronized by Charles Baudelaire and Oscar Wilde in their time — and its small, unostentatious bar is a choice meeting place for the lions of modern French literature.

Raphael
17 Av. Kléber, 75016 Paris ☎45-02-16-00 610356. Map 6F2 to 88 rms 88 Métro Kléber.
Location: On one of the avenues radiating from Étoile and the Arc de Triomphe. The smallest of the Parisian *palaces* (luxury hotels), the Raphael has a curiously unreal atmosphere heightened by dark wood paneling, heavy tapestries, thick carpets, and a huge painting of a seascape by Turner. This and its discreet location may be what appeals to the international movie stars and producers who stay here regularly. It's also located coveniently close to the film-world's offices, which are clustered around the Étoile and the Champs-Élysées.

Regent's Garden
6 Rue Pierre-Demours, 75017 Paris ☎45-74-07-30 640127. Map 6D3 to 40 rms 39 Métro Ternes.
Location: A quiet street in a residential area. The Regent's Garden lives up to its name by possessing a real garden, as opposed to the courtyard found in so many Parisian hotels, complete with statues and fountains. The building itself is typical of the showy *grand bourgeois* architecture of the mid-19thC. Its cavernous rooms, the lofty ceilings of which sport decorative moldings, are furnished in appropriate style, with brass bedsteads and large mirrors. The bathrooms, on the other hand, are equipped with thoroughly 20thC conveniences. The 17e may seem a little far from the hub of things, but the Rue Pierre-Demours is in fact only a few minutes' walk from the Arc de Triomphe.

Relais Christine
3 Rue Christine, 75006 Paris ☎43-26-71-80 202606. Map 9I8 to 51 rms 51 Métro Mabillon.
Location: A tiny backwater in the heart of the Latin Quarter, close to Pl. St-Michel. The Rue Christine not only boasts an excellent movie theater and the **Photogalerie** restaurant, but one of the area's most distinguished hotels, the Relais Christine. The 16thC building, once a monastery, became a publisher's book depot among other things before being transformed into a hotel in 1979. It's comfortable, spacious and tastefully decorated rooms, several of which are split-level apartments, are individually furnished with period pieces. Those on the lower floors are a trifle dim, although room 1 on the ground floor has a stone wall and a fine carved door. Other features include parking in the hotel courtyard, automatic shoe-cleaning machines, and color TV, minibar and direct-dial telephones in all the rooms — which will strike you as only fair when you come to peruse the bill.

Résidence Charles-Dullin
10 Pl. Charles-Dullin, 75018 Paris ☎42-57-14-55 290532. Map 4D9 to 76 rms 76 Métro Anvers.
Location: A quiet little square in Montmartre. The recently-opened Résidence Charles-Dullin, where you can rent one-, two- and three-room flats by the week, is not strictly speaking a hotel. Nevertheless it is an ideal place for the couple or family, for instance, who want to try out the joys of French cooking for themselves: each flat has a fully-equipped kitchen. Otherwise, the services provided are those of any good quality hotel.

Résidence Foch
10 Rue Marbeau, 75016 Paris 45-00-46-50 630886 to 25 rms 25 Métro Porte-Maillot.
Location: In the expensive residential area of the 16e. This small and exclusive luxury hotel is tucked away in the secluded calm of a tiny street near Paris' millionaires' row, Av. Foch, a minute or two's stroll from the Bois de Boulogne, and very near the excellent **Le Petit Bedon** restaurant. Résidence Foch is furnished with pleasant antiques, has an intimate bar, and includes, among its attractive rooms, a large and brightly lit split-level suite on the top floor.

Résidence Lord Byron
5 Rue de Châteaubriand, 75008 Paris 43-59-89-98 649662. Map 7F4 to 31 rms 24 Métro Étoile.
Location: Close to the Arc de Triomphe and Champs-Élysées. One of the quietest and most pleasant places to stay near the Champs-Élysées, which is a minute's walk away, and a must for anyone shunning the sometimes over-fussy service of the area's bigger hotels in the same high class. The furniture and decor are discreet and relaxing. There is an attractive inner courtyard with trelliswork, which many of the rooms overlook.

Ritz
15 Pl. Vendôme, 75001 Paris 42-60-38-30 220262. Map 8G7 164 rms 164 Métro Pyramides.
Location: Superbly located in the exclusive and beautiful Pl. Vendôme. Arguably the most famous hotel in the world, the Ritz lives up to its reputation, seeming to exude luxury, attentiveness and just the right amount of old-fashioned charm. Nor has it rested on its laurels like many other long-famous hotels, but has been sensitively renovated: the huge and splendid original baths remained, while the telephones were computerized. The benefits of staying at the Ritz are many: kind and unobtrusive service, beautiful period furnishings, a lovely inner garden, several chic bars, and an exceptionally good restaurant, **L'Espadon**.

Royal Monceau
35 Av. Hoche, 75008 Paris 45-61-98-00 650361. Map 2E4 220 rms 220 Métro Courcelles.
Location: Between the Arc de Triomphe and the attractive Monceau Park. Not long ago this luxury hotel came under new management and was given a complete overhaul. It is a favorite with international business clients, but all who can afford the Monceau would most certainly enjoy its serene, pastel charm and excellent features. In addition to its lovely, very "unhotel-like" rooms and attentive staff, the Monceau also boasts two haute cuisine restaurants, both of which are favorites with many Parisians. Offering Italian fare, there is the well-known **Il Carpaccio**, situated in the hotel's main building. In the courtyard is the round, glass-enclosed **Le Jardin**, offering superb, imaginatively prepared gourmet fare and white-gloved service. In addition, there are also two elegant cocktail bars. The hotel also features **Les Thermes**, an exclusive fitness club which includes a swimming pool (a rare feature in a Paris hotel), a sauna and gym, massage, hydrotherapy, and its own separate health-conscious restaurant. The Royal Monceau is also well equipped to cater to the corporate traveler and has several fine rooms especially suitable for conference or banqueting functions in addition to a fully-equipped business center.

St-André-des-Arts
66 Rue St-André-des-Arts, 75006 Paris 43-26-96-16. Map 9I8 35 rms 15. Métro St-Michel.
Location: On the Left Bank, between the St-Germain-des-Prés and Latin Quarters. Fun-loving, amusing clientele and a friendly welcome are what make this establishment memorable; the accommodations, however, are unfortunately nothing special. The hotel is remarkably well located for exploring the Left Bank.

St-James et Albany
202 Rue de Rivoli, 75001 Paris 42-60-31-60 213031. Map 8G7 to 207 rms 207 Métro Tuileries.
Location: Overlooking the Tuileries Gardens. For years, the Hôtel St-James et Albany, parts of which date from the time of Louis XIV, chugged along in its old-fashioned way with its own select band of aristocratic habitués (as one would expect of a hotel with a name so wonderfully redolent of London's clubland).

Then, after a long period of closure for alterations, it reopened in 1981, revealing an unusually successful combination of the old and the new in fittings and furniture. The refurbished and well-managed hotel, with its own excellent restaurant, **Le St James**, is now giving its prestigious neighbors on the Rue de Rivoli some stiff competition.

St-Simon
14 Rue de St-Simon, 75007 Paris ☎45-48-35-66 203277. Map 8I6 34 rms 34. Métro Rue-du-Bac.
Location: In a calm street just off the Bd. St-Germain. Quiet, cozy, intimate, welcoming, discreet and lived-in are all adjectives that have been liberally applied to this 19thC hotel, and there is no reason to dispute these assessments. The St-Simon, which was always remarkable for its period furnishings, was taken over in 1976 by a Swedish couple, the Lindqvists, whose hobby is antiques; since then, they have been gradually adding new pieces to the rooms. A delightful and consequently extremely popular hotel.

de Seine
52 Rue de Seine, 75006 Paris ☎46-34-22-80. Map 9I8 30 rms 30 Métro St-Germain-des-Prés, Odéon, Mabillon.
Location: On the Left Bank, in an attractive, quiet, art gallery-filled street just a few yards from the bustling Latin Quarter. The Hôtel de Seine is one of Paris's best-kept secrets. Run by the multilingual Monsieur Edouard with friendliness and great efficiency, the hotel itself is not fancy, but is, however, clean, secure and well-maintained. It is excellent value for money and offers useful features such as direct-dial telephones and breakfast brought to your room. The hotel is an easy walk from the *quai*, and is a fine base from which to explore all the nooks and crannies of the Latin Quarter, including some of the more famous nearby sights such as the Cathedral of Notre-Dame, the Church of St-Germain-des-Prés, and the atelier of Delacroix. For that other favorite French pastime, eating and café-hopping, the Hôtel de Seine is also ideally placed. A myriad restaurants and cafés are virtually outside your door, in addition to the Rue de Seine's superb food shops and dazzling open-air food market. As one might expect with all these advantages, the Hôtel de Seine serves many regular guests, so be advised to reserve well in advance.

Sofitel-Paris-Invalides
32 Rue St-Dominique, 75007 Paris ☎45-55-91-80 250019. Map 7H5 112 rms 112 Métro Invalides.
Location: In a quiet position on the Left Bank, just across the river from the Place de la Concorde. Part of the Sofitel chain, this hotel was built in the early 1970s and has since been entirely refurbished. Luxuriously appointed, it combines ultra-modern facilities with the well-bred patina of the Faubourg-St-Germain, a district full of embassies and ministries. It is within easy reach of many Paris highlights, such as the *Musée Rodin*, the *Musée d'Orsay*, the *Eiffel Tower* and *Les Invalides*. It has a high-quality restaurant, **Le Dauphin**.

Solférino
91 Rue de Lille, 75007 Paris ☎47-05-85-54. Map 8H7 to 34 rms 30. Métro Solférino.
Location: In St-Germain, tucked between the Seine and the Bd. St-Germain. The Solférino is a charming, old-fashioned and modest hotel with prettily and tastefully decorated, high-ceilinged bedrooms, a delightful little *salon* and a veranda for breakfasting. The faithful, mainly English and American, clientele are expecially appreciative of the warm welcome extended by the Solférino's friendly staff.

Splendid Étoile
1 bis Av. Carnot, 75017 Paris ☎47-66-41-41 280773. Map 6E3 57 rms 53 Métro Étoile.
Location: Right on the bustling Place Charles-de-Gaulle. This building is a fine 19thC mansion, entirely renovated inside and out in 1976. As a hotel it is comparatively small, with 57 spacious and elegantly furnished bedrooms. Some of the rooms look directly on to the *Arc de Triomphe*, but the windows are double-glazed so you can enjoy the sensation of being at the hub of Paris without suffering the attendant noise. There are conference facilities, an "English" bar and a fashionable restaurant called **Le Pré-Carré**, often frequented by show-business people and other well-known faces.

Suède
31 Rue Vaneau, 75007 Paris 47-05-00-08 200596. Map 14J6 to 41 rms 37 AE CB DC VISA Métro Sèvres-Babylone.
Location: In a plush area between Rue de Varenne and Rue de Babylone. Cool elegance distinguishes this hotel, which is just as it should be since it backs onto the gardens of the Prime Minister's official residence, the Hôtel Matignon. If you want to try to glimpse the man, or simply admire the towering plane trees that grow here, ask for a room on the second or third floor. The hotel also has a large, gently lit lounge in the Directoire style and a pretty little inner courtyard where morning or afternoon refreshment may be taken.

Terminus Nord
12 Bd. Denain, 75010 Paris 42-80-20-00 660615. Map 5E10 to 220 rms 125 AE CB DC VISA Métro Gare du Nord.
Location: Opposite the Gare du Nord. Prices vary considerably in this large and completely renovated hotel — which, by the way, has nothing to do with the adjoining restaurant of the same name — depending on whether or not you choose to have a private bathroom. If you do, you get a TV set as well. Rooms facing the street are insulated from noise. As a special bonus, the management does not charge for local telephone calls. Extremely convenient location for anyone in transit to or from the capital via the Gare du Nord.

Terrass'
18 Rue Joseph-de-Maistre, 75018 Paris 46-06-72-85 280830. Map 4C8 106 rms 106 AE CB DC VISA Métro Blanche.
Location: On the edge of Montmartre. The hotel rooms with the best views in Paris are undoubtedly to be found in this first-class establishment, which is perched on one of the outcrops of the Butte de Montmartre. From the hotel you can see the Panthéon, the surprisingly tall Opéra, Les Invalides, the Arc de Triomphe and, of course, the Eiffel Tower. Otherwise the Terrass', built in 1912 but modernized more than once since then, and being the only four-star hotel in Montmartre, provides all the services one would expect to find in a good hotel — though it does manage to charge marginally less for them than its rivals located in other parts of the city.

Tuileries
10 Rue St-Hyacinthe, 75001 Paris 42-61-04-17 240744. Map 8G7 to 26 rms 26 AE CB VISA Métro Pyramides.
Location: Close to Pl. Vendôme and within easy reach of Av. de l'Opéra and the Tuileries Gardens. You won't find a much quieter street in the center of Paris than the tiny Rue St-Hyacinthe: it is scarcely used by vehicles at all except those looking for a parking space. The Hôtel des Tuileries, which occupies a late 18thC building with a superb carved wooden front door, was recently modernized with care, and each room was decorated differently. Downstairs, though, there is still plenty of warm, old-fashioned velvet.

Université
22 Rue de l'Université, 75007 Paris 42-61-09-39 260717 OREM ref. 310. Map 8I7 to 20 rms 28. Métro Rue-du-Bac.
Location: On the Left Bank, between Bd. St-Germain and the Seine. Despite its rather steep prices, this hotel is reserved well ahead by people who want to stay in style in the antique-dealing and publishing end of St-Germain-des-Prés. The establishment, which occupies a 17thC *hôtel particulier* (private house), has been completely refurbished, and is filled with antiques and tapestries. The rooms are decorated with individual style and the breakfast lounge, hall, and tiny courtyard are charming.

Vieux Marais
8 Rue du Plâtre, 75004 Paris 42-78-47-22. Map 10H10 30 rms 21 AE Métro Rambuteau.
Location: On one of the less picturesque streets in the Marais. This charming quarter was a virtual slum 25yrs ago. Now in the process of renovation, it contains some of the priciest property in town, but it does not yet have its fair share of hotels, so the Vieux Marais, modernized in 1979, is a welcome addition. The amiable Rumiel family have done a good job of decorating it, brightening up the five-floor building with flowery wallpaper, matching curtains (made by Madame Rumiel herself), and light-colored bathrooms. The direct-dial telephones are rare for the price.

Eating in Paris

French cuisine is renowned as the finest in the world; the superb standard of cooking in the average French household is matched by the unequaled quality of France's restaurants. Whereas provincial restaurants reflect local produce and traditions, those of Paris act as a focus for the rest of the country, bringing together the individual and varied regional cuisines, being continually interested in change and innovation, and constantly striving for new limits of perfection. In Paris, with a little judicious choosing, you can quite simply have the gastronomic experience of a lifetime, whether it is a perfectly smoked Auvergne ham in a crowded wine bar, or a five-course extravaganza in one of the city's revered establishments.

Cooking in France is regarded not as a necessity but as an art, and its leading exponents, such as Paul Bocuse, Michel Guérard and Roger Vergé, are held in god-like esteem. They are the modern-day successors of the immortalized 19th and early 20thC chefs Carême and Escoffier, masters of *grande* or *haute cuisine*; but whereas Escoffier, for all his technical brilliance, put many strictures on French cuisine, many of today's great chefs are breaking free from his rules and regulations and seeking entirely new directions.

This style of cooking, pioneered in France since the war by such chefs as Alexandre Dumaine, André Pic and Fernard Point, is termed just that: *nouvelle cuisine*. (The term *nouvelle cuisine* had in fact been used previously in the 1740s during a similar culinary seachange.) In keeping with the modern trend away from rich, heavy food, and with the emphasis on absolute freshness, *nouvelle cuisine* at its best is lighter and tastier than traditional French cuisine, and is often characterized by unusual combinations of high-quality ingredients, and carefully presented, smaller and more manageable portions. *Nouvelle cuisine* is not a total culinary revolution, because although the ideas are different the methods remain the same, but it is a far-reaching adaptation to today's requirements of classic French cooking.

It must not be thought, however, that *nouvelle cuisine* has entirely swept traditional French cookery aside. On the contrary, the classic dishes will always remain, as will the excellent and more than ever popular *cuisine bourgeoise* that is the root of all French cooking. Regional cookery too, the individual cuisines of every part of France, still flourishes, as a visit to Normandy or Nice, Alsace or the Auvergne or to many of the regionally-inspired restaurants of Paris will tell you.

In Paris, all these varieties can be sampled. For a good insight into *nouvelle cuisine* try **Jacqueline Fénix**; for a Provençal fish soup try **Pierre Vedel**; for food from the Auvergne try **L'Ambassade d'Auvergen**; from the southwest try **Le Trou Gascon**; from the Landes try **Le Repaire de Cartouche**; for mushrooms try **Au Quai d'Orsay**; for *choucroute* try **Baumann**; for classic cuisine try **Lasserre**; or for good plain *cuisine bourgeoise* try **Le Procope** or **Le Trumilou**. (See *Restaurants*.)

Of course, it's not just French cuisine that can be sampled in Paris. Like all major capital cities, Paris is cosmopolitan, and although in our selection of the city's restaurants we have concentrated almost solely on French cooking, the food of many different nations is also to be found. Some parts of Paris have a remarkably ethnic flavor, such as the Belleville/Ménilmontant quarter where you can find North African dishes, or the Marais, which is packed with Jewish restaurants.

Some of the best foreign restaurants to be found in town are: for Chinese/Vietnamese, **Délices de Szechuen** (*40 Av. Duquesne, 7e ☎43-06-22-55*); **Pagoda** (*50 Rue de Provence, 9e ☎48-74-81-48*); for Indian, **Anarkali** (*4 Pl. Gustave-Toudouze, 9e ☎48-78-39-84*); **Indra** (*10 Rue Cdt-Rivière, 8e ☎43-59-46-40*); for North African, **Abel** (*15 Rue St-Vincent-de-Paul, 10e ☎48-78-41-88*); **Timgad** (*21 Rue Brunel, 17e ☎457-4-23-70*); for Japanese, **Nikko Hôtel** (**Benkay**) (*61 Quai de Grenelle, 15e ☎45-75-62-62*); for Italian, **Au Châteaubriant** (*23 Rue Chabrol, 10e ☎48-24-58-94*); **Gildo** (*153 Rue de Grenelle, 7e ☎45-51-54-12*); for Russian, **Daru** (see *Restaurants*); **Dominique** (*19 Rue Bréa, 6e ☎43-27-08-80*).

A resumé of cooking styles in Paris restaurants

Grande cuisine

Though the simpler classic dishes will survive no matter what, *grande cuisine* (also known as *haute cuisine*) on a grand scale has gone into irreversible decline as labor costs have risen and people have become fussier about their digestions and waistlines. The cooking may necessitate 50 or more scullions in the kitchen preparing rich and complicated dishes. Definitely food for a treat rather than for every day.

Nouvelle cuisine

The four main tenets of France's most recent school of cookery are that produce should be: fresh and of the highest quality; under- rather than over-cooked whenever possible; undisguised by rich, indigestible sauces; and often imaginatively combined with other ingredients. Particularly in Paris, however, one must beware of chefs who have exploited the cult of *nouvelle cuisine* by serving badly thought-out and often outlandish combinations of ingredients in amounts so tiny that they do not even cover the exiguous centers of the basketweave-patterned crockery that in such places seems to be *de rigueur*. Less unscrupulous and more dedicated chefs tend to re-interpret the well-established favorites of *cuisine bourgeoise* while retaining the better elements of *nouvelle cuisine*.

Cuisine bourgeoise

This can be classical, traditional or mainstream cooking, often with a regional flavor. It is the alchemy that turns a tough old bird or gristly cut of meat into a dish that melts in your mouth. *Cuisine bourgeoise* has never been more popular; an increasing number of Paris restaurants that once served nothing but *grande cuisine*, then tried pure *nouvelle cuisine*, now offer lighter versions of such stalwarts as *coq au vin*, *blanquette de veau*, *civet de lièvre*, and so on.

Regional cookery

One of the great fountainheads of mainstream French cooking, regional dishes have as their keynotes extraordinary variety and the ingenious use of mundane ingredients. Languedoc's *cassoulet* is an example, being made from white haricot beans, sausages, pork and preserved goose. Regional cookery lends character to some of Paris' best restaurants.

Ethnic cookery

Chinese (usually Vietnamese in disguise), unashamed Vietnamese, Italian, Russian and Jewish are the main non-French cuisines to be found in Paris, as well as North African food, from the former French colonies of Morocco, Tunisia and Algeria.

Choosing a restaurant

There is little doubt that in Paris practically any mood or gastronomic whim can be catered to. Apart from the restaurants proper, upon which the selection on the following pages concentrates, there are many other types of eating houses providing snacks and lighter meals. Since few people can even eat, let along enjoy, two full-blooded French meals a day, it is a good idea if eating out to try a place of this sort for lunch, and visit a restaurant in the evening, or vice versa.

Brasseries are restaurants-cum-cafés, often with a long bar, which serve both large and light meals; some of the most famous, including **Lipp** and **La Coupole**, are included in our selection of restaurants. So-called drugstores (little like their American originals) are popular too and, like *brasseries*, provide continuous service throughout the day. The ordinary café, always close at hand, is an excellent place for anything from a huge French bread sandwich or a *croque monsieur* (toasted ham-and-cheese sandwich) to a midday *plat du jour*, often scrawled in whitewash on the window.

The more prestigious *salons de thé* and their recent offshoots, sometimes called *tarteries*, specialize in tarts, quiches and pizzas, and also serve wine. Hamburger chains are firmly established in Paris, but a more indigenous and imaginative version of fast food is the *croissant* in various unorthodox guises (stuffed with anything from cheese to raspberries and bananas). *Crêpes*, too, make delicious take-out food.

Perhaps the very best place for a gourmet snack, however, is one of the cafés that serves excellent wine by the glass with sandwiches (often open ones) of equally high quality. Six of these are described in detail in *Restaurants*: **Café de la Nouvelle Mairie, La Cloche des Halles, L'Écluse I** and **II, Au Rubis** and **Le Val d'Or**.

Choosing somewhere for a pleasant snack is unlikely to prove problematic or disappointing, but taking pot-luck with restaurants is more hazardous, though it can just as easily turn out to be a real find as a disaster. Look carefully at the menu in the window of the restaurant. If the chef takes any trouble there will be a few *plats du jour*, *specialités* or unusual dishes; a drab list of easily refrigerated escalopes, chops and steaks bodes ill. A packed restaurant is always a good sign, but this is no golden rule, as some good and less expensive restaurants are half-empty in the evening, while fashionable establishments do not fill up until 9pm. Bear in mind that if you have chosen a restaurant in advance, particularly if it is a well-established one, it is always worth making a reservation.

The menu

At first sight, a French menu can be a mystifying document. But, particularly if you are trying to estimate the likely cost, there are several things for which you should look. Does the set menu (*menu à prix fixe* or *menu conseillé*), if available, include drink (*boisson comprise* or *b.c., vin compris* or *v.c.*), and is it free or *suppléments* on the dishes you want? If not, you may find yourself paying substantially more than the basic price. Fortunately service now has to be included by law.

The set menu is often very good value at more expensive restaurants. The choice of dishes may be rather limited, but the difference in price compared with the same fare *à la carte* is often considerable, even if portions are occasionally smaller.

The menu at a restaurant which offers only *à la carte* fare needs careful scrutiny too, because sometimes normally inexpensive dishes such as side salads may be offered at a disproportionately inflated price.

Restaurants that offer both set-price and *à la carte* menus often keep the former on a separate card and you may find you have to ask specifically for this.

A full five-course meal in France begins with hors-d'oeuvre, then continues with an *entrée* (often a fish dish), main course (often a *plat du jour*) and sometimes salad, before cheese, and finally a dessert. A true feast, but if all that sounds too much for your palate to cope with, you can order a main course with either a starter or dessert from the *à la carte* menu. See *Menu decoder in Words and phrases* p205.

As you are handed the menu, you will probably be asked if you want an aperitif. The French prefer not to knock out their taste buds with a whiskey or dry Martini (the properly mixed version of which is unknown outside a few deluxe hotel bars). Instead they order a *kir* (blackcurrant liqueur — *cassis* — with white wine) or a *kir royal* (with champagne).

Wines in Paris

The wine you choose when eating out depends very much on your choice of restaurant and in Paris you can find the richest variety in the world. Among these you will also find differing degrees of seriousness about wine, ranging from the establishments that push the wine with the highest profit margin to some like **L'Écluse** where their primary interest is in featuring 15 Bordeaux, and offering light meals to match.

Although there is much talk about asking the advice of a wine-waiter (*sommelier*), in fact there are hardly two-dozen Paris restaurants that have one who is properly qualified.

A restaurant need not have a *sommelier* to keep a good wine list, however. It is often worthwhile asking advice from the owner, who is not infrequently the person who greets and seats the customers, and is probably also the one who buys the wines.

There are two methods a helpful waiter may use when suggesting wine. The professional, with good experience in judging and serving people, will pick up numerous hints about the customer that will help determine the category of wine to recommend. Others will suggest wines within a moderate price range, await the customer's reaction, then recommend something of greater or lesser price accordingly.

You should always look at the wine list for an idea of the price range and qualities offered before asking advice. There are invariably some bargains, but they are not always easy to find. On average the mark-up is about three times higher than the price you will pay in a wine store.

French wines are classified into *Appellation Contrôlée*, VDQS (*Vins Délimités de Qualité Supérieure*), *Vin de Pays* or *Vin de Table*. None of these are a guarantee of quality, but simply mean that each category must conform to certain criteria of origin, vinification and grape variety. The criteria are more strict for *Appellation Contrôlée* than VDQS, and so on down the scale, and prices reflect this. Good values, however, can be found in each category. *Vin de Pays*, literally "country wine" offers the best values in many restaurants. These wines are from lesser districts, but are made according to strict rules. Often they are labeled by their grape variety — Cabernet Sauvignon, Chardonnay etc — which is not usually the case with *Appelletion Contrôlee* wines.

In choosing wines, the so-called *Réserve du Patron* should be avoided. In nearly all Paris restaurants it is of very poor quality and simply not worth the risk. You should also be wary of ordering a "*petit Bordeaux*," for similar reasons.

The reputation of the grower, château or *négociant* is another extremely important criterion, particularly with Burgundies. If a name is not familiar, it is often wiser to choose according to the year because a good vintage VDQS can often be better quality, and value, than a mediocre vintage of an *Appellation Contrôlée*. Most wine in the lower categories is blended by the shippers and does not carry vintage dates. *Vin de Table* is commonly served in carafes or jugs called "*pichets*." VDQS is being slowly phased out, leaving *AC* and *Vin de Pays* as the two categories.

An important consideration when choosing the wine is the type of cuisine. The more thoughtful restaurateurs will pick their wine list with their cooking in mind; thus a *nouvelle cuisine* establishment will favor lighter, more elegant wines than one serving robust regional cooking. Unfortunately in many restaurants fashion, ignorance or sheer laziness dictate the choice. It is hard to create adventurous wine and food matches when the wine list features only the tired standbys.

Wine and food

Choosing wine to go with food is primarily a matter of common sense. A meal is a progression of tastes, and for this reason a dry wine is often chosen at the beginning of a meal to accompany the more simple-tasting first course. This progression may also be a cause of difficulties with cheese: some are too fatty or strong-tasting for the delicate old red that was drunk with the main course. Ordering a white or young red would be an anticlimax and, consequently, it is rare that a wine is specifically ordered to go with the cheese.

It is often worthwhile to be adventurous, however, following the guidance of your palate. And to this end it is interesting that the Lyonnais sometimes drink a light chilled Beaujolais with oysters; and one of Paris' best wine waiters dispels the myth than no wine goes with salad vinaigrette, suggesting that a young Chinon or Beaujolais agree perfectly well.

When eating regional food, it pays to pick a wine from the same area. Some partnerships are enshrined in gastronomic legend: red Bordeaux with lamb, Muscadet with shellfish. Others are less obvious but equally enjoyable: in the Loire Valley they enjoy salmon with a light red, such as Chinon or Saumur Champigny. Dishes from Provence, with their emphasis on strong olive oil, tomato and herb flavors, are well matched by Provençal and Rhône wines. The cuisine of the Lot and Dordogne, built around rich foods such as preserved duck and goose and truffles, is complemented by the red wines of Bergerac, Cahors and Duras.

It is risky, even in Paris, to order very fine wines in a restaurant: too much depends on unknowable factors such as the skill of the cellarman and the sense of the *sommelier*.

Vintages

A vintage chart is a blunt instrument: it cannot reveal the exceptions to the general. Modern winemaking is capable of overcoming adverse conditions that a couple of decades ago would have wiped out the year's crop. In most vintages careful and clever châteaux proprietors will make better wine than their neighbors. Fashion has its influence, too: the excitement about the very fine 1982 vintage in Bordeaux has overshadowed the almost equally good wines of 1983, which are consequently cheaper.

Vintage chart

A guide to the major areas and the general qualities of recent vintages. See key below.

	1978	1979	1980	1981	1982	1983	1984	1985	1986	1987
Red Bordeaux										
Médoc/Graves	●✱	●✱	◑✱	●✱	●✱	●	○✱	●	●	○
Pomerol/St-Emilion	●✱	●✱	◑✱	●✱	●✱	●		●	●	◑
White Bordeaux										
Sauternes & sweet	◑✱	◑✱	◑✱	●✱	◑✱	●✱	○✱	●	●	◑
Graves & dry	●✱	◑✱	◑✱	●✱	●✱	●✱	○✱	●✱	◑✱	●
Red Burgundy and neighbors										
Côte d'Or	●✱	◑✱	◑✱	○	●	●	◑	●	◑	●
Beaujolais	●✱	◑✱	○✱	●✱	◑✱	●✱	◑✱	●✱	◑✱	●✱
White Burgundy and neighbors										
Côte d'Or	●✱	◑✱	◑✱	◑✱	◑	●✱	◑✱	◑✱	◑✱	○
Chablis	●✱	◑✱	◑✱	◑✱	◑	●✱	◑✱	●✱	●✱	◑
Alsace	●✱	●	◑✱	◑✱	◑✱	●✱	◑✱	●✱	◑✱	●
Rhone	●✱	●✱	◑✱	●✱	○✱	●	◑✱	●	◑	●

Above-average vintages of other white wines
Mâcon-Villages, 1982, 1983, 1985, 1986; **Loire** (sweet – Anjou, Touraine), 1976, 1978, 1979, 1981, 1985; **Upper Loire** (dry – Pouilly-Fumé, Sancerre), 1981, 1983, 1984, 1986; **Muscadet**, the newest vintage is best.

Key: ● above average to outstanding ◑ average
○ acceptable ✱ for drinking now

Restaurants listed by arrondissement

1er
André Faure
Bistro de la Gare-I
La Cloche des Halles
L'Écluse de Halles
L'Espadon
Gérard Besson
Le Grand Véfour
Le St James
Pharamond
Au Pied de Cochon
Pierre Traiteur
Rôtisserie Rivoli
Au Rubis to
Le Vert Galant
Willi's to

2e
Aux Crus de Bourgogne to
Delmonico
Le Vaudeville to

3e
L'Alisier to
L'Ambassade d'Auvergne
La Taverne des Templiers

4e
La Taverne du Sergent Recruteur
Le Trumilou to

5e
Atelier Maître Albert
Le Balzar
La Bûcherie to
Café de la Nouvelle Mairie
Chez Toutoune
Clavel to
Dodin Bouffant to
Au Pactole to
La Tour d'Argent

6e
L'Assiette au Boeuf-I to
Bistro de la Gare-II
Le Chat Grippé to
Le Cherche Midi
Claude Sainlouis
La Closerie des Lilas
L'Écluse-I
La Hulotte
Lapérouse
Lipp
La Macrobiothèque
Le Muniche
Le Petit Zinc
Polidor

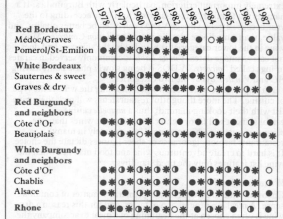

Le Pot d'Etain
Le Procope to
Sur Les Quais

7^{e}
Bistrot d'Orsay to
Bistrot de Paris
Chez Françoise
Chez Ribe
Le Jardin
Le Maconnais
Au Quai d'Orsay
Relais Saint-Germain
Le Sancerrois
Thoumieux
Le Télégraphe to

8^{e}
L'Assiette au Boeuf-II to
Bateaux-Mouches
Baumann-Marbeuf to
Baumann-Napoléon to
Bistro de la Gare-III
Boulangerie St-Phillipe to
La Boutique à Sandwiches to
Le Bristol
Chez Edgard
Daru to
Don Camillo Rive Droite
L'Écluse-II
Germain
Lasserre
Laurent
Le Lord Gourmand to
La Marcande
Maxim's
Le Moulin du Village
Au Petit Montmorency to
Les Princes
Régence-Plaza
Taillevent
Le Val d'Or
Au Vieux Berlin to

9^{e}
À l'Annexe to
L'Assiette au Boeuf-III to
L'Auberge
Bistro de la Gare-IV
Chartier
L'Écluse Opera
Le Grand Café
Le Petit Riche

10^{e}
Brasserie Flo
Julien
Terminus Nord

11^{e}
Le Repaire de Cartouche to

12^{e}
Le Terroir
Le Trou Gascon to

14^{e}
L'Auberge de l'Argoat
La Coupole
Le Duc to
L'Entrepôt
Pavillon Montsouris to
Le Pouilly
Tarte Julie to

15^{e}
L'Aquitaine
Le Clos Morillons
Morot-Gaudry
Pierre Vedel
Le Restaurant du Marché

16^{e}
Au Clocher du Village to
Le Petit Bedon
Le Pré Catelan
Le Vivarois

17^{e}
Chez Gorisse

18^{e}
Beauvilliers
Le Maquis

Neuilly-sur-Seine
Jacqueline Fénix

L'Alisier
26 Rue de Montmorency, 3^{e}
*42-72-31-04. Map **10H10** to Last orders 10pm. Closed Sat lunch, Sun. Métro Rambuteau.*
Brass coat-hangers, tiled floor, discreet prints, velvet bench seats, attentive service: this restaurant owned by Jean-Lue and Jean-François Dodeman has all the ingredients of a typical cozy Parisian bistro. But there is a difference: the food is several cuts above average, in quality, imagination and value. Local habitués (craftsmen, jewelers) appreciate the delicious *foie gras de canard*, interesting fish dishes (*filets de Saint-Pierre au paprika, suprême de volailles au truffe, saumon farci aux olives et poivrons*), and excellent desserts.

L'Ambassade d'Auvergne
22 Rue du Grenier-St-Lazare, 3^{e}
*42-72-31-22. Map **10H10** Last orders 11.30pm. Métro Arts-et-Métiers.*
The vast majority of café-owners in Paris hail from the Auvergne. When they have something to celebrate, they will, as often as not, head for this invitingly rustic "embassy" of Auvergnat tradition to savor the dishes of their — or their parents' — childhood. It's the only place in Paris

that regularly serves such specialties as *mourtayrol* and *estofinado*. The Auvergnat cheeses, which owner Joseph Petrucci obtains from his wife's relations, are quite superb.

André Faure
40 Rue du Mont-Thabor, 1er 42-60-74-28. Map 8G7 (lunch) (dinner). Last orders 10pm. Closed Sun, Aug. Métro Concorde.
This conveniently located restaurant (just by Pl. de la Concorde) offers nourishing fare at very modest prices. The emphasis is on straightforward *cuisine bourgeoise* rather than on great subtlety.

À l'Annexe
15 Rue Chaptal, 9e 48-74-65-52. Map 4D8 to Last orders 10pm. Closed Sat, Sun, Aug. Métro St-Georges.
Habitués of this atmospheric bistro range from office workers to the elderly residents of the quiet and respectable little streets surrounding it, only a minute or two from the glitter and glare of Pigalle. The food is on the light side, with fish dishes a strong point. You are served by a waitress of the old school — once on the right side of her, you're firm friends.

L'Aquitaine
54 Rue de Dantzig, 15e 48-28-67-38 Last orders 11.30pm. Closed Sun, Mon. Métro Convention.
There are few pleasures greater than eating on the first-floor terrace of L'Aquitaine, overlooking La Ruche, the "*cité des artistes*" where Soutine, Modigliani and Chagall worked. Sample the superb cuisine of winsome Christiane Massia, a deceptively fragile-looking feminist, who has publicly crossed swords with that self-confessed king of *phallocrates*, Paul Bocuse. With the help of an all-female team of assistant cooks — and her husband Michel, for the fine selection of wines and Armagnacs — she treats typically southwestern ingredients with an idiosyncratically light touch. *Confits* come with sorrel purée; a discreet Roquefort sauce is served with steamed turbot.

L'Assiette au Boeuf-I
22 Rue Guillaume-Apollinaire, 6e 42-60-88-44. Map 8I7 to Last orders 1am. Métro St-Germain-des-Prés.
L'Assiette au Boeuf-II
123 Av. des Champs-Élysées, 8e 47-20-01-13. Map 7F4 to Last orders 1am. Métro George V.
L'Assiette au Boeuf-III
20 Bd. Montmartre, 9e 47-70-91-35. Map 8F8 to Last orders 1am. Métro Richelieu-Drouot.
The three Paris restaurants of this name are all part of Michel Oliver's empire (see **Bistro de la Gare I-IV** and **Bistro de Paris**). **L'Assiette au Boeuf-II** was, in fact, the first of Michel Oliver's successful chain (its modern decor is just beginning to date) while **L'Assiette au Boeuf-II** is the latest addition.

Atelier Maître Albert
1-5 Rue Maître-Albert, 5e 46-33-13-78. Map 16J10 Last orders midnight. Closed for lunch and Sun. Métro Maubert-Mutualité.
When a formula works, it's a good idea to stick to it, which is precisely what M. Crouzier has done at his maze-like, low-lit restaurant. For years, contented Left Bankers have flocked back for the very reasonably-priced set dinner (no lunch) offering plenty of choice: five starters, seven main dishes, two cheeses and seven desserts, washed down by, perhaps, a well-chosen Gamay de Touraine. In summer there's air conditioning; in winter the superb old fireplace springs to life with a blaze of logs.

L'Auberge
164 Rue Montmartre, 9e 42-36-71-09. Map 9F9 Last orders 11.30pm. Closed Sat, Sun, Aug. Métro Rue Montmartre.
Despite its pretty-pretty half-timbered front, this is not a tourist trap (although located in an area that abounds in them). The excellent cuisine is vaguely *nouvelle* (smoked salmon, *feuilleté d'escargots au champagne foie gras*), the decor cozy, and the service friendly if a trifle slow — but then with staff costs being high, a leisurely pace is often the price that has to be paid for inexpensive food — in this case, a bargain set menu.

L'Auberge de l'Argoat
27 Av. Reille, 14e 45-89-17-05. Last orders 10pm. Closed Sun, Mon. Métro Porte-d'Orléans.
Despite a recent change of chef, the warm atmosphere still prevails in this unjustly little-known restaurant. Jeanine Gaulon, who now presides over the kitchen, has brought her own style to the menu, while still

giving pride of place to fish and marrying it with recondite combinations such as raw fish with fresh ginger. This change of chef was perhaps just what was needed to make this family restaurant known to a wider clientele.

Le Balzar
49 Rue des Écoles, 5e ☎43-54-13-67. Map ***15J9*** *Last orders 12.30am. Closed Aug. Métro Maubert-Mutualité.*
Solid, traditional fare is served here by expert waiters in waistcoats and long aprons. But people eat at the old-fashioned Latin Quarter brasserie (or have a drink in its small café section) not so much for the food as to watch — or be watched by — famous actors and actresses, television personalities, talent-spotters and members of the literary world.

Bateaux-Mouches ✿
Pont de l'Alma, 8e ☎42-25-96-10. Map ***7G4*** *AE VISA*
Open all year for dinner. Closed Nov 15 to March 1. Lunch only Sat and Sun Nov 15 to Easter. Métro Alma-Marceau.
Eating on a Bateaux-Mouches cruiser as it chugs up and down the River Seine may not appeal to everyone, but it is a romantic and remarkably neat way to combine traffic-free sightseeing with good classical food. The two formulas available — a moderately priced lunch trip and a more expensive and lavish dinner outing (tie and jacket are required) — are both very good value, considering that they include the price of the very pleasant river trip. Now, it is possible to spend tea-time on board. One week reservation (Tues, Thur, Sat 3.30pm to 5.45pm).

Baumann-Marbeuf
15 Rue Marbeuf, 8e ☎47-20-11-11. Map ***7F4*** *to AE VISA Last orders 1am. Métro Franklin-D-Roosevelt.*
Baumann-Napoléon
38 Av. de Friedland, 8e ☎42-27-99-50. Map ***7E4*** *to AE VISA Last orders 1am. Métro Étoile.*
The food at both of these restaurants, owned by Guy-Pierre Baumann, is predominantly Alsatian: many varieties of sauerkraut (with fish, with *pot au feu, à l'orientale*, etc.), shoulder of pork with red cabbage, and a good selection of wines and *alcools blancs* (fruit spirits) from Alsace. At the Baumann-Napoléon you can also try some interesting fish dishes and recipes from centuries gone by, such as Menon's *cuisses de canard à la moutarde* (1742).

Beauvilliers
52 Rue Lamarck, 18e ☎42-54-19-50. Map ***4C8***
Last orders 10.30pm. Closed Sun, Mon lunch, Sept. Métro Lamarck-Caulaincourt.
One has the sense, when dining at Beauvilliers, of being a guest in a calm and beautiful private house, and that is precisely the effect that owner Edouard Carlier has striven to create. The restaurant is filled with lovely things: antique silver, porcelain, flowers, and Carlier's own superb (and growing) collection of prints. The house itself stands on the hillside of Montmartre and has a delightful terrace. The food, served either indoors or on the terrace, matches the surroundings — Carlier aims for top quality, and usually achieves it.

Bistro de la Gare-I
30 Rue St-Denis, 1er ☎42-26-82-80. Map ***9H9*** *VISA Last orders 1am. Métro Châtelet-Les-Halles.*
Bistro de la Gare-II
59 Bd. du Montparnasse, 6e ☎48-24-49-61. Map ***14K7*** *VISA Last orders 1am. Métro Montparnasse-Bienvenue.*
Bistro de la Gare-III
73 Av. des Champs-Élysées, 8e ☎43-59-67-83. Map ***7F4*** *VISA Last orders 1am. Métro George V.*
Bistro de la Gare-IV
38 Bd. des Italiens, 9e ☎42-46-15-74. Map ***9F8*** *VISA Last orders 1am. Métro Richelieu-Drouot.*
Raymond Oliver of **Le Grand Véfour** spawned a son, Michel, who combines an infectious love of food (as can be seen from his cooking programs on French TV) with business acumen. He has now built up an empire of seven restaurants (four Bistros de la Gare and three **Assiettes au Boeuf**) that have proved to be among Paris' best stand-bys for people who want a reliable, quick meal when going to a show or movie. They provide — till 12.30 or 1am and every day of the year — limited but carefully balanced set menus of reasonable price. There is a slightly greater choice at the more expensive **Bistros de la Gare** than at the **Assiettes au Boeuf**; at both, the main qualities are good meat and interesting desserts.

The most interesting atmosphere in any of Michel Oliver's establishments is to be found at **Bistro de la Gare-II**. Formerly the Restaurant Rougeot, it boasts one of the finest Art Nouveau decors in Paris (mini-landscapes in *faïence*, mirrors, stained-glass ceiling).

Bistrot d'Orsay
3 Rue Surcouf, 7e ☎45-51-48-48. Map 13H5 to AE DC VISA Last orders 10pm. Closed Mon, Sun evening, July. Métro Invalides.
This establishment adjoins the fashionable restaurant **Au Quai d'Orsay** (not the Foreign Ministry, which is also popularly known as Quai d'Orsay). Seated at its old-fashioned horseshoe bar or at a table, you can tuck into *cuisine bourgeoise* in a lively, almost party-like atmosphere, surrounded by attractive Second-empire decor. Cheaper but no more downscale than the Quai itself.

Bistrot de Paris
33 Rue de Lille, 7e ☎42-61-16-83. Map 8H7 VISA Last orders midnight. Closed Sat, Sun. Métro Solférino.
The fashionable gastronomic meeting place, the Bistrot de Paris is the jewel in Michel Oliver's substantial crown (see also **Assiette au Boeuf I-III** and **Bistro de la Gare I-IV**). Tables are packed, the conversation animated, the decor ravishing, and the food good. Service, though, can be a trifle slow and casual; and the bill undoubtedly reflects not only the food, but the famous faces.

Boulangerie St-Philippe
73 Av. Franklin-D-Roosevelt, 8e ☎43-59-78-76. Map 7G5 to VISA Closed for dinner and Sat. Métro Franklin-D-Roosevelt.
Elbow your way through the crowds of gourmet shoppers and office workers buying snacks in this busy bakery, and you'll find a pleasant little lunch restaurant serving surprisingly sophisticated *plats du jour*. The butter and cream used in these dishes, and in the delicious desserts and pastries, comes from Echiré, which has an *appellation*, like a wine-producing area. Quality is commensurate.

La Boutique à Sandwiches
12 Rue du Colisée, 8e ☎43-59-34-32. Map 2F5 to Last orders 1am. Closed Sun, Aug. Métro Franklin-D-Roosevelt.
This is the kind of restaurant that one occasionally discovers by a happy chance and then remains passionately devoted to. There is hidden treasure behind its rather modest name and exterior. Two Alsatian brothers, Claude and Hubert Schick, with the help of relations, run the place with great dash, flair and friendliness. The ground-floor section is a sandwich boutique, but an unusually good one, selling some 40 different varieties, all made to order. Upstairs is a cozy dining room where you can count on the kind of wholesome cooking, lovingly prepared, for which Alsace is famous. Especially delicious are the *pickelfleisch* (salt beef) and *raclette valaisanne* (fondu cheese with potatoes, pickles and charcuterie). The equally irresistible desserts include a mouth-watering *streusel* (crumble). Located just off the Champs-Élysées and open late, this is a useful stand-by for movie-goers.

Brasserie Flo
7 Cour des Petites-Écuries, 10e ☎47-70-13-59. Map 5F10 AE DC VISA Last orders 10.30pm. Métro Château-d'Eau.
One of Jean-Claude Bucher's five Paris restaurants (see also **Julien, Terminus Nord** and **Le Vaudeville**), Brasserie Flo reflects his Alsatian origins in its food and drink, and there is beer drawn from the barrel, a rarity in Paris. The turn-of-the-century decor, with its old brass luggage racks and hat-stands, is equally reminiscent of France's most Germanic province. Despite, or because of, the brasserie's cramped seating and reasonable prices, it attracts a lot of well-known faces.

Le Bristol
112 Rue du Faubourg-St-Honoré, 8e ☎42-66-91-45. Map 7F6 AE DC Last orders 10.30pm. Métro Champs-Élysées-Clemenceau.
It's the decor and the clientele that are most distinctive and distinguished here (see also *Hotels*). The dining room, gently lit from above and lined with *Régence* wood paneling, is one of the most elegant to be found in any luxury Parisian hotel. Your neighbors at the next table are likely to be members of the more staid international jet-set (politicians, chief executives, elderly heiresses). If you don't care about the setting or the company, you can always fall back on Emile Tabourdiau's excellent cuisine, which is best described as discreetly *nouvelle*.

La Bûcherie
41 Rue de la Bûcherie, 5ᵉ 43-54-78-06. Map ***19J9*** *to* AE VISA *Last orders 12.30am. Open as salon de thé 3-7.30pm. Métro Maubert-Mutualité.*

This restaurant can be a bit cramped, but on a cold winter's evening, with the logs crackling in the grate and lots of convivial neighbors, few would object. Amiable, bear-like Bernard Bosque is an inventive cook: witness his interpretation of fish *á l'oseille*, in which he replaces sorrel with the equally tart but distinctive rhubarb. His desserts are light and delicious, and his wine list strong, featuring both well-known and less familiar vintages.

Café de la Nouvelle Mairie
19 Rue des Fossés-St-Jacques, 5ᵉ 43-26-80-18. Map ***15K9*** *Last orders midnight. Closed Sat, Sun, Aug. Métro Luxembourg.*

A few minutes' walk from the Luxembourg Gardens is this attractive intact prewar café, kept spick and span by the two new owners from Touraine and Aveyron. Their small selection of good hot snacks and sandwiches is really only a pretext for cracking open a bottle (or two) from their succinct but excellent range of Beaujolais and Loire wines, or for trying his superb old rum.

Chartier
7 Rue de Faubourg Montmartre, 9ᵉ 47-70-86-29. Map ***9F9*** *Last orders 9.30pm. Métro Rue Montmartre.*

Hurry to get a last glimpse of Paris' sole surviving mid-19thC *bouillon decor* (*bouillons* were popular restaurants, or soup kitchens) before it becomes transmogrified, with taste of course, into a chic "eatery." The atmosphere is very much the same as it must have been 100yrs ago, and prices don't seem to have risen much either. The Bohemian atmosphere, and not the food, is what going to Chartier's is all about.

Le Chat Grippé
87 Rue d'Assas, 6ᵉ 43-54-70-00. Map ***15K8*** *to* AE VISA *Last orders 10.30pm. Closed Sat lunch, Mon, Aug. Métro Vavin.*

A small, elegant establishment in the hinterland of the Luxembourg Gardens, an area not over-endowed with restaurants. The proprietor, Marc Prunières, provides a broad-based menu, geared to seasonal availability. Strong points in his repertoire include *foie gras au ratafia de champagne*, and some mouth-watering desserts such as *"pastis" quercymois avec sorbet à la pomme*.

Le Cherche Midi
22 Rue du Cherche Midi, 6ᵉ 45-48-27-44. Map ***14J7*** *Last orders midnight. Métro Sèvres-Babylone.*

If you want a change from French cuisine and like the idea of an Italian meal, this friendly, informal restaurant would be a good choice. There is a small but consistently good-quality menu offering a variety of fresh pastas, as well as such dishes as Parma ham, and *carpaccio* made with mushrooms, celery and parmesan. The decor has a homey touch, with large primitive paintings of country scenes. It is advisable to reserve in advance.

Chez Edgard
4 Rue Marbeuf, 8ᵉ 47-20-51-15. Map ***7F4*** AE CB VISA *Last orders 1am. Closed Sun. Métro Franklin-D-Roosevelt.*

Perhaps the most startling thing about this excellent if rather noisy restaurant, which is located in the plush business quarter of Av. George V and constantly bulges at the seams with personalities from politics, the movies and commercial radio, is its wide spectrum of prices. The food is not the bargain it once was, but you can still eat a three-course meal for a reasonable price, depending on what you choose from the *à la carte* selection. The fare is simple but imaginative, and the sweet whiff of the sea as you walk in bears witness to the freshness of the shellfish displayed outside.

Chez Françoise
Aérogare des Invalides, 7ᵉ 47-05-49-03. Map ***13H5*** AE VISA *Last orders midnight. Closed Sun evening and Aug. Métro Invalides.*

Conveniently tucked away in the Invalides Air Terminal, this is a rather old-fashioned-looking buffet, with skylight and potted plants. However, it provides reliable and far from dull dishes, as well as inexpensive wines, for the air traveler wishing to leave the capital with a pleasant taste in the mouth.

Chez Gorisse
84 Rue Nollet, 17ᵉ 46-27-43-05. Map ***3C6*** VISA *Last orders 10pm. Closed Sun. Métro La Fourche.*

This restaurant went through a difficult period after the departure of Rémy Pommerai who had been in charge for several years. It is now run by Dominique Terrasson, who has given it a new lease on life. It has a cozy and old-fashioned atmosphere and reasonable prices. The cooking is a mixture of such down-to-earth dishes as *navarin d'agneau pot-au-feu* and more inventive ones such as *brioche à la moelle*.

Chez Ribe
15 Av. de Suffren, 7e 45-66-53-79. Map 12I3 Last orders 10.30pm. Closed Sun, Aug, week of Christmas and New Year. Métro Champ-de-Mars.
Radio and TV people working in the area like this well-redecorated former *bougnat* (coal merchant's shop and café). Owner Antoine Pérès cooks most of the dishes, which are generously served, while his diet-conscious wife Mireille is in charge of starters and desserts. The style is fairly traditional with regional touches, though there are also more modern dishes such as raw marinated scallops (when in season) and veal with limes.

Chez Toutoune
5 Rue de Pontoise, 5e 43-26-56-81. Map 10J10 Last orders 10.45pm. Closed Sun, Aug 8-Sept 8. Métro Maubert-Mutualité.
Good food cuts across class divisions (in France at least), which probably explains Chez Toutoune's wide spectrum of customers, from casually-dressed students to elderly *bourgeois* couples complete with pearls and Légion d'honneur rosettes. The exceptionally friendly atmosphere is effortlessly created by the blonde Toutoune herself. The formula is a lavish five-course set menu chalked up each day on a blackboard: a soup, a good choice of *entrées* and main dishes, two cheeses in peak condition, and a battery of desserts. The *cuisine* is sophisticated provincial. Toutoune is now a TV star. She presents everyday her "*menu du jour* and recipes" on Channel 2.

Claude Sainlouis
27 Rue du Dragon, 6e 45-48-29-68. Map 8I7 Last orders 11pm. Closed Sun, Aug, Easter, Christmas, New Year. Métro St-Germain-des-Prés.
When owner Claude Sainlouis (real name, Claude Piau) gave up his job as a stuntman and took up catering, he decided he wasn't going to take any more risks. For the last 20yrs or so, he has been serving an immutable menu of salad, expertly grilled steak and chocolate mousse for (almost) a song. His caution paid off: the place is permanently packed with people out for an evening in St-Germain-des-Prés.

Clavel
65 Quai de la Tournelle, 5e 46-33-18-65. Map 16J10 to Last orders 10.30pm. Closed Sun evening, Mon, last 3 weeks in Aug. Métro Maubert-Mutualité.
Formerly L'Ambroisie, the creation of master chef Bernard Pacaud, this restaurant was taken over in August 1986 by Eric Piras and Mme Clavel, who have kept up the sophisticated standards of their predecessor. There is no special regional emphasis but a wide variety of dishes, with ingredients chosen according to seasonal availability.

La Cloche des Halles
28 Rue Coquillière, 1er 42-36-93-89. Map 10G9 Last orders 8pm. Closed Sun. Métro Les Halles.
Serge Lesage is keeping up the standards of his predecessor by continuing to lavish top-quality ham (raw, cooked on the bone, and *persillé*), quiches, pâtés, tarts, sandwiches of every description and, last but not least, excellent wines (Beaujolais and Burgundy in particular) on the happy habitués, many from the nearby Banque de France, of this bustling café.

Au Clocher du Village
8bis Rue Verderet, 16e 42-88-35-87 to Last orders 10.30pm. Closed Sat lunch, Sun. Métro Louvre.
A picture-postcard place with the atmosphere of an old *auberge*, located in a charming little village square and decorated with plants and the works of Sunday painters. The menu is commensurately rustic (hot sausage, veal with cream sauce) and the wines are solid.

Le Clos Morillons
50 Rue des Morillons, 15e 48-28-04-37. Map 19D4. Last orders 10.15pm. Closed Sat lunch, Sun. Métro Convention.
Located in a rather bleak backwater of the 15e, this establishment was taken over in 1984 by brothers Philippe and Marc Delacourcelle,

who offer a selection of seasonal food, tending to lightness and prepared with great finesse. They specialize in wines of the Loire valley.

La Closerie des Lilas
*171 Bd. du Montparnasse, 6e ☎43-26-70-50. Map **15L8**. Last orders 12.30am. Métro Vavin.*

La Closerie has always been, and is still, the haunt of literati, artists and plain hacks, though nowadays they tend to congregate in the bar and brasserie section. The restaurant proper, which has a pleasant terrace, accommodates an altogether more *bourgeois* crowd, and its food is suitably classical.

La Coupole
*102 Bd. du Montparnasse, 14e ☎43-20-14-20. Map **14K7** Open noon-2am. Closed Aug. Métro Montparnasse-Bienvenue.*

La Coupole is Paris' largest brasserie, and an institution. It probably serves the most motley crowd of customers to be found in any Paris eating place: they range from besuited politicians, movie-producers, painters and students to photographers and bevies of very attractive girls who appreciate the excellent exposure afforded by La Coupole's open plan with its long, broad aisles. The waiters are particularly hard-boiled, the food competent if undistinguished, and the noise, when the evening is in full swing (around 11pm), deafening. But it's all worth it for the show.

Aux Crus de Bourgogne
*3 Rue Bachaumont, 2e ☎42-33-48-24. Map **9G9** to Last orders 10.30pm. Closed Sat, Sun. Métro Les Halles.*

The formula of this bistrot has remained unchanged since 1930, no doubt because of its success. Francis Larcier took over the direction a few years ago after the death of his grandmother, who had reigned for 50 years. He decided to keep the traditional Les Halles atmosphere. The setting of brown woodwork and mirrors remains the same, and the *foie gras* is still excellent value, as is the fresh lobster and the *coq au vin* with mushrooms. Many of the hearty dishes survive from the days when the market traders used to call in here before going to work.

Daru
*19 Rue Daru, 8e ☎42-27-23-60. Map **2E4** to Last orders 11pm. Closed Sun, Mon, Aug. Métro Courcelles.*

White Russians, many of them taxi-drivers, used to recall the "good old days" over a glass of vodka and a *zakouski* in this grocery/snack bar opposite the Russian Orthodox Church. Although most of them have since departed this world, the Daru remains a repository of Russian tradition, boasting a score of Russians and Polish vodkas as well as a passable French brand, Tersa. There is also tasty food for every purse, from *tarama* and *borstch* to smoked salmon and caviar.

Delmonico
*39 Avenue de l'Opéra, 2e ☎42-61-44-26. Map **8F7** Last orders 10pm. Closed Sat, Sun. Métro Opéra.*

This is the restaurant of the Hôtel Edouard VII, superbly located a stone's throw from the Place de l'Opéra. Outwardly the building retains its original splendid Belle Epoque style, but the English monarch would no longer recognize the interior, which has been thoroughly modernized. The restaurant is quietly elegant and verdant with potted plants. The chef, Claude Monteil, practices a cuisine that is broadly *nouvelle* in orientation.

Dodin Bouffant ✿
*25 Rue Frederic-Sauton, 5e ☎43-25-25-14. Map **15J9** to Last orders midnight. Closed Sun, Aug, two days over Christmas and New Year. Métro Maubert-Mutualité.*

Jacques Manière, among Paris' most iconoclastic, outspoken and warm-hearted chefs, made Dodin Bouffant one of the finest — and certainly cheapest for quality — restaurants in the capital. It was he who installed the saltwater tanks in the cellar, where oysters, mussels, clams, the rare *violet*, and other shellfish co-exist peacefully before expiring at your command. Manière retired in 1981, and the chef is now Philippe Valin, who had survived the blisteringly tough training he had been put through by Manière (an ex-army man). With the restaurant's former *maître de'hôtel*, Maurice Cartier, Valin has kept the Manière ensign flying: in other words, Dodin Bouffant still provides wonderful fish combinations, both as starters and as main courses, a sumptuous *plateau de fruits de mer* of utter freshness, unusual meat dishes, featherlight desserts, and wines that are no less than a gift.

Don Camillo Rive Droite
92 Rue La Boétie, 8e ☎43-59-08-20. Map 7F4 Last orders 11.30pm. Closed Sat, Sun, Aug. Métro St-Philippe-du-Roule.
Le Tout Paris goes for this restaurant's extravagant Art Deco fittings, winter garden, and clever mixture of cooking genres: *cuisine minceur* (apparently preferred by more male than female customers), *cuisine bourgeoise*, and straightforward, good sea-food. The *arbiter elegantiae* is now none other than Guy-Louis Duboucheron, who owns the ultra-fashionable **L'Hôtel** (see *Hotels*).

Le Duc
243 Bd. Raspail, 14e ☎43-22-59-59. Map 14M7 to Last orders 10.30pm. Closed Sat, Sun, Mon. Métro Denfert-Rochereau.
If, like Fats Waller, your favorite dish is fish, make a point of eating at Paul and Jean Minchelli's establishment, which is regarded by many as being the finest seafood-only restaurant in town. Paul, who has written an authoritative cookery book on the subject, was one of the first chefs to approach the preparation of fish with a completely fresh and inventive eye, and, among other things, to take his cue from the Japanese and explore the possibilities of raw fish. In his hot dishes, the fish is always cooked to perfection (just a second or two underdone), and never swathed in a strong sauce of the kind that destroys delicate flavors.

L'Écluse-I
15 Quai des Grands-Augustins, 6e ☎46-33-58-74. Map 9I9 Open noon-2pm. Métro St-Michel
L'Écluse-II
64 Rue François-1er, 8e ☎47-20-77-09. Map 7G4 Open noon-2pm. Métro George V.
Écluse Opera
4 Rue Halévy, 9e ☎47-42-62-33. Map 8F7 Open noon-2pm. Métro Opera.
Écluse de Halles
Rue Mondétour, 1er ☎47-03-30-73. Map 9H9 Open noon-2pm. Métro Châtelet-Les-Halles.
This chain, originally started by Georges Bardawil, has recently been taken over by a trust, which has nevertheless preserved the initial spirit. The more sophisticated **L'Écluse-II**, like its namesake, is a wine bar restricted to Bordeaux — open bottles of which are ingeniously topped up with nitrogen to stop them deteriorating, so that the very best wines can be served by the glass. At off-peak hours **L'Écluse-I** is one of the most relaxing place in which to sit and read, work or chat. The good selection of vintages available at reasonable prices can be accompanied by excellent "super-snacks": *carpaccio*, *foie gras*, smoked salmon, *saucisson sec*, goat's cheese, and a superbly rich and sticky chocolate cake that connoisseurs cross Paris to sink their teeth into. **L'Écluse-II**, frequented by photographers, journalists and models, has a similar range of classy tidbits to enhance the wines.

L'Entrepôt
7/9 Rue Francis-de-Pressensé, 14e ☎45-40-60-70. Map 14M5 Dinner only. Open 8.30pm. Last orders midnight. Métro Pernéty.
The fashionable haunt for younger intellectuals, photographers, actors and journalists has recently come under new management. The functional steel and glass setting is somewhat cold in its effect, but this is made up for by the warm reception and the hearty cuisine, which is much the same as it always was. The movie theater that used to be in the same complex has long since closed.

L'Espadon
15 Pl. Vendôme, 1er ☎42-60-38-30. Map 8G7 Last orders 11pm. Métro Tuileries.
The wonderfully atmospheric restaurant of the **Ritz** (see *Hotels*), with its gentle lighting and *trompe-l'oeil*, was presided over by Escoffier at the turn of the century, and until fairly recently it maintained standards worthy of the great man. In the last few years, however, there has been a slight decline, from superlative to just plain good. Unfortunately the prices are still as high as ever.

Gérard Besson
5 Rue du Coq-Héron, 1er ☎42-33-14-74. Map 10G9 Last orders 10.30pm. Closed Sat, Sun, July. Métro Les Halles.
The lunchtimes menu served by Gérard Besson, owner-chef of easily the best restaurant in the Les Halles area, is such good value it verges on the philanthropic. After things to nibble with your apéritif, you get a choice of three starters, such as a

chunky *soupe de poissons* with saffron, four main courses, *fromage blanc*, and one of six desserts, like pistachio profiteroles, washed down by, perhaps, half a bottle of Château Capbern (a Saint-Estèphe *cru bourgeois*). Coffee follows, with *petits fours*, and a bill so light for the quality it almost flutters away. *À la carte* prices are higher.

Besson, who comes from Bourg-en-Bresse and has worked with Alain Chapel, has a classical yet very personal style that contrasts refreshingly with the striving-after-effect of which some *nouvelle cuisine* chefs are guilty. He also lays down his own wines (45,000 bottles), then offers them at bargain prices, especially the Bordeaux, when ready for drinking.

Germain

19 Rue Jean-Mermoz, 8ᵉ ☎43-59-29-24. Map 7F5 Last orders 10pm. Closed Sun. Métro Franklin-D-Roosevelt.

It's hard to grab a table here, and one can see why, as the value for money is quite exceptional for the area. In a genuine bistro setting with imitation-leather seats and original paintings on the walls, habitués (art dealers, fashion designers and models, among others) enjoy simple cooking.

Le Grand Café

4 Bd. des Capucines, 9ᵉ ☎47-42-75-77. Map 4F8 Open 24hrs a day. Métro Quatre-Septembre.

This is the best of the handful of Paris brasseries that serve full-blown meals 24hrs a day. Its clientele are hungry local shift- and night-workers (mainly journalists), topping up with solid or liquid nourishment.

Le Grand Véfour

17 Rue de Beaujolais, 1ᵉʳ ☎42-96-56-27. Map 9G8 Last orders 10.30pm. Closed Sat lunch, Sun, Aug. Métro Pyramides.

If you walk out of the Paris Royal at its N end, you will pass, under the arcade, a muskily-lit restaurant that looks like a rare fossil from another age. This is the world-famous Le Grand Véfour, formerly home ground of much-traveled author and cook Raymond Oliver, now the property of M. Taittinger, of champagne fame. Its decor, which dates from the Directoire, is, in fact, one of the oldest extant restaurant interiors in Paris, if not the oldest (it is classified as a historical monument). The excellent food of the new chef J.C. Lhonneur, pupil of Robuchon, one of the great French chefs, is classical, as you might expect. Bordeaux are, of course, staggeringly well-represented on the wine list.

La Hulotte

29 Rue Dauphine, 6ᵉ ☎46-33-75-92. Map 9I8 AE VISA Last orders 10.30pm. Closed Sun, Mon, Aug. Métro Mabillon.

This restaurant's snug little upstairs dining-room is a haven of reliability in the shark-infested waters of Quartier Latin catering. A basket of brown bread served, unusually for Paris, with a little dish of butter and a jug of good cheap wine will keep your hunger and thirst at bay as you wait.

Jacqueline Fénix

42 Av. Charles-de-Gaulle, Neuilly-sur-Seine ☎46-24-42-61 Last orders 10pm. Closed Sat, Sun, Christmas week, Aug. Métro Porte-Maillot.

This chic and inviting restaurant is only 5mins' walk from Porte Maillot. Much of its becoming decor is the work of the comely Jacqueline Fénix herself, who runs the establishment jointly with moustachioed chef Michel Rubod. Rubod, once a professional gardener, uses vegetables and herbs with imagination. A stickler for fresh ingredients, he is most at home in a *nouvelle cuisine* idiom.

Le Jardin

100 Rue du Bac, 7ᵉ ☎42-22-81-56. Map 8I6 Last orders 10.30pm. Closed Sun. Métro Rue-du-Bac.

Even in Paris vegetarian cooking is becoming increasingly popular, as is proved by this well-patronized vegetarian restaurant on the Left Bank. You have to pass through a shop selling books and health foods and down a corridor into a serene, skylit courtyard dining room decorated with stone sculptures, a fountain and an abundance of plants. The cuisine at this restaurant is sophisticated and creative, marrying the best of health food with the imaginativeness of the *nouvelle* style, as evidenced by dishes such as *salade orientale* which features saffron rice, avocado, mushrooms, green beans and delicate strands of Japanese hiziki seaweed all in a light vinaigrette dressing. The menu is by no means spartan — fish, "biological" wine, teas and tempting desserts are also on offer.

Julien
16 Rue du Faubourg-St-Denis, 10e
47-70-12-06. Map ***5F10***
AE VISA Last orders 1.30am. Closed July. Métro Strasbourg-St-Denis.
Paul Bucher, owner of five Parisian eating places, has single-handedly done more than anyone to save authentic restaurant decors from the modernizer's axe. Though both **Brasserie Flo** and **Le Vaudeville** are museum pieces in their own way, the jewel in Bucher's crown must be Julien, which sports some of Paris' most fabulous Art Nouveau designs — and is accordingly much favored by extrovert admen and showbiz people. The food is classical and straightforward, with a slight Alsatian bias.

Lapérouse
51 Quai de Grands Augustins, 6e
43-26-68-04. Map ***9I9***
AE CB Last orders 1am. Métro Odéon.
The décor of this restaurant facing the Seine is redolent of a bourgeois interior of the 19thC, with its concealed doors, overladen woodwork and private rooms for four to eight diners, often frequented by politicians and writers. The cuisine is classic: *foie gras de canard, ris de veau à l'oseille, feuilleté aux poires*. A memorable place to dine.

Lasserre
17 Av. Franklin-D-Roosevelt, 8e
43-59-53-43. Map ***7F5***
Last orders 10.30pm. Closed Sun, Mon lunch, Aug. Métro Franklin-D-Roosevelt.
The essence of Lasserre, like that of the equally famous **La Tour d'Argent**, is found particularly in the decor, tableware and superlative service. The food is excellent and deeply traditional. It is a haven for the extremely rich, old-fashioned gourmets who almost seem to use it as their canteen. In Lasserre your caviar or *foie gras* is wheeled processionally to your table and each empty oyster shell is spirited away by a deft waiter.

Laurent
41 Av. Gabriel, 8e 47-23-79-18. Map ***8G6*** *AE*
Last orders 11pm. Closed Sat lunch, Sun. Métro Concorde.
Well-bred opulence is the keynote of this distinguished establishment, occupying a delectable pavilion in the parkland setting off the Champs-Élysées — all white and gold stucco on the outside, Second-Empire elegance inside, with a garden at the back where one can feast under the chestnut trees on a summer day. After a period of closure the restaurant came under new ownership in 1976 and, after a total overhaul, was re-opened in 1977 under the direction of Edmond Ehrlich, a native of Vienna and a graduate of the élite hotel school in Lausanne. Under his aegis Laurent has blossomed once again into one of the truly great restaurants of Paris, with an appropriately VIP clientele. The menu is half *nouvelle cuisine*, half more traditional fare. Dishes that the restaurant is particularly proud of include lobster salad and a dessert called *les deux soufflés Laurent* (a hot and a cold soufflé served together). In choosing from one of the 600 wines available you can turn for advice to Philippe Bourguignon, one of the top *sommeliers* of France. Service is exceptionally good. In the evening, candlelight and a pianist add to the festive atmosphere. Prices are commensurately high, but in relative terms the value is good.

Lipp
151 Bd. St-Germain, 6e 45-48-53-91. Map ***8I7*** *Open 9am (for breakfast)-1am (main meals from noon). Closed first two weeks over Christmas and New Year. Métro St-Germain-des-Prés.*
This delightfully intact turn-of-the-century brasserie attracts the capital's intellectual, political and showbiz élite in far greater swarms than any other Parisian restaurant, however chic. The previous owner, Roger Cazes, died in 1987, and the Lipp is now run by his niece, Mme Perrochon. She has followed the tradition of her uncle and is no doubt as careful as he was in seating clients. The unknown usually get sent up to the first floor (where the occasional celebrity is to be spotted) but they can, if so inclined, brave the small, crowded café section by the entrance. Impeccable service by long-aproned and long-serving waiters, reliable *plats du jour*, and the herd instinct explain Lipp's phenomenal success.

Le Lord Gourmand
9 Rue Lord-Byron, 8e 45-62-66-06. Map ***6F3*** *AE VISA Last orders 10.30pm. Closed Sat lunch, Sun, Christmas week. Métro Étoile.*
Roland Borne offers some of the best food to be had in the vicinity of the Champs-Élysées. This restaurant has been newly decorated throughout

and maintains a well balanced menu, rich in creation. The desserts are extremely good, in particular the chocolate cake. One of the best places in the capital to go for a tête-à-tête celebration.

Le Mâconnais
10 Rue du Bac, 7e ☎42-61-21-89. Map 8H7 Last orders 10.30pm. Closed Sat lunch, Sun, one week at Easter, three weeks in Aug, Christmas. Métro Rue-du-Bac.
This cozy bistro specializes in cuisine of the region around Mâcon and Lyon. Some of its strong points are *salade mâconnaise, fricassée d'escargots, jambonneau aux lentilles* and a variety of excellent charcuteries. There is a pleasantly *fin-de-siècle* feel to the smallish bar and dining area, humming with the chatter of publishers, literati, antique dealers and other Left Bank folk. The charming and energetic proprietors, Monsieur and Madame Lefebvre, are friendly hosts, and the place has a warm and relaxed atmosphere.

La Macrobiothèque
17 Rue de Savoie, 6e ☎43-25-04-96. Map 9I8 Last orders 10pm. Closed Sun. Métro Odéon, Saint-Michel.
One need not be a health-food addict to enjoy La Macrobiothèque, a small and reliable whole food restaurant situated in a rustic 17thC building. For 12 years now, Pierre, the welcoming proprietor, has been serving tasty vegetarian meals to a steady stream of regular customers who are attracted by La Macrobiothèque's hearty cooking, large portions and affordable prices.

Le Maquis
69 Rue caulaincourt, 18e ☎42-59-76-07. Map 4C8 Last orders 10.30pm. Closed Sun, Mon. Métro Lamark-Caulaincourt.
Montmartre — and in particular the streets bordering that center of kitsch art, the Place du Tertre — is not a good area for eating, as some of the bad habits of picture-vendors seem to have rubbed off on restaurant owners. Ten minutes' walk down the Butte, however, this attractively decorated bistro offers an inexpensive set lunch and interesting *à la carte* food — unfussy, up-to-date, colorful and light. Two other exceptions to the rule about the quality of food in Montmartre are **Beauvilliers** and **Les Semailles**.

La Marcande
52 Rue Miromesnil, 8e ☎42-65-19-14. Map 7F5 AE CB VISA Last orders 10pm. Closed Sat, Sun, three weeks in Aug. Métro Miromesnil.
This elegantly appointed restaurant affords diners a view not only over a delightful courtyard garden, but also over part of the kitchens. Behind the glass partitions a smart team of chefs prepares some of the most imaginative food to be had in this part of town, such as *papillote de Saint-Jacques au foie gras, galette de pigeonneau aux truffes*, and *ragoût de champignon des bois*. The walls are hung with a changing exhibition of modern paintings.

Maxim's
3 Rue Royale, 8e ☎42-65-27-94. Map 8G6 AE VISA Last orders 1am. Closed Sun. Métro Concorde.
The reputation of this world-famous restaurant had waned somewhat by the time it was taken over a few years ago, in the face of much scepticism, by fashion designer Pierre Cardin. In the event, those who said that a cobbler should stick to his last were proved wrong. Cardin has kept Maxim's essential character as a top-class restaurant (with top-class prices), and has maintained and renovated its marvelous Art Nouveau decor. At the same time his ownership has given a new zest to this establishment, which is again enjoying a fashionable clientele.

Morot-Gaudry
8 Rue de la Cavalerie, 15e ☎45-67-06-85. Map 12J3 VISA Last orders 10.30pm. Closed Sat, Sun. Métro La Motte Piquet-Grenelle.
Majestically located, à **La Tour d'Argent**, on the top floor of a ship-like 1920s building with a wonderful view of the nearby Eiffel Tower, this restaurant is much favored by bigwigs from UNESCO (also nearby). French food gurus can't seem to decide whether Jean-Pierre Morot-Gaudry's cuisine is *nouvelle* or not. No matter: his concoctions have the stamp of true originality (calf's liver with raspberries, crab *boudin*, red mullet with chanterelles). There is an excellent set menu of six dishes with different wines, and a venerable collection of Calvados.

Le Moulin du Village
Cité Berryer, 23-25 Rue Royale, 8e ☎42-65-08-47. Map 8G6

Last orders 10.30pm. Closed Sat evening, Sun. Métro Concorde.
Probably the largest selection of little-known wines in Paris is to be found here. Englishman Steven Spurrier, who part-owns the place, runs a very well-stocked wine shop a little farther down the Cité Berryer. The restaurant is in a mews, almost invisibly tucked away off the Rue Royale, a marvelously calm and unpolluted spot for outdoor eating in summer. Le Moulin du Village features *nouvelle cuisine*.

Le Muniche
27 Rue de Buci, 6e ☎46-33-62-09. Map 918 Last orders 3am. Métro Mabillon.
This large, bustling, noisy and cramped brasserie, which serves hearty food (for example, *choucroute, charcuterie*), is the canteen of Left Bank literati, who can be seen exchanging pleasantries from table to table before, perhaps, drifting down to the live jazz club below, **Le Furstenberg** (under the same management, and well air-conditioned).

Au Pactole
44 Bd. St-Germain, 5e ☎46-33-31-31. Map 16J10 to Last orders 11pm. Closed Sat lunch, Sun. Métro Maubert-Mutualité.
Lunch is the best time to eat here because, with luck, the sun will be streaming through the windows of the attractive covered terrace. The formerly rather somber décor has given way to brighter tones of orange and yellow. Roland Magne is an inventive yet unfussy cook with a penchant for unusual combinations (kid with mint, lamb with violets). His set menu is a wonderful bargain.

Pavillon Montsouris
20 Rue Gazan, 14e ☎45-88-38-52 to Last orders 10.30pm. Métro Cité-Universitaire.
This restaurant, located in the Parc Montsouris, has changed its former charming name, *Le Jardin de la Paresse*, to a more prosaic one, and Yvan Courault, who took over in June 1987, has given it a face-lift, with pleasing results. You dine in a large verandah shaded by trees, and in summer there is a terrace facing the park. The menu created by chef Michel Bouvier includes such dishes as *galettes feuilletées de moules* and *filet de lapereau au basil*. Excellent value.

Le Petit Bedon
38 Rue Pergolèse, 16e ☎45-00-23-66. Map 6E2 Last orders 10.15pm. Closed Sat, Sun, Aug. Métro Argentine.
The very well-heeled quarter of Av. Foch had no really good restaurant untill recently, when one of Paris' most gifted and inventive young chefs, Christian Ignace, who was trained by Raymond Oliver (of **Le Grand Véfour**), took over Le Petit Bedon. His cuisine might loosely be called *nouvelle*, but it steers clear of the chi-chi terminology (e.g., *petits légumes*), contrast for contrast's sake, and the microscopic portions that are continuing to give the school a bad name. Ignace, a man drawn more toward ingredients like lamb's tongues, carp and teal than caviar or *foie gras*, has proved himself to be a master of subtle combination.

Au Petit Montmorency
5 Rue Rabelais, 8e ☎42-25-11-19. Map 7F5 to Last orders 10.30pm. Closed Sat, Sun, Aug. Métro Miromesnil.
Daniel Bouché calls his cooking "*cuisine buissonnière*" ("truant cooking"), by which he means he follows no school but his own. That may sound pretentious but it's results that count. A faithful and rather chic clientele comes back again and again for such inventive delights as rabbit with sea-urchins, beef cheek with calf's foot, or coffee and whiskey ice cream. The decor is pleasantly old-fashioned.

Le Petit Riche
25 Rue Le Peletier, 9e ☎47-70-68-68. Map 4E8 Last orders 12.15am. Closed Sun. Métro Le Peletier.
The new management of this restaurant has not, thankfully, tampered with its quite exceptional decor, which, with its decorated frosted windows, large mirrors and brass luggage-racks, is somewhat more Edwardian than Belle Epoque. Nor has the management changed the strong emphasis on Loire wines: a good selection is still available, and this must be one of the very few Paris restaurants serving Bourgueil in carafes. But not all is at it was; indeed, the reasonably-priced food is a distinct improvement on previous offerings, which had become stuck in a deep rut. It clearly combines ancient and modern, and is generously served.

Le Petit Zinc
25 Rue de Buci, 6e ☎46-33-51-60.

Map 9I8 Last orders 3am. Métro Mabillon.
Probably the best restaurant in town open until 3am, Le Petit Zinc has a pleasant, old-fashioned bistro atmosphere, a short menu of *plats bourgeois*, and some unpretentious wines. A haunt of insomniacs, it is under the same management as **Le Muniche**.

Au Pied de Cochon
6 Rue Coquillière, 1er ☎42-36-11-75. Map 9G9 Open 24hrs a day. Métro Les Halles.
The bold red awning bearing the name Au Pied de Cochon is one of the landmarks of Les Halles, unchanged amid the whirlwind of redevelopment that has transformed the district in the past decade. The restaurant retains the authentic atmosphere of the old Les Halles — a bustling, friendly, no-nonsense place. The oysters and other seafood are to be recommended, as is the onion soup.

Pharamond
24 Rue de la Grande-Truanderie, 1er ☎42-33-06-72. Map 10H9 Last orders 10pm. Closed Sun, Mon lunch, July, Métro Les Halles.
This gem of a restaurant, with its Art Nouveau *faïence* and mirrors, was formerly in the heart of the fruit-and-veg section of Les Halles market (now banished to Rungis); it's now surrounded by a plethora of trendy, here-today-gone-tomorrow clip-joints that have proliferated in and around the Forum des Halles. Pharamond used to be famed mainly for its succulent tripe and *andouillette*, but it now features some more modern dishes on its varied menu.

Pierre Traiteur
10 Rue de Richelieu, 1er ☎42-96-09-17. Map 9F8 Last orders 10pm. Closed Sat, Sun, Aug. Métro Richelieu-Drouot.
A rather noisy, upscale bistro that offers a tempting choice between Auvergnat food (such as the rare *estofinado*, made from wind-dried cod) and more sophisticated fare (raw sea-bass with chives). There is a commendable selection of lesser-known wines.

Pierre Vedel ✿
19 Rue Duranton, 15e ☎45-58-43-17 Last orders 10pm. Closed Sat, Sun, July 14-Aug 15, week of Christmas and New Year. Métro Boucicaut.
Genuine Mediterranean restaurants do not lie thick on the ground in Paris, so all the more reason to be thankful for the existence of this welcoming bistro. Vedel himself, who comes from the fishing port of Sète, naturally feels most at home with seafood (excellent garlicky lobster soup, fillet of *rascasse* in saffron-flavored aspic), but he also has a talent for inventive vegetable dishes, for example, stuffed cabbage and a gamut of combined vegetable mousses.

Polidor ✿
41 Rue Monsieur-le-Prince, 6e ☎43-26-95-34. Map 15J8 Last orders 1am. Métro Odéon.
Price has little to do with fashion, and the fact that Polidor gives away a three-course set meal for a ludicrously low price does not deter Claire Bretécher or Serge Reggiani from bestowing their custom on the place. Little has changed since the time of previous habitués such as Verlaine, Valéry and Joyce: there are still lace curtains, numbered napkin lockers (some in use), a spiral staircase, and even waitresses in turn-of-the-century dress. The new owner, André Maillet, comes from the Somme, in the north of France, and used to be a butcher. It's been packed ever since. Good *cuisine bourgeoise*.

Le Pot d'Etain
22 Rue des Canettes, 6e ☎43-26-42-68. Map 9J8 Last orders midnight. Métro Mabillon, St-Germain-des-Prés.
A pleasantly rustic atmosphere characterizes this restaurant, housed in a building with rough stone walls and wooden beams. The cuisine is catholic enough for most tastes, and good value. Fondue is a strong point and so are the fish dishes. There is even a fish tank in a back dining room — but strictly for decoration.

Le Pouilly
96 Rue Daguerre, 14e ☎43-22-60-18. Map 14M7 Last orders 9pm. Closed Sat, Sun, Aug. Métro Denfert-Rochereau.
One of the places to which the people working in the 195m (650ft) Tour Maine-Montparnasse escape at lunchtime in order to restore their sanity and sate their appetites is this quiet, almost provincial bistro. Located at the Montparnasse end of

the equally provincial Rue Daguerre (home of the movie-maker Agnès Varda and subject of a documentary by her), it serves good, uncomplicated food.

Le Pré Catelan ⏢
Route de Suresnes, Bois de Boulogne, 16e ☎45-24-55-58 IIII ▭ ■ ⏢ 🚗 AE ⦶ ⊚ VISA Last orders 10.30pm. Closed Sun evening, Mon, one week in Feb.
Most well-heeled Parisians abandon the capital during *le weekend*. Many of those who don't, and who hanker after tiptop food in an accessible pastoral setting, make for this establishment in the Bois de Boulogne. It was transformed a few years ago from an ailing eating place into a palatial summerhouse of a restaurant by the well-known caterer and pastry cook, Gaston Lenôtre. His nephew, Patrick Lenôtre, took over as chef and turned it into Paris' finest outdoor restaurant. Patrick has since left to run his own restaurant and been succeeded as chef by Denis Bernal, who has kept up the same standards. His cooking is stylish and decorative—thus mirroring the clientele. In winter there's cozy, indoor dining in front of an open fire.

Les Princes ⏢
31 Av. George V, 8e ☎47-23-54-00. Map 7F4 IIII ▭ ≡ ⏢ 🚗 AE ⦶ ⊚ VISA Last orders 11.30pm. Métro George V.
That Les Princes, in the **Hôtel George V** (see *Hotels*), is the least starchy restaurant in a luxury Parisian hotel is due, in large part, to its manager M. Frison, who is neither stuffy nor obsequious. The clientele here includes admen and movie-producers with pretty women in tow. The food combines the aristocratic (*tournedos de poisson au poivre noir, foie gras de canard au torchon*) with peasant food (salt pork with lentils), and with, for France, the exotic (angels on horseback). In summer you can eat in the George V's lovely flower-filled courtyard.

Le Procope
13 Rue de l'Ancienne-Comédie, 6e ☎43-26-99-20. Map 9I8 III to IIII ▭ ■ AE ⦶ VISA Last orders 1am. Closed July. Métro Odéon.
No other restaurant in Paris has been going as long as the Procope, which opened in 1686 (as a café to start with). Previous customers include La Fontaine, Voltaire, Benjamin Franklin, Jean-Jacques Rousseau, Robespierre, Napoleon, Balzac, George Sand and Huysmans. Although recently renovated, its two floors have retained their warm, original atmosphere. The fare is traditional *cuisine bourgeoise* with a good selection of sea food. Unfortunately you can no longer eat here at bargain prices, as you could before the recent overhaul and change of management.

Au Quai d'Orsay
49 Quai d'Orsay, 7e ☎47-05-69-09. Map 7H5 IIII ■ (lunch) ▭ (dinner) ≡ ⏢ AE ⦶ ⊚ VISA Last orders 11pm. Métro Invalides.
Mushroom freaks should make a beeline for this restaurant which prides itself on its selection of fungi, including (depending on the time of year) *cèpes, chanterelles*, hedgehog mushrooms, saffron milk-caps and oyster mushrooms. The very copiously served *cuisine bourgeoise* on offer has recently made some concessions to "modernity," perhaps to please the restaurant's very fashion-conscious clientele.

Régence-Plaza ⏢
25 Av. Montaigne, 8e ☎47-23-78-33. Map 7G4 IIII ▭ ≡ ⏢ 🚗 AE ⦶ ⊚ VISA Last orders 10.15pm. Métro Franklin-D-Roosevelt.
People go to the Régence-Plaza, the more expensive of the **Hôtel Plaza-Athénée's** two restaurants, to savor the glittering company as much as the food. Manager M. Roland uses the experience he gained at **La Tour d'Argent** to good effect: he is an expert at organizing the arrangement of diners so that the celebrities whom ordinary customers have come to see are sprinkled evenly over the whole dining room. In summer the inner courtyard is a marvelous, verdant jungle of plants. The cuisine is a mixture of classical and new styles, and the wine list is superb.

Relais Saint-Germain ✿
190 Bd. St-Germain, 7e ☎45-48-11-73. Map 8I7 III ■ ⦶ VISA Last orders 11pm. Métro Rue-du-Bac.
The covered terrace of this restaurant is a good vantage point from which to observe the exotic parade that roves between the Café Flore at St-Germain-des-Prés and the Escurial at Rue du Bac. The cuisine is good (with the emphasis on fish, especially home-made smoked salmon) and excellent value for money; and the chef makes excellent *charlotte au chocolat*.

Le Repaire de Cartouche
8 Bd. Filles-du-Calvaire. 11e ☎47-00-25-86. Map 11H12 III to

Last orders 9.45pm. Closed Sat lunch, Sun, July 24-Aug 22. Métro Filles-du-Calvaire.
Raymond Pocous, a printer by trade, presides over this pleasant and relaxed, two-level old restaurant. He may have a strong Paris accent but his heart is in the Landes, in southwest France, where he spent his early childhood. The menu is suitably atavistic, though without any of the heaviness that often mars the cuisine of that area. His smoked duck breast (not only the best cuts, but gizzards and hearts), and renowned Chalosse beef are all eminently digestible. Pocous has a contagious enthusiasm for his fine selection of Bas-Armagnacs.

Le Restaurant du Marché
59 Rue de Dantzig, 15e ☎48-28-31-55. AE Ⓓ VISA Last orders 11.30pm. Métro Convention.
Under the same friendly management as **L'Aquitaine** down the road, this partly old-fashioned, partly modern establishment sets out, like the preceding restaurant, **Le Repaire de Cartouche**, to acquaint the customers with the hearty fare of the Landes, in southwest France, much of which revolves around goose and duck. This is one of the few places in Paris where you'll get a *garbure* (on request in winter), the soup that is a meal in itself (with ham, various vegetables including cabbage, and a sprinkling of Roquefort).

Rôtisserie Rivoli
Hôtel Inter-Continental, 3 Rue de Castiglione, 1er ☎42-60-37-80. Map 8G7 AE Ⓓ VISA Last orders 10.30pm. Métro Tuileries.
This restaurant is unusual for a luxury hotel (it's part of the **Hôtel Inter-Continental**: see *Hotels*) in that it offers a set menu which, in view of its copiousness and high quality, is very good value indeed — particularly in summer, when there is the additional bonus of eating on the hotel's celebrated and often celebrity-packed Italian-style patio. Chef Jean-Jacques Barbier shows a refreshing interest in the kitchen garden, and his two *plats du jour*, themselves traditional rather than inventive, are imaginatively served with two, and sometimes three, vegetables.

Au Rubis
10 Rue du Marché-St-Honoré, 1er ☎42-61-03-34. Map 8G7 to Open 7am-10pm. Closed Sat, Sun, Aug. Métro Pyramides.
Owner Léon Gouin has retired, but the success of his tiny wine bar has not abated. You still have to get there early to stake out your table for the lunchtime *plat du jour*; and if all you want is a glass of one of the many wines available and an excellent open sandwich, you still have to fight your way to the bar in true English-pub style.

Le St James
6 Rue de 29-Juillet, 1er ☎42-60-31-60. Map 8G7 AE Ⓓ VISA Last orders 10pm. Closed Sat, Sun. Métro Tuileries.
The most discreet of all good hotel restaurants in Paris (it adjoins the **Hôtel St-James et Albany**, see *Hotels*) and ideal for a low-profile business lunch or *dîner à deux* (with piano). In summer, food is also served in the pleasant courtyard overlooking the hotel's 17thC rear facade. Chef Jean-Pierre Lauret offers a catholic range of excellent dishes (and a very reasonable set menu) that features *cuisine nouvelle*.

Le Sancerrois
12 Rue du Champ-de-Mars, 7e ☎45-55-13-47. Map 13I4 AE VISA Last orders 9pm. Closed Sat evening, Sun, Aug. Métro École-Militaire.
People from the nearby TV studios appreciate the quiet atmosphere of this friendly, unpretentious café-restaurant. The food is Auvergnat, and the handful of wines (some available by the glass in the café section) mainly Loire and Beaujolais, and all impeccably chosen.

Sur Les Quais
53 Quai des Grands-Augustins, 6e ☎43-25-45-94. Map 9I9 Last orders 11.30pm. Closed Sat lunch, Sun. Métro Odéon.
This chic and unostentatious restaurant has become in a short time a highly fashionable rendezvous for the young Parisian set. The hostess is Valerie-Anne Giscard d'Estaing, daughter of the ex-President and author of a number of cookery books. She has brightened up the restaurant, formerly called La Cannelle, and given it a new name that alludes to the Marlon Brando film *On the Waterfront*. The service is discreet and attentive, the cuisine classic and of high quality.

Taillevent
15 Rue Lamennais, 8e ☎45-63-39-94. Map 7F4 Last

orders 10pm. Closed Sat, Sun, Aug. Métro Étoile.
Taillevent, named after one of the first great French cooks who lived in the 14thC, is run by Jean-Claude Vrinat with all the skill you would expect of a business-school graduate, and he has made it one of the capital's top five or six restaurants. He follows new cooking trends, and will occasionally send his chef off for a refresher course with the Troisgros brothers or Michel Guérard. Vrinat is also always on the look-out for excellent lesser-known wines to fill out his incredible wine list. He buys some of his cheeses direct from the farm, which is most unusual for this class of establishment. Taillevent is much frequented by politicians and top businessmen. The decor is suitably discreet. Reserve weeks —even months — ahead.

Tarte Julie
8 Rue Jolivet, 14ᵉ ☎43-20-70-34. Map ***14L6*** *to* *Open noon-11pm. Closed Sun, Mon. Métro Edgar-Quinet.*
Lissom, sun-tanned young mums wearing Hermès scarves, who frequent the nearby branch of Habitat, mingle here, amid Habitat-style furniture, with secretaries working in the Tour Maine-Montparnasse. There is a wide selection of very good salads, well-filled *pizze*, tarts and ice creams at reasonable prices. The tarts and *pizze* can also be bought to take away — indeed Tarte Julie started out as a shop. A good place for a lunchtime or afternoon break if you are in the area.

La Taverne du Sergent Recruteur ✿
41 Rue St Louis-en-l'Ile, 4ᵉ ☎43-54-75-42. Map ***10J10*** *Open for dinner only. Last orders 12.30am. Closed Sun. Métro Pont Marie.*
In the 18th century when the French army was short of men it would employ a *sergent recruteur* (recruiting sergeant), a sly character who would ply his victims with food and drink until they were so befuddled that they signed his enlistment papers without objection. At this restaurant, on the romantic Ile St-Louis, you get similar lavish treatment but without the penalty. Before you come here make sure that you have a big appetite. There is no *à la carte*, only a fixed-price menu of remarkably good value. You start with a generous salad, a basket of sausage and a crook of pâté. Then comes a choice of main dishes, followed by a cheese board and finally a dessert. The dining room is just the sort of place where one can imagine the recruiting sergeant at work: leaded windows, stone-flagged floor, heavy wooden beams and stone arches.

La Taverne des Templiers
106 Rue Vieille du Temple, 3ᵉ ☎42-78-74-67. Map ***11H11*** *Last orders 10pm. Closed Sat, Sun, Aug. Métro Filles du Calvaire.*
Curiously, this part of the old and picturesque Marais quarter contains almost no restaurants of any quality. But here is the exception. The Taverne des Templiers occupies a building dating from the year 1229 and restored in 1500. It was therefore originally put up not long after the Marais was drained by the Knights Templar, and quite possibly members of the order frequented the building. Today's customers dine in a wonderfully atmospheric room, beneath a superb beamed ceiling. The food, scrupulously prepared under the supervision of the patron, Guy Bertrand, is a mixture of *nouvelle cuisine* and more traditional dishes.

Le Télégraphe ✿
41 Rue de Lille, 7ᵉ ☎40-15-06-65. Map ***8H7*** *to* *Last orders 12.45am. Closed Sun. Métro Solférino.*
A new Left Bank restaurant, only a stone's throw from the Musée d'Orsay, the Télégraphe has in a very short time acquired a high reputation. Publishers, journalists and politicians gather here to talk shop. The superb décor is the work of François-Joseph Graf: arcades, columns, stained-glass windows, woodwork with an Art Nouveau touch and a pleasant verandah looking onto a little garden. The cuisine is very *à la mode*, with dishes, such as *compôte de lapereau en gelée d'échalotes* and *aiguillettes de canard aux cinq épices*. Prices are reasonable for what you get.

Terminus Nord
23 Rue de Dunkerque, 10ᵉ ☎42-85-05-15. Map ***5D10*** *Last orders 12.30pm. Métro Gare-du-Nord.*
Cafés and restaurants near stations tend to treat their irregular, hurried and captive clientele in less than gentlemanly fashion. A notable exception is the Terminus Nord, the fifth restaurant in the stable of Jean-Paul Bucher (see **Brasserie Flo, Julien** and **Le Vaudeville**). An ideal

place at which to eat before taking a train from the Gare du Nord opposite, this brasserie offers food that is good enough to attract swarms of gourmets who have no intention of leaving town.

Le Terroir
22 Rue Chaligny, 12e ☎43-07-47-66. Map **17K14** *Last orders 9.30pm. Closed Sat evening, Sun, Aug. Métro Reuilly-Diderot.*
This constantly packed bistro serves a mixture of *cuisine bourgeoise* and of specialties from the Sud-Ouest (such as excellent foie gras and *confits d'oie*). Regulars include doctors from a nearby hospital.

Thoumieux
79 Rue St-Dominique, 7e ☎47-05-49-75. Map **13H5** *Last orders 11.30pm. Closed Mon, July 15-Aug 15. Métro La Tour Maubourg.*
No one would claim that this spacious, vaguely Art Deco restaurant, attached to a hotel of the same name, did what its name suggests in French — *tout mieux* (everything better); but it does do an honest job of serving good traditional food.

La Tour d'Argent
15 Quai de la Tournelle, 5e ☎43-54-23-31. Map **16J0** *Last orders 10pm. Closed Mon. Métro Maubert-Mutualité.*
This penthouse restaurant is world famous. Eccentric but shrewd ex-playboy Claude Terrail has, over the years, perfected the art of giving his customers what they want: the pleasure of a table overlooking the illuminated Notre-Dame (but reserve well ahead); of dealing with a *sommelier* who looks delighted, not petulant, if they choose the cheapest wine on his list (the finest classical cellar in Paris); and the convenience and style of walking out of the elevator afterwards straight into their proferred coats, then out to find their cars purring at the curbside. Service of this caliber and the very high quality of La Tour d'Argent's cuisine cost a great deal; it is Paris' most expensive restaurant.

Le Trou Gascon
40 Rue Taine, 12e ☎43-44-34-26 to Last orders 10pm. Closed Sat, Sun. Métro Daumesnil.
The acclaimed chef, Alain Dutournier, who created this restaurant, has turned it over to his wife, who has continued in the same style. The restaurant offers a most unusual blend of new ideas and provincial (Gascon) tradition; and an equally rare selection of wines (some 450) ranging from prestigious Bordeaux to humble, little-known *crus*, all annotated in detail on the city's most compulsively readable wine list. Throw in the amazing collection of Armagnacs, and the restaurant's turn-of-the-century decore (a riot of mirrors and moldings), and you have the makings of a memorable meal.

Le Trumilou
84 Quai de l'Hôtel-de-Ville, 4e ☎42-77-63-98. Map **10I10** *to Last orders 11pm. Closed Mon. Métro Pont-Marie.*
Although the former proprietors retired in 1987, this little bistro has retained the homey atmosphere that it always had. The new owner has understood how to maintain tradition and keep a faithful clientele. Thus one still finds the same solid *cuisine bourgeoise*, served by waitresses in small white aprons.

Le Val d'Or
28 Av. Franklin-D-Roosevelt, 8e ☎43-59-95-81. Map **7F5** *Restaurant closed for dinner; snacks only served in evening till 9pm. Closed Sat, Sun. Métro St-Philippe-du-Roule.*
Youthful Géraud Rongier moved several years ago from his tiny **La Cloche des Halles** to this larger café near St-Philippe-du-Roule. On the ground floor he provides cold snacks (including, in many people's opinion, the very best sandwiches in town), and in the mirror-filled basement hot lunches of exceptional value are served. At both levels, a small but very reliable selection of wines is available (mainly Beaujolais and Burgundy).

Le Vaudeville
29 Rue Vivienne, 2e ☎42-33-39-31. Map **9F8** *Last orders 2am. Métro Bourse.*
Once upon a time this was a dreary, half-empty Art Deco brasserie, haunted by tired journalists working nearby. In stepped Jean-Paul Bucher (see **Brasserie Flo, Julien and Terminus Nord**) with his magic wand to restore the establishment's Egyptian-style walls and opaque fittings to their former glory and put professionals in charge of the kitchens. It now offers very good classical cuisine at highly competitive

prices — and open until 2am it is a boon for people wanting a bite after a show. As the quality of the Sylvaner wine has greatly improved since the Alsatian Bucher took over, the hacks have been nursing less ferocious hangovers.

Le Vert Galant
42 Quai des Orfèvres. 1er ☎43-26-83-68. Map 9I9 [price] [AE] [DC] [MC] [VISA] Last orders 10.30pm. Closed Sat. Métro Pont Neuf, Cité.

The name *Vert Galant* refers to the popular King Henry IV, whose equestrian statue stands a stone's-throw away on the Pont Neuf. The pleasure-loving monarch would have appreciated having a restaurant named after him, especially one in such an enviable position as this, on the Ile de la Cité overlooking the Seine and backing onto the tranquil Place Dauphine. The upstairs dining room has a superb view of the river, and in summer one can dine on the ground-floor terrace. The cuisine here is predominantly in the classical French style. There is a distinguished clientele, including lawyers from the nearby Palais de Justice, publishers, writers and show-business people.

Au Vieux Berlin
32 Av. George V, 8e ☎47-20-88-96. Map 7F4 [price] to [price] [AE] [DC] [VISA] Last orders 11pm. Closed Sat, Sun. Métro George V.

Movie and showbiz people (Serge Gainsbourg, Jacques Dutronc) appreciate the discretion and attentive service available at this accurate reproduction of a prewar Berlin eating house (complete with pianist and candles in the evening). The food, though mainly German (plenty of game in season, pumpkin soup with bacon, knuckle of pork with pease pudding), has an attractively light and — dare one say it? — French touch.

Le Vivarois [Δ]
192 Av. Victor-Hugo, 16e ☎45-04-04-31. Map 6F2 [price] [AE] [DC] [VISA] Last orders 10pm. Closed Sat, Sun, Aug. Métro Rue de la Pompe.

This is the most unusual of the city of Paris' pantheon of first-class restaurants, run by a true eccentric, chef-patron Claude-Peyrot, and frequented by well-heeled gourmands, often political. Peyrot is no disciple of *nouvelle cuisine*, rather a past-master at dishes that are traditional in the best sense (i.e., not overcomplicated or smothered in heavy sauces). His aim is not flashy inventiveness but utter perfection of both raw materials and the end-product — and he usually succeeds. A very interesting wine list with a very interested wine waiter to explain it.

Willi's
13 Rue des Petits-Champs, 1er ☎42-61-05-09. Map 9G8 [price] to [price] [CB] Open 11am-10pm. Closed Sat, Sun. Métro Bourse.

Willi's (named after owner Mark Williamson) is a fairly faithful copy of a typical London wine bar, except that the number of wines (99, and many available by the glass) and the quality of the food served (Anglo-French) are much higher than one would normally expect in Britain. It is crowded with English expatriates and tweedy French Anglophiles, who doubtless appreciate being served by attentive and well-bred young ladies.

Cafés

The café is one of the most civilized institutions ever invented. It is a living stage, a forum for debate, a club, a home away from home. Paris was among the earliest cities to establish a café society, and it remains one of the few where traditional café life still thrives; in fact the French capital without its cafés would be unthinkable. In them revolutions have been plotted, poems written, philosophies born. As literary and artistic circles have migrated from one district to another, so different cafés have had their spells as fashionable meeting places. Some of the famous ones have disappeared, others have been ruined by modernization, but many are still virtually intact.

The more than 10,000 cafés in Paris cater, between them, to almost every need a Parisian might have. An often staggering range of alcoholic, soft and hot drinks is available; solid fare includes croissants, hard-boiled eggs and sandwiches, and sometimes hot snacks and even sit-down meals, especially at lunchtime. You can make local and sometimes trunk (*inter*) calls, though both will cost much more than from the public phone booths that have recently sprung up in increasing numbers in the streets of Paris. The main brands of French cigarettes can be found in most cafés, but *cafés-tabacs* (recognizable by their red lozenge sign) sell a wide range of cigarettes, cigars, pipe- and even chewing-tobacco, snuff, stamps, envelopes, postcards, pens and state lottery tickets (including the bingo-like *Loto*). If the letters PMU are displayed outside, it means the *café-tabac* turns into a betting shop on certain days, and you can have a flutter on the horses via the state tote system. Other café amusements may include pinball machines (known as "flippers"), electronic games, juke-boxes, miniature soccer, American pool and French billiards. You can even use them for their public rest rooms (for the price of a coffee), and the standard of these has improved greatly over the last decade or so.

In the Middle Ages young men went in search of the Grail; today the café is the quest of a young man in search of an artistic education.

George Moore, *Vale*, 1914

There are free attractions, too. You can read, write, work or just while away the time with or without friends for as long as you like (except in one or two cafés on the Bd. St-Michel, where notices fiercely warn you that your order will be automatically renewed every hour!). Cafés with terraces are good vantage points from which to observe the passers-by on, say, the Champs-Élysées or one of the busy boulevards like the Bds. Montmartre, des Italiens, des Capucines, Haussmann, Clichy, Pigalle, St-Germain, St-Michel and du Montparnasse. But expect to be asked to pay a stiffer price here: you're paying not only for the refreshment, the seat and the service, but for the prime location.

If you simply want to rest your feet or appease the children, look for a side-street café, which will be quieter and cheaper, as well as providing friendlier and more personal service.

Remember that most cafés have a two-tiered price system, depending on whether you drink at the bar or occupy a table. Usually, the price difference is not enormous. However, at some more expensive establishments the cement-stained building workers knocking back their *pastis* at the bar will pay up to 50% less than the well-heeled customers sitting on the terrace — cafés are democratic, too. Watch out for the price of certain drinks — non-French beer, bottled mineral water, Coca Cola, whiskey and vodka, to name but a few.

A word about the different types of café you're likely to encounter. *Buvettes*, which are getting rarer every day, are grocery shops or wine merchants with a counter (*zinc*) but usually no tables; here, and at the almost extinct *bougnats* (tiny, Spartan cafés run by coal-and-wool merchants), you will find the authentic flavor of prewar Paris.

The already mentioned *cafés-tabacs* differ from other cafés in that their prices may be fractionally lower and their atmosphere a little livelier. Brasseries, "drugstores" and "pubs" (the last two bear little relation to the American or British originals) are large and generally serve hot meals throughout the day.

Lastly, at the more elegant end of the spectrum, there are *salons de thé*. When they double up as *pâtisseries* they tend to cater to maiden aunts and usually do not serve alcoholic drinks. Sometimes, however, run-of-the-mill cafés with social ambitions arrogate the title *salon de thé*. Genuine *salons de thé*, if you can afford them, are the best places for a good Continental breakfast.

As in restaurants, tipping in cafés is no longer a problem: at the tables, the tip is clearly included on the ticket the waiter gives you, or else he will add it on himself. At the bar, there is generally a notice indicating whether it is included or not. If in doubt, ask.

Interesting cafés in Paris are far too numerous to list exhaustively, but here are a few favorites arranged according to area.

Left Bank

Montparnasse

Still the center of Bohemian life in Paris, though many of the café decors have been ruined. Genuine artists, intellectuals, writers, movie people and hangers-on of every description gather in **La Coupole** (see Restaurants), or **Le Select** (*99 Bd. du Montparnasse*), which has hardly changed since it was frequented by Erik Satie, Francis Poulenc, Robert Desnos and Foujita. Across the way, **Le Dôme** (*108 Bd. du Montparnasse*) is still cashing in on its reputation as a favorite watering hole of Modigliani, Stravinsky, Picasso and Hemingway. Unfortunately, its hybrid 1920s decoration has destroyed the charm of its former atmosphere. Five minutes' walk along the boulevard is the still lively **Closerie des Lilas** (see Restaurants). Behind Montparnasse station is **Les Mousquetaires** (*77 Av. du Maine*), a marvelous, cavernous café-cum-billiard hall.

St-Germain-des-Prés

Two of the most famous of all cafés, **Les Deux Magots** and **Le Flore** (*170 and 172 Bd. St-Germain respectively*), are to be found right in the heart of this district. The list of their customers past and present reads like a roll call of French *vie intellectuelle* over the last century: Rémy de Gourmont, Jarry, Huysmans, Barres, Maurras, Giraudoux, Sartre, de Beauvoir, Breton, Camus and the Prévert brothers, to name but a few. The Existentialist movement was born in one or other of them, or both, as were many of Sartre's philosophical and literary works — he preferred writing on a café table rather than on a desk. Nowadays, however, times have changed and only the wealthier literati can afford to hold court regularly at the two cafés, and most of the cafés' day-to-day customers belong to the most trendy international set.

On the other side of the boulevard there is still plenty of action at **Lipp** (see Restaurants). The high priests of modern French intellectual life, such as *nouveau philosophe* Bernard-Henri Lévy and novelist Philippe Sollers, have retreated to the quieter waters of the English "pub" around the corner, **The Twickenham** (*70 Rue des Sts-Pères*). Another "pub" in the area is the vast **Pub St-Germain-des-Prés** (*17 Rue de l'Ancienne-Comédie*), which boasts an unrivaled range of draft and bottled beers, teas and whiskeys, and is open all day and all night. Also in the Rue de l'Ancienne-Comédie is the famous **Le Procope**, the first-ever café in Paris, which opened its doors to the public as far back as 1686. Though it is open for a few hours in the afternoon, its prime function is now as a restaurant (see Restaurants).

The man regarded by many as the finest *pâtissier* in Paris, **Christian Constant**, has a *salon de thé* in his shop nearby (*26 Rue du Bac*).

St-Michel

The cafés on the Bd. St-Michel itself are no longer as interesting as they used to be, and two of them have been turned into McDonalds, though there are several around the Place St-Michel that are popular with the Latin Quarter crowd. However, you can take refuge nearby at **L'Écluse-I, Le Balzar**, or **Café de la Nouvelle Mairie** (see *Restaurants*). There are also two afternoon-only *salons de thé* within easy reach: **La Bûcherie** (see *Restaurants*) and **The Tea Caddy** (*14 Rue St-Julien-le-Pauvre*), where you'll enjoy better scones, muffins and cinnamon toast than you're ever likely to encounter in a café or tea shop in Britain.

Right Bank

Champs-Élysées

There are only two cafés of any real interest actually on the Champs-Élysées: **Fouquet's** (*no. 99*) and **L'Alsace** (*no. 39*). At the first, you pay withering prices for the privilege of joining starlets on its terrace; the real movie stars can be found in the hushed and old-fashioned (no unaccompanied ladies) bar within. L'Alsace is a brasserie which has the merit of serving genuine Alsatian beer, wine and food 24hrs a day. Not far from the Champs-Élysées there are several good establishments which serve refreshments and snacks outside meal times, notably **Le Val d'Or**, the bar of **Aux Vieux Berlin, L'Écluse-II**, and **Boulangerie St-Philippe**. These are all described under *Restaurants*.

Opéra — Boulevard Haussmann

Once the hub of café society, this is now mainly a business quarter, and becomes pretty bleak after the early evening. But French office-workers being as demanding as they are, most cafés are reliable, particularly those that are found lurking down side streets.

One of the most celebrated establishments in Paris is, of course, the **Café de la Paix** (*12 Bd. des Capucines*). It emerged from meticulous restoration a few years ago with its deliciously ornate green and gold decor, designed by Charles Garnier, architect of the Opéra opposite, and with its clientele (wealthy tourists for the most part) unscathed. Some of the best coffee, home-made croissants and other pastries are to be found at the smart but stark *salon de thé* of **Fauchon** (*26 Pl. de la Madeleine*), Paris' most famous food store. Here you proceed as in Italy; you decide whether you want a pastry or not, pay for it and/or for a coffee at the cash desk, hand over your ticket at the counter, collect your order and eat it standing up at one of the pedestal tables. After a day's shopping in *Faubourg-St-Honoré*, treat yourself to tea at **Angélina** (*226 Rue de Rivoli*); where the patisserie are delectable concoctions of cream, chocolate and meringue. A number of cafés serve good wines and snacks: as well as **Au Rubis** (see *Restaurants*), there is **Ma Bourgogne** (*133 Bd. Haussmann*), frequented by French executives, and **Le St-Amour** (*4 Rue de Rome*), a friendly and rollicking café usefully located near the big department stores on the Bd. Haussmann.

Les Halles

Now, sadly, only a shadow of its former self, "*le ventre de Paris*" is in such a state of ferment — with cafés and restaurants mushrooming overnight and disappearing without trace within a month — that it is safe to recommend only the gilt-edged stock.

Opposite the excellent **La Cloche des Halles** (see *Restaurants*) is a pleasant old-fashioned café with nothing extraordinary about it except its name, **La Promenade de Vénus** (*44 Rue du Louvre*), which resulted in its being selected by André Breton as the meeting place for fellow Surrealists. Around the corner, the best-known Les Halles restaurant, **Au Pied de Cochon** (*6 Rue Coquillière*), still serves fairly pricey but uneven food 24hrs a day every day of the year.

Le Marais

If you wander around this fascinating old quarter, which has retained an almost provincial calm, you're bound to find several small cafés, filled with regulars and rich in character. On the beautifully intact 17thC Pl. des Vosges, there is the cozy and altogether trendier **Ma Bourgogne** (*no. 19*), which serves reasonably good wines. But for a really wide and reliable selection of vintages, try **La Tartine** (*24 Rue de Rivoli*) on the southern edge of Le Marais; this bustling, smoke-filled café has not changed much since Lenin and Trotsky drank there. Also on the periphery is a very good *pâtisserie/salon de thé* called **Clichy** (*5 Bd. Beaumarchais*).

Montmartre — Pigalle

All self-respecting painters have long since fled the Pl. du Tertre in Montmartre, crammed now with terrible paintings of sad-eyed children and dogs, and Pigalle has become a sex-shop jungle haunted by tough Brazilian transvestites. In both areas, cafés have turned the exploitation of tourists into a fine art, but as soon as you move away from the bright lights you may find a genuine Montmartrois café.

One such establishment is the delightful **Aux Négociants** (*27 Rue Lambert*), where excellent and inexpensive wines flow freely as regulars converse, conveniently gathered around the tiny, horseshoe-shaped bar.

Nightlife and the arts

From the panhandling mimes in the piazza at Beaubourg to the idolized divas at the *Opéra*, Paris remains a compelling magnet for performers and their followers from every French-speaking country, and much of the rest of Europe as well. The center of established culture is the monumental state Opéra, the glorious Baroque interior of which is accessible to even the most hard-up devotee, though the price of a good ticket can be exorbitant. Around it lie the Boulevard theaters. Just as plush are the grand movie theaters along the Champs-Élysées, which sometimes even show French movies with English subtitles. The Left Bank shelters most of the revival and avant-garde movie theaters and the ancient Marais quarter now thinks itself the home of the *café-théâtre*.

Although not cheap, most prices are reasonable, and a great many concerts are free. Informality is the rule for all but the grandest occasions. Beware of late summer, when almost all theaters close for a month or two. Many theaters need reservations a week or two in advance, but **SOS Théâtres** (☎*42-25-67-07*) or **Chèque-Théatre** (☎*42-46-72-40*) provide last-minute assistance. For music bookings try **FNAC** (*Rue de Rennes, 6ᵉ* ☎*45-44-39-12 or Rue Pierre-Lescot, Forum des Halles, 1ᵉʳ* ☎*42-61-81-18*). Indispensable publications are *Pariscope* and *l'Officiel des Spectacles*, published every Wed.

As for less serious nightlife, "Gay Paree" still conjures up visions of cancan dancers, champagne and a cosmopolitan sophistication unique to the French capital. Since the Belle Époque, the combination of Bohemian artists, international café society and madcap expatriates has given Paris a slightly naughty but very glamorous after-dark reputation.

While a considerable bourgeois element has crept in and the favored nightlife among certain natives is eating out, Paris is still very lively indeed after dark. The chief and cheapest spectator sport, people-watching, can be accomplished in many cafés, particularly on the Left Bank (see *Cafés*). At the most expensive end of the scale, the spectacular revues with feathered and sequined scantily-clad beauties are flourishing as never before.

Parisians have always loved dancing, so clubs and discos are crowded and colorful. Like revues and cabarets, they tend to charge by the drink (*consommation*) rather than by the combination of admission fee plus drink. Prices can range from inexpensive at the more popular discos to vastly expensive at the most lavish nightclubs. Bar-hopping is not really a Parisian diversion, although many good bars welcome customers for the apéritif hour, and for a late-night drink. Cabarets and jazz clubs, with their echoes of the postwar era, are largely unchanged since the 1950s, and they can offer both nostalgia and entertainment, although it should also be said that Paris has always been *the* center for jazz in Europe.

Visible nightlife is concentrated mainly in St-Germain and the Latin Quarter on the Left Bank, and in Pigalle, its side streets crammed with sex shows and tattoo parlors, on the Right Bank. While prostitution is not illegal, soliciting is. Thus, prostitutes displaying their charms in the Bois de Boulogne and around the Rue St-Denis meet with some indifference from the police. Though there are still plenty of prostitutes in evidence, the Rue St-Denis is now becoming rather chic, part of the transition catalyzed by the influx of trendy shops and restaurants around the *Forum des Halles*. Ladies of the night (and day) also hang out in more stylish districts, such as around the Opéra and along the Rue Daunou.

It is a good idea to reserve ahead wherever possible.

Ballet

In recent years, great efforts have been made to liberate the dance from the traditional gold standard of the Opéra. More informal space is offered to foreign and touring companies of every kind, especially during festivals. Every July, there is open-air ballet in the Cour Carrée of the Louvre.

Carré Sylvia Montfort
106 Rue Briançon, 15ᵉ ☎45-31-28-34. Métro Porte-de-Vanves.
Off the beaten boulevard perhaps, but worth an expedition south.

Éspace Marais
22 Rue Beautrellis, 4ᵉ ☎42-71-10-19. Map ***11****J11. Métro Sully-Morland.*
Simple, unconventional and often exciting.

Opéra
Pl. de l'Opéra, 9ᵉ ☎47-42-57-50. Map ***8****F7. Métro Opéra.*
Home of French ballet, shared with the **National Opera**. Magnificent setting (see *Sights*).

Théâtre de la Ville
2 Pl. du Châtelet, 4ᵉ ☎42-74-22-77. Map ***10****I9. Métro Châtelet.*
Base for the larger visiting companies.

Bars

A night in a bar is not a Parisian habit. Bars are always crowded before dinner for an apéritif, or very late after everything else has closed. They tend to open around 5pm and may stay open till dawn. Unlike many other cities, there are no legal closing hours in Paris.

Some of the more sophisticated bars are found in the smart hotels, notably **L'Hôtel**, the bar of which resembles an indoor garden, the **Plaza-Athénée**, the **Crillon**, the **Ritz** and the **George V** (for addresses see *Hotels*).

Prices are high for spirits or champagne, considerably less for pastis or a wine-based drink such as *kir*. Nonalcoholic drinks are just as popular among the French as the more intoxicating variety, such as the refreshing *citron pressé*.

Alexandre
*Av. George V, 8e ☎47-20-17-82. Map **6**F4. Métro George V.*
Comfortable, civilized and elegant piano bar.

Bar du Lénox
*9 Rue de L'Université, 7e ☎42-96-10-95. Map **8**I7. Métro Rue du Bac.*
A 1930s décor provides an agreeable setting for a quiet and relaxed rendezvous.

Bedford Arms
*17 Rue Princesse, 6e ☎46-33-25-60. Map **15**J8. Métro St-Germain-des-Prés* AE Φ VISA
Based on the French idea of an English pub, very lively, popular with journalists and movie types.

Closerie des Lilas
*171 Bd. Montparnasse, 6e ☎43-26-70-50. Map **15**L8. Métro Vavin* AE Φ VISA
The ghost of Hemingway lingers in the bar, which still attracts assorted artists and literati. Boasts a good brasserie. (See also *Restaurants*.)

La Coupole
*102 Bd. Montparnasse, 14e ☎43-20-14-20. Map **14**K7. Métro Vavin* CB
A cultural landmark and watering hole for three generations of artists. Motley, crowded, noisy; frequented by politicians, beautiful girls, journalists, students, *cinéastes*, anybody. (See also *Restaurants*.)

Fouquet's
*99 Champs-Élysées, 8e ☎47-23-70-60. Map **6**F3. Métro George V* AE Φ
Liveliest bar on the Champs-Élysées, with a friendly mix of regulars and tourists. (See also *Cafés*.)

Harry's Bar
*5 Rue Daunou, 2e ☎42-61-71-14. Map **8**F7. Métro Opéra.*
"Sank Roo Doe Noo," as popular with Parisians as with visiting Anglophones, stocks 160 types of whiskey and harks back to the Lost Generation when such distinguished drinkers as Hemingway and Fitzgerald graced the stools. Good piano bar in the basement. Opened in 1911, it closes only on Christmas Day.

Rosebud
*11bis Rue Delambre, 14e ☎43-35-38-54. Map **16**L7. Métro Vavin.*
Once a rendezvous for Montparnasse artists and writers, such as Sartre and Simone de Beauvoir; now slightly run-down. Good chili.

Le Village
*7 Rue Gozlin, 6e ☎43-26-80-19. Map **15**I8. Métro St-Germain-des-Prés.*
A dim echo of prewar St-Germain.

Cabarets

Caveau des Oubliettes
*11 Rue St Julien le Pauvre, 5e ☎43-54-94-97. Map **15**J9. Métro St-Michel.*
Fake decor and costumed waiters but a real Latin Quarter atmosphere with authentic old French songs of love and life.

Chez Félix
*23 Rue Mouffetard, 5e ☎47-07-68-78. Map **16**K10. Métro Cardinal-Lemoine.*
Candlelit 14thC cellar with Brazilian music; dancing in the basement.

Club des Poètes
*30 Rue de Bourgogne, 7e ☎47-05-06-03. Map **8**H6. Métro Invalides* VISA
Totally Parisian idea — selected poems are sung, acted, danced and mimed.

Crazy Horse Saloon
*12 Av. George V, 8e ☎47-23-32-32. Map **7**F4. Métro George V* AE Φ VISA
Strip show without the strip. Dancers, with crazy names like Vanilla Banana and Tootsie Roll, are

already *déshabillée*, their charms enhanced with artistic lighting and risqué costumes. Excellent entertainment by magicians; good dancing. The Crazy Horse Saloon is crowded, uncomfortable and very expensive.

Don Camilo ✿
*10 Rue des Sts-Pères, 7e ☎42-60-32-84. Map **8**I7. Métro St-Germain-des-Prés* AE Φ
Variety show with elegance, and excellent dining available for a cabaret.

Au Lapin Agile ✿
*22 Rue des Saules, 18e ☎46-06-85-87. Map **4**C8. Métro Lamarck-Caulaincourt.*
Haunt of Montmartre artists such as Renoir and Picasso, now devoted to tourists, but still retaining some of the charms of Vieux Paris.

Le Milliardaire
*68 Rue Pierre-Charron, 8e ☎42-25-25-17. Map **7**F4. Métro Franklin-D-Roosevelt* AE Φ VISA
The sexiest strip, after the **Crazy Horse**.

Cafés-théâtres

The heyday of the *café-théâtre* is past, although it has certainly retained its refreshing informality. At some you eat, at others you can drink.

If you are lucky, the show may turn out to be almost as good as the food.

Blancs-Manteaux
*15 Rue des Blancs-Manteaux, 4e ☎48-87-15-84. Map **10**H10. Métro Rambuteau.*

Café d'Edgar
*58 Bd. Edgar-Quinet, 14e ☎43-20-85-11. Map **14**L7. Métro Edgar-Quinet.*

Café de la Gare
*41 Rue du Temple, 3e ☎42-78-52-51. Map **10**H10. Métro Hôtel-de-Ville.*

Petit Casino
*17 Rue Chapon, 3e ☎42-78-36-50. Map **10**H10. Métro Rambuteau.*

Point Virgule
*7 Rue Sainte-Croix-de-la-Bretonnerie, 4e ☎42-78-67-03. Map **10**H10. Métro Hôtel-de-Ville.*

Casinos

Except for a few exclusive and very private gaming clubs, it is not possible to gamble in Paris. The nearest good casino is at Enghien, 16km (10 miles) NW of the city.

Concerts

The range of music is almost matched by the spread of its habitat. Conventional *salles* vie with theaters, museums, gardens, grand houses and, best of all, the old churches of Paris, including **La Madeleine**, **St-Germain-des-Prés**, **St-Julien-le-Pauvre**, and **St-Roch**. Favorites are the summer Sun evening recitals at **Notre-Dame**. As for pop concerts, the really big ones are held at **Olympia**, both for French and for foreign performers, and there are also smaller venues. For listings of programs see *l'Officiel des Spectacles* or *Pariscope*.

IRCAM (Experimental Institute)
*31 Rue St-Merri, 4e ☎42-77-12-33. Map **10**H10. Métro Rambuteau.*

Maison de Radio-France
116 Av. du Président-Kennedy, 16e ☎45-24-15-16. Métro Ranelagh.

Salle Gaveau
45 Rue la Boétie, 8e ☎45-63-20-30. Map 2F5. Métro Miromesnil.

Salle Pleyel
252 Rue du Faubourg-St-Honoré, 8e ☎45-63-88-73. Map 7E4. Métro Ternes.

Théâtre des Champs-Élysées
15 Av. Montaigne, 8e ☎47-20-38-37. Map 7G4. Métro Alma-Marceau.

Théâtre Musical de Paris
See under *Opera*.

Rock venues

Élysées Montmarte
72 Bd. de Rochechouart, 9e ☎42-52-86-46.

Le Gibus See under *Discos*.

Olympia
28 Bd. des Capucines, 2e ☎47-42-25-49.

Le Palace See under *Discos*.

Dancing

The last tango in Paris still lives on. Dancing with strangers is viewed as a simple, entertaining diversion, just like taking tea in a café.

Adison Square Gardel
23 Rue du Cdt-Mouchotte, 14e ☎43-21-54-58. Map 14L6. Métro Gaité AE VISA
Tea dancing, a throwback to the 1930s in this Franco-American atmosphere, and tangos at night. There's more modern music on offer as well.

Le Balajo
9 Rue de Lappe, 11e ☎47-00-07-87. Map 11I12. Métro Bastille.
Street cleaners, *concièrges*, and a host of beautiful people slumming.

Club 79
79 Champs-Élysées, 8e ☎47-23-68-75. Map 6F3. Métro George V.
Large basement dance hall in a chic location.

La Coupole
102 Bd. Montparnasse, 14e ☎43-20-14-20. Map 14K7. Métro Montparnasse-Bienvenue.
Dancing down in the basement to old-fashioned tangos and waltzes. A motley crowd for politicians to showbiz personalities to artists and students.

Discos

The very word *discothèque* is, of course, French. Paris' discos tend to be wonderfully flashy affairs, with glittery decor and glittery people, throbbing lights, pulsating music, and a generally frenetic atmosphere. Some are more sedate, but only slightly so.

Les Bains
7 Rue du Bourg-l'Abbé, 3e ☎48-87-01-80. Map 10G10. Métro Étienne-Marcel.
Amusing setting in a former public bath house. All types: punks, mods, rockers, cowboys, lots of young people.

Bus Palladium
6 Rue Fontaine, 9e ☎48-74-54-99. Map 4D8. Métro Blanche.
Hot, crowded, loud, friendly. For dancing till you drop.

Le Gibus
18 Faubourg du Temple, 10e ☎47-00-78-88. Map 11G11. Métro République.
The wildest, most far-out young crowd, all costumed in the finery of yesterday and tomorrow. The closest to a New York or London disco; today's rock music.

La Main Jaune
Porte de Champerret, 17e ☎47-63-26-47. Métro Porte-de-Champerret.
Roller disco on the edge of the freeway.

Le Palace
*8 Rue du Faubourg-Montmartre, 9e ☎42-46-10-87. Map **9**F9. Métro Rue Montmartre* AE DC VISA
Still going strong, Paris' best and most popular disco where absolutely anyone and everyone goes. Chic crowd — Paloma Picasso, fashion designers — mingles with hairdressers, perhaps in drag, and, in fact, *Le Tout Paris*. Gay nights, black nights and live concerts.

Salle Wagram
*39 Av. de Wagram, 17e ☎43-80-30-03. Map **6**E3. Métro Ternes.*
Huge former *salle de spectacles*, now transformed into one of the city's most chic discos.

La Scala
*188bis Rue de Rivoli, 1e ☎42-61-64-00. Map **9**H9. Métro Palais-Royal.*
Spacious discotheque equipped with all the latest electronic gadgetry and stunning lighting effects.

Jazz clubs

Once the refuge of American jazz musicians between the wars, and after World War II, Paris still retains its love for jazz, although sometimes with a slightly tired air. Nostalgic.

Le Bilboquet
*13 Rue St Benoît, 6e ☎45-48-81-84. Map **8**I7. Métro St-Germain-des-Prés.*
A jazz hot-spot and an institution, with blues predominating.

Le Cambridge
*17 Av. de Wagram, 17e ☎43-80-34-12. Map **6**E3. Métro Ternes, Étoile.*
Program of exclusively traditional jazz.

Caveau de la Huchette
*5 Rue de la Huchette, 5e ☎43-26-65-05. Map **15**J9. Métro St-Michel* DC
In the heart of the student-jammed Latin Quarter, very popular, excellent live music, dancing.

Jazz-club Lionel Hampton
*Hôtel Meridien, 81 Bd. Gouvion-St-Cyr, 17e ☎47-58-12-30. Map **6**E1. Métro Porte-Maillot* AE DC MC VISA
Top jazz musicians and laid-back atmosphere.

London Tavern
*3 Rue du Sabot, 6e ☎45-48-42-39. Map **8**J7. Métro St-Germain-des-Prés.*
Imitation English pub, but genuine jazz.

Le Montgolfier
*Sofitel Paris, 8-12 Rue Louis Armand, 15e ☎40-60-30-30. Map **18**D3. Métro Corentin-Celton.*
Jazz and vertigo combined on the 23rd floor of this modern hotel.

Le Petit Journal
*71 Bd. St-Michel, 5e ☎43-26-28-59. Map **10**I9. Métro St-Michel.*
New Orleans jazz.

Movie theaters

Foreign movies are either dubbed in French (VF) or presented in the original version, with subtitles (VO). The **Gaumont, Pathé** and **Paramount** chains along the Champs-Élysées are best for the new movies, while the independents of the Left Bank, headed by the **Olympic** and **Action** organizations, present a motley and dazzling selection of revivals from every continent.

Cinemathèque Française
*Palais de Chaillot, Av. Albert-de-Mun, 16e ☎47-04-24-24. Map **12**H2. Métro Trocadéro. Closed Mon. Center Georges Pompidou (5th floor). Rue Beaubourg, 4e ☎42-78-35-57. Métro Rambuteau. Closed Tues.*
France's two national film theaters, sometimes obscure, always fascinating.

Gaumont Les Halles
*1-3 Rue Pierre-Lescot, Forum des Halles (Niveau 3), 1er ☎40-26-12-12. Map **10**H9. Métro Châtelet-Les-Halles.*

Six screens in the new Forum, most modern and convenient of the commercial movie theaters.

La Géode
*26 Av. Corentin Cariou, 20e ☎40-05-70-00. Map **19**C5. Métro Porte de la Villette.*
Amazing movie theater in a steel sphere, with wrap-around screen (see also *Parc de la Villette* in *Sights*)

Les 14-Juillet Bastille
*4 Bd. Beaumarchais, 11e ☎43-57-90-81. Map **11**I12. Métro Bastille.*
Three screens, representing the conscience of French independent cinema.

Kinopanorama
*60 Av. De La Motte Picquet, 15e ☎43-06-50-50. Map **12**J3. Métro La Motte Picquet.*
One of the most elegant of Parisian movie theaters, equipped with Dolby stereo.

La Pagode
*57bis Rue de Babylone, 7e ☎47-05-12-15. Map **13**J5. Métro St-François-Xavier.*
In an impressive Chinese pavilion, this is unquestionably the most beautiful movie theater in the city of Paris.

République Cinémas
*18 Rue du Faubourg-du-Temple, 11e ☎48-05-51-33. Map **11**G11. Métro République.*
Unremittingly experimental.

Le Grand Rex
*1 Bd. Poissonière, 2e ☎42-36-83-93. Map **4**F9. Métro Bonne-Nouvelle.*
Giant theater with 2,800 seats, for big, spectacular movies.

Studio 28
*10 Rue de Tholozé, 18e ☎46-06-36-07. Map **4**C8. Métro Place Blanche.*
Cherished movies of the past — Bunuel, Marx Brothers, W.C. Fields *et al.*

Leo 3 Luxembourg
*67 Rue Monsieur-Le-Prince, 6e ☎46-33-97-77. Map **15**J8. Métro Odéon.*
Three screens, each with a regular midnight showing — a boon for insomniacs, shift-workers or those who dislike rush-hour travel. Deservedly popular.

Vendôme-Opéra
*32 Av. de l'Opéra, 2e ☎47-42-97-52. Map **9**G8. Métro Opéra.*
Specializes in operatic movies.

Nightclubs

In Paris, as elsewhere, club normally means "private," although there are varying degrees of privacy, particularly for visitors. If you are young, or pretty, or well-dressed (ideally all three), however, the chances are you won't be turned away. Otherwise, hotel *concièrges* are often helpful. Private clubs are stuffy about male dress, and ties are expected. Women, however, can be as far out as they like.

Club Olivia Valère
*40 Rue du Colisée, 8e ☎42-25-11-68. Map **7**F5. Métro St-Philippe-du-Roule.*
Lively nightclub popular with the very young and not far from the Champs-Élysées.

Castel ✿
*15 Rue Princesse, 6e ☎43-26-90-22. Map **15**J8. Métro St-Germain-des-Prés* AE
For many years the Castel has been, and still is today, Paris' very best, very private club. Castel is supervised by Jean Castel, who is often referred to as the King of the Paris Night. The club has the prettiest girls in town, not to mention good food. There is an excellent bar and "canteen" on the main floor, with more elegant dining upstairs. There's a disco down in the basement and a video room with airplane seats on an upper floor, plus a music room. This is a real experience — if you are lucky enough to get through the door.

Le Garage
*41 Rue Washington, 8e ☎45-63-21-27. Map **7**F4. Métro George V.*
This bar/disco can be found only a stone's throw away from the Champs-Élysées.

Régine's
*49 Rue Ponthieu, 8e ☎43-59-21-60. Map **7**F5. Métro Franklin-D-Roosevelt* AE
A slightly *démodé* but still glamorous night spot. Good food, international jet set.

Studio 102
*2 Av. des Champs-Élysées, 8e ☎42-89-31-41. Map **6**F3. Métro George V* VISA
This club is a Movie studio during the day, and transforms itself into a discotheque at night, with an atmosphere reminiscent of the 60s. Metallic décor with black predominating.

Opera

The most opulent of the arts has a fitting setting in the magnificent *Opéra*. The huge stage can play to over 2,000 spectators under the Chagall ceiling. Few other theaters in Paris have the facilities to deal with the scope of an opera production. Reserve seats at least two weeks in advance.

Opéra
*Pl. de l'Opéra, 9e ☎47-42-57-50. Map **8**F7. Métro Opéra.*

Opéra-Comique (Salle Favart)
*5 Rue Favart, 2e ☎42-96-06-11. Map **9**F8. Métro Richelieu-Druout.*

Théâtre Musical de Paris-Châtelet
*Pl. du Châtelet, 1er ☎42-33-00-00. Map **10**I9. Métro Châtelet.*

Revues

(See *Cabarets*.) Parisian revues blend nudity with entertainment and unabashed glamor. The formula differs, but establishments usually require customers to spend generously on drinks or dinner. The clientele tends to be made up of expense-account executives entertained by Parisian businessmen, or, perhaps, tourists gawking at the feathers, the sequins and skin.

Alcazar de Paris
*62 Rue Mazarine, 6e ☎43-29-02-20. Map **9**I8. Métro Odèon* AE Ⓓ VISA
Slightly raunchy review, often with transvestites, often satirical. It helps to be able to understand French.

Crazy Horse Saloon See *Cabarets*.

Folies Bergère ✿
*32 Rue Richer, 9e ☎42-46-77-11. Map **4**E9. Métro Cadet, Le Peletier.*
Strictly a theater, with no dinner or drinks required. Payment is simply made by buying a ticket for a seat. Glorious history of Maurice Chevalier, Mistinguett and the stars of Paris, now rather sad.

Lido
*116 Champs-Élysées, 8e ☎45-63-11-61. Map **6**F3. Métro George V* AE Ⓓ VISA
Paris' most lavish revue, with good dancers, acrobats, and magician. Very expensive; mediocre food.

Moulin Rouge
*Pl. Blanche, 9e ☎46-06-00-19. Map **4**D7. Métro Blanche* AE Ⓓ
Immortalized by Toulouse-Lautrec. The same management as the **Lido** (above) but cheaper.

Paradis Latin
*28 Rue du Cardinal-Lemoine, 5e ☎43-25-28-28. Map **16**K10. Métro Cardinal-Lemoine* AE Ⓓ
Wonderful architecture in an old Eiffel warehouse, with a spectacle devised by Jean-Marie Rivière, old-time master of ceremonies.

Theaters

Over a hundred theaters offer more variety than quality — Paris has always preferred the revue, but theater-lovers keep trying.

Antoine-Simone Berriau
*14 Bd. de Strasbourg, 10e ☎42-08-77-71. Map **5**F10. Métro Strasbourg-St-Denis.*
Upper-crust "Boulevard" theater.

La Cartoucherie
Route de la Pyramide, Bois de Vincennes, 12e ☎43-74-24-08/43-74-99-61. (See Vincennes for map location.) Métro Château-

de-Vincennes, then bus no. 306.
There are three theaters grouped in the pleasant surroundings of the Bois de Vincennes.

La Comédie Française
2 Rue de Richelieu, 1er ☎40-15-00-15. Map ***9****H8. Métro Palais-Royal.*
Respectable seat of the French classics; Molière, Racine and other well-established playwrights are performed.

Lucernaire Centre
53 Rue Notre-Dame-des-Champs, 8e ☎45-44-57-34. Map ***14****K7. Métro Vavin.*
Up to six small-scale plays staged in a day.

Odéon
Pl. Paul Claudel 6e ☎43-25-70-32. Map ***15****J8. Métro Odéon.*
Another national theater, bolder than its rival, the *Comédie Française.*

Théâtre National de Chaillot
Pl. du Trocadéro, 16e ☎47-27-81-15. Map ***12****H2. Métro Trocadéro.*
Famous in the 1950s, and today for its technical facilities.

Théâtre Renaud-Barrault
Av. Franklin Roosevelt, 8e ☎42-56-60-70. Map ***7****G5. Métro Champs-Élysées Clemenceau.*
Founded by the legendary couple of French theater, Jean-Louis Barrault and Madeleine Renaud, this theater is devoted to 20thC drama.

Shopping

Paris gave the world the boutique, the small specialty shop that still embodies the intimate character of Parisian shopping. Entire *quartiers* are blanketed with boutiques, the specialties of which range from antiques to zippers. There are good department stores, but it is the boutiques that exhibit the individuality, variety and flair that makes Paris Europe's most seductive city for shopping.

Fine tailoring, luxurious fabrics and the indefinable chic of Parisian clothing is epitomized by the haute couture and designers' ready-to-wear. But Paris fashion is also translated into reasonably priced clothing found in hundreds of small boutiques. Everything to do with fashion is a good buy, provided it is of French origin, mainly because you cannot get the same thing elsewhere at the same price. French perfume, cosmetics, home accessories and lingeries make Paris the woman's ultimate shop window, while men's and children's wear take a distinct second place.

Food and everything related to it — kitchen gadgets, cookbooks, herbs, linens — are especially close to the French heart, with a huge variety available in even the smallest neighborhood shops.

The French are themselves careful shoppers, unhurried by high-pressure sales techniques. While sales personnel have a reputation for indifferent service, things have improved markedly in recent years.

Much of the 8e is devoted to expensive fashion, primarily the Champs-Élysées, Av. Victor-Hugo, Av. Montaigne and the Faubourg-St-Honoré. Off the Champs-Élysées run several arcades filled with shops. The Faubourg-St-Honoré combines luxury shopping with small boutiques in a highly concentrated area. Around the Opéra cluster jewelers, shoe stores and perfumeries.

Trendier and less expensive is the area blossoming around Les Halles, where the old food market once lived. The Forum des Halles, an underground shopping center, combines designer boutiques with colorful, avant-garde fashion, plus furniture, *batterie de cuisine* and interesting home accessories. Adjacent streets are jammed with a collection of original shops with offbeat merchandise.

An eclectic mélange of designer fashion and trendy boutiques is found in St-Germain on the Left Bank, which tends to be slightly less expensive than the Right Bank. All the flea markets offer used clothing and army-surplus goods.

Department stores remain open from 9.30am-6.30pm without interruption Mon-Sat, and some are open until 8pm on Wed. Smaller boutiques generally open Mon-Sat 10am-6pm, although they may close for an hour at lunch. While neighborhood shops often observe the traditional Mon closing, stores in the center stay open. And, while Aug was once the universal vacation month, now most of the larger shops stay open throughout the summer.

Foreign visitors should ask for the *détaxe*, a refund of the French excise tax, returnable upon leaving the country with the purchases. Also, many shops advertise "duty-free" goods, meaning this tax is deducted from the price on the spot. Be wary of this, for the basic price may be raised. Comparison-shopping is useful, particularly when buying perfumes and choosing designer accessories.

Cuisine

Cookware

Paris is a cook's heaven. No other city can compare with the array of food-related objects, often cheaper than and sometimes simply unobtainable elsewhere. Department stores all have large cookware departments, but it is more fun to go directly to the major specialists. Be prepared to pay cash, and ask for shipping and *détaxe* information.

Dehillerin ✿
18 Rue Coquillière, 1er. Map 9G9. Métro Étienne-Marcel.
The Dehillerin is perhaps the best restaurant supply house in the world, this store also sells happily on a smaller scale. Outstanding buys in copper, carbon steel knives, casseroles of all description. Free catalog (also in English) and amiable service from Gaston. Excellent shipping service.

MORA
13 Rue Montmartre, 1er. Map 9G9. Métro Étienne-Marcel.
Smaller selection is offered than in the above supply house, but still a store for true professionals. You may find the cool, even casual service difficult to take.

A. Simon
36 Rue Étienne-Marcel, 2e. Map 9G9. Métro Etienne-Marcel.
Divided into two stores, one with metalware, electrical appliances and knives; the other devoted to pottery, glassware and a reasonable selection of porcelain. Good colorful displays and helpful personnel make shopping here a pleasure.

Food and drink

Every neighborhood has its *charcuteries*, selling pork products, prepared foods and a bit of everything, and its *fromageries*, *caves* and *pâtisseries*. The areas around the Pl. de la Madeleine and Les Halles are particularly exciting.

Androuet
41 Rue d'Amsterdam, 8e. Map 3E7. Métro St-Lazare.
Owned by Pierre Androuet, this store is a temple to cheese. Special boxes for traveling.

Battendier
8 Rue Coquillière, 1er. Map 9G9. Métro Étienne-Marcel AE VISA
A chic *charcuterie* known for its sausages, ham and pâtés.

Bertillon
31 Rue St Louis-en-l'Ile, 4e. Map 10J10. Métro Pont-Marie.
Superb ice cream and sorbets, made from the freshest fruits that change with the seasons.

Cantin Marie-Anne
12 Rue de Champ-de-Mars, 7e. Map 13I4. Métro École-Militaire.
The place to come for traditional cheeses. Mouthwatering selection.

Caves de la Madeleine
24 Rue Boissy d'Anglas, 8e. Map 8G6. Métro Madeleine
This store is nestled in a delightful mews and run by Englishman Steven Spurrier. A wide selection of wines and spirits. Gift-wrapping and a delivery service.

Fauchon
28 Pl. de la Madeleine, 8e. Map 8F6. Métro Madeleine
One of the world's most celebrated food stores, with two large boutiques, Fauchon carries over 20,000 products. Wonderful gift service; will ship anywhere.

La Ferme St-Hubert
21 Rue Vignon, 8e. Map 8F7. Métro Madeleine.
Superb cheeses; helpful service.

Hédiard
21 Pl. de la Madeleine, 8e. Map 8F6. Métro Madeleine
A smaller Fauchon, with exotic products and spices, rare fruits and an outstanding wine selection. Five Paris branches.

Labeyrie
6 Rue Montmartre, 2e. Map 9G9. Métro Étienne-Marcel.
Foie gras, truffles, confits of duck and goose, and all the wonderful foods of the Landes region.

Legrand
1 Rue de la Banque, 2e. Map 9G8. Métro Bourse.
Reasonably priced wines and alcohol, and interesting culinary products.

Lenôtre
44 Rue d'Auteuil, 16e. Métro Michelange-Auteuil.
Now a famous chef, Lenôtre was first a caterer and then became a really outstanding *pâtissier*. Excellent chocolates, ice cream and prepared food.

À l'Olivier
23 Rue de Rivoli, 4e. Map 10I10. Métro Hôtel-de-Ville.
Oil of every imaginable variety, including sheeps' feet oil (for mechanics), but, above all, olive oil.

Piètrement
10 Rue Montmartre, 1er. Map 9G9. Métro Étienne-Marcel.
Foie gras, truffles, dried mushrooms. Charming service.

Poilâne
8 Rue de Cherche-Midi, 6e. Map 14J7. Métro St-Sulpice. 49 Bd. de Grenelle, 16e. Map 12I2. Métro Bir-Hakeim. Forum des Halles, 1er. Map 10H9. Métro Châtelet-Les Halles.
Baked in wood-fueled ovens, containing no preservatives, Lionel Poilâne's crusty loaves are the best in Paris.

Soleil de Provence
6 Rue du Cherche-Midi, 6e. Map 14J7. Métro St-Sulpice.
Fruity olive oil, honeys and olive oil soap.

Department stores

Bazar de l'Hôtel de Ville
55 Rue de la Verrerie, 4e. Map 10I10. Métro Hôtel-de-Ville
Excellent sporting goods, garden tools, books, records, and a dazzling array of hardware.

Bon Marché
38 Rue de Sèvres, 7e. Map 14J6. Métro Sèvres-Babylone
A true department store comprising fresh foods along with clothing, home furnishings and a wide selection of linens.

FNAC
Forum des Halles, 1er. Map 10H9. Métro Châtelet-Les-Halles. 136 Rue de Rennes, 14e. Map 14K6. Métro Montparnasse-Bienvenue. 26 Av. Wagram, 8e. Map 6E3. Métro Charles-de-Gaulle-Étoile.
This store sells discount records, books, small appliances, sports goods, photo equipment. The Forum store specializes in records, audiovisual supplies, photo goods and sports goods; Montparnasse concentrates on video and books; and Av. Wagram stocks the largest selection of audiovisual goods to be found in Paris.

Galeries Lafayette
40 Bd. Haussmann, 9e. Map 8F7. Métro Chaussée-d'Antin, Auber. Maine-Montparnasse Centre, 14e. Map 14K6. Métro Montparnasse-Bienvenue
A serious attempt to update its fashion image has succeeded in

turning both branches of this store into trendy fashion spots, with vast home furnishings departments and a wide selection of porcelain, glassware and cookware. A variety of good, slick ideas, and an abundance of color.

Printemps
64 Bd. Haussmann, 9e. Map 8F7. Métro Havre-Caumartin, Auber AE CB Φ MC VISA
Elegant, with deluxe ready-to-wear on the "Rue de La Mode," and a magnificant stained-glass cupola that is a historical monument. Wide range of lingerie, gourmet boutiques, and a top-floor restaurant renowned for its Art Nouveau decor.

Samaritaine ✿
Pont Neuf, 1er. Map 9H9. Métro Pont-Neuf AE Φ MC VISA
An old-fashioned store noted for its uniforms (chefs' clothes and bartenders' outfits), sports goods and household items. The 10th story of Magasin 2 offers an unparaleled panoramic view over the city.

Aux Trois Quartiers
17 Bd. de la Madeleine, 8e. Map 8F7. Métro Madeleine AE CB Φ MC VISA
A quiet store with polite sales personnel and attentive service. A wide selection of gifts, pleasant accessories and linens. Rarely crowded. Recently totally renovated.

Drugstores

These have nothing to do with American-style drugstores, although they all have pharmacies. Parisian drugstores are mini-shopping centers, meeting places and classy emergency shops that often include movie theaters and restaurants among their distractions. Open daily from 9am to after midnight, they have counters devoted to books, perfume, food, gifts, toys and tobacco. Excellent selection of newspapers and periodicals in foreign languages.

149 Bd. St-Germain 6e. Map 8I7. Métro St-Germain-des-Prés AE Φ MC VISA

133 Av. des Champs-Élysées 8e. Map 6F3. Métro George V AE Φ MC VISA

1 Av. Matignon 8e. Map 7F5. Métro Franklin-D-Roosevelt AE CB Φ MC VISA

Fashion

Bargains

Couturiers and ready-to-wear designers often sell last season's styles, with or without the labels (*dégriffé*), at half-price. The Rue St-Placide, 6e (*Métro Sèvres-Babylone*) and Rue d'Alesia, 14e (*Métro Alesia*) are lined with discount stores for men, women and children.

Bab's ✿
89bis Av. des Ternes, 17e. Map 6D2. Métro Porte-Maillot. 29 Av. Marceau, 16e. Map 6G3. Métro Alma-Marceau AE MC VISA
Nina Ricci, Guy Laroche and others. Georgeous silk blouses.

Bidermann ✿
114 Rue de Turenne, 3e. Map 11H11. Métro Filles-du-Calvaire.
Suits for men by St Laurent and others.

Gigi's Soldes ✿
30 Pl. du Marché-St-Honoré, 1er. Map 8G7. Métro Tuileries AE Φ VISA
French and Italian shoes, superb boots for men and women.

MicMac ✿
13 Rue Laugier, 17e. Map 6D3. Métro Ternes.
Last year's collection at knock-down prices.

Le Mouton à 5 Pattes ✿
8-10 and 48 Rue St-Placide, 6e. Map 14J6&7. Métro St-Placide.
All sorts of bargains are to be found in this store, from last year's shoes and boots to imperceptibly flawed suits and dresses.

La Solderie
85 Rue de la Boetie, 8e. Map 7F4. Métro St Augustin.
Goods by high-class couturiers, such as St Laurent and Chanel, at cut prices.

Children's clothing

Paris is renowned for its stylish and chic children's clothes. Exquisite layettes and hand-embroidered gowns can still be found in Paris but children's fashions are extremely expensive. Many designers (**Dior, Hechter** and others) makes a children's line. The best selection is in department stores. **Baby Dior** has a very upscale range of children's wear from birth upward.

Men's clothing

French styling combines English conservatism with Italian flair. Many couturiers design men's lines (see women's *Couturier boutiques*). Men's clothing is not a good buy in France, with a few exceptions.

Arnys
*14 Rue de Sèvres, 7e. Map **14**J6. Métro Sèvres-Babylone* AE Φ MC VISA

Charvet
*28 Pl. Vendôme, 1er. Map **8**G7. Métro Opéra, Tuileries, Madeleine* AE Φ VISA

Daniel Hechter
*12 Faubourg-St-Honoré, 8e. Map **8**G6. Métro Concorde* AE Φ MC VISA

Gianni Versace
*59ter Rue Bonaparte, 6e. Map **14**J7. Métro St-Germain-des-Prés* AE VISA

Island
*4 Rue Vide-Gousset 2e. Map **9**G9. Métro Bourse* AE Φ VISA

Stanley Bertin
*22 Place St-André-des Arts, 6e. Map **9**I9. Métro St-Michel.*

Western House
*13 Av. de la Grande Armée, 17e. Map **6**E2. Métro Étoile.*

Unisex fashion

Altona
*8 Rue de l'Odéon, 6e. Map **15**J8. Métro Odéon* VISA
Utilitarian chic cavalry jackets, oversized trousers, canvas goods, sweaters.

Opox Rapax
*12 Rue de la Ferronnerie, 1er. Map **9**H9. Métro Châtelet. 64 Rue de Rennes, 6e. Map **14**J7. Métro St-Germain-des-Prés* AE VISA
Imaginative pants and sweaters.

Women's fashion See *Women's clothing*

Household accessories, china, glass and silver

Au Bain Marie
*12 Rue Boissy d'Anglas 8e. Map **8**G6. Métro Concorde* AE
Charming, old-fashioned objects and linens.

Baccarat
*30bis Rue du Paradis, 10e. Map **5**E10. Métro Château-d'Eau* AE VISA
World-renowned crystal, beautiful gifts. Also a fascinating museum of the history of crystal.

Christofle
*12 Rue Royale, 8e. Map **8**G6. Métro Madeleine* AE Φ MC VISA
Magnificent silver flatware in modern and retro patterns.

Lalique
*11 Rue Royale, 8e. Map **8**G6. Métro Madeleine* VISA
Collection of crystal, particularly frosted Art Nouveau and Deco patterns.

Limoges-Unic ✿
*12 and 58 Rue du Paradis, 10e. Map **5**E10. Métro Château-d'Eau* AE Φ VISA
Outlet for France's famed porcelain.

Puiforcat
*131 Bd. Haussmann, 8e. Map **8**F6. Métro-St-Augustin* Φ VISA
Well-designed silver, good selection of gifts.

Jewelry

As in fashion, Paris has the haute couture of jewelry (*haute joaillerie*) and the ready-to-wear. Both are extremely stylish, a wide and interesting range is offered and, compared with the rest of the world, items are competitively priced.

The "hautes" are, broadly speaking, grouped together, all clustered around the Pl. Vendôme.

Boucheron
*26 Pl. Vendôme, 1er. Map **8**G7. Métro Opéra, Concorde* AE Φ VISA

Cartier
*13 Rue de la Paix, 1er. Map **8**F7. Métro Opéra* AE Φ VISA

Ilias Lalaounis
*364 Rue St-Honoré, 1er. Map **8**G7. Métro Opéra, Madeleine* AE Φ

Van Cleef et Arpels
*22 Pl. Vendôme, 1er. Map **8**G7. Métro Opéra-Pyramides* AE Φ

Zolotas
*370 Rue St-Honoré, 1er. Map **8**G7. Métro Madeleine, Concorde* AE Φ

Jewelry boutiques

Comptoir du Kit
*42 Galerie Vivienne, 2e. Map **9**F8. Métro Bourse* VISA

Fabrice
*33 and 54 Rue Bonaparte, 6e. Map **9**I8. Métro St-Germain-des-Prés* AE Φ VISA

Impertinence
*20 Rue du Bac, 7e. Map **8**I7. Métro Rue du Bac.*

Mademoiselle Zaza
*29 Boulevard Raspail, 7e. Map **14**J7. Métro Sèvres-Babylone.*

Leather goods

La Bagagerie ✿
*41 Rue du Four, 6e. Map **15**J8. Métro St-Germain-des-Prés. 12 Rue Tronchet, 8e. Map **8**F7. Métro Madeleine. 74 Rue de Passy, 16e. Métro Muette* AE Φ VISA

Hermès
*24 Faubourg-St-Honoré, 1er. Map **8**F6. Métro Madeleine* AE Φ VISA

Lancel
*43 Rue de Rennes, 6e. Map **14**J7. Métro St-Germain-des-Prés. 4 Rond Point des Champs-Élysées, 8e. Map **14**J7. Métro Franklin-D-Roosevelt* AE Φ VISA

Louis Vuitton
*78bis Av. Marceau, 8e. Map **6**F3. Métro Charles-de-Gaulle-Étoile.*

Lingerie

Beautiful French underwear is considered nearly as important as outerwear, and men's underwear is sexy as well. Lingerie shops often sell swimsuits.

Chantal Thomass
11 Rue Madame, 6e. Map 14J7. Métro St Sulpice CB

Erès
2 Rue Tronchet, 8e. Map 8F7. Métro Madeleine AE ⊕ VISA

Les Nuits d'Elodie
1bis Av. MacMahon, 17e. Map 6E3. Métro Charles-de-Gaulle-Étoile.

Sabbia Rosa
71 Rue des Sts-Pères, 7e. Map 8I7. Métro Sèvres-Babylone AE ⊕ VISA

Markets

Flea markets

Each weekend Paris blossoms with flea markets on the periphery selling mainly antiques of varying quality, old clothes, books, and just plain junk. Open Sat, Sun and sometimes Mon, they invite bargaining. Most vendors will not accept credit cards, but many will ship. The most famous flea market is the *Marché aux Puces* at Porte de Clignancourt.

Marché d'Aligre Pl. d'Aligre, 12e. Métro Ledru-Rollin
Puces de Didot Av. Georges Lafenêstre. Métro Porte-de-Vanves
Puces de Kremlin-Bicêtre La Route de Paris. Métro Porte-d'Italie
Puces de Montreuil Porte de Montreuil. Métro Porte-de-Montreuil

Food markets

Every neighborhood has its street market selling mainly food. Straw baskets and kitchen gadgets can also be good buys. In addition there are several streets known for outdoor food shops, primarily the Rue Mouffetard (*Métro Censier-Daubenton*) and the Rue Cler (*Métro École-Militaire*). These are some of the better, more central markets.

Av. President-Wilson 16e. *Map 6G3*. Métro Alma-Marceau
Av. de Saxe 7e. Map 13J4. Métro École-Militaire
Bd. de Grenelle 15e. Map 12J3. Métro La Motte Picquet-Grenelle *Cité Berryer* 26 Rue Royale, 8e. Map 8G6. Métro Madeleine

Miscellaneous markets

Animals
Quais de Louvre and Mégisserie 1er. Map 9H8&I9. Métro Palais-Royal, Pont-Neuf
Birds
Pl. Louis-Lépine 4e. Map 9I9. Métro Cité. Sun
Books (bouquinists)
Quais des Grands-Augustins, Conti and Malaquais 6er. Map 9I8. Métro St-Michel
Quais de Louvre and Mégisserie 1er. Map 9H8&I9. Métro Palais-Royal, Pont-Neuf
Quai Voltaire 6e. Map 8H7. Métro Rue-de-Bac
Flowers
Pl. Louis-Lépine Quai de la Corse, 4e. Map 9I9. Métro Cité
Pl. de la Madeleine 1er. Map 8F6. Métro Madeleine
Pl. des Ternes 8e. Map 6E3. Métro Ternes
Stamps
Av. Gabriel 1er. Map 7F5. Métro Franklin-D-Roosevelt
Textiles
Marché St-Pierre Pl. St-Pierre. Map 4D9. Métro Anvers

Perfume and cosmetics

Many shops offer "duty-free" perfumes, meaning that the price is lowered by the excise tax, and many just offer discounts. Comparison-shopping is useful, since the best prices are at the duty-free airport shop, although the selection there is certainly more limited.

Dozens of shops surround the Opéra, all selling the major brands of cosmetics and perfumes. These are the slightly more unusual ones.

L'Artisan Parfumeur
*84bis Rue de Grenelle, 6e. Map **8**I6. Métro Rue-du-Bac* AE
Charming, unusual scents such as grapefruit and cinnamon, lovely pot-pourris and gifts for men and women.

Dans un Jardin
*71 Rue la Boétie, 8e. Map **7**F5. Métro St-Philippe-du-Roule, Miromesmil* VISA
Custom-made perfumes and unusual gifts.

Guerlain
*68 Champs-Élysées, 8e, Map **6**F3. Métro George V. 2 Pl. Vendôme, 1er Map **8**G7. Métro Tuileries. 29 Rue de Sèvres, 6e. Map **14**J7. Métro Sèvres-Babylone.*

Roger et Gallet
*62 Faubourg-St-Honoré, 8e. Map **8**F6. Métro Madeleine* AE Φ VISA
Lovely soaps, eau de toilette, bath accessories for men and women.

Sur la Place
*12 Pl. St-Sulpice, 6e. Map **14**J7. Métro St-Sulpice.*
Old-fashioned bath jellies, algae from Brittany, natural beauty products.

Michel Swiss ✿
*16 Rue de la Paix, 1er. Map **8**F7. Métro Opéra* AE Φ VISA

Shoes

Most shoe stores carry goods for men and women, and many stock handbags and luggage. While the well-known labels are expensive. Paris is still a wonderful place for shoes.

Bally
*11 Bd. de la Madeleine, 1er. Map **8**F7. Métro Madeleine. 35 Bd. des Capucines, 9e. Map **8**F7. Métro Opéra* AE Φ MC VISA *Twenty other branches.*

Carel
*4 Rue Tronchet, 8e. Map **8**F7. Métro Madeleine* AE Φ MC VISA *Various other branches.*

Céline
*58 Rue de Rennes, 6e. Map **14**J7. Métro St-Germain-des-Prés. 24 Rue François-1er, 8e. Map **7**G4. Métro Franklin-D-Roosevelt. 3 Av. Victor-Hugo, 16e. Map **6**F2. Métro Charles-de-Gaulle-Étoile* AE Φ VISA

Robert Clergerie
*5 Rue du Cherche-Midi, 6e. Map **14**J7. Métro Sèvres-Babylone* AE VISA

Jocelyn
*Arcades du Lido, 76-78 Champs-Élysées, 8e. Map **7**F4. Métro George V* AE CB Φ MC VISA

Mancini
*72 Av. Victor-Hugo, 16e. Map **6**F2. Métro Victor-Hugo* AE Φ MC
Ready-made and made-to-measure shoes (you must allow at least two weeks).

Maud Frizon
*7 Rue de Grenelle, 6e. Map **14**J7. Métro Sèvres-Babylone. 83 Rue des Sts-Pères, 6e. Map **8**I7. Métro St-Germain-des-Prés* AE Φ VISA

Charles Jourdan
*12 Rue du Faubourg-St-Honoré, 8e. Map **8**G6. Métro Concorde. 5 Bd. de la Madeleine, 1er. Map **8**F7. Métro Madeleine. 60 Rue de Rennes, 6e. Map **14**J7. Métro St-Germain-des-Prés. 86 Av. Champs-Élysées, 8e. Map **7**F4. Métro Franklin-D-Roosevelt. Forum des Halles, 1er. Map **8**I7. Métro Les Halles* AE Φ MC VISA

Stephane Kélian
*62 Rue des Sts-Pères, 6e. Métro St-Germain-des-Prés. Forum des Halles, 1er. Map **8**I7. Métro Châtelet-Les-Halles* VISA

Andrea Pfister
*4 Rue Cambon, 1er. Map **8**G7. Métro Concorde. 56 Rue du Four, 6e. Map **15**J8. Métro Mabillon* AE Φ MC VISA

Sacha
*15 Rue de Turbigo, 1er. Map **10**G9. Métro Étienne-Marcel. 24 Rue de Buci, 6e. Map **9**I8. Métro St-Germain-des-Prés. 43 Bd. Haussmann, 9e. Map **8**F7. Métro Havre-Caumartin* AE Φ VISA

St-Laurent See *Couturier boutiques*.

Textiles

The backbone of the fashion industry, French textiles are sumptuous, beautifully designed and often reasonably priced.

Alexandra
*95 Faubourg-St-Honoré, 8e. Map **8**G6. Métro Concorde.*

Bouchara ✿
*54 Bd. Haussmann, 9e. Map **8**F7. Métro Havre-Caumartin* VISA
Five other branches also.

Max
*70 Champs-Élysées, 8e. Map **7**F4. Métro George V* AE VISA

Rodin
*36 Champs-Élysées, 8e. Map **7**F4. Métro Franklin-D-Roosevelt* VISA

Toys

For toy shops see *Paris for children*.

Women's clothing

Boutiques

Paris is renowned for its boutiques, which are liberally scattered around the city. A selection is listed below, but you will certainly make you own discoveries.

Agnes B
*3 Rue du Jour, 1er. Map **9**G9. Métro Les Halles* AE Φ
Smart quilted coats, sportswear and wild colors.

Anastasia
*18 Rue de l'Ancienne-Comédie, 6e. Map **8**I8. Métro Odéon* AE
Capes, romantic country clothes with a Russian flair.

Autour du Monde
*12 Rue des Francs-Bourgeois, 8e. Map **11**I11. Métro Saint-Paul* CB
Fashionable sportswear for the younger generation. Sometimes crowded.

Dorothée Bis
*17 Rue de Sèvres, 6e. Map **14**J7. Métro Sèvres-Babylone. 10 Rue Tronchet, 9e. Map **8**F7. Métro*

*Madeleine. Forum des Halles, 1er. Map **10**H9. Métro Châtelet-Les-Halles* AE VISA
Young, inventive clothes in bright colors and avant-garde styles.

Boutique Lacoste
*Galerie du Claridge, 74 Champs-Élysées, 8e and branches. Map **7**F4. Métro George V* AE Ⓓ VISA
The entire range of Lacoste clothes and luggage is available here, all emblazoned with the ubiquitous crocodile motif.

Cacharel
*165 Rue de Rennes, 6e. Map **14**J7. Métro St-Sulpice. 34 Rue Tronchet, 9e. Map **8**F7. Métro Madeleine. 7 Rue de Passy, 16e. Map **6**I2. Métro Passy* AE Ⓓ MC VISA
Young, classical clothes, never quite in or out of style.

Chantal Thomass
*5 Rue du Vieux-Colombies, 6e. Map **14**J7. Métro St Sulpice* CB
Revival of very sexy and feminine styles.

Chloé
*3 Rue de Gribeauval, 7e. Map **8**I7. Métro Rue-du-Bac. 60 Rue Faubourg-St-Honoré, 1er. Map **8**G6. Métro Concorde* AE Ⓓ MC VISA
Trendsetting and elegant clothes designed by Karl Lagerfeld.

Comme des Garçons
*40 Rue Étienne Marcel, 2e. Map **10**G9. Métro Étienne Marcel* AE CB VISA
This is Japan's most strikingly original fashion house, with beautifully made clothes. The cutting edge of avant garde fashion, like the pages of *Vogue* come to life.

Coulountjios ✿
*3 Rue du Cygne, 1er. Map **9**H9. Métro Les Halles.*
Exciting furs with hand-painted linings.

France Faver
*79 Rue des Sts-Pères, 6e. Map **8**I7. Métro Sèvres-Babylone* AE MC VISA
Semi-made-to-measure clothing, elegant and refined. Lovely hats.

France Rive Droite
*Galerie du Claridge, 74 Champs-Élysées. Map **7**F4. Métro George V* AE Ⓓ MC VISA
Ready-to-wear clothes and accessories bearing designer labels are among the choice goods available in this exclusive and central shopping precinct.

Daniel Hechter
*12 Faubourg-St-Honoré, 8e. Map **8**G6. Métro Concorde* AE Ⓓ MC VISA
This boutique specializes in young, classic, well-cut sportswear. Four other branches.

Kenzo ✿
*3 Pl. des Victoires, 2e. Map **9**G8. Métro Bourse* AE VISA
One of Paris's most innovative designers, Kenzo introduces offbeat styles often later adopted by the stuffier couturiers. Fabric and workmanship not always of high quality.

Laïmoun ✿
*2 Rue de Tournon, 6e. Map **15**J8. Métro Odéon* AE MC VISA
A very special boutique-find in the Latin Quarter. Everything here is designed in Lebanon and is finely crafted from beautiful, hand-woven fabrics. Items range from casually elegant day wear to sumptuous caftan-style gowns, all with sophisticated styling adapted from traditional Lebanese garments. Laïmoun also feature unusual accessories and at-home items.

Thierry Mugler
*10 Pl. des Victoires, 2e. Map **9**G8. Métro Bourse* AE Ⓓ VISA
Tough chic.

Maud Perl
*47 Quai des Grands Augustins, 6e. Map **9**I8. Métro Odéon, Saint-Michel* VISA
If you are saving your money for a Paris creation that is both elegant and versatile, this is it. Designed by Maud Perl, all the clothes in this boutique are fashioned out of hand-dyed silk — every texture and color imaginable — from subtle and luminous earth tones and pastels to those of a brilliant, jewel-like hue, each in textures ranging from nubby raw silk to the shimmering and nearly diaphanous. Every item is a well-made classic, eminently wearable for nearly any occasion.

Georges Rech ✿
*54 Rue Bonaparte, 6e. Map **14**J7. Métro St-Germain-des-Prés. 23 Av. Victor-Hugo, 16e. Map **6**F2. Métro Charles-de-Gaulle-Étoile* AE Ⓓ VISA
Smart, wearable clothes co-ordinated in chic, elegant ensembles.

Sonia Rykiel
4 and 6 Rue de Grenelle, 6e. Map 8I7. Métro St-Sulpice. 70 Faubourg-St-Honoré, 8e. Map 8G6. Métro Concorde AE
Sleek, unlined knits and accessories, plus feathered and sequined evening wear. Original and amusing. Also mohair jackets and angora sweaters.

Ventilo
59 Rue Bonaparte, 6e. Map 14J7. Métro St-Germain-des-Prés AE Φ VISA
Handsome dresses and separates in unusual fabrics.

Victoire
12 Pl. des Victoires, 1er. Map 9G8. Métro Bourse AE Φ VISA
Top designers, very chic with relaxed sales personnel. Co-ordinated accessories. A favorite with fashion editors.

Couturier boutiques

Designers' clothing, ready-to-wear and at much lower prices than the haute couture, is still expensive but stunning, with high-quality styling and fabrics and an excellent standard of workmanship.

Pierre Balmain
44 Rue François-1er, 8e. Map 7G4. Métro Franklin-D-Roosevelt AE Φ
Slightly boring collection, but attractively simple and always safe.

Pierre Cardin
27 Av. Victor Hugo, 16e. Map 6F2. Métro Étoile AE Φ
Eccentric women's fashions; men's clothing as well.

Chanel
31 Rue Cambon, 1er. Map 8G7. Métro Concorde AE
Little suits, quilted handbags, jewelry; a direct reflection of the couture.

Christian Dior
26-32 Av. Montaigne, 8e. Map 7G4. Métro Alma-Marceau AE Φ VISA
Discreet daytime dresses, glamorous evening wear; sportswear in the boutique **Tricots**.

Louis Féraud
2 Pl. Porte Maillot, 17e. Map 6E2. Métro Port Maillot. 88 Faubourg-St-Honoré, 1er. Map 8F5. Métro Champs-Élysées-Clemenceau AE Φ VISA
A favorite of showbiz clients, noted for long gowns and evening wear.

Givenchy
3 Av. George V, 8e. Map 7G4. Métro Alma-Marceau. 66 Av. Victor-Hugo, 8e. Map 6F2. Métro Victor-Hugo AE Φ
Once an elegant, creative designer but without a good collection for several seasons. Wide selection of classics.

Lanvin
22 Faubourg-St-Honoré, 1er. Map 8G6. Métro Concorde AE Φ VISA
Attractive cocktail and evening dresses. A far cry from the famous couture house of the 1920s.

Ted Lapidus
35 Rue François-1er, 8e. Map 7G4. Métro Franklin-D-Roosevelt AE Φ MC VISA
Good casualwear, especially coats, and lovely fabrics. Classic and fanciful designs in a variety of colors. Five other branches.

Guy Laroche ✿
27 Av. Montaigne, 8e. Map 7G4. Métro Alma-Marceau Φ VISA
The least expensive designers' ready-to-wear; nothing too way out but everything very wearable if you like a "good," timeless look. Four other boutiques.

Hanae Mori
17 Av. Montaigne, 8e. Map 7G4. Métro Franklin-D-Roosevelt AE
Sumptuous silks, Japanese-inspired design. A collection of skirts and jackets. Free alteration service.

Nina Ricci
39 Av. Montaigne, 8e, Map 7G4. Métro Franklin-D-Roosevelt AE Φ VISA
Safe fashions in beautiful fabrics. Irresistible accessories for the evening. Conservative suits in a variety of fabrics. Sales models in basement.

St-Laurent Rive Gauche
6 Pl. St Sulpice, 6e. Map 14J7. Métro St Sulpice AE Φ VISA
Still supreme after more than 30yrs. Elegant, classic, with dash and versatility. Top quality fabrics and impeccable cuts. Collectible fashions that can be built on each season. Four other branches.

Haute couture

Opulent, made-to-measure clothing is the specialty that made the Paris fashion industry the best and most famous in the world. Each couturier has a distinct style which can be seen during the showings, normally in Jan (for summer) and July (for winter clothing) when the new collections are modeled for prospective clients. Tickets for these fashion showings can be obtained through hotel *concierges*, or directly from the couture houses. *Concierges* can also arrange a private video presentation of any of the main couture houses' current collection.

Pierre Balmain
44 Rue François-1er, 8e ☎47-20-35-34. Map **7** *F4. Métro Franklin-D-Roosevelt* AE Φ

Pierre Cardin
27 Av. Victor Hugo, 16e ☎45-01-69-53. Map **6** *F2. Métro Étoile* AE Φ

Chanel
31 Rue Cambon, 1er ☎42-61-54-55. Map **8** *G7. Métro Madeleine, Opéra* AE

Christian Dior
30 Av. Montaigne, 8e ☎47-23-54-55. Map **7** *G4. Métro Alma-Marceau* AE Φ

Louis Féraud
88 Faubourg-St-Honoré, 8e ☎42-65-27-29. Map **8** *F6. Métro Madeleine* AE Φ MC VISA

Ted Lapidus
35 Rue François-1er, 8e ☎47-20-56-14. Map **7** *G4. Métro Franklin-D-Roosevelt* AE Φ MC VISA

Clothing sizes

When shops give clothing sizes in inches or centimeters, use the following conversion scale to determine the correct size

12 *in*	16	20	24	28	32	36	40	44	48
30 *cm*	40	50	60	70	80	90	100	110	120

When standardized codes are used, although these may be found to vary considerably, the following provides a useful guide.

Women's clothing sizes

UK/US sizes	8/6	10/8	12/10	14/12	16/14	18/16
French sizes	38/34N	40/36N	42/38N	44/40N	46/42N	48/44N
Bust in/cm	31/80	32/81	34/86	36/91	38/97	40/102

Men's clothing sizes

European code (suits)	44	46	48	50	52	54	56
Chest in/cm	34/86	36/91	38/97	40/102	42/107	44/112	46/117
Collar in/cm	13½/34	14/36	14½/37	15/38	15½/39	16/41	16½/42
Waist in/cm	28/71	30/76	32/81	34/86	36/91	38/97	40/102
Inside leg in/cm	28/71	29/74	30/76	31/79	32/81	33/84	34/86

Men's and women's shoe sizes

UK/US sizes	3/4½	4/5½	5/6½	6/7½	7/8½	8/9½	9/10½	10/11½	11/12½
European	36	37	38	39	40	41	42	43	44

Guy Laroche
29 Av. Montaigne, 8ᵉ ☎47-23-78-72. Map **7***G4. Métro Alma-Marceau*
AE Φ VISA

Hanae Mori
17 Av. Montaigne, 8ᵉ ☎47-23-52-03. Map **7***G4. Métro Alma-Marceau*
AE

Nina Ricci
39 Av. Montaigne, 8ᵉ ☎47-23-78-88. Map **7***G4. Métro Franklin-D-Roosevelt* AE Φ VISA

Yves St-Laurent
5 Av. Marceau, 16ᵉ ☎47-23-72-71. Map **6***G3. Métro Alma-Marceau.*

Jean-Louis Scherrer
51 Av. Montaigne, 8ᵉ ☎43-59-55-39. Map **7***G4. Métro Alma-Marceau.*

Torrente
9 Faubourg-St-Honoré, 1ᵉʳ ☎42-66-14-14. Map **8***G6. Métro Concorde*
AE Φ MC

Emmanuel Ungaro
2 Av. Montaigne, 8ᵉ ☎47-23-61-94. Map **7***G4. Métro Alma-Marceau*
AE Φ VISA

Biographies

A list of the famous whose names are linked with Paris would be endless. The following personal selection pays particular attention to those mentioned in this book.

Balzac, Honoré de *(1799-1850)*
Author of the great series of novels and stories called *La Comédie Humaine*. Many of these portray intimately the life of Paris, its inhabitants and their social mores.

Barrault, Jean-Louis *(born 1910)*
Author, outstanding artist of mime and director, who became internationally famous after his performance in Marcel Carne's celebrated movie *Les Enfants du Paradis* (1944).

Chevalier, Maurice *(1888-1972)*
Actor, dancer and singer, who often appeared in English-speaking movies as the embodiment of urbane Parisian charm.

Clemenceau, Georges *(1841-1929)*
Politician and journalist. Known as "the tiger" because of his tough belligerence. Clemenceau was Premier in 1906-09 and 1917-20.

Cocteau, Jean *(1889-1963)*
A flamboyant genius who achieved fame as an artist, novelist (*Les Enfants Terribles*), screenwriter and movie director (*La Belle et la Bête*) and playwright (*Orphée*).

Colbert, Jean-Baptiste *(1619-83)*
Most effective of Louis XIV's ministers. His wise financial policies greatly enriched the state.

Colette *(1873-1954)*
Author of vividly sensual and perceptive novels, such as *Chéri* and *La Chatte*. She lived for a time in the Palais-Royal.

De Gaulle, Charles *(1890-1970)*
Soldier and statesman. After leading the Free French during the war, he headed a provisional government from 1944-46. In 1958 he

came out of retirement to lead France again and draw up a new constitution, resigning in 1969.

Dreyfus, Alfred *(1859-1935)*

Jewish army officer imprisoned in 1894 on a false charge of treason. The subsequent attempts by Zola and others to exonerate him split France into bitterly opposed factions and opened up an ugly blister of anti-semitism.

Gambetta, Léon Michel *(1838-82)*

French leader during the Franco-Prussian War of 1870-71. He is famous for his daring escape from Paris by balloon when the city was under siege.

Geneviève, Saint *(c.422-512)*

Patron saint of Paris. She calmed the Parisians by correctly predicting that Attila the Hun would not attack the city in AD451. Ten years later, she smuggled in food when Paris was besieged by the Franks.

Giscard d'Estaing, Valéry *(born 1926)*

Finance minister under de Gaulle. Leader of Independent Republican Party from 1967. President of France 1974-81.

Haussmann, Georges Eugène *(1809-91)*

As Prefect of the Seine under Napoleon III, he re-shaped large areas of Paris, creating boulevards, squares, parks and bridges. His grand, triumphal style is now an integral part of the city's personality.

Hugo, Victor *(1802-85)*

A towering figure in French literature and the leader of the Romantic movement in France. Author of *Notre-Dame de Paris* (*The Hunchback of Notre Dame*) and *Les Misérables*, he was also a member of parliament. As writer and politician he was a fierce champion of liberty and justice.

Lafayette, Marquis de *(1757-1834)*

A dashing and glamorous figure who fought against Britain in the American War of Independence, commanded the Paris National Guard after the fall of the Bastille, and was the main author of the Declaration of Rights.

Malraux, André *(1901-76)*

Novelist, art historian, revolutionary fighter, resistance hero and de Gaulle's Minister of Culture from 1958-69.

Mansart, François *(1598-1668)*

Architect who created the Classical style in French architecture, for example the Hôtel Carnavalet, and gave his name to the high-pitched Mansard roof.

Mansart, Jules Hardouin- *(1645-1708)*

Great nephew of François and chief architect to Louis XIV. His designs include the Grand Trianon and the Dôme church.

Mazarin, Jules *(1602-61)*

Cardinal and statesman. Chief Minister of France during the regency of Anne of Austria, mother of Louis XIV.

Mitterrand, François *(born 1916)*

Leader of the Socialist Party and President of the Republic since 1981. His election was hailed with wild celebration in the streets of Paris by young supporters of the Left.

Piaf, Edith *(1915-63)*

Singer, actress and cabaret performer, whose small size and lively personality won her the nickname "*La Môme*" (the sparrow), and whose inspired rendering of such songs as *La Vie en Rose*, *Milord* and *Je ne regrette rien* seemed to epitomize the spirit of Paris.

Pompadour, Marquise de *(1721-64)*

Mistress of Louis XV and a ruthless political intriguer. For 20yrs she unofficially controlled the French government. A lavish partron of the arts, she also helped to lead France into financial, political and military disaster.

Pompidou, Georges *(1911-74)*
De Gaulle's successor as president, he remained in office until his death. Many of the new building developments in Paris have resulted from his campaign to "modernize" the city.

Proust, Marcel *(1871-1922)*
One of the most influential novelists of all time. His fame rests on a seven-part work, *À la Recherche du Temps Perdu* (*Remembrance of Things Past*), a minutely detailed and searching autobiographical work. Proust was born in Paris and lived there for most of his life.

Richelieu, Armand Jean du Plessis *(1585-1642)*
Cardinal and effective ruler of France under Louis XIII, he greatly increased the power of France and the crown. He was an energetic patron of literature and founded the Académie Française.

Robespierre, Maximilien *(1758-94)*
Revolutionary leader and architect of the Reign of Terror, he was executed in his turn on the guillotine.

Sartre, Jean-Paul *(1886-1980)*
Novelist, playwright, existentialist philosopher, left-wing polemicist and doyen of the Left Bank intelligentsia. He expounded his ideas in philosophical works such as *L'Être et le Néant* (*Being and Nothingness*) and in novels such as *Les Chemins de la Liberté* (*Roads to Freedom*).

Paris for children

Paris is a city of adult pleasures where the world of childhood innocence is a restricted domain — and perhaps all the more cherished on that account. The needs of children are catered to in many imaginative ways, and Paris can be a rich and exciting place for the young. But it can also be frustrating and claustrophobic, especially for active and restless youngsters. The perfect illustration is the Parisian park. Although the city has a large amount of green space per inhabitant, much of it is in the form of small, well-tailored public gardens bristling with signs telling visitors to keep off the grass. The inevitable children's play area, with its sandbox and sometimes slide and swings, is a welcome feature but no substitute for the open space where children can kick a ball or roll in the grass. On the positive side, the larger parks offer more exciting distractions such as donkey rides and miniature farms, and there are many fun places for children: zoos, museums, theaters, circuses.

Having children with you in Paris means careful planning if they are to get the best out of their stay. A good way to keep abreast of children's events is to read the section "Pour les jeunes" in the weekly event guide called *l'Officiel des Spectacles*.

Parks and zoos

Top of the list is the **Jardin d'Acclimatation** ( ) which is a veritable children's paradise on the edge of the *Bois de Boulogne* offering enough distractions to please the most demanding youngster, including a puppet show, distorting mirrors, an archery range, miniature golf (minigolf), driving in mini-cars organized by the police, a dolphinarium and a small zoo. Kids will enjoy riding there on a miniature train from Porte Maillot. The rest of the Bois is not ideal for children, for the most part, but there is a boating lake.

The Bois de *Vincennes* also has boating lakes and the best zoo in the city. Another but less exciting zoo is to be found in the *Jardin des Plantes*. Other parks to take children to are: the *Buttes Chaumont*, with dramatic scenery, grass to walk on, roller-skating, boating and donkey rides; the *Champ-de-Mars*, with a playground for skate-boards and roller-skating, donkey-rides, and puppet shows; the *Luxembourg* gardens, which is excellent, with donkey rides, a pond for toy boats and a large marionette theater; the *Palais de Chaillot* gardens, E side, for an underground acquarium and small playground; **Ranelagh Gardens** (*Av. Raphael, 16^e*) for a playground, cycling and roller-skating track, donkey rides, merry-go-round, puppet shows; the highly imaginative Jardin d'Enfants in the park of *Les Halles*; and the *Tuileries* gardens, which has small play areas, donkey rides, puppet shows and two ponds for toy boats.

Museums and workshops

The main museums that give special emphasis to children and with supervised activities are the *en Herbe* museum in the Jardin d'Acclimatation, the **Musée des Enfants** (part of the *Art Moderne de la Ville de Paris* museum), the *Arts Décoratifs* museum and the *Pompidou Center*. But for sheer old-fashioned fun there is no museum that can beat the *Grévin* with its waxworks and conjuring show. Other museums that children enjoy visiting are: the *Arts et Traditions Populaires* museum with everyday objects from past life in France, including toys; the *Palais de la Découverte*, a science museum with a planetarium, the **Army Museum** at *Les Invalides*; the *Marine* museum; and the technical museum in the *Conservatoire des Arts et Métiers*, with its push-button working models of machines.

There are a number of workshops offering a range of crafts and activities for children. Here are some of them.

L'Abécédaire 68 Rue Crozatier, 12e ☎43-43-25-36
Ateliers des Enfants 32 Rue de la Solidarite, 19e ☎42-05-61-73
Centre Franco-Americain 261 Bd. Raspail, 14e ☎43-35-21-50
Mosaïque l'Atelier des Enfants 13 Cité Dupont, 11e ☎43-57-93-37
Etude et Action Atelier 31 Rue Chapon, 3e ☎42-77-09-00
Maison des Jeunes et de la Culture 4 Rue J. Jacques Rousseau, 1er ☎42-60-20-24. (Branches also in 6e, 10e, 11e, 13e, 14e, 15e, 16e, 17e, 18e and 20e)

Theaters, movies, circuses and other events

Apart from the puppet shows in the parks (see opposite), there are many theaters that stage special performances for children. A list of these, along with other children's events such as children's movies and circuses, can be found in the "Pour les jeunes" section of *l'Officiel des Spectacles*. For a list of café-theaters which often have matinées for children, see *Nightlife*.

Other ideas

Most children enjoy climbing up to the high vantage points of Paris (*Tour Eiffel*, *Tour Montparnasse*, *Arc de Triomphe*, *Notre-Dame*, *Sacré-Coeur*) or, by contrast, plunging underground into the Sewers — *Égouts* and *Catacombs*, but the latter is not for the squeamish.

The Sunday bird market on the *Ile de la Cité* is always crowded, and river and canal trips are also popular with the young. And if you go up to *Montmartre* you can take them on the funicular railroad. There are also annual events that are great attractions for kids, such as the Fête du Pont-Neuf, Marais Festival and Feux de St-Jean (see *Calendar of events* in *Planning* for full list).

Toy shops

French toys can be sophisticated, well-designed and expensive. Many are quite beautiful, particularly marionettes, model cars and boats, and dolls.

Ali Babba 29 Av. de Tourville, 7e ☎45-55-10-85. Métro École-Militaire AE ⊕ VISA
Farandole 48 Av. Victor-Hugo, 8e ☎45-01-72-32. Métro Victor-Hugo
Jouets Montparnasse 33 Bd. Edgar-Quinet, 14e ☎43-20-98-79
Le Ciel est à tout le monde 10 Rue Gay-Lussac, 5e ☎46-33-21-50
Le Nain Bleu 406 Rue St-Honoré, 1er ☎42-60-39-01. Métro Concorde AE VISA

For information on children's clothes see *Shopping*.

Baby sitters

The following operate baby-sitting services.

Catholic Institute 21 Rue d'Assas, 6e ☎42-22-41-80
General Association of Paris Medical Students 91 Bd. de l'Hôpital, 13e ☎45-86-52-02. (Daily 2-7pm)
Kid Service 17 Rue Molière, 1er ☎42-96-04-16
Maman Poule 13 Rue Paul-Chatrousse, 92200 Neuilly ☎47-47-78-78

For information about sports, including roller-skating and skate-boarding, see *Sports and activities*.

Sports and activities

In a city as devoted to urban pleasures as Paris it is perhaps surprising to find that there is a rich choice of sports both for those who want to take part and for those who prefer to watch. Within the city boundaries, where space is at a premium, it is easier to pursue indoor than outdoor sports, but on the periphery a full range of open-air sports is available.

Pursuing a sport in Paris can be an expensive business, but is not necessarily so. Many facilities, often in the form of multi-purpose leisure complexes, are provided by the City of Paris, and these can be used by the public at relatively low cost. For details contact **Allô Sports** (*☎42-76-54-54*). For a list that includes private multi-purpose clubs get in touch with the organization **CIDJ** (*101 Quai Branly, 75015 Paris ☎45-66-40-20*). Some sporting facilities are also listed in the weekly magazines *L'Officiel des Spectacles* and *Pariscope* and in the English magazine *Passion*, published approximately every six weeks. The best way to keep abreast of events is to read the daily sports newspaper *L'Équipe*.

Conveniently, the 16e contains the major tennis and soccer stadiums **Roland Garros** and **Parc des Princes**, as well as **Longchamp** and **Auteuil** racecourses in the Bois de Boulogne. The main arena for spectator sport is the **Palais Omnisports de Bercy** near the Gare de Lyon, where you can see anything from basketball and judo to motorcycle racing and show jumping.

As a starting point, the following section is an A-Z guide to the main sports, games and other leisure activities in and around Paris.

Athletics
There are numerous centers in Paris where you can practice athletics. Contact the **Fédération Française d'Athlétisme** (*10 Rue de Faubourg-Poissonnière, 75010 Paris ☎47-70-90-61*) or write to **Bureau des Sports** (*17 Bd. Morland, 75181 Paris*) for a list of stadiums.

Auto racing
One of the world's geat auto-racing circuits is at **Le Mans**, about 184km (115 miles) sw of Paris, where the 24hr road race takes place every year in mid-June.

For further information contact the **Fédération Française de Sport Automobile** (*136 Rue de Longchamp, 75016 Paris ☎ 47–27–97–39*).

Bicycling
Cycle racing is another French mania culminating in the annual Tour de France which finishes in Paris in July. A good idea is to make use of the *Train plus vélo* scheme offered by the French National Railways (SNCF) which gives you a day's excursion with bicycle rental thrown in.

For general inquiries get in touch with the **Fedération Française du Cyclisme** (*43 Rue de Dunkerque, 75010 Paris ☎42-85-41-20*).

Boating
Pleasure boats can be rented at the following parks:
Bois de Boulogne Métro Porte-Dauphine.
Bois de Vincennes Métro Château-de-Vincennes.
Parc de Buttes-Chaumont Métro Buttes-Chaumont.

Boules
This game, and its close relative, *pétanque*, are national obsessions in France. Walk into almost any park in Paris on a Sat or Sun afternoon, and you will find a series of amateur matches in progress on any convenient patch of earth or gravel. To find out more contact:
Lique de l'Ile de France de la Fédération Française de Pétanque et de Jeu Provençal 9 Rue Duperré, 75009 Paris ☎48-74-61-63

Bowling
The largest alley is the **Bowling de Paris** (*Jardin d'Acclimatation, Bois de Boulogne ☎47-47-77-55*). Other "bowlings" are advertised in *L'Officiel des Spectacles* and *Pariscope*.

Boxing
Both the English and French varieties of boxing are practiced in Paris.

For the former contact the **Fédération Française de Boxe** (*62 Rue Nollet, 75017 Paris ☎48-78-14-93*), and for the latter the **Fédération Française de Boxe Française-Savate et Disciplines Assimilées** (*25 Bd. des Italiens, 75002 Paris ☎47-42-82-27*).

Bridge
There are several good bridge clubs in Paris where you can also play backgammon and gin rummy:
Bridge Club de Paris 68 Bd. de Courcelles, 17e ☎47-63-68-31
Bridge Club Étoile 99 Rue de la Pompe, 16e ☎45-53-54-40

For further information contact the **Fédération Française de Bridge** (*73 Av. Charles de Gaulle, 92200 Neuilly ☎47-38-24-40*).

Chess
You will find that chess is played in many Paris cafés as well as in special clubs. The **Ligue d'Ile de France d'Échecs** (*33-37 Quai de Grenelle, 15ᵉ ☎45-78-98-43*) can provide information.

Dance
Whether your bent is toward classical ballet, flamenco, rock or folk, there is sure to be a dance center in Paris to suit you. Ask at the **Fédération Française de la Danse** (*12 Rue St-Germain-l'Auxerrois, 75001 Paris ☎42-36-19-61*).

Fishing
Fédération Interdépartementale des Associations de Pêche et de Pisciculture (*8 Rue Léon Frot, 11ᵉ ☎43-48-36-34*) for information.

Football (soccer)
The main Paris stadium is the **Parc des Princes** (*Porte de St-Cloud, 16ᵉ*) near the s end of the Bois de Boulogne, where such events as the French Cup Final (either May or June) are held.

For more details contact the **Fédération Française de Football** (*60bis Av. d'Iéna, 75016 Paris ☎47-20-65-40*) or the **Ligue-Parisienne de Football** (*5 Pl. de Valois, 75001 Paris ☎42-61-56-47*).

Gardens
There are floral gardens in the **Bois de Vincennes** and the **Bois de Boulogne**, and the **Parc de Bagatelle** also forms part of the latter. Also worth a visit are the **Jardin des Plantes** and the **Jardin Fleuriste** (*Porte d'Auteuil*) where all the capital's flowers are grown. There is also a greenhouse with exotic and tropical plants, as well as a palm house.

Many châteaux in the Ile de France have beautiful gardens and are worth a visit.

Among the more unusual gardens are the **Albert Kahn Gardens**, on the banks of the Seine in Boulogne-Billancourt, and the rose museum at L'Häy-les-Roses, just outside Paris.

Golf
Most of the best golf courses belong to clubs, which will admit players on payment of a green fee and where you can also rent clubs and other golfing equipment. Public golf courses also welcome visitors.

For further details about golfing facilities contact the **Fédération Française de Golf** (*69 Av. Victor-Hugo, 75016 Paris ☎45-00-62-20*).

Gymnastics
There are plenty of gymnasiums in Paris. For a list contact **Allô Sports** (☎42-76-54-54) or the **Fédération Française d'Education Physique et de Gymnastique Volontaire** (*2 Rue de Valois, 75001 Paris ☎42-96-12-80*).

Health clubs
Although there are many health clubs in Paris, most are open to members only. However, **La Sauna du Louvre** (*274 Rue St-Honoré, 1ᵉʳ ☎42-60-61-26*) is open to visitors. Many hotels have saunas and other health facilities for residents. For exercise classes, including aerobics and "dancersize," go to **Espace Vit'Halles** (*48 Rue Rambuteau, 4ᵉ ☎42-77-21-71*).

Horseback racing

The principal racecourses are **Longchamp** (*Bois de Boulogne*) and **St-Cloud** (*12km (8 miles) w of Paris*) for flat-racing, and **Auteuil** (*Bois de Boulogne, Métro Porte d'Auteuil*) for steeple-chasing. Other courses in or near Paris are found at Chantilly, Enghien, Evry, Maisons-Laffitte and Vincennes.

Longchamp is a superb racecourse, and has a restaurant overlooking the track. The biggest racing event, the Prix de l'Arc de Triomphe, is held there on the first Sun in Oct.

Ice-skating

There are several ice-rinks in Paris where skates can also be rented. One is the **Gaîté Montparnasse** (*16 Rue Vercingétorix, 14e ☎43-21-60-60*). For a list of the many other rinks and for more specific information try the **Fédération Française des Sports de Glace** (*42 Rue du Louvre, 75001 Paris ☎42-61-51-38*).

Language courses

Courses can be booked from your country of origin; the French Embassy will have general information as well as details of how to apply.

The following associations organize courses for all ages and all levels.

Alliance Française 101 Bd. Raspail, 75006 Paris ☎45-44-38-28
Eurocentre de Paris 13 Passage Dauphine, 75006 Paris ☎43-25-81-40

Riding

There are many riding stables in the Paris region, although they tend to be in the outlying areas, such as the Bois de Boulogne and the Bois de Vincennes. Contact the **Ligue Équestre de Paris** (*51 Rue Dumont d'Urville, 75016 Paris ☎45-00-48-74*) — afternoons only — for details of horse shows.

Roller-skating

It's as much fun to watch the skills of others as it is to participate at a number of outdoor roller-skating and skate-boarding *pistes* such as the big concourse at the **Palais de Chaillot**. Or try a roller-skating discotheque like **La Main Jaune** (*Pl. de la Porte Champerret, 17e ☎47-63-26-47*) where you can rent skates for the evening — open to children during the day.

Rugby

For rugby union contact the **Fédération Française de Rugby** (*7 Cité d'Antin, 75009 Paris ☎48-74-84-75*). Important rugby (as well as soccer) fixtures are held at the **Parc des Princes** (*Métro Porte de St-Cloud*).

Skate-boarding

As with roller-skating you can skate-board on the concourse of the Palais de Chaillot as well as other unofficial *pistes*, or you can choose a special skate-board park.

Squash

Though squash is an increasingly popular sport in France, there are still relatively few courts in the center of Paris, and they usually require membership. There are excellent courts at **Tour Montparnasse** (*37 Av. du Maine, 15e ☎45-38-66-20*) and at **Le Squash Front de Seine** (*21 Rue Gaston-de-Cavaillet, 15e ☎45-75-35-37*).

Swimming
Details of municipal pools can be obtained from **Allô Sports** (*☎42-76-54-54*). Information is also available from the **Fédération Française de Natation — Comité de l'Ile de France** (*148 Av. Gambetta, 75020 Paris ☎43-64-17-02*). Meanwhile here is a selection.

Deligny Quai Anatole-France, 7ᵉ ☎45-51-72-15, a very popular place which also has other sports facilities and a bar-restaurant.
Molitor (municipal) 2 Av. de la Porte-Molitor ☎46-51-02-73
Oberkampf 160 Rue Oberkampf, 11ᵉ ☎43-57-56-19
Piscine Municipal de Neuilly 50 Rue Pauline-Borghese, Neuilly ☎47-22-69-59

Tennis
Both municipal courts (for example in the Luxembourg gardens) and many private ones are available. Information from **Allô Sports** (*☎42-76-54-54*). Tennis clubs open to visitors include the following.

Club Multisports des Damiers 48 Pl. des Saisons, La Défense ☎47-74-63-39
Stade Français Porte de St-Cloud, 2 Rue de Commandant Guilbaud, 16ᵉ ☎46-51-66-53

For a complete list of municipal courts (there are almost 200) write to **Bureau des Sports** (*17 Bd. Morland, 75181 Paris*).

Walking and rambling
Contact the **Fédération Française de Randonnée Pédestre** (*8 Av. Marceau 75008 ☎47-23-62-32*) for information.

Zoos
A selection of zoos is listed below. They are all featured individually in the *A-Z of sights and places of interest*.

Bois de Vincennes Métro Château-de-Vincennes
Jardin d'Acclimatation, Bois de Boulogne Métro Porte-Maillot
Jardin des Plantes Métro Jussieu

Excursions

Paris has always been the center of power, politics and the arts in France, and over the centuries great châteaux have grown up within easy striking distance of the city. Several important cathedral towns are also close at hand, as well as pretty villages and many magnificent forests, a famous feature of the Ile de France. All these sights make easy one-day excursions from Paris for the modern visitor. Here we describe in full five of the best-known sights near Paris: Chartres, Fontainebleau, Reims, Rouen and Versailles. However, there are others to choose from:

Barbizon 58km (35 miles) SE of Paris. By train, from Gare du Lyon; by car, on A6 or N7. Small village close to Fontainebleau famed for its artistic associations in the 19thC when several Romantic painters settled there. They included Rousseau and Miller whose studios are open to the public. The inn where they gathered, Pierre Ganne's, also stands.

Beauvais 76km (45 miles) N of Paris. By train, from Gare du Nord; by car, on N1. Though the center of Beauvais was destroyed

in a 1940 air raid, the Gothic cathedral miraculously survived.
Chantilly 50km (30 miles) N of Paris. By train, from Gare du Nord; by car, on N16. Famed for its cream, its hand-worked lace, and its racecourse, but most of all for its elegant château.
Compiègne 82km (50 miles) NE of Paris. By train, from Gare du Nord; by car, on A1. The impressive palace here was a favorite royal hunting residence, and is surrounded by the majestic Compiègne Forest, where in 1918 and 1940 two very different armistices were signed.
Malmaison 15km (10 miles) W of Paris. By Métro/RER to Rueil-Malmaison; by car, N13 via La Défense. The château of Napoleon and Josephine, now a fascinating museum.
St-Germain-en-Laye 21km (12 miles) W of Paris. By Métro/RER to St-Germain-en-Laye; by car, on N13. Smart suburb of Paris; old streets, château, museum of French national antiquities.
Senlis 51km (30 miles) NE of Paris. By train, from Gare du Nord; by car, on A1. Old town with narrow streets, a ruined royal castle and a lovely 12thC cathedral.
Vaux-le-Vicomte 60km (35 miles) SE of Paris. By train, from Gare du Lyon; by car, on N5. Fabulous château and spacious grounds designed by Le Vau, Le Brun and Le Nôtre, still privately owned.

Chartres

88km (55 miles) SW of Paris. Population: 41,250. Getting there: By train, from Gare Montparnasse; by car, N10 or A11; by bus, tours from Cityrama (3 Pl. des Pyramides, 1er ☎42-60-30-14) and Paris-Vision (3 Rue d'Alger, 1er ☎42-60-31-25) i 7 Cloître Notre-Dame ☎(16) 37-21-54-03.

Chartres Cathedral

✗ (compulsory in crypt). Cathedral open daily Mar-Sept 7am-7.30pm. Oct-Feb 7.30am-7pm. Opening hours of crypt, tower and treasury vary according to season.

No one who has seen the cathedral of Notre-Dame at Chartres will ever forget the experience, for it is a building of potent beauty, a representation of the New Jerusalem on earth, as well as a shrine to the Virgin Mary. The building as it now stands was erected on the site of an earlier church which burned down in 1194, leaving only the crypt with its precious relic, the **Sancta Camisia** (now in the treasury), said to be the garment which the Virgin was wearing when she gave birth to Jesus. The fire and the survival of the relic were taken to be a sign from the Virgin that she wanted a more impressive shrine. Accordingly, enormous donations poured in from all over Christendom, and a huge army of craftsmen set to work, completing the basic structure of the cathedral in the extraordinary short span of about 25yrs. This rapidity explains the unique unity of the building as an architectural and esthetic whole.

The cathedral overflows with visual riches, but one of its most famous features is the abundant **stained glass** ★ which includes three staggering rose windows. The imagery of the stained glass, its graceful tracery depicting legends of saints, could by itself occupy many hours of study. Another attraction is the curious **maze** set into the floor of the nave near the W door, to which many people attribute an esoteric significance. The rich sculpture around the **portals** should also not be missed, nor the intricately worked **screen** ☆ separating the choir from the ambulatory. If you have time, climb up to the roof, via a stairway on the N side, for a dizzying view to the N and W through the flying buttresses. It is worthwhile taking one of the excellent English lecture tours of the cathedral conducted by the resident English guide, Malcolm Miller.

Other buildings worth visiting include the churches of **St-Pierre, St-André, St-Martin-au-Val** and **St-Aignan** and the Bishops' Palace, now the **Musée des Beaux-Arts** (▣ *open 10am-noon, 2-6pm; closed Tues*), containing many fine works of art from medieval ivories to 18thC paintings.

The town

The newer part of the town to the S and W is not particularly remarkable, but the old district along the banks of the River Eure is beautiful and unspoiled. Here you can wander past old stone bridges, half-timbered houses and gardens reflected in the water, with the cathedral visible at every turn above the jumble of rooftops.

Hotels

Le Grand Monarque (*22 Pl. des Épars, 28000 Chartres ☎(16) 37-21-00-72* ▮▮□), grand and sedate; also **Ouest** (*3 Pl. P-Semard, 28000 Chartres ☎(16) 37-21-43-27* ▮□).

Restaurants

Le Buisson and Ardent (*10 Rue au Lait ☎(16) 37-34-04-66* ▮□ *to* ▮▮▮▮): delicious and interesting food in an old Chartres house. **Le Grand Monarque** (*22 Pl. des Epars ☎(16) 37-21-00-72* ▮▮▮▮), the hotel restaurant serves exceptionally good *nouvelle cuisine*; reserve in advance.

Cafés

Le Moulin (*21 Rue de la Tannerie*), by the river; also **Salon de Thé Bergamote** (*opposite N door of cathedral*).

Fontainebleau ★

65km (40 miles) SE of Paris. Population: 19,600. Getting there: By train, from Gare de Lyon to Fontainebleau station, then bus to the palace; by car, on the A6 or the N7; by bus, tours with Cityrama (4 Pl. des Pyramides, 1er ☎(42-60-30-14) or Paris-Vision (3 Rue d'Alger, 1er ☎42-60-31-25) ℹ 31 Place Napoléon Bonaparte ☎64-22-25-68.

The palace

☎64-22-34-39 ▣ ✗ Open daily 9.30am-12.30pm, 2-5pm. Closed Tues.

As a former royal residence, the palace of Fontainebleau is just as interesting as Versailles and possesses a much more subtle beauty; even the name has a magical quality, deriving from a fountain in the grounds of the palace, *fontaine belle eau* (fountain of beautiful water). The town too has its charm, a place of well-heeled grace and elegance with leafy avenues and large, quietly prosperous houses. All around it lies the lovely Fontainebleau forest.

If you have time to spare before visiting the palace, take a walk (allow 45-50mins) through the thickly wooded park and approach the palace through the **formal garden** ☆ with its carp pond, its great parterres designed by Le Nôtre in 1664 and its curious statues, which include a pair of sphinxes.

A royal residence from the 12thC, Fontainebleau saw the birth of two French Kings, Philippe le Bel and Louis XIII. But the palace is linked particularly with the colorful François I (1494-1547), rake, military adventurer, friend of Leonardo da Vinci and one of the greatest royal patrons of the arts in French history. In

1528 he knocked down most of the existing medieval edifice and began to build a new château according to Renaissance principles which had influenced him while he was campaigning in Italy. All over the building, carved in stonework and paneling, you will see the fire-breathing salamander that was his emblem. Henry II, Catherine de Medici and Henry IV added to the palace.

Most of the French sovereigns lived for a time at Fontainebleau, and the palace has witnessed a rich pageant of history: Louis XIV's decision to revoke the Edict of Nantes was made there; Pope Pius VII lived a virtual prisoner in the palace between June 1812 and Jan 1814; Napoleon I made Fontainebleau his favorite residence after the Tuileries, and it was here that he came when he abdicated in 1814 before departing for Elba.

Fontainebleau has been described as a "rendezvous of châteaux" for it is really a sprawling conglomeration of buildings of different periods, built around five courtyards. Before entering, take a walk around the palace. On the N side is the charming **Garden of Diana** ☆ with its fountain decorated with a statue of the goddess. Traveling counter-clockwise, pass into the White Horse Courtyard, or **Courtyard of Farewells** ☆ which was the scene of Napoleon's farewell to his guard. Note the graceful double-horseshoe staircase with its hermetic caduceuses carved in the stonework of the balustrade.

To the right of the stairway is an arch leading into the **Fountain Courtyard** looking onto the Carp Pond. Notice on the right the two stone statues of fierce-looking Fô dogs guarding the entrance to the Empress Eugénie's Chinese salons.

Through another archway to the W is the **gilded door** ☆ which is one of the most famous features of the palace. This huge gateway, with its three superimposed loggias, was the first structure to be completed when rebuilding began in 1528.

From here the way leads NE along the facade of the ballroom. Turn left to stand between the **Oval Courtyard** to the SW, with its domed gateway, and the **Courtyard of the Kitchens** to the NE. The gateway to the latter is decorated by two huge **Hermes heads** in stone.

Arguably the most remarkable room in the palace is the **François I Gallery** ★ which was decorated in the years 1534-37 by a team of Italian artists and craftsmen. The walls are adorned with 14 frescoes surrounded by rich decorative stucco work and illustrating events or allegorical subjects connected with the reign of François I. One shows an elephant decorated with fleur-de-lys as an allegory of the king's wisdom; another, symbolizing the unity of the state, depicts François I presenting a pomegranate, symbol of concord, to representatives of different classes. Another splendid Renaissance-style room is the vast **ballroom** ☆ which was designed by Philibert Delorme under Henry II. It has deep, arched bays, frescoes of mythological scenes and a coffered ceiling, the design of which is reflected in the woodwork of the floor.

The rooms known as the **apartments of the King and Queen** are a rich confection of different periods, much of the decoration being in the overblown 19thC style of King Louis-Philippe.

Equally ornate is the series of **Napoleonic rooms**, including the Emperor's Throne Room, bedroom and council chamber. Notice that the Napoleonic bee emblem of industry and discipline figure prominently in the decoration.

Those interested in Napoleon and in militaria should visit the **Musée Napoléonien d'Art et d'Histoire Militaire** (*88 Rue St-Honoré; open Tues-Sat 2-5.30pm*) which has a splendid collection of military paraphernalia.

The forest

Ideally your visit to Fontainebleau should be a two-day affair, one to visit the palace and town, another to explore the forest. This great expanse of woodland is a remarkable natural phenomenon. Over the millennia a strange alchemy of glacial action and erosion has produced a surreal terrain of hills, ravines and extraordinary rock formations. Giant boulders with organic-looking contours lie everywhere, some resembling stranded whales, others sculptures by Henry Moore. No wonder the forest has been used as a setting for more than 100 movies in which it has served to represent, among other things, the terrain of the Holy Land, the Wild West and the Switzerland of William Tell.

Hotels

Aigle Noir 🏨 (*Pl. Napoléon-Bonaparte, 77300 Fontainebleau* ☎*64-22-32-65* ▮▮▮▮); **Napoléon** (*9 Rue Grande, 77300 Fontainebleau* ☎*64-22-20-39* ▮▮□).

Restaurants

Aigle Noir (see *Hotels* above); **François 1er** (*3 Rue Royale* ☎*64-22-24-68* ▮□ *to* ▮▮□).

Reims

143km (89 miles) NE *of Paris. Population: 183,600. Getting there: By train, from Gare de l'Est; by car, on the A4; by bus, tours with Cityrama (4 Pl. des Pyramides, 1er ☎42-60-30-14) and Paris-Vision (3 Rue d'Alger, 1er ☎42-60-31-25)* **i** *1 Rue Jadart ☎(16) 26-47-04-60.*

Reims is famous for two main reasons: its Gothic cathedral and the fact that it is the capital of the Champagne Country and the place where many of the big producers have their cellars. On a day excursion from Paris, try to get there early because the town has much to offer, but if possible avoid going on a Mon or Tues, when the most interesting museums are closed.

Despite the heavy damage Reims suffered in World War I, it has remained a gracious place with quietly elegant streets, solid houses, wide boulevards, fashionable shops and a lively air. Particularly fine is the **Place Royale** ☆ which was built with Classical simplicity as one unit in the 18thC.

Reims was an important city in Roman times, and some fine monuments of that era remain; the most striking is the **Mars Gate** near the station. This three-arched edifice is thought to have been the largest of its kind in the Roman Empire. The mythological themes carved on it include the story of Romulus and Remus, and local etymology has it that the latter was the founder of the city — hence the name. The Roman forum also survives, in the center of the **Place du Forum**, and includes among other things an imposing vaulted colonnade which has been beautifully restored.

Notre-Dame Cathedral ★ (*open 8am-7pm*), begun in 1211, is one of the chain of great Gothic churches which includes Chartres, Amiens and Notre-Dame de Paris. Its special importance lies in the fact that all but three kings of France were crowned there. It was one of Joan of Arc's triumphs to take the Dauphin to Reims, escorting him with an army of 12,000 men through English-held territory, so that he could be crowned as Charles VII there in 1429.

The cathedral is not as overwhelming as that of Chartres, but it has a graceful splendor. The W facade, with its three portals and its sculpture, has eroded over the centuries, but some fine statues still survive, notably the angel to the right of the center door, whose face bears a curiously mischievous smile.

Inside, the cathedral has the typical majesty and grace of its era, with the characteristic soaring ribbed ceiling. The large rose window at the W end retains its original 13thC stained glass; most of the original glass was destroyed in World War I, but some of the modern glass is of a very high standard, most notably the three windows by Chagall at the E end, and the intriguing windows in the S transept depicting aspects of the Champagne industry.

The **Palais du Tau** (☎*26-47-49-37* ▣ *open daily 10am-noon, 2-6pm; closed Tues in winter*) is a museum containing the cathedral treasury. It was once a royal residence, and dates from the 12thC. It was damaged in World War I and has been extensively restored. Other churches include the 11thC **Basilica of St-Remi** ☆ and the small 20thC **Chapelle Foujita**, in Rue de Champ-de-Mars, which was designed and decorated by the Japanese artist Leonard Foujita, who lives in France.

A delightful museum is the **Hôtel Le Vergeur** ☆ (*36 Pl. du Forum* ☎*(16) 26-47-20-75* ▣ *open Tues-Sun 2-6pm*) in a lovely rambling house, parts of which date from the 13thC. The museum was formerly the residence of the art collector and traveler Hugues Krafft, and the contents range from antique furniture and works of art to a priceless collection of original Dürer engravings of the *Apocalypse* and the *Passion of Christ*. The museum also illustrates the history of Reims and the garden contains a fascinating collection of old facades and doorways.

Other interesting museums are the **Musée St-Denis** (*8 Rue Chanzy,* ☎*(16) 26-47-28-44* ▣ *open daily 10.30am-noon, 2-6pm; closed Tues*), and the **Ancien Collège des Jesuites** (*1 Pl. Museux* ▣ *open Mon, Tues, Thurs, Fri 10am-noon, 2pm-6pm*). The Museé St-Denis is a fine arts museum with a collection of sculpture, furniture, objets d'art and French paintings from the 17thC to modern times, which includes works by most of the great French painters. The Ancien Collège des Jesuites is a 17thC building with some magnificent rooms, a fine art and furniture collection and a planetarium (*Sat 3pm, Sun 2.15pm, 3.30pm, 4.45pm*).

If you are interested in champagne, a prime focus of a visit to Reims must be the cellars of one or more of the producers dotted around the suburbs of the town. At the premises of Piper-Heidsieck, for example, you descend 18m (54ft) below ground and then proceed in wagons pulled by an electric car through catacombs flanked by stacks of bottles. En route an audiovisual program is run on champagne production.

The easiest way to visit the cellars and vineyards of Reims and also of Épernay, 24km (15 miles) to the S, is to take a day trip by bus from Paris. These are arranged by Cityrama, Paris-Vision and other tour operators. If you have your own car, the brochure *The Champagne Road*, from the Tourist Office in Reims, gives details to enable you to choose your route.

The following champagne cellars in Reims and Épernay welcome visitors. Asterisks indicate appointments required.

REIMS **Abel Lepitre*** (*2 Av. du Gl-Giraud*); **Besserat de Bellefon*** (*Allée du Vignoble*); **Charles Heidsieck*** (*46 Rue de la Justice*); **Veuve Clicquot-Ponsardin** (*1 Pl. des Droits-de-l'Homme*); **George Goulet*** (*4 Av. du Gl-Giraud*); **Heidsieck & Co Monopole** (*83 Rue Coquebert*); **Henriot & Co*** (*3 Pl. des Droits-de-l'Homme*); **Krug*** (*5 Rue Coquebert*); **Lanson Père & Fils*** (*12 Bd. Lundy*); **Louis Roederer*** (*21 Bd. Lundy*); **G.H. Mumm & Co** (*34 Rue du Champ-de-Mars*); **Piper-Heidsieck** (*51 Bd. Henri-Vasnier*); **Pommery & Greno** (*5 Pl. Gl-Gouraud*); **Ruinart Père & Fils*** (*4 Rue des Crayères*); **Taittinger** (*9 Pl. St-Nicaise*).

ÉPERNAY **De Castellane*** (*57 Rue du Verdun*); **G.H. Martel & Co*** (*46 Av. Champagne*); **Mercier** (*75 Av. Champagne*); **Moët & Chandon** (*20 Av.*

Champagne); **Perriet-Jouët** (*26 Av. Champagne*); **Pol Roger★** (*1 Rue Henri-Lelarge*).

Hotels

Frantel (*31 Bd. P-Doumer, 51100 Reims ☎(16) 26-88-53-54* ▮▮▯), a stylish modern hotel with above-average service; **La Paix** (*9 Rue Buirette, 51100 Reims ☎(16) 26-40-04-08* ▮▯), quiet, comfortable and modern, good restaurant; **Boyer "Les Crayères"** (*64 Bd. Vasnier ☎(16) 26-82-80-80* ▮▮▮▮) an elegant hotel with a delightful garden and one of the best restaurants in France, offering superb *nouvelle cuisine*.

Restaurants

Les Ormeaux (*306 Av. Laon ☎(16) 26-09-89-18*); **Le Vigneron** (*Pl. Paul Jamot ☎(16) 26-47-00-71), cuisine Champenoise*.

Rouen

140km (87 miles) NW of Paris. Population: 118,350. Getting there: By train, from Gare St-Lazare; by car, on the A13, N14 or N15 ℹ 25 Pl. Cathédrale ☎(16) 35-71-41-77.

For centuries the capital of the powerful duchy of Normandy and the last bridging point of the Seine, Rouen has been an important prize and has suffered regular sieges and ransacking, culminating in severe damage from heavy bombing by both sides in the Second World War. Despite this, it has retained an intimate domestic atmosphere, some superb church and secular architecture, fine museums, and a bustling social and shopping center. It is an ideal city for walking. The following route takes in most of the main sights, some of which are described more fully opposite.

Begin at the Pl. de la Cathédrale, a short walk from the railroad station or parking lots. After visiting the **cathedral**, leave by the W door, and follow Rue St-Romain, along the N side. The overhanging buildings date from before 1525 when local law forbade the style to prevent streets from becoming too dark. On the right, notice the **Vieille Maison** of 1466 and the restored **Archbishop's Palace**. Note the plaque recording that Joan of Arc was condemned here in 1431 and then officially rehabilitated 25yrs later.

Across the Rue de la République is the ornate church of **St-Maclou** 🏛 ✝ which shows the limit reached by the Flamboyant style. Pass along Rue Martainville and Rue Damiette, to see the sculpted facade of the superb **Hôtel d'Etancourt** in the Pl. du Lieutenant-Aubert, and the enormous abbey of **St-Ouen**. Note particularly the stained glass and the exhilarating **Portail des Marmousets**. Leave the abbey gardens by the restored 18thC **Hôtel de Ville** and across Pl. du Général-de-Gaulle to reach the shaded **Pl. du Rougemare**, where there are pleasant cafés.

Rue du Cordier leads from the square to Rue du Donjon, where the **Joan of Arc Tower** (🎫 *open 10am-noon, 2-5pm or 5.30pm; closed Thurs and hols*) is found. This donjon with its pepperpot roof is all that remains of a castle built in 1204. In it is the somber, bare room where Joan of Arc was brought before her accusers.

After leaving the tower, turn back along Rue du Donjon, then turn right into Rue Jacques Villon at the end of which, on the left, is the old church of St-Laurent, which houses the **Secq des Tournelles Museum**. The **Beaux-Arts Museum** is on the opposite side of the street. After this museum the walk takes you right to Rue Thiers, then left to Rue Jeanne d'Arc until you reach the Rue du Gros Horloge, which leads, on the right, to the **Place du Vieux Marché**. This square, where Joan of Arc was burned at the stake, combines tall timbered houses with some wonderfully successful modern architecture — a mixture also illustrated by the 16thC stained glass in the light and airy modern church.

Returning from the square to the Rue du Gros Horloge, walk along as far as the **Gros Horloge** itself and the **Belfry Museum**. Then continue along the street as far as the Rue du Bec which leads to the delightful **Palais de Justice**. However, only the central block remains from the 16thC when it was built for Normandy's parliament. From here, by turning right along Rue aux Juifs and then right again into Rue des Carmes, it is easy to get your bearings to return to the Pl. de la Cathédrale where the walk began.

Rouen Cathedral (Notre-Dame) 🏛 ✝ ★

Crypt and Lady Chapel 🎫 ✗ compulsory. Tours 10am, 11am, 2.15pm, 3pm, 4pm, 5pm during June-Sept and Easter, except Sun morning and other hols; rest of year Sat 2.15pm, 3pm, 4pm, Sun 3.15pm, 4pm, 5pm.

Rouen's cathedral soars above the city in extravagant confidence. The main W facade climbs from the solid base of the St-Romain Tower on the N side and the two outer portals, sole remnants of the cathedral that burned down in 1201, to a dramatic skyline, the late 15thC work of Guillaume Pontis. It reaches its climax in the **Tour de Beurre** (Butter Tower) on the S side, which was paid for by indulgences granted to allow citizens to eat butter during Lent; the ornate decoration, always in proportion, typifies the Flamboyant style. The cathedral's interior is more austere but just as harmonious, highlights being the **11thC crypt** and the **Lady Chapel**, with its 14thC windows and Renaissance tombs of the two cardinals of Amboise.

Secq des Tournelles Museum ☆

Rue Jacques Villon, in the old church of St-Laurent 🎫 Open 10am-noon, 2-6pm. Closed Tues, Wed morning and hols. (Ticket also gives entry to Beaux-Arts and Gros Horloge Belfry.)

This unusual museum houses a collection of all sorts of ironwork, displayed perfectly in the church. The arches are hung with *auberge* and tradesmen's signs, and the alcoves and galleries are full of tools, jewelry and locks.

Beaux-Arts Museum

Rue Jacques Villon 🎫 (For times and tickets, see Secq des Tournelles Museum.)

A considerably richer collection than the average provincial art gallery; the most interesting rooms are reached by turning left from the entrance hall. The outstanding exhibit, kept alone in an alcove, is Gerard David's *Virgin and Saints*, a work of great calmness and sensitivity. Other notable paintings include collections of Delacroix, Géricault, Jouvenet, Monet and Sisley, and single works by Ingres, Velázquez and Clouet.

Gros Horloge and Belfry Museum

🎫 (For times and tickets, see Secq des Tournelles Museum.)

The enormous and colorful Renaissance clock straddles the street named after it, adorning a gatehouse completed in 1527, inside which is the Belfry Museum where you can examine the workings of the clock, made in the late 14thC, as well as two 13thC bells. The highlight is the view of the city and Seine valley after the long climb up a spiral staircase.

Hotels

Cathédrale (*12 Rue St-Romain, 76000 Rouen ☎(16) 35-71-57-95* ▮☐) is a traditional hotel; **Frantel** (*Rue Croix de Fer, 76000 Rouen ☎(16) 35-98-06-98 ⊙ 180949* ▮▮▮▮) is modern with every facility.

Restaurants

Bertrand Warin (*7 Rue Pie ☎(16) 35-89-26-69 ▮□ to ▮▮□ closed Sun evening, Mon, Aug*) has traditional Norman decor and a garden where you can have aperitifs or coffee; **Au Bois Chenu** (*23 Pl. Pucelle D'Orléans ☎35-71-19-54*) **La Couronne** (*31 Pl. du Vieux-Marché ☎(16) 35-71-40-90 ▮▮□*), reputedly the oldest *auberge* in France, specializes in classical French cuisine.

Versailles ★

24km (15 miles) sw of Paris. Population: 97,150. Getting there: By train, from Gare des Invalides, Gare Montparnasse; by car, on the N10; by bus, tours with Cityrama (4 Pl. des Pyramides, 1er ☎42-60-30-14) and Paris-Vision (214 Rue de Rivoli, 1er ☎42-60-30-01) i 7 Rue Reservoirs ☎39-50-36-22.

The palace

✉ ✗ in English and French ✗ compulsory in some parts of building ☕ For full details and opening times, write to Services des Visites, Château de Versailles, 78000 Versailles. For times of guided visits ☎39-50-58-32. State apartments open daily 9.45am-5pm; Grand Trianon 9.45am-5pm; Petit Trianon 2-6pm; gardens open dawn to dusk.

The palace of Versailles is perhaps the greatest monument to absolute monarchy ever built. It is overwhelming, fascinating, unforgettable, but to many people not exactly beautiful. Louis XIV, the Sun King who built it, was extremely vain and his palace is an expression of egomania in stone, plaster and gold leaf.

The site was first occupied by a hunting lodge and then by a small brick-and-stone château built by Louis XIII which his son Louis XIV enlarged into the present building, the work continuing from 1661 for about half a century. The architects were first Le Vau, then Jules Hardouin-Mansart. The decoration was supervised by Le Brun and the gardens were planned by Le Nôtre, creator of the *Tuileries* gardens. At the height of the building work 36,000 men and 6,000 horses were employed.

In 1682 Louis decided to make Versailles the court residence and seat of government, and it retained this function until the Revolution. Thus Versailles was the capital of France for over a century. It was the scene of a glittering court which in its heyday included a thousand nobles who lived in the palace itself, along with a vast retinue of servants.

Approaching the palace from the station and the Av. de Paris, the grand stables are to the right and left of the vast **Place d'Armes** in front of the palace. Passing through the great wrought-iron gates, the visitor enters the enormous courtyard with its equestrian statue of *Louis XIV*, erected by King Louis-Philippe, in the middle. Enter by the doorway on the right of the courtyard, and follow the stairway to the upper chapel vestibule, from where the **chapel** ☆ can be seen. Dedicated to St Louis (King Louis XI of France), it is a frothy confection in white and gold with a sumptuously painted ceiling.

From here you pass into the series of **State apartments** ☆ leading into the astonishing **Hall of Mirrors** ☆ where the 17 windows that overlook the gardens are matched on the opposite wall by a row of arches filled with reflecting glass.

Beside the Hall of Mirrors are the sumptuous **King's apartments** ☆ with the bed where each morning and night the monarch's *levée* and *couchée* took place in front of the assembled courtiers. Louis XIV died of gangrene on this bed on Sept 1, 1715.

At the opposite end of the Hall of Mirrors are the **Queen's apartments** ☆ followed by the **Coronation Room** and then the S wing, the first floor of which is taken up almost entirely by the **Hall of Battles**, built by Louis-Philippe, containing 33 paintings of war scenes. Also on the first floor are several rooms, including the **private apartments of the King and Queen** ☆

The **Royal Opera** ☆ which occupies the end of the N wing, can also be visited only on a guided tour. Its interior is entirely of wood, ornately carved and painted in gold, blue and pink.

The gardens

To understand Versailles fully it is necessary to appreciate that the whole complex, palace and gardens, is a kind of symbolic Utopia in which one theme is constantly emphasized: that of a solar deity around which everything revolves, just as the state revolves around the king. This comes across particularly clearly in the **gardens** ☆ which were laid out by Le Nôtre in a series of highly formal terraces adorned with parterres, statues, vases and fountains. Here nature is subdued as a demonstration of the power of the Sun King who, in the gardens, is represented as Apollo.

Bear this in mind as you approach the main focus of the garden, the fountain of Apollo, through a long avenue, flanked by statues and with a carpet of lawn stretching down the middle. The figure of Apollo in his chariot emerges out of the water, just as in legend the sun rose out of the sea at daybreak. If you want to witness the amazing spectacle of the illuminated **fountains** ☆ in operation, telephone for details of times and tickets (☎*39-50-36-22*).

Beyond the fountain of Apollo stretches the **Grand Canal**, on which there once sailed a flotilla of small-scale ships and gondolas. Today you can rent a boat to row on the canal in more modest style. The waterway forms a cross, the northern arm of which leads to where the **Grand Trianon** ☆ and **Petit Trianon** ☆ are situated. These are worth a visit, the former with its pink marble colonnade and lavish interior, the latter more elegant and restrained with its exquisite theater in which Marie-Antoinette used to act. Close by is the **hamlet**, a collection of mock-rustic buildings where the same queen used to play at leading the simple life.

The town

The name of Versailles is so closely linked with the palace that the town itself tends to be neglected by tourists. It is worth knowing, however, that Versailles is one of the earliest examples of what we now call town planning. It was built by royal command in the 17thC after its layout had been carefully designed. Its regular, grid-like pattern of streets and squares (exemplified in the elegant Pl. Hoche) inspired the designers of such cities as St Petersburg, Washington and Karlsruhe. Today it preserves a wealth of domestic architecture from the time of Louis XV and XVI. Two churches worth visiting are **Notre-Dame**, built by J.H. Mansart in the 1680s, and **St-Louis**, built by Mansart de Sagonne in the mid-18thC.

Hotel

St-Louis (*28 Rue St-Louis, 78000 Versailles* ☎*39-50-23-55* II□).

Restaurants

Boule d'Or (*25 Rue de Maréchal Foch* ☎*39-50-22-97* II□ *to* III□); **La Flotille** (*Parc du Château* ☎*39-51-41-58*), a delightful café near the E end of the canal in the palace gardens; **Trois Marches** (*3 Rue Colbert* ☎*39-50-13-21* IIII).

A guide to French

This glossary covers the basic language needs of the traveler: for pronunciation, essential vocabulary and simple conversation, finding accommodations, visiting the bank, shopping, using public transportation or a car, and for eating out.

Pronunciation

It is impossible to give a summary of the subtlety and richness of the French language, but there are some general tips about pronunciation that should be remembered.

French tends to be pronounced in individual syllables rather than in rhythmic feet, so that the word *institution* has four stresses in French and only two in English. In French the voice usually rises at the ends of words and sentences whereas it drops in English. French vowels and consonants are shorter, softer and more rounded than their English counterparts.

The French language is full of characteristic sounds — the r, the u, the frequent eau sound and the nasal sounds (e.g., an, en, ien, in, ain, on, un). The best way to acquire these is to speak English whilst mimicking a strong French accent. The great poet Verlaine used this method with his English pupils.

Vowels

a		short, as in h*a*t; e.g., h*a*ricot
	before i	long, as in h*ay*; e.g., *ai*mer
	before m, n	as the *o* in h*o*t; e.g., d*a*nse
e	at beginning of word	as the *e* in let; e.g., *e*xemple
	at end of syllable	as the *ir* in *irk*; e.g., r*e*pas
	before m, n	as the *a* in *a*rm; e.g., *em*ploi
	before r or z at end of word	as the *a* in l*a*dy; e.g., cherch*er*, ven*ez*
é		as the *a* in b*a*by; e.g., b*é*b*é*
è		as the *ai* in *ai*r; e.g., fr*è*bre
i		as the *ee* in s*ee*k; e.g., r*i*re
	before m, n	as the *a* in p*a*n; e.g., v*in*
o		short, as in s*o*ng; e.g., t*o*mate
	before i	as in *wh* in *wh*ite; e.g., s*oi*f
	before n	as the *or* in t*or*n; e.g., L*on*dres
u		as the *u* in t*u*ne; e.g., j*u*pe

Consonants

c	before a,o,u	hard, as in *c*at; e.g., *c*anard
	before e,i,y	as the *s* in *s*ight; e.g., *c*èpe
	before h	as the *sh* in *sh*ock; e.g., *ch*ic
ç		as the *c* in fa*c*et; e.g., fa*ç*on
g	before a,o,u	as in *g*un; e.g., *g*az
	before e,i,y	as the *dg* in le*dg*e; e.g., *G*i*g*i
	before n	as the *n* in o*n*ion; e.g., Co*gn*ac
h		never sounded
j		as the *s* in lei*s*ure; e.g., *j*upe
m,n	at end of word	not sounded, except with slight nasal twang; e.g., no*m* —
r		rolled in back of throat
s	at end of word	usually silent; e.g., Pari*s*
t	at end of word	usually silent; e.g., tô*t*
x	at end of word	usually silent; e.g., pri*x*

Letter groups

(e) au (x)	as in *oh*; e.g., gât*eaux*
ail (le)	as in *eye*; e.g., vol*aille*
(a) (e) in	as in p*an*, plus nasal twang; e.g., p*ain*
(a) (e) ine	as en in m*en*; e.g., Madel*eine*
il (le) at end of word	usually *ee* as in s*ee*; e.g., rou*ille* (except ville, pronounced "veel")
ine	as in gr*een*; e.g., poitr*ine*

Reference words

Monday	lundi
Tuesday	mardi
Wednesday	mercredi
Thursday	jeudi
Friday	vendredi
Saturday	samedi
Sunday	dimanche

January	janvier
February	février
March	mars
April	avril
May	mai
June	juin
July	juillet
August	août
September	septembre
October	octobre
November	novembre
December	décembre

1	un	11	onze	21	vingt-et-un
2	deux	12	douze	22	vingt-deux
3	trois	13	treize	30	trente
4	quatre	14	quatorze	40	quarante
5	cinq	15	quinze	50	cinquante
6	six	16	seize	60	soixante
7	sept	17	dix-sept	70	soixante-dix
8	huit	18	dix-huit	80	quatre-vingts
9	neuf	19	dix-neuf	90	quatre-vingt-dix
10	dix	20	vingt	100	cent

First	premier, -ière
Second	second, -e
Third	troisième
Fourth	quatrième
. . . .o'clock	. . . .heures
Quarter-past	. . . .et quart
Half past	. . . .et demie
Quarter to	. . . .moins le/un quart
Quarter to six	six heures moins le quart

Mr	monsieur/M.
Mrs	madame/Mme
Miss	mademoiselle/Mlle
Ladies	dames
Men/gentlemen	hommes/messieurs

Basic communication

Yes	oui (si, for emphatic contradiction)
No	non
Please	s'il vous plait
Thank you	merci
I'm very sorry	je suis désolé/ pardon, excusez-moi
Excuse me	pardon/excusez-moi
Not at all/you're welcome	de rien
Hello	bonjour, salut (familiar), allo (on telephone)
Good morning	bonjour
Good afternoon	bonjour
Good night	bonsoir/bonne nuit
Goodbye	au revoir, adieu (final or familiar)
Morning	matin (m)
Afternoon	après-midi (m/f)
Evening	soir (m)
Night	nuit (f)
Yesterday	hier
Today	aujourd'hui
Tomorrow	demain
Next week	la semaine prochaine
Last week	la semaine dernière
. . . .days ago	il y a . . . .jours
Month	mois (m)
Year	an (m)/année (f)
Here	ici
There	là
Over there	là-bas
Big	grand, -e
Small	petit, -e
Hot	chaud, -e
Cold	froid, -e
Good	bon, bonne
Bad	mauvais, -e
Well	bien
Badly	mal
With	avec
And	et
But	mais
Very	très
All	tout, -e
Open	ouvert, -e
Closed	fermé, -e
Left	gauche
Right	droite
Straight ahead	tout droit
Near	près/proche
Far	loin
Up	en haut
Down	en bas
Early	tôt
Late	tard
Quickly	vite
Pleased to meet you.	Enchanté.
How are you?	Comment ça va? (Formal: comment allez vous?)
Very well, thank you.	Très bien, merci.
Do you speak English?	Parlez-vous anglais?

Words and phrases

I don't understand.
comprends pas.
I don't know. Je ne sais pas.
Please explain. Pourriez-vous m'expliquer?
Please speak more slowly. Parlez plus lentement, s'il vous plaît.
My name is . . . . Je m'appelle . . . .
I am American/English. Je suis americain, -e/anglais, -e.
Where is/are? Où est/sont . . . ?
Is there a . . . .? Y a-t-il un, une . . . .?
What? Comment?
How much? Combien?

That's too much. C'est trop.
Expensive cher (chère)
Cheap pas cher/bon marché
I would like . . . . je voudrais . . . .
Do you have . . . .? Avez-vous . . . .?
Just a minute. Attendez une minute. (On telephone: ne quittez pas!)
That's fine/OK. Ça va/OK/ ça y est/d'accord.
What time is it? Quelle heure est-il?
I don't feel well. Je ne me sens pas bien/j'ai mal.

Accommodations

Making a reservation by letter

Dear Sir, Madam,
Monsieur, Madame,
I would like to reserve one double room (with bathroom), one twin-bedded room
Je voudrais réserver une chambre pour deux personnes (avec salle de bain), une chambre avec deux lits
and one single room (with shower) for 7 nights from
et une chambre pour une personne (avec douche) pour 7 nuits à partir
12th August. We would like bed and breakfast/half board/full board,
du 12 août. Nous désirons le petit déjeuner/la demi-pension/pension,
and would prefer rooms with a sea view.
et préférerions des chambres qui donnent sur la mer.
Please send me details of your terms with the confirmation.
Je vous serais obligé de m'envoyer vos conditions et tarifs avec la confirmation.
Yours sincerely,
Veuillez agréer, Monsieur, l'expression de mes sentiments distingués.

Arriving at the hotel

I have a reservation. My name is . . . .
J'ai une réservation. Je m'appelle . . . .
A quiet room with bath/shower/toilet/wash basin
Une chambre tranquille avec bain/douche/toilette/lavabo
. . . .overlooking the sea/park/street/back.
. . . .qui donne sur la mer/le parc/la rue/la cour.
Does the price include breakfast/service/tax?
Ce prix comprend-il le petit déjeuner/le service/les taxes?
This room is too large/small/cold/hot/noisy.
Cette chambre est trop grande/petite/froide/chaude/bruyante.
That's too expensive. Have you anything cheaper?
C'est trop cher. Avez-vous quelque chose de moins cher?
Where can I park my car? Où puis-je garer ma voiture?
Is it safe to leave the car on the street? Est-ce qu'on peut laisser la voiture dans la rue?

Floor/story étage (m)
Dining room/restaurant salle à manager (f) restaurant (m)
Lounge salon (m)
Porter portier/concierge (m) porteur (station)
Manager directeur (m)
Do you have a room? Avez-vous une chambre?
What time is breakfast/dinner? À quelle heure est le petit déjeuner/ diner?
Can I drink the tap water? L'eau du robinet est-elle potable?
Is there a laundry service? Y a-t-il un service de blanchisserie?
What time does the hotel close? À quelle heure ferme l'hôtel?
Will I need a key? Aurai-je besoin d'une clé?

Is there a night porter? Y a-t-il un portier de nuit?
I'll be leaving tomorrow morning. Je partirai demain matin.
Please give me at call at . . . . Voulez-vous m'appeler à . . .
Come in! Entrez!

Shopping

Where is the nearest/a good . . . .? Où est le . . . .le plus proche?/Où y a-t-il un bon . . . .?
Can you help me/show me . . . ? Pouvez-vous m'aider/voulez-vous me montrer . . . ?
I'm just looking. Je regarde.
Do you accept credit cards/travelers cheques? Est-ce que, vous prenez des cartes de credit/chèques de voyage?
Can you deliver to . . . .? Pouvez-vous me le livrer à . . . .?
I'll take it. Je le prends.
I'll leave it. Je ne le prends pas.
Can I have it tax-free for export? Puis-je l'avoir hors taxe pour exportation?
This is faulty. Can I have a replacement/refund? Celui-ci ne va pas. Voulez-vous me l'échanger?
I don't want to spend more than . . . Je ne veux pas mettre plus de . . . .
I'll give . . . .for it. Je vous donne . . . .
Can I have a stamp for . . . .? Donnez-moi un timbre pour . . . .s'il vous plaît.

Shops

Antique shop antiquaire (m/f)
Art gallery galérie d'art (f)
Bakery boulangerie (f)
Bank banque (f)
Beauty parlor salon de beauté (m)
Bookstore librairie (f)
Butcher boucherie (f)
Horse butcher boucherie chevaline (f)
Pork butcher charcuterie (f)
Tripe butcher triperie (f)
Cake shop pâtisserie (f)
Chemist/pharmacy/drugstore pharmacie (f) (m)
Clothes shop magasin de vétements/de mode (m)
Dairy crèmerie (f)
Delicatessen épicerie fine (f) charcuterie (f)
Department store grande surface (f)/grand magasin (m)
Fish store marchand de poisson/poissonier (m)
Florist fleuriste (m/f)
Greengrocer marchand de légumes/primeurs (m)
Grocer épicier (m)
Haberdasher mercier (m)
Hairdresser coiffeur (m)
Hardware store droguerie (f)
Jeweler bijouterie/joaillerie (f)
Market marché (m)
Newsstand marchant de journaux (m)
Optician opticien (m/f)
Perfumery parfumerie (f)
Photographic shop magasin de photographie (m)
Post office bureau de poste (m)
Shoe shop magasin de chaussures (m)
Souvenir shop magasin de cadeaux/souvenirs (m)
Stationer papeterie (f)
Supermarket supermarché (m)
Tailor tailleur (m)
Tobacconist bureau de tabac (m)
Tourist office syndicat d'initiative (m)
Toy shop magasin de jouets (m)
Travel agent agence de voyage (f)

At the bank

I would like to change some dollars/pounds/travelers cheques.
Je voudrais changer des dollars/livres/chèques de voyage.
What is the exchange rate?
Quel est le taux?/le cours du change?
Can you cash a personal check?
Pouvez-vous encaisser un chèque personnel?
Can I obtain cash with this credit card?
Puis-je obtenir de l'argent avec cette carte de crédit?
Do you need to see my passport?
Voulex-vous voir mon passeport?

Some useful goods

Antiseptic cream crème antiseptique (f)
Aspirin aspirine (f)
Bandages pansements (m)bandes (f)
Band-Aid sparadrap (m)

Words and phrases

Cotton coton hydrophile (m)
Diarrhea/upset stomach pills comprimés (m) pour la diarrhée/ l'estomac dérangé
Indigestion tablets comprimés pour l'indigestion
Insect repellent anti-insecte (m)
Laxative laxatif (m)
Sanitary napkins serviettes hygiéniques (f)
Shampoo shampooing (m)
Shaving cream crème à raser (f)
Soap savon (m)
String ficelle (f)
Sunburn cream crème écran solaire (f)
Sunglasses lunettes de soleil (f)
Suntan cream/oil crème solaire (f) /huile bronzante (f)
Tampons tampons (m)
Tissues mouchoirs en papier (m)
Toothbrush brosse à dents (f)
Toothpaste (pâte) dentifrice (f)
Travel sickness pills comprimés pour les maladies de transport

---

Bra soutien-gorge (m)
Coat manteau (m)
Dress robe (f)
Jacket veste/jaquette (f)
Pants slip (m)
Pullover pull (m)
Shirt chemise (f)
Shoes souliers (m)/ chaussures (f)
Skirt jupe (f)
Socks chaussettes (f)
Stockings/tights bas/collants (m)
Swimsuit maillot de bain (m)
Trousers pantalon (m)

Film film (m)/pellicule (f)
Letter lettre (f)
Money order mandat (m)
Postcard carte postale (f)
Stamp timbre (m)
Telegram télégramme (m)

Driving

Gas station station-service (f)
Fill it up. Le plein, s'il vous plaît.
Give me . . . .francs worth. Donnez m'en pour . . . .francs.
I would like . . . .liters of gasoline. Je voudrais . . . .litres d'essence.
Can you check the . . . .? Voulez-vous vérifier . . . .?
There is something wrong with the . . . . Il y a quelque chose qui ne va pas dans le . . . .
Battery batterie (f)
Brakes freins (m)
Exhaust échappement (m)
Lights phares (m)
Oil huile (f)
Tires pneus (m)
Water eau (f)
Windshield pare-brise (m)
My car won't start. Ma voiture ne veut pas démarrer.
My car has broken down/had a flat tire. Je suis tombé en panne/J'ai eu une crevaison.
The engine is overheating. Le moteur chauffe.
How long will it take to repair? Il faudra combien de temps pour la réparer?

Car rental

Is full/comprehensive insurance included? Est-ce que l'assurance tous-risques est comprise?
Is it insured for another driver? Est-elle assurée pour un autre conducteur?
Unlimited mileage kilométrage illimité
Deposit caution(f)
By what time must I return it? À quelle heure devrais-je la ramener?
Can I return it to another depot? Puis-je la ramener à une autre agence?
Is the gas tank full? Est-ce que le réservoir est plein?

Road signs

Aire (de repos) highway rest stop
Autres directions other directions
Centre ville town center
Chaussée deformée irregular surface
Déviation diversion
Passage à niveau level crossing
Passage protégé priority for vehicles on main road
Péage toll point
Priorité à droite priority for vehicles coming from the right
Ralentir slow down
Rappel remember that a previous sign still applies
Route barrée road blocked
Sortie de secours emergency exit
Stationnement interdit no parking
Stationnement toléré literally, parking tolerated
Toutes directions all directions
Verglas (black) ice on road

Other methods of transportation

Aircraft avion (m)
Airport aéroport (m)
Bus autobus (m)
Bus stop arrêt d'autobus (m)
Coach car (m)
Ferry/boat ferry/bâteau/bac (m)
Ferry port port du ferry/bâteau/bac (m)
Hovercraft hovercraft/aéroglisseur (m)

Station gare (m)
Train train (m)
Ticket billet (m)
Ticket office guichet (m)
One-way billet simple
Round trip billet aller-retour
Half fare demi-tarif
First/second class première/seconde classe
Sleeper/couchette wagon-lit (m)

When is the next . . . .for . . . .? À quelle heure est le prochain . . . . pour . . . .?
What time does it arrive? À quelle heure arrive-t-il?
What time does the last . . . .for . . . .leave? À quelle heure part le dernier . . . .pour . . . .?
Which platform/quay/gate? Quel quai/port?
Is this the . . . .for . . . .? Est-ce que c'est bien le . . . .pour . . . .?
Is it direct? Where does it stop? C'est direct? Où est-ce qu'il s'arrête?
Do I need to change anywhere? Est-ce que je dois changer?
Please tell me where to get off? Pourrez-vous me dire ou je devrai descendre?
Take me to . . . . Conduisez-moi à . . . .
Is there a dining car? Y a-t-il un wagon-restaurant?

Food and drink

Have you a table for . . . .? Avez-vous une table pour . . . .?
I want to reserve a table. Je veux réserver une table.
A quiet table. Une table bien tranquille.
A table near the window. Une table près de la fenêtre.
Could we have another table? Est-ce que nous pourrions avoir une autre table?
Set menu Menu prix-fixe
I did not order this Je n'ai pas commandé cela
Bring me another . . . . Apportez-moi encore un . . . .
The check please L'addition s'il vous plaît
Is service included? Le service, est-il compris?

Breakfast petit déjeuner (m)
Lunch déjeuner (m)
Dinner dîner (m)
Hot chaud
Cold froid
Glass verre (m)
Bottle bouteille (f)
Half-bottle demi-bouteille
Beer/lager bière (f)/lager (m)
Draft beer bière pression
Orangeade/lemonade sirop d'orange/de citron (m)
Mineral water eau minérale (f)
Carbonated gazeuse
Noncarbonated non-gazeuse
Fruit juice jus de fruit (m)
Red wine vin rouge (m)
White wine vin blanc
Rosé wine vin rosé
Vintage année (f)

Dry sec
Sweet doux (of wine)
Salt sel (m)
Pepper poivre (m)
Mustard moutarde (f)
Oil huile (m)
Vinegar vinaigre (m)
Bread pain (m)
Butter beurre (m)
Cheese fromage (m)
Milk lait (m)
Coffee café (m)
Tea thé (m)
Chocolate chocolat (m)
Sugar sucre (m)
Steak biftek (m)
well done bien cuit
medium à point
rare saignant
very rare bleu

Menu decoder

Agneau lamb
Agneau de pré salé young lamb grazed in fields bordering the sea
Aiglefin haddock
Aigre-doux sweet and sour
Aiguillettes thin slices
Ail garlic
Ailerons chicken wings
Aïoli garlic mayonnaise

Allumettes puff pastry strips garnished or filled
Alouette lark
Ananas pineapple
Anchoïade anchovy paste, usually served on crispy bread
Anchois anchovies
Andouillette chitterling sausage
Anguille eel

Words and phrases

Arachides peanuts
Artichaut artichoke
Asperges asparagus
Assiette assortie mixture of cold hors d'oeuvre
Baguette long bread loaf
Banane banana
Barbue brill
Barquette pastry boat
Basilic basil
Baudroie monkfish
Belons flat shelled oysters
Betterave beetroot
Beurre butter
Biftek beefsteak
Bignorneaux winkles
Bisque shellfish soup
Blanchailles whitebait
Blanquette "white" stew thickened with egg yolk
Bombe elaborate ice cream
Bouchée tiny vol-au-vent
Boudin (noir ou blanc) (black or white) sausage pudding
Bouillabaisse Mediterranean fish soup which must include fresh fish and saffron
Bouillon broth
Bourride Provençal soup of mixed fish with *aïoli*
Brandade de morue purée of salt cod, milk and garlic (Provençal dish)
Brioche soft bread
(à la) Broche spit-roasted
Brochet pike
Brochette (de) meat or fish on a skewer
Cabillaud cod
Calmar squid
Canard duck
Carré (d'agneau) loin (of lamb)
Cassis blackcurrants
Cassoulet casserole from Languedoc with beans, *confit d'oie* and pork
Cèpes prized wild, dark brown mushrooms
Cervelles brains
Champignons mushrooms
Chanterelles, girolles apricot-colored mushroom
Chantilly whipped cream with sugar
Chicorée curly endive/chickory
Chou light puff pastry/cabbage
Choucroute pickled white cabbage/ sauerkraut
Choufleur cauliflower
Citron lemon
Citron vert lime
Civet de lièvre jugged hare
Colin hake
Concombre cucumber
Confit meat covered in its own fat, cooked and preserved
Confit d'oie preserved goose
Confiture jam
Contre-filet sirloin steak
Coquillages shellfish
Coquille St Jacques scallops, usually cooked in wine
Côte, côtelette chop, cutlet
Coupe ice cream dessert
Crabe crab
Crème cream
Crêpe thin pancake
Cresson watercress
Crevettes grises shrimps
Crevettes roses prawns
Croque-monsieur toasted cheese-and-ham sandwich
Croustade small bread or pastry mold with a savory filling
(en) Croûte cooked in a pastry case
Cru raw
Crudités selection of raw sliced vegetables
Cuisses (de grenouilles) (frogs) legs
Cuit cooked
Culotte de boeuf rump of beef
Darne thick slice, usually of fish
Daube meat slowly braised in a rich wine stock
Daurade sea bream
Dindon turkey
Écrevisses freshwater crayfish
Émincé thinly sliced
Endive endive
Épaule (d'agneau) shoulder (of lamb)
Éperlans smelts
Épices spices
Épinards spinach
Escabèche various fish, fried, marinated and served cold
Escargots snails
Estouffade a stew marinated and fried then slowly braised
Estragon taragon
Faisan pheasant
Farci stuffed
Faux filet sirloin steak
Fenouil fennel
Feuilleté light flaky pastry
Filet fillet
Flageolets fava beans
Flétan halibut
Foie liver
Foie gras goose liver
(au) Four cooked in the oven
Fourré stuffed
Frais, fraîche fresh
Fraises strawberries
Framboises raspberries
Frappé surrounded by crushed ice
Fricadelle kind of meat ball
Frit fried
Frites chips/french fries
Fritots fritters
Fruits de mer seafood
Fumé smoked
Galantine cooked meat, fish or vegetables served cold in a jelly
Galette flaky pastry case
Gambas large prawns
Garbure very thick soup
Garni garnished

Gâteau cake
Gibier game
Gigot (d'agneau) leg (of lamb)
Glace ice cream
Glacé iced, frozen, glazed
(au) Gratin crisp browned topping of breadcrumbs and cheese
Grenouilles frogs
Grillé grilled
Grive thrush
Hachis minced
Harengs herrings
Haricot stew with vegetables/beans
Haricots verts green beans
Homard lobster
Huile (d'olive) (olive) oil
Huîtres oysters
Jambon ham
Laitue lettuce
Langouste spiny lobster or crayfish
Langoustines Dublin bay prawns
Langue (de boeuf) (ox) tongue
Lapin rabbit
Légumes vegetables
Lièvre hare
Loup de mer sea bass
Magret (de canard) breast (of duck)
Maïs sweetcorn
Maquereaux mackerel
Marcassin young wild boar
Marrons chestnuts
Matelote freshwater fish stew
Merlin whiting
Morilles edible dark-brown fungi
Morue cod
Moules mussels
Moules marinière mussels cooked with white wine and shallots
Museau de porc pig's snout
Navarin stew of lamb and young root vegetables
Noix nuts, usually walnuts
Noix de veau rump of veal
Oeufs eggs
Oie goose
Oignons onions
Oseille sorrel
Oursins sea urchins
Palourdes clams
Pamplemousse grapefruit
(en) Papillote cooked in oiled or buttered paper
Pâte pastry
Paupiette thin slices of meat or fish rolled up and filled
Pêche peach
Perdreau partridge
Persil parsley
Petit salé salted pork
Petits fours tiny cakes and sweets
Petits pois peas
Pieds de porc pigs' trotters
Pignons pine nuts
Piments doux sweet peppers
Pintade guinea fowl
Pissaladière bread dough or pizza covered with tomatoes
Pissenlits dandelion leaves, used in salads
Pistou vegetable soup with a paste of garlic, basil and oil
Poché poached
Pochouse fish stew
Poire pear
Poireaux leeks
Poisson fish
Poitrine de porc belly of pork
Pomme apple
Pomme (de terre) potato
Porc pork
Poularde capon
Poulet young spring chicken
Poulpe octopus
Poussin very small baby chicken
Primeurs young vegetables or wines
(à la) Provençale with tomatoes, garlic, olive oil, etc
Quenelles light dumplings of fish or poultry
Queue de boeuf oxtail
Quiche egg- and milk-based open pie
Radis radishes
Raie skate
Raifort horseradish
Ris (de veau) (calf's) sweetbreads
Riz rice
Rognons kidneys
Romarin rosemary
Rôti roast
Rouget red mullet
Rouille garlic and chili sauce usually served with fish soups
Safran saffron
Saint Pierre John Dory
Salade Niçoise salad including tomatoes, beans, potatoes, black olives and tuna
Sanglier wild boar
Saucisses fresh wet sausage
Saucisson dry sausage (salami-type)
Sauge sage
Saumon salmon
Selle (d'agneau) saddle (of lamb)
Suprême de volaille chicken breast and wing fillet
Tapenade purée of black olives and olive oil
Tête (de veau) (calf's) head
Thon tuna fish
Thym thyme
Timbale dome-shaped mold or the pie cooked within it
Tournedos small thick round slices of beef fillet
Tourte covered tart
Tranche slice
Truffes truffles
Truite trout
Truite saumonée salmon trout
(à la) Vapeur steamed
Veau veal
Viande meat
Vinaigrette oil-and-vinegar dressing
Volaille poultry
Vol-au-vent puff pastry case

Index

With the exception of a few of the most notable, such as the Deux Magots café and the Crillon hotel, individual hotels, restaurants, cafés and shops have not been indexed, because they appear in alphabetical order within their appropriate sections. The sections themselves, however, have been indexed. Similarly, although most streets are listed in the gazetteer and not in the index, a few exceptions, such as the Champs-Élysées, are indexed as well.

Page numbers in **bold** type indicate the main entry; those in *italic* refer to the illustrations and plans.

Index

Gazetteer of street names

Numbers after the street name refer to pages on which the street is mentioned in the book. Map references refer to the maps that follow this gazetteer.

It has not been possible to label every street drawn on the maps, although of course all major streets and most smaller ones have been named. However, even streets not labeled have been given map references in this gazetteer, because this serves as an approximate location which will nearly always be sufficient for you to find your way.

PARIS

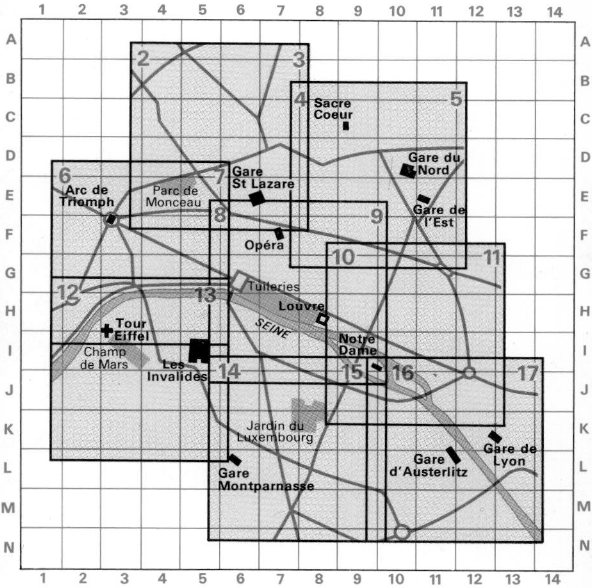

LEGEND

City Maps

0 100 200 300 400 500m.

- Major Place of Interest
- Other Important Building
- Built-up Area
- Park
- Cemetery
- Named church, church
- Mosque
- Synagogue
- Hospital
- Emergency Hospital
- Information Office
- Post Office
- Police Station
- Parking Lot
- Metro Station
- One Way Street
- Stepped Street
- No Entry
- Arrondissement Boundary
- 10 Adjoining Page No.

Area Maps

- Place of Interest
- Built-up Area (Paris centre)
- Surrounding built-up area
- Wood or Park
- Cemetery
- Superhighway (with access point)
- Superhighway under construction
- Main Road - Four Lane Highway
- Other Main Road
- Secondary Road
- Railroad
- R.E.R.
- Airport

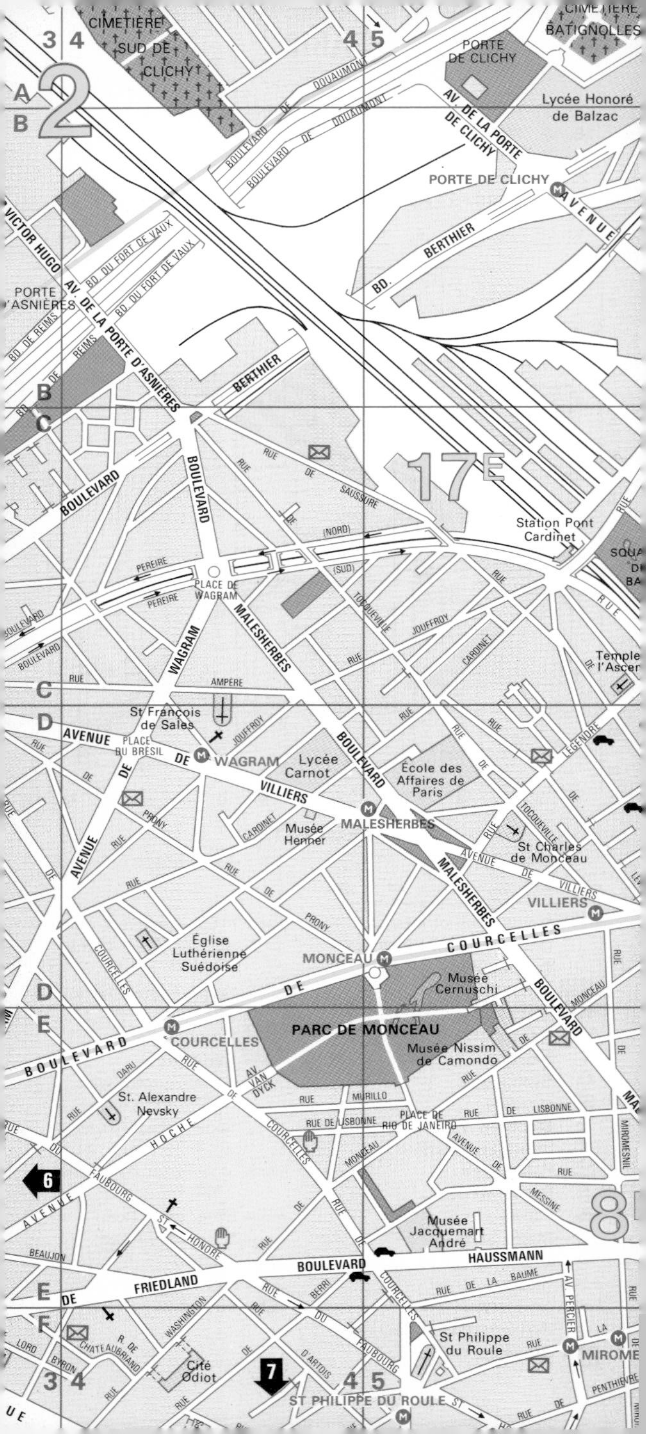

CIMETIÈRE SUD DE CLICHY
CIMETIÈRE BATIGNOLLES
PORTE DE CLICHY
Lycée Honoré de Balzac
BOULEVARD DE DOUAUMONT
AV. DE LA PORTE DE CLICHY
PORTE DE CLICHY
AVENUE
BD. BERTHIER
AV. VICTOR HUGO
BD. DU FORT DE VAUX
PORTE D'ASNIÈRES
AV. DE LA PORTE D'ASNIÈRES
BD. DE REIMS
BERTHIER
17E
RUE DE SAUSSURE
Station Pont Cardinet
BOULEVARD
PLACE DE WAGRAM
PEREIRE
MALESHERBES
TOCQUEVILLE
JOUFFROY
CARDINET
Temple de l'Ascension
AMPÈRE
St François de Sales
AVENUE DE VILLIERS
PLACE DU BRÉSIL
WAGRAM
Lycée Carnot
École des Affaires de Paris
LEGENDRE
Musée Henner
MALESHERBES
St Charles de Monceau
VILLIERS
PRONY
Église Luthérienne Suédoise
MONCEAU
COURCELLES
Musée Cernuschi
PARC DE MONCEAU
Musée Nissim de Camondo
BOULEVARD DE COURCELLES
DARU
St. Alexandre Nevsky
AV. VAN DYCK
MURILLO
RUE DE LISBONNE
PLACE DE RIO DE JANEIRO
HOCHE
MIROMESNIL
MESSINE
8E
AVENUE
FAUBOURG
ST HONORÉ
Musée Jacquemart André
BEAUJON
BOULEVARD HAUSSMANN
FRIEDLAND
RUE DE LA BAUME
AV. PERCIER
BERRI
WASHINGTON
CHATEAUBRIAND
LORD BYRON
St Philippe du Roule
MIROMESNIL
Cité Odiot
D'ARTOIS
PENTHIÈVRE
ST PHILIPPE DU ROULE
6
7

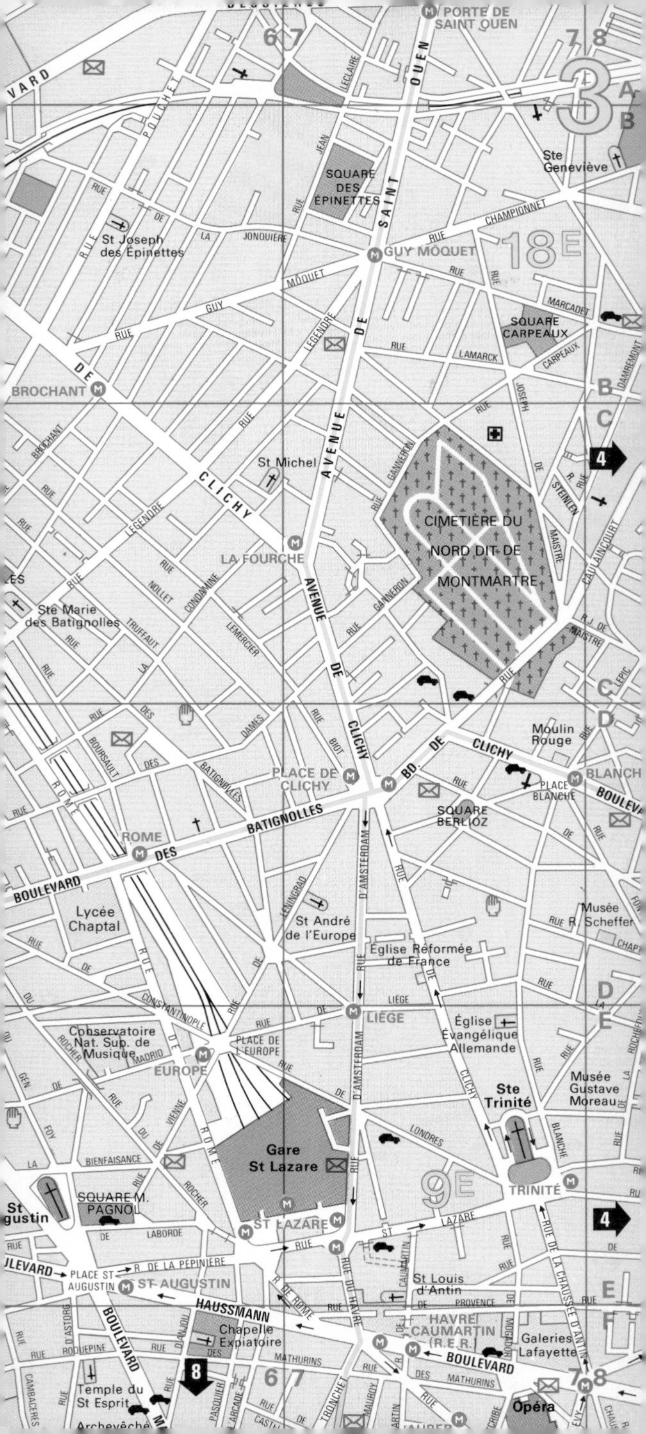

PORTE DE SAINT OUEN
SQUARE DES ÉPINETTES
St Joseph des Épinettes
Ste Geneviève
GUY MÔQUET
18E
SQUARE CARPEAUX
BROCHANT
St Michel
LA FOURCHE
CIMETIÈRE DU NORD DIT DE MONTMARTRE
Ste Marie des Batignolles
AVENUE DE SAINT OUEN
AVENUE DE CLICHY
RUE GUY MÔQUET
RUE LEGENDRE
RUE LAMARCK
RUE CHAMPIONNET
RUE MARCADET
RUE DES DAMES
RUE NOLLET
RUE DES BATIGNOLLES
Moulin Rouge
PLACE DE CLICHY
BD. DE CLICHY
BLANCHE
PLACE BLANCHE
SQUARE BERLIOZ
ROME
BOULEVARD DES BATIGNOLLES
Lycée Chaptal
St André de l'Europe
Église Réformée de France
Musée R. Scheffer
LIÈGE
Église Évangélique Allemande
Conservatoire Nat. Sup. de Musique
PLACE DE L'EUROPE
EUROPE
Ste Trinité
Musée Gustave Moreau
Gare St Lazare
SQUARE M. PAGNOL
9E
TRINITÉ
St Augustin
ST LAZARE
PLACE ST AUGUSTIN
ST AUGUSTIN
St Louis d'Antin
BOULEVARD HAUSSMANN
HAVRE CAUMARTIN (R.E.R.)
Chapelle Expiatoire
Galeries Lafayette
Temple du St Esprit
Opéra
RUE DE LA CHAUSSÉE D'ANTIN
RUE D'AMSTERDAM
RUE DE ROME
RUE DU HAVRE
RUE DES MATHURINS
BOULEVARD MALESHERBES
3
4
8

Temple de Montmartre
Musée d'Art Juif
LAMARCK CAULAINCOURT
CIM. ST VINCENT
Musée de Montmartre
Basilique du Sacré Cœur
St Pierre de Montmartre
PL. DU TERTRE
SQ. JEHAN RICTUS
SQUARE WILLETTE
ABBESSES
PL. SAINT PIERRE
PL. CHARLES DULLIN
ANVERS
Moulin Rouge
BLANCHE
PLACE BLANCHE
St Jean de Montmartre
BOULEVARD DE CLICHY
PIGALLE
PLACE PIGALLE
BOULEVARD DE ROCHECHOUART
Lycée J. Decour
Musée R. Scheffer
AVENUE TRUDAINE
RUE VICTOR MASSÉ
RUE CONDORCET
RUE DE LA TOUR D'AUVERGNE
RUE DE MAUBEUGE
ST GEORGES
Musée Gustave Moreau
9E
RUE DE BELLEFOND
SQUARE DE MONTHOLON
TRINITÉ
N.D. de Lorette
N.D. DE LORETTE
RUE LAMARTINE
RUE DE CHÂTEAUDUN
CADET
Musée du Grand Orient de France
RUE LA FAYETTE
LE PELETIER
Folies Bergère
RUE DE PROVENCE
RUE RICHER
Galeries Lafayette
CHAUSSÉE D'ANTIN
Rédemption
St Eugène Ste Cécile
Hôtel des Ventes
PASS. JOUFFROY
Conservatoire Nat. d'Art Dramatique
RICHELIEU DROUOT
HAUSSMANN
Musée Grévin
R. CITÉ BERGÈRE
BD. DES ITALIENS
BD. MONTMARTRE
RUE MONTMARTRE
BD. POISSONNIÈRE
CAPUCINES
Opéra Studio
PASS. DES PANORAMAS
PLACE DE L'OPÉRA
OPÉRA
BONNE NOUVELLE
GAL. MONTMARTRE
RUE DU QUATRE SEPTEMBRE
QUATRE SEPTEMBRE
FEYDEAU
La Bourse
BOURSE
RUE ST AUGUSTIN
RUE DES JEÛNEURS
2E
R. DE LOUVOIS
SQUARE LOUVOIS
Bibliothèque National
RUE RÉAUMUR
SENTIER

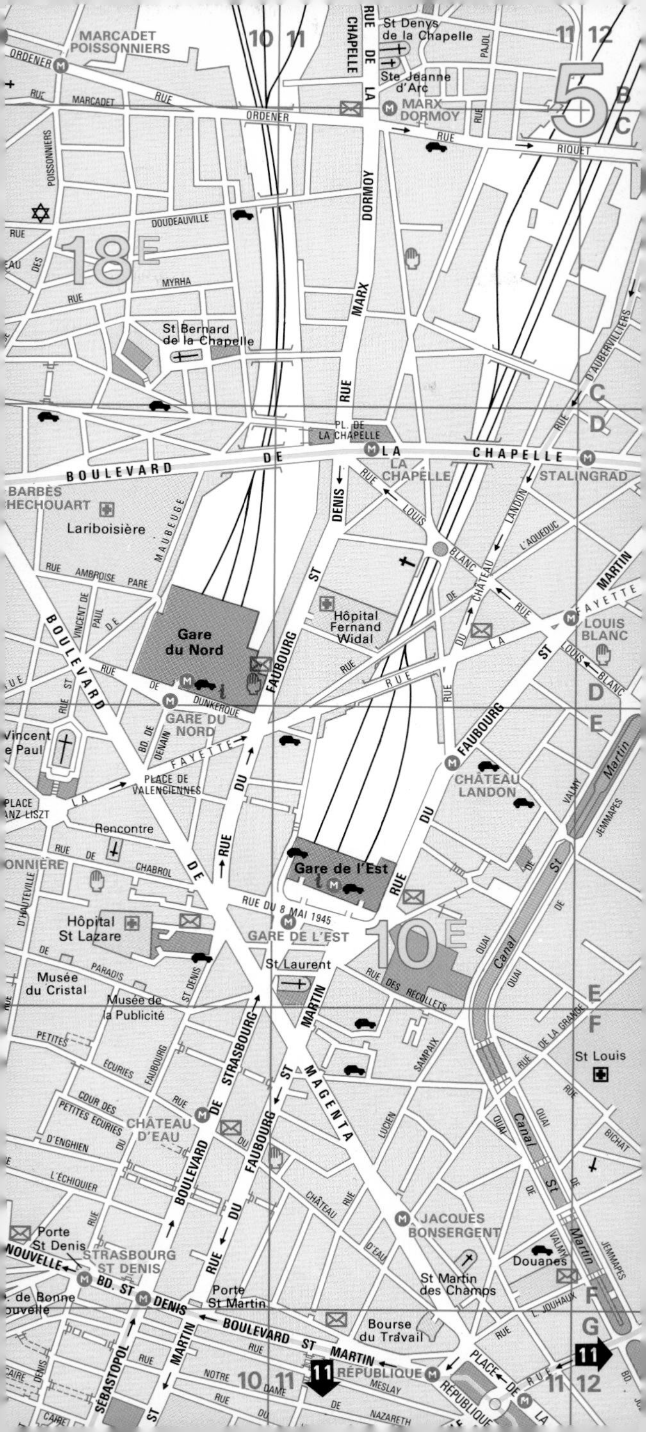

MARCADET POISSONNIERS
ORDENER
RUE MARCADET
RUE ORDENER
10 11
RUE DE LA CHAPELLE
St Denys de la Chapelle
Ste Jeanne d'Arc
MARX DORMOY
PAJOL
11 12
5
B
C
RUE RIQUET
POISSONNIERS
DOUDEAUVILLE
18E
MYRHA
RUE MARX DORMOY
St Bernard de la Chapelle
RUE D'AUBERVILLIERS
PL. DE LA CHAPELLE
BOULEVARD DE LA CHAPELLE
LA CHAPELLE
STALINGRAD
C
D
BARBÈS ROCHECHOUART
Lariboisière
MAUBEUGE
RUE ST DENIS
RUE LOUIS BLANC
RUE LANDON
L'AQUEDUC
RUE AMBROISE PARÉ
RUE DE CHÂTEAU
MARTIN
FAYETTE
LOUIS BLANC
Hôpital Fernand Widal
BOULEVARD
VINCENT DE PAUL
Gare du Nord
FAUBOURG
RUE LA
RUE DE DUNKERQUE
GARE DU NORD
D
E
Vincent de Paul
BD. DE DENAIN
FAYETTE
RUE DU FAUBOURG ST MARTIN
CHÂTEAU LANDON
VALMY
Martin
JEMMAPES
PLACE FRANZ LISZT
PLACE DE VALENCIENNES
Rencontre
RUE DE CHABROL
Gare de l'Est
RUE DU 8 MAI 1945
GARE DE L'EST
Hôpital St Lazare
10E
QUAI
Canal St Martin
RUE DE PARADIS
St Laurent
Musée du Cristal
Musée de la Publicité
RUE DES RÉCOLLETS
E
F
PETITES ÉCURIES
FAUBOURG
BOULEVARD DE STRASBOURG
MAGENTA
SAMPAIX
RUE DE LA GRANGE
St Louis
COUR DES PETITES ÉCURIES
CHÂTEAU D'EAU
LUCIEN
RUE BICHAT
D'ENGHIEN
L'ÉCHIQUIER
CHÂTEAU
RUE D'EAU
JACQUES BONSERGENT
Porte St Denis
STRASBOURG ST DENIS
St Martin des Champs
Douanes
F
BD. ST DENIS
Porte St Martin
L. JOUHAUX
G
BD. de Bonne Nouvelle
BOULEVARD ST MARTIN
Bourse du Travail
11
SÉBASTOPOL
RÉPUBLIQUE
PLACE DE LA RÉPUBLIQUE
MESLAY
NOTRE DAME
10 11
11 12
RUE DE NAZARETH

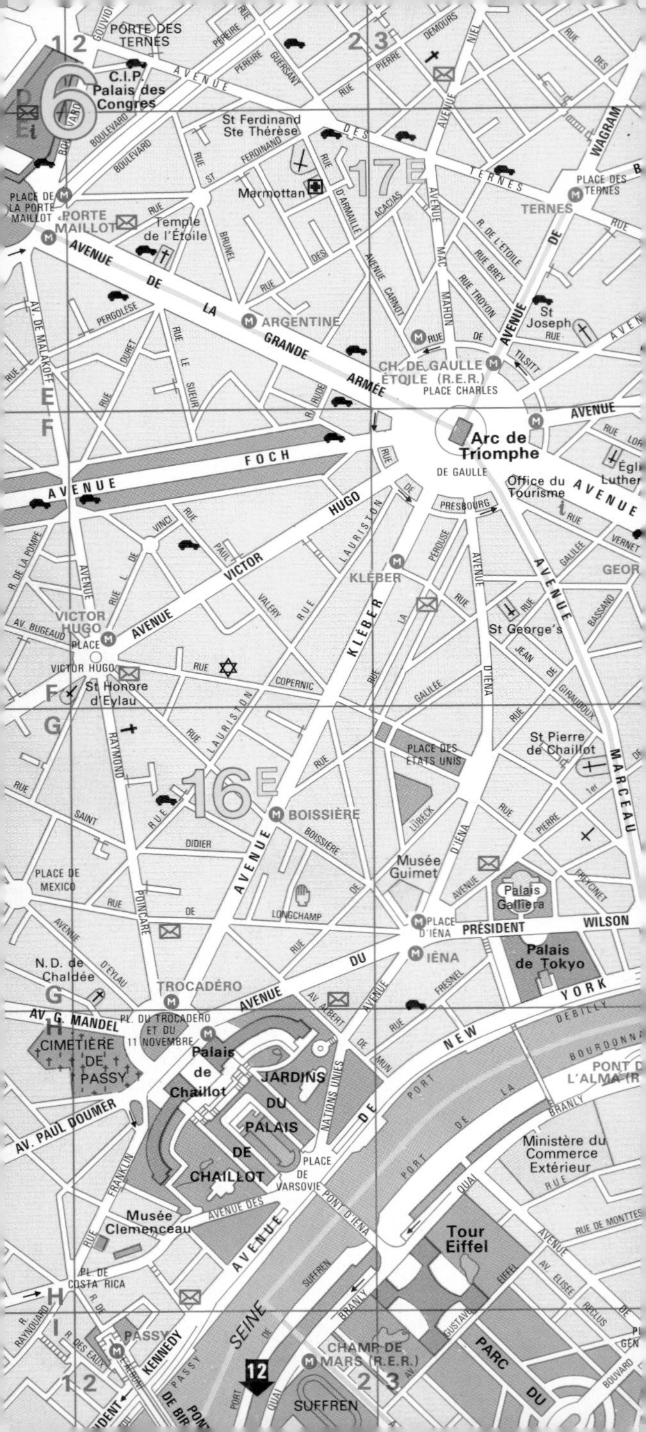

PORTE DES TERNES
C.I.P. Palais des Congres
St Ferdinand Ste Thérèse
Marmottan
17E
PLACE DES TERNES
TERNES
PLACE DE LA PORTE MAILLOT
PORTE MAILLOT
Temple de l'Étoile
AVENUE DE LA GRANDE ARMÉE
ARGENTINE
St Joseph
CH. DE GAULLE ÉTOILE (R.E.R.)
PLACE CHARLES DE GAULLE
Arc de Triomphe
Office du Tourisme
AVENUE FOCH
AVENUE VICTOR HUGO
KLÉBER
AVENUE KLÉBER
VICTOR HUGO
PLACE VICTOR HUGO
St Honore d'Eylau
RUE COPERNIC
St George's
St Pierre de Chaillot
PLACE DES ÉTATS UNIS
16E
BOISSIÈRE
PLACE DE MEXICO
Musée Guimet
Palais Galliera
PLACE D'IÉNA
PRÉSIDENT WILSON
IÉNA
Palais de Tokyo
N.D. de Chaldée
TROCADÉRO
AVENUE DU
NEW YORK
AV. G. MANDEL
PL. DU TROCADERO ET DU 11 NOVEMBRE
CIMETIÈRE DE PASSY
Palais de Chaillot
JARDINS DU PALAIS DE CHAILLOT
AV. PAUL DOUMER
PONT DE L'ALMA
Ministère du Commerce Extérieur
PLACE DE VARSOVIE
PONT D'IÉNA
Musée Clemenceau
Tour Eiffel
PL. DE COSTA RICA
SEINE
PASSY
KENNEDY
CHAMP DE MARS (R.E.R.)
12
SUFFREN
PARC DU

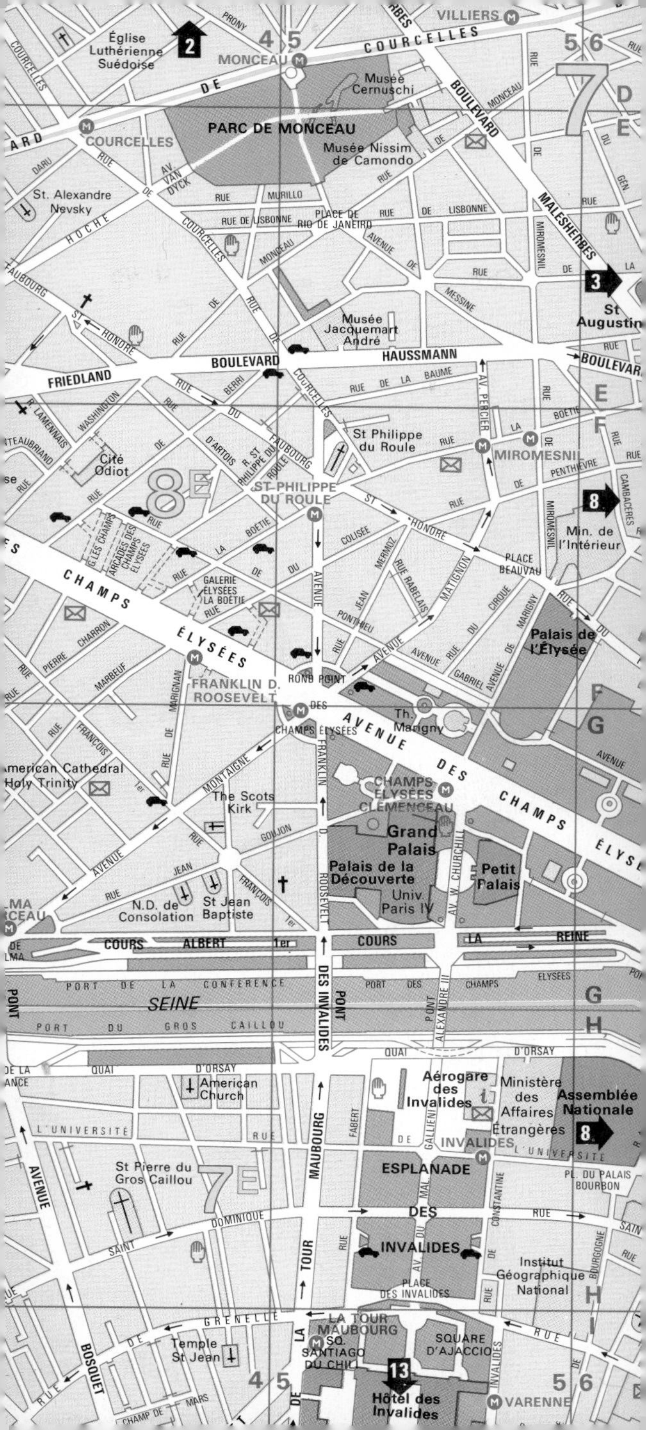

Église Luthérienne Suédoise
2
PRONY
4 5
MONCEAU
VILLIERS
COURCELLES
5 6
7
D
E
DE
Musée Cernuschi
PARC DE MONCEAU
COURCELLES
BOULEVARD
MONCEAU
Musée Nissim de Camondo
DARU
AV. VAN DYCK
St. Alexandre Nevsky
RUE MURILLO
HOCHE
RUE DE LISBONNE
PLACE DE RIO DE JANEIRO
RUE DE LISBONNE
MALESHERBES
MIROMESNIL
AVENUE
MONCEAU
FAUBOURG
ST HONORE
RUE
MESSINE
3
St Augustin
Musée Jacquemart André
BOULEVARD
HAUSSMANN
FRIEDLAND
BERRI
RUE DE LA BAUME
AV. PERCIER
LAMENNAIS
WASHINGTON
CHATEAUBRIAND
D'ARTOIS
R. ST PHILIPPE DU ROULE
St Philippe du Roule
MIROMESNIL
BOETIE
PENTHIEVRE
Cité Odiot
8E
ST-PHILIPPE DU ROULE
CAMBACERES
8
Min. de l'Intérieur
COLISÉE
MERMOZ
RUE RABELAIS
MATIGNON
PLACE BEAUVAU
G.LES CHAMPS
ARCADES DES CHAMPS ÉLYSÉES
GALERIE ÉLYSÉES LA BOÉTIE
JEAN
PONTHIEU
CIRQUE
MARIGNY
Palais de l'Élysée
CHAMPS
ÉLYSÉES
PIERRE CHARRON
MARBEUF
RUE DU
GABRIEL
ROND POINT
FRANKLIN D. ROOSEVELT
DES CHAMPS ÉLYSÉES
AVENUE DES CHAMPS
Th. Marigny
F
G
FRANÇOIS
MARIGNAN
MONTAIGNE
American Cathedral Holy Trinity
CHAMPS ÉLYSÉES CLÉMENCEAU
The Scots Kirk
GOUJON
Grand Palais
Palais de la Découverte
Univ. Paris IV
AV. W. CHURCHILL
Petit Palais
JEAN GOUJON
FRANÇOIS 1er
FRANKLIN D. ROOSEVELT
N.D. de Consolation
St Jean Baptiste
ALMA MARCEAU
COURS ALBERT 1er
COURS LA REINE
PORT DE LA CONFERENCE
SEINE
PORT DU GROS CAILLOU
PONT DES INVALIDES
PORT DES CHAMPS ELYSEES
PONT ALEXANDRE III
H
QUAI D'ORSAY
American Church
Aérogare des Invalides
Ministère des Affaires Étrangères
Assemblée Nationale
L'UNIVERSITÉ
FABERT
GALLIENI
INVALIDES
PL. DU PALAIS BOURBON
St Pierre du Gros Caillou
7E
MAUBOURG
ESPLANADE DES INVALIDES
CONSTANTINE
BOURGOGNE
DOMINIQUE
SAINT
TOUR
Institut Géographique National
PLACE DES INVALIDES
GRENELLE
LA TOUR MAUBOURG
SQ. SANTIAGO DU CHILI
SQUARE D'AJACCIO
BOSQUET
Temple St Jean
13
Hôtel des Invalides
VARENNE
CHAMP DE MARS

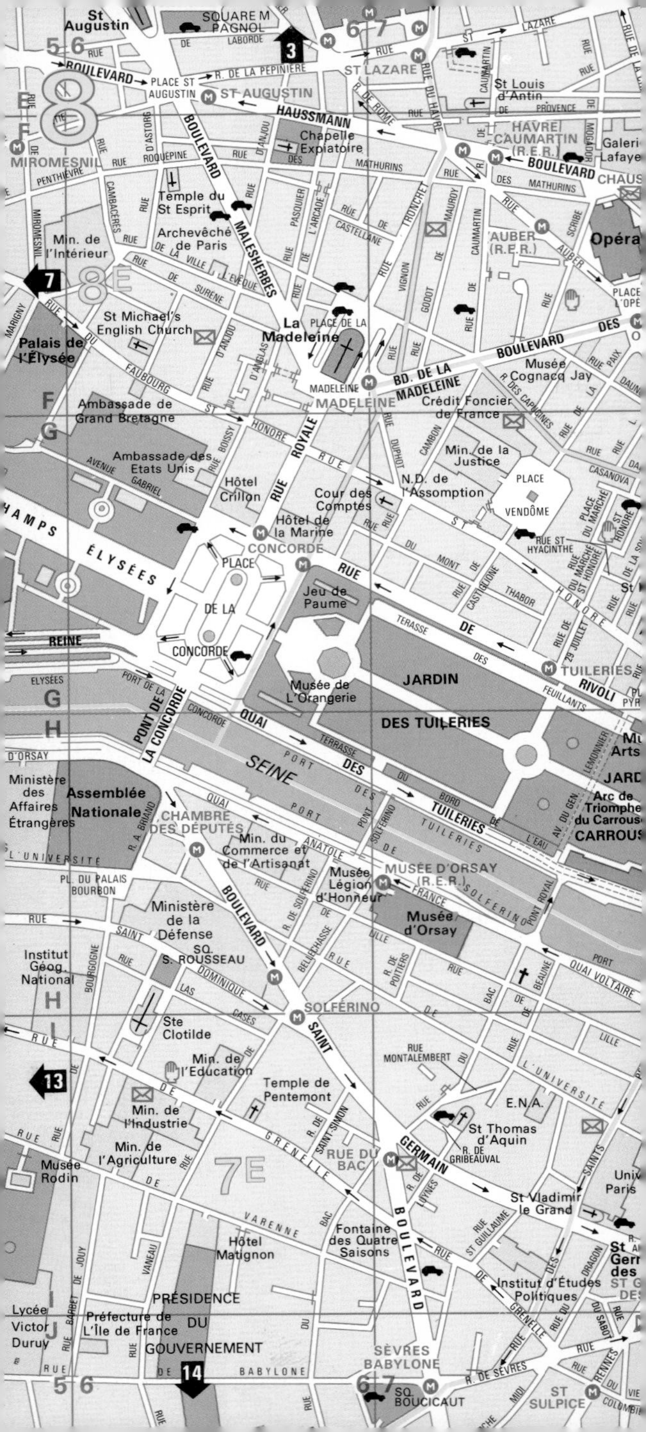
St Augustin
SQUARE M PAGNOL
RUE DE LABORDE
3
6 7
5 6
RUE LAZARE
ST LAZARE
8
BOULEVARD
PLACE ST AUGUSTIN
R. DE LA PEPINIERE
ST AUGUSTIN
R. DE ROME
RUE DU HAVRE
CAUMARTIN
St Louis d'Antin
PROVENCE
RUE MOGADOR
HAUSSMANN
Chapelle Expiatoire
HAVRE CAUMARTIN (R.E.R.)
Galeries Lafayette
MIROMESNIL
RUE ROQUÉPINE
D'ASTORG
RUE D'ANJOU
RUE DES MATHURINS
BOULEVARD
CHAUS
PENTHIÈVRE
CAMBACÉRÈS
Temple du St Esprit
Archevêché de Paris
PASQUIER
L'ARCADE
RUE CASTELLANE
TRONCHET
MAUROY
CAUMARTIN
AUBER (R.E.R.)
RUE AUBER
SCRIBE
Opéra
MIROMESNIL
Min. de l'Intérieur
RUE DE LA VILLE L'EVEQUE
RUE DE SURÈNE
MALESHERBES
VIGNON
GODOT
8E
7
PLACE DE L'OPÉRA
MARIGNY
Palais de l'Élysée
RUE DU FAUBOURG
St Michael's English Church
La Madeleine
PLACE DE LA MADELEINE
BOULEVARD DES
BD. DE LA MADELEINE
Musée Cognacq Jay
RUE DE LA PAIX
DAUNOU
R. DES CAPUCINES
Ambassade de Grand Bretagne
ST HONORÉ
Crédit Foncier de France
F
G
Ambassade des Etats Unis
AVENUE GABRIEL
RUE BOISSY
RUE ROYALE
DUPHOT
CAMBON
Min. de la Justice
N.D. de l'Assomption
PLACE VENDÔME
CASANOVA
Hôtel Crillon
Cour des Comptes
Hôtel de la Marine
PLACE DU MARCHÉ ST HONORÉ
CHAMPS ÉLYSÉES
CONCORDE
RUE ST HYACINTHE
RUE DU MONT THABOR
CASTIGLIONE
PLACE DE LA CONCORDE
Jeu de Paume
RUE DE RIVOLI
TERASSE DES FEUILLANTS
RUE DU 29 JUILLET
TUILERIES
REINE
ELYSÉES
PORT DE LA CONCORDE
PONT DE LA CONCORDE
Musée de L'Orangerie
JARDIN DES TUILERIES
QUAI DES TUILERIES
PORT DES TUILERIES
SEINE
PORT
H
D'ORSAY
Ministère des Affaires Étrangères
Assemblée Nationale
R. A. BRIAND
QUAI ANATOLE DE FRANCE
PONT SOLFERINO
CHAMBRE DES DÉPUTÉS
Min. du Commerce et de l'Artisanat
BORD DE L'EAU
LEMONNIER
AV. DU GEN.
Musée des Arts
JARDIN
Arc de Triomphe du Carrousel
CARROUSEL
L'UNIVERSITÉ
PL. DU PALAIS BOURBON
Musée Légion d'Honneur
MUSÉE D'ORSAY (R.E.R.)
Musée d'Orsay
PONT ROYAL
RUE DE SOLFERINO
Ministère de la Défense
BOULEVARD
R. DE SOLFERINO
BELLECHASSE
RUE DE LILLE
R. DE POITIERS
QUAI VOLTAIRE
RUE SAINT DOMINIQUE
SQ. S. ROUSSEAU
Institut Géog. National
BOURGOGNE
RUE LAS CASES
SOLFÉRINO
RUE DU BAC
BEAUNE
Ste Clotilde
Min. de l'Education
RUE MONTALEMBERT
L'UNIVERSITÉ
13
Temple de Pentemont
E.N.A.
Min. de l'Industrie
R. DE SAINT-SIMON
St Thomas d'Aquin
R. DE GRIBEAUVAL
Min. de l'Agriculture
RUE DE GRENELLE
RUE DU BAC
SAINT GERMAIN
R. DE LUYNES
SAINTS PÈRES
Musée Rodin
7E
St Vladimir le Grand
Université Paris
RUE DE VARENNE
BAC
RUE ST GUILLAUME
St Germain des Prés
Hôtel Matignon
Fontaine des Quatre Saisons
VANEAU
BARBET DE JOUY
Institut d'Études Politiques
RUE DES SAINTS PÈRES
RUE DU DRAGON
GRENELLE
DU SABOT
PRÉSIDENCE DU GOUVERNEMENT
Lycée Victor Duruy
Préfecture de l'Île de France
RUE DU BAC
BOULEVARD
RUE DE RENNES
SÈVRES BABYLONE
R. DE SÈVRES
RUE DE BABYLONE
14
5 6
6 7
SQ. BOUCICAUT
ST SULPICE
MIDI
VIEUX COLOMBIER
I
J

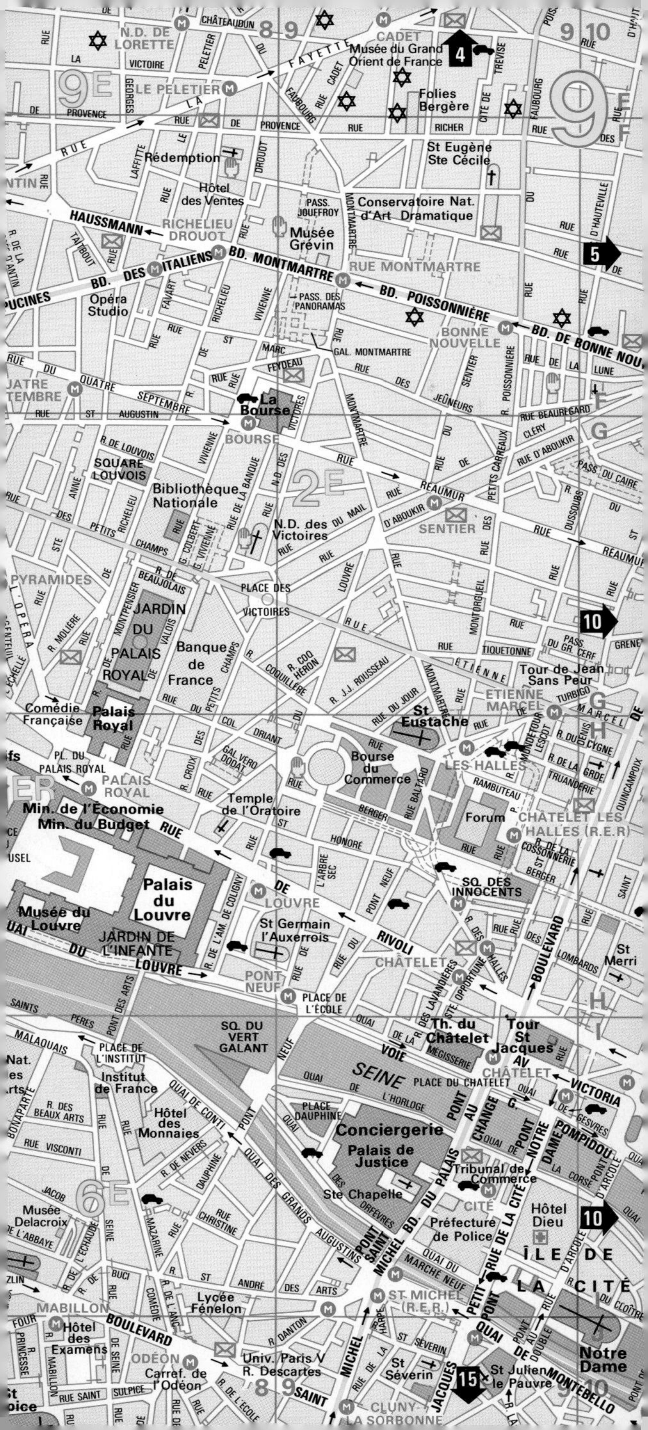
N.D. DE LORETTE
CHÂTEAUDUN
CADET
Musée du Grand Orient de France
4
9E
LE PELETIER
PROVENCE
RICHER
Folies Bergère
St Eugène Ste Cécile
Rédemption
Hôtel des Ventes
PASS. JOUFFROY
Conservatoire Nat. d'Art Dramatique
HAUSSMANN
RICHELIEU DROUOT
Musée Grévin
BD. DES ITALIENS
BD. MONTMARTRE
RUE MONTMARTRE
BD. POISSONNIÈRE
BD. DE BONNE NOUVELLE
5
Opéra Studio
PASS. DES PANORAMAS
GAL. MONTMARTRE
BONNE NOUVELLE
QUATRE SEPTEMBRE
La Bourse
BOURSE
RUE ST AUGUSTIN
R. DE LOUVOIS
SQUARE LOUVOIS
Bibliothèque Nationale
2E
RÉAUMUR
SENTIER
N.D. des Victoires
PYRAMIDES
PLACE DES VICTOIRES
JARDIN DU PALAIS ROYAL
Banque de France
10
TIQUETONNE
Tour de Jean Sans Peur
ÉTIENNE MARCEL
Comédie Française
Palais Royal
St Eustache
Bourse du Commerce
LES HALLES
PL. DU PALAIS ROYAL
PALAIS ROYAL
Min. de l'Économie
Min. du Budget
Temple de l'Oratoire
Forum
CHÂTELET LES HALLES (R.E.R)
Palais du Louvre
Musée du Louvre
JARDIN DE L'INFANTE
LOUVRE
St Germain l'Auxerrois
RIVOLI
SQ. DES INNOCENTS
CHÂTELET
St Merri
PONT NEUF
PLACE DE L'ÉCOLE
SQ. DU VERT GALANT
Th. du Châtelet
Tour St Jacques
SEINE
PLACE DU CHÂTELET
VICTORIA
PLACE DE L'INSTITUT
Institut de France
Hôtel des Monnaies
QUAI DE CONTI
PLACE DAUPHINE
Conciergerie
Palais de Justice
Ste Chapelle
Tribunal de Commerce
CITÉ
Hôtel Dieu
Préfecture de Police
ÎLE DE LA CITÉ
6E
Musée Delacroix
BD. DU PALAIS
PONT ST MICHEL
ST MICHEL (R.E.R.)
Lycée Fénelon
MABILLON
Hôtel des Examens
BOULEVARD ST GERMAIN
ODÉON
Carref. de l'Odéon
Univ. Paris V R. Descartes
St Séverin
St Julien le Pauvre
Notre Dame
QUAI DE MONTEBELLO
15
CLUNY-LA SORBONNE
8 9
9 10

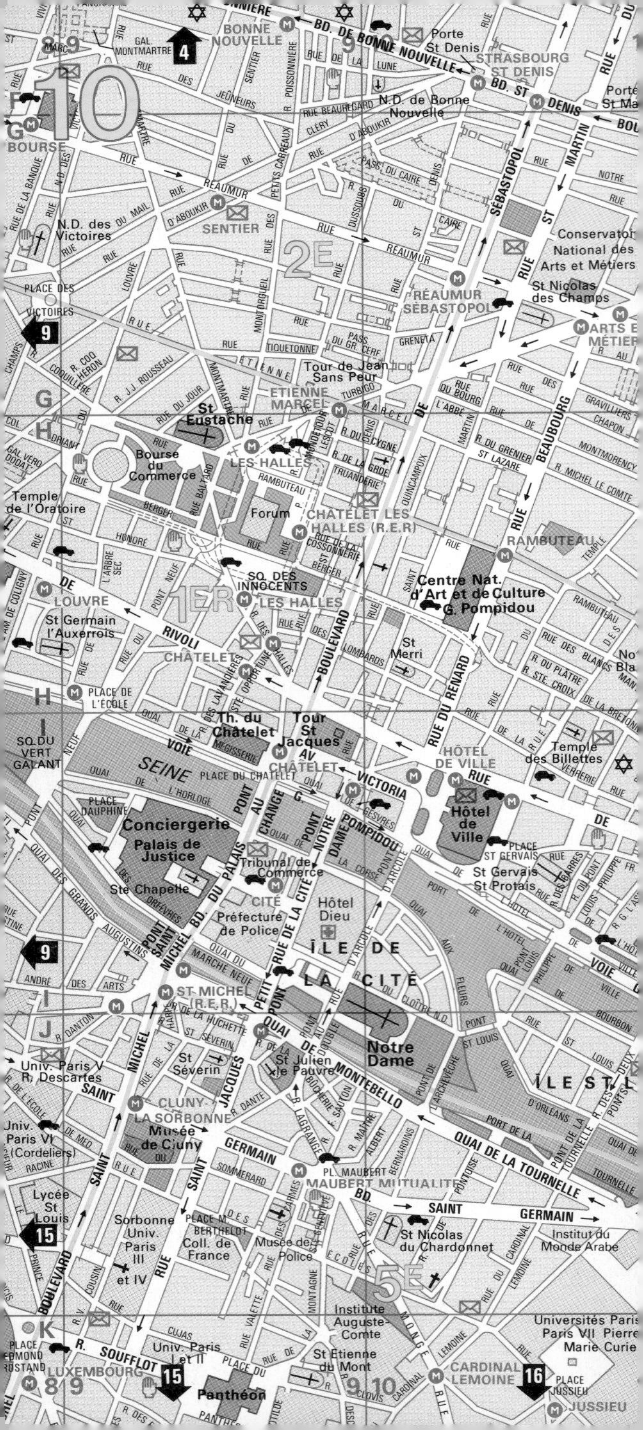
10
BOURSE
BONNE NOUVELLE
BD. DE BONNE NOUVELLE
Porte St Denis
STRASBOURG ST DENIS
BD. ST DENIS
N.D. de Bonne Nouvelle
RUE RÉAUMUR
SENTIER
N.D. des Victoires
PLACE DES VICTOIRES
2E
RÉAUMUR SÉBASTOPOL
Conservatoire National des Arts et Métiers
St Nicolas des Champs
ARTS ET MÉTIERS
Tour de Jean Sans Peur
ETIENNE MARCEL
St Eustache
Bourse du Commerce
LES HALLES
Forum
CHÂTELET LES HALLES (R.E.R)
RAMBUTEAU
Temple de l'Oratoire
SQ. DES INNOCENTS
Centre Nat. d'Art et de Culture G. Pompidou
LOUVRE
St Germain l'Auxerrois
1ER
RIVOLI
CHÂTELET
St Merri
BOULEVARD
RUE DU RENARD
BEAUBOURG
PLACE DE L'ÉCOLE
Th. du Châtelet
Tour St Jacques
SQ. DU VERT GALANT
SEINE
PLACE DU CHATELET
AV VICTORIA
HÔTEL DE VILLE
Hôtel de Ville
Temple des Billettes
PLACE DAUPHINE
Conciergerie
Palais de Justice
Ste Chapelle
Tribunal de Commerce
CITÉ
Préfecture de Police
Hôtel Dieu
ÎLE DE LA CITÉ
St Gervais St Protais
PONT AU CHANGE
PONT NOTRE DAME
PONT D'ARCOLE
PONT ST MICHEL
ST MICHEL (R.E.R.)
Notre Dame
St Séverin
St Julien le Pauvre
QUAI DE MONTEBELLO
ÎLE ST L
QUAI DE LA TOURNELLE
Univ. Paris V R. Descartes
Univ. Paris VI (Cordeliers)
CLUNY-LA SORBONNE
Musée de Cluny
BD. SAINT GERMAIN
PL. MAUBERT
MAUBERT MUTUALITÉ
Lycée St Louis
Sorbonne Univ. Paris III et IV
Coll. de France
Musée de Police
St Nicolas du Chardonnet
Institut du Monde Arabe
5E
Institute Auguste-Comte
Universités Paris Paris VII Pierre Marie Curie
PLACE EDMOND ROSTAND
LUXEMBOURG
RUE SOUFFLOT
Univ. Paris I et II
St Etienne du Mont
Panthéon
CARDINAL LEMOINE
PLACE JUSSIEU
JUSSIEU
4
9
15
16

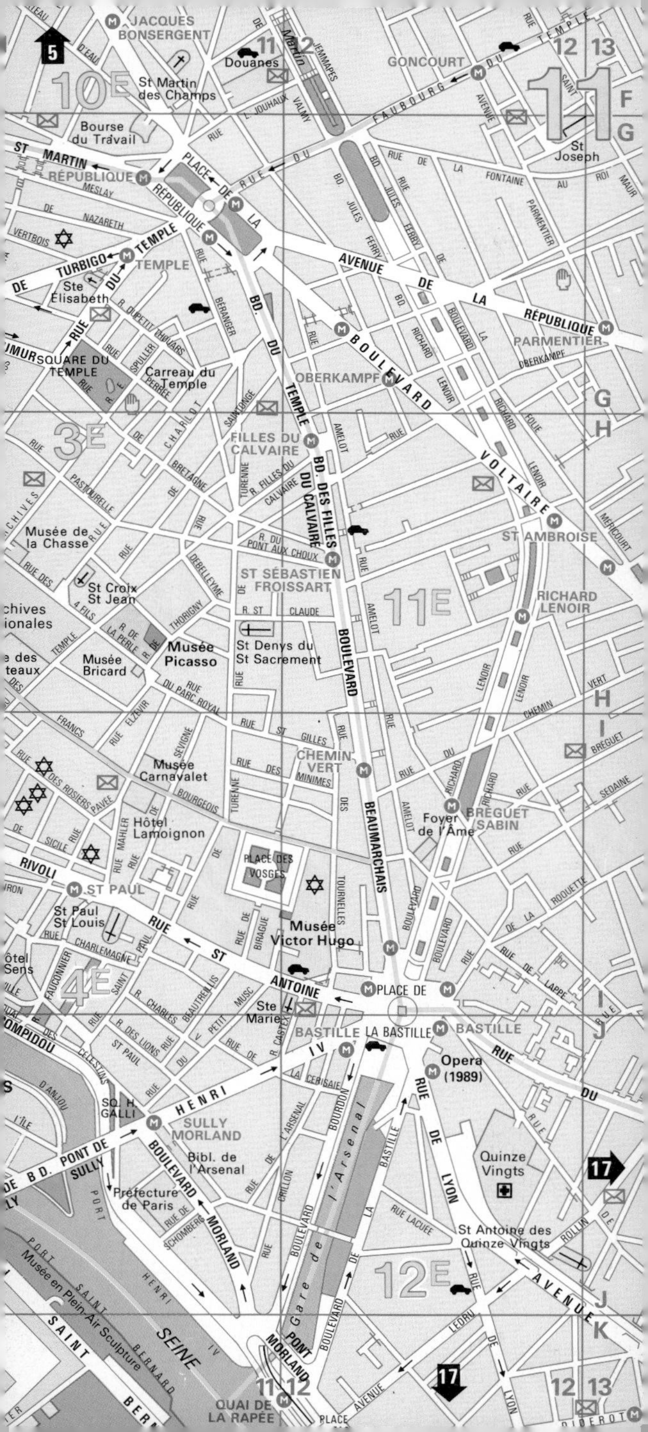

5
JACQUES BONSERGENT
10E
St Martin des Champs
11
12
Douanes
JEMMAPES
VALMY
L. JOUHAUX
GONCOURT
FAUBOURG DU TEMPLE
12
13
11
F
G
Bourse du Travail
ST MARTIN
RÉPUBLIQUE
MESLAY
PLACE DE LA RÉPUBLIQUE
RUE DU
BD. JULES FERRY
RUE DE LA FONTAINE AU ROI
St Joseph
MAUR
PARMENTIER
DE NAZARETH
VERTBOIS
TURBIGO
RUE DU TEMPLE
TEMPLE
AVENUE DE LA RÉPUBLIQUE
PARMENTIER
OBERKAMPF
DE
Ste Elisabeth
R. DUPETIT THOUARS
BERANGER
BD. DU TEMPLE
BOULEVARD VOLTAIRE
BD. RICHARD LENOIR
BOULEVARD RICHARD LENOIR
SQUARE DU TEMPLE
SPULLER
PERREE
Carreau du Temple
OBERKAMPF
G
H
3E
CHARLOT
SAINTONGE
FILLES DU CALVAIRE
AMELOT
FOLIE
RUE PASTOURELLE
BRETAGNE
TURENNE
R. FILLES DU CALVAIRE
BD. DES FILLES DU CALVAIRE
Musée de la Chasse
R. DU PONT AUX CHOUX
ST AMBROISE
MÉRICOURT
RUE DES ARCHIVES
DEBELLEYME
ST SÉBASTIEN FROISSART
St Croix St Jean
4 FILS
RICHARD LENOIR
11E
Archives Nationales
THORIGNY
R. ST CLAUDE
LA PERLE
Musée Picasso
St Denys du St Sacrement
Musée Bricard
BOULEVARD
RUE DU PARC ROYAL
VERT CHEMIN
H
I
FRANCS
ELZEVIR
RUE ST GILLES
BRÉGUET
SÉVIGNÉ
CHEMIN VERT
RUE DES MINIMES
SEDAINE
Musée Carnavalet
DES ROSIERS
PAVÉE
BOURGEOIS
BEAUMARCHAIS
BRÉGUET SABIN
Foyer de l'Âme
Hôtel Lamoignon
MAHLER
SICILE
RIVOLI
PLACE DES VOSGES
TOURNELLES
ROQUETTE
ST PAUL
St Paul St Louis
CHARLEMAGNE
RUE ST ANTOINE
RUE DE BIRAGUE
Musée Victor Hugo
RUE DE LAPPE
Hôtel de Sens
4E
FAUCONNIER
R. CHARLES V
BEAUTREILLIS
MUSC
PETIT
Ste Marie
R. CASTEX
PLACE DE LA BASTILLE
BASTILLE
BASTILLE
I
J
POMPIDOU
CELESTINS
R. DES LIONS ST PAUL
HENRI IV
LA CERISAIE
Opera (1989)
RUE DU
D'ANJOU
L'ÎLE
SQ. H. GALLI
SULLY MORLAND
BOURDON
L'ARSENAL
RUE DE LYON
BD. PONT DE SULLY
BOULEVARD MORLAND
Bibl. de l'Arsenal
Quinze Vingts
17
Préfecture de Paris
SCHOMBERG
CRILLON
Gare de l'Arsenal
RUE LACUÉE
St Antoine des Quinze Vingts
ROLLIN
12E
AVENUE
J
K
PORT
SAINT BERNARD
Musée en Plein-Air Sculpture
SEINE
HENRI IV
PONT MORLAND
LEDRU
17
QUAI DE LA RAPÉE
11
12
PLACE
12
13
DIDEROT

12
23
6
G
H
I
J
K
L
LONGCHAMP
PLACE D'IÉNA
PRÉSIDENT
WILSON
IÉNA
Palais de Tokyo
TROCADÉRO
AVENUE
DU
YORK
NEW
DEBILLY
BOURDONNAIS
PONT DE L'ALMA (R.E.R.)
AV. G. MANDEL
DU TROCADERO ET DU 11 NOVEMBRE
CIMETIÈRE DE PASSY
Palais de Chaillot
JARDINS DU PALAIS DE CHAILLOT
NATIONS UNIES
AV. ALBERT
FRESNEL
BRANLY
AV. PAUL DOUMER
PLACE DE VARSOVIE
PONT D'IÉNA
Ministère du Commerce Extérieur
QUAI
Tour Eiffel
RUE DE MONTTESSUY
AV. ELISEE RECLUS
FRANKLIN
16E
AVENUE DES
Musée Clemenceau
PL. DE COSTA RICA
AVENUE
SUFFREN
SEINE
PASSY
R. RAYNOUARD
R. DES EAUX
KENNEDY
PONT DE BIR HAKEIM
CHAMP DE MARS (R.E.R.)
GUSTAVE EIFFEL
PARC DU CHAMP
PLACE GEN. GOURAUD
BOUVARD
SUFFREN
Ministère des Transports
AV. DU PRÉSIDENT
POMPIDOU
CYGNES
GRENELLE
ALLÉE DES
RUE JEAN REY
AV. JOSEPH BOUVARD
RUE DE LA FÉDÉRATION
R. DESAIX
CHARLES FLOQUET
BIR HAKEIM
RUE DU DOCTEUR FINLAY
BD.
RUE EMERIAU
PLACE DUPLEIX
St Léon
VILLAGE SUISSE
DUPLEIX
DE
Totem
Reflet
Lutécien
Nikko
Perspective
Panorama
SQUARE HÉRICART
RUE CHARLES
LOURMEL
VIOLET
THÉATRE
COMMERCE
LA MOTTE PICQUET GRENELLE
Foyer de Grenelle
FRÉMICOURT
AVENUE ÉMILE ZOLA
AV. ÉMILE ZOLA
CHARLES MICHELS
LINOIS
SAINT
DU THÉATRE
NIVERT
15E
PLACE DU COMMERCE
COMMERCE
PLACE VIOLET
ENTREPRENEURS
St Jean Baptiste de Grenelle
Temple de Résurrection
CROIX
MADEMOISELLE
RUE DE JAVEL
L'ÉGLISE
FÉLIX FAURE
SQUARE ST LAMBERT
Boucicaut
JARDIN DURANTON
BOUCICAUT
AVENUE
CONVENTION
L'ABBÉ GROULT

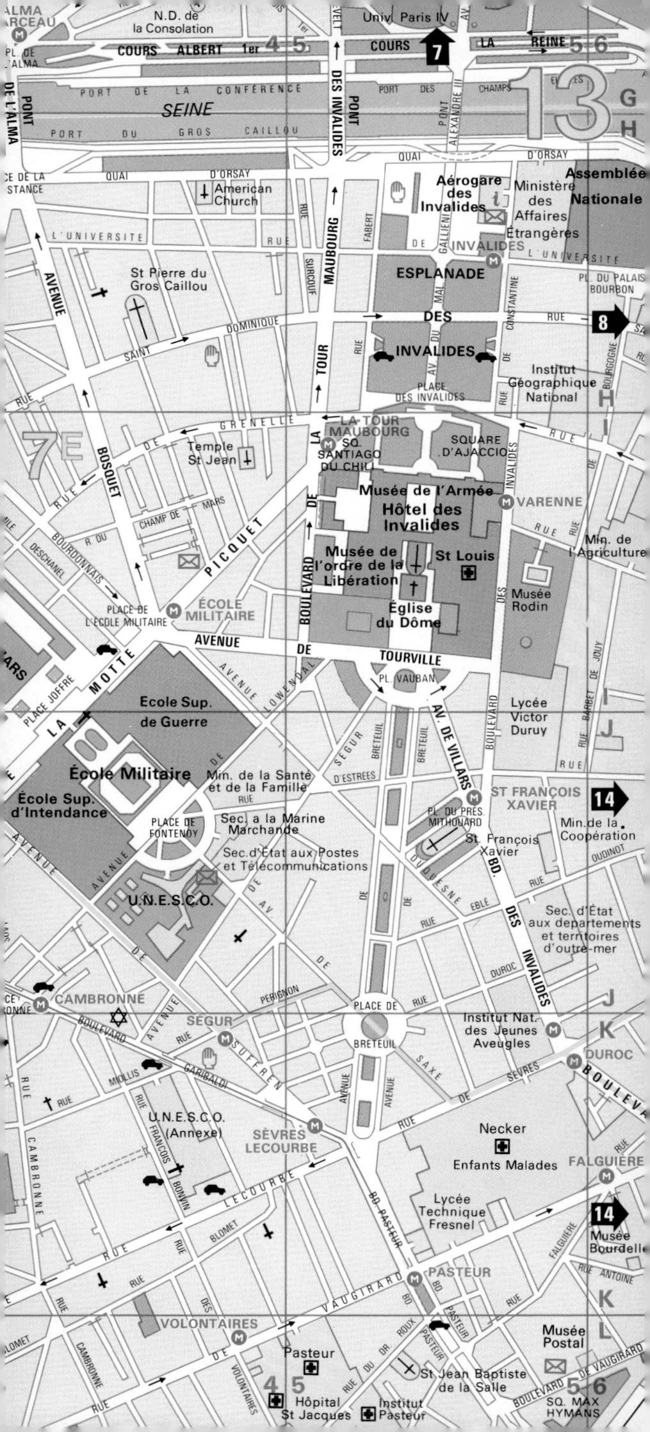
ALMA MARCEAU
N.D. de la Consolation
Univ. Paris IV
COURS ALBERT 1er
COURS LA REINE
4 5
5 6
7
13
G
H
PL. DE L'ALMA
PONT DE L'ALMA
PORT DE LA CONFÉRENCE
SEINE
PORT DU GROS CAILLOU
PONT DES INVALIDES
PORT DES CHAMPS ÉLYSÉES
PONT ALEXANDRE III
QUAI D'ORSAY
QUAI D'ORSAY
American Church
Aérogare des Invalides
Ministère des Affaires Étrangères
Assemblée Nationale
RUE DE L'UNIVERSITE
RUE FABERT
RUE SURCOUF
MAUBOURG
DE INVALIDES
L'UNIVERSITE
PL. DU PALAIS BOURBON
St Pierre du Gros Caillou
AVENUE
ESPLANADE DES INVALIDES
RUE DOMINIQUE
SAINT
RUE
TOUR
AV. DU MAL GALLIENI
RUE DE CONSTANTINE
8
Institut Géographique National
PLACE DES INVALIDES
BOURGOGNE
H
I
RUE DE GRENELLE
7E
BOSQUET
Temple St Jean
LA TOUR MAUBOURG
SQ. SANTIAGO DU CHILI
SQUARE D'AJACCIO
INVALIDES
Musée de l'Armée
Hôtel des Invalides
VARENNE
RUE DE VARENNE
Min. de l'Agriculture
CHAMP DE MARS
R. DU BOURDONNAIS
DESCHANEL
PICQUET
BOULEVARD DE
Musée de l'ordre de la Libération
St Louis
Musée Rodin
DES
PLACE DE L'ECOLE MILITAIRE
ÉCOLE MILITAIRE
Église du Dôme
AVENUE DE TOURVILLE
AVENUE LOWENDAL
PL. VAUBAN
MOTTE
LA
PLACE JOFFRE
Ecole Sup. de Guerre
SEGUR
BRETEUIL
AV. DE VILLARS
BOULEVARD
Lycée Victor Duruy
RUE BARBET DE JOUY
J
École Militaire
Min. de la Santé et de la Famille
D'ESTREES
ST FRANÇOIS XAVIER
14
École Sup. d'Intendance
RUE
PLACE DE FONTENOY
Sec. a la Marine Marchande
PL. DU PRES. MITHOUARD
St. François Xavier
Min. de la Coopération
Sec. d'État aux Postes et Télécommunications
DUQUESNE
OUDINOT
BD. DES INVALIDES
AVENUE
U.N.E.S.C.O.
EBLÉ
RUE
Sec. d'État aux departements et territoires d'outre-mer
AV. DE
DE
DUROC
CAMBRONNE
PERIGNON
PLACE DE BRETEUIL
J
K
AVENUE
SÉGUR
Institut Nat. des Jeunes Aveugles
BOULEVARD GARIBALDI
SUFFREN
SAXE
DUROC
BOULEVARD
MOLLIS
RUE DE SEVRES
U.N.E.S.C.O. (Annexe)
SÈVRES LECOURBE
Necker Enfants Malades
FALGUIÈRE
RUE FRANCOIS BONVIN
LECOURBE
BD. PASTEUR
Lycée Technique Fresnel
14
Musée Bourdelle
BLOMET
FALGUIERE
RUE ANTOINE
PASTEUR
VAUGIRARD
K
L
VOLONTAIRES
Musée Postal
Pasteur
RUE DU DR ROUX
St Jean Baptiste de la Salle
BOULEVARD DE VAUGIRARD
4 5
5 6
Hôpital St Jacques
Institut Pasteur
SQ. MAX HYMANS
CAMBRONNE
VOLONTAIRES

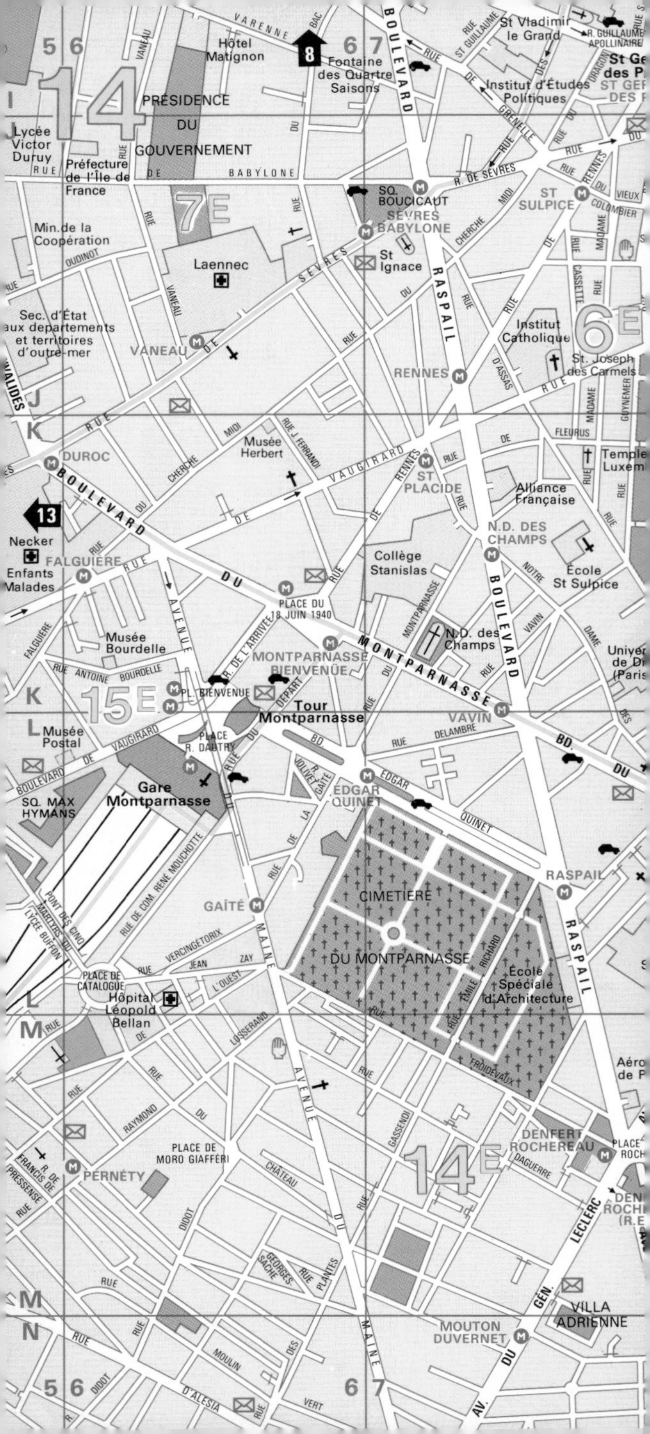

5 6
6 7
14
VARENNE
BAC
8
Hôtel Matignon
Fontaine des Quartre Saisons
BOULEVARD
St Vladimir le Grand
R. GUILLAUME APOLLINAIRE
RUE ST GUILLAUME
Institut d'Études Politiques
GRENELLE
PRÉSIDENCE DU GOUVERNEMENT
Lycée Victor Duruy
Préfecture de l'Île de France
BABYLONE
R. DE SÈVRES
SQ. BOUCICAUT
SÈVRES BABYLONE
ST SULPICE
7E
Min. de la Coopération
OUDINOT
Laennec
St Ignace
RASPAIL
CHERCHE MIDI
VANEAU
Sec. d'État aux departements et territoires d'outre-mer
SÈVRES
Institut Catholique
6E
St. Joseph des Carmels
RENNES
D'ASSAS
FLEURUS
MADAME
CASSETTE
COLOMBIER
VIEUX
GUYNEMER
INVALIDES
J
K
DUROC
Musée Herbert
RUE J FERRANDI
VAUGIRARD
ST PLACIDE
Temple Luxem
Alliance Française
13
Necker
Enfants Malades
FALGUIÈRE
N.D. DES CHAMPS
Collège Stanislas
École St Sulpice
NOTRE DAME
PLACE DU 18 JUIN 1940
MONTPARNASSE
N.D. des Champs
VAVIN
Musée Bourdelle
RUE ANTOINE BOURDELLE
MONTPARNASSE BIENVENÜE
R. DE L'ARRIVÉE
DÉPART
PL. BIENVENÜE
15E
Tour Montparnasse
Musée Postal
L
DELAMBRE
BD. DU
PLACE R. DAUTRY
BOULEVARD DE VAUGIRARD
Gare Montparnasse
SQ. MAX HYMANS
JOLIVET
GAÎTE
EDGAR QUINET
RUE DE LA GAÎTE
RUE DE COM. RENÉ MOUCHOTTE
PONT DES CINQ MARTYRS DU LYCÉE BUFFON
CIMETIÈRE DU MONTPARNASSE
GAÎTE
VERCINGÉTORIX
JEAN ZAY
L'OUEST
PLACE DE CATALOGUE
Hôpital Léopold Bellan
RUE ÉMILE RICHARD
École Spéciale d'Architecture
M
LOSSERAND
FROIDEVAUX
AVENUE DU MAINE
RAYMOND
PLACE DE MORO GIAFFERI
GASSENDI
DENFERT ROCHEREAU
DAGUERRE
14E
PERNÉTY
R. DE FRANCIS DE PRESSENSÉ
CHÂTEAU
DIDOT
GEORGES SACHE
RUE PLANTES
LECLERC
AV. DU GÉN.
VILLA ADRIENNE
MOUTON DUVERNET
N
MOULIN DES
D'ALÉSIA
VERT
Aéro de P

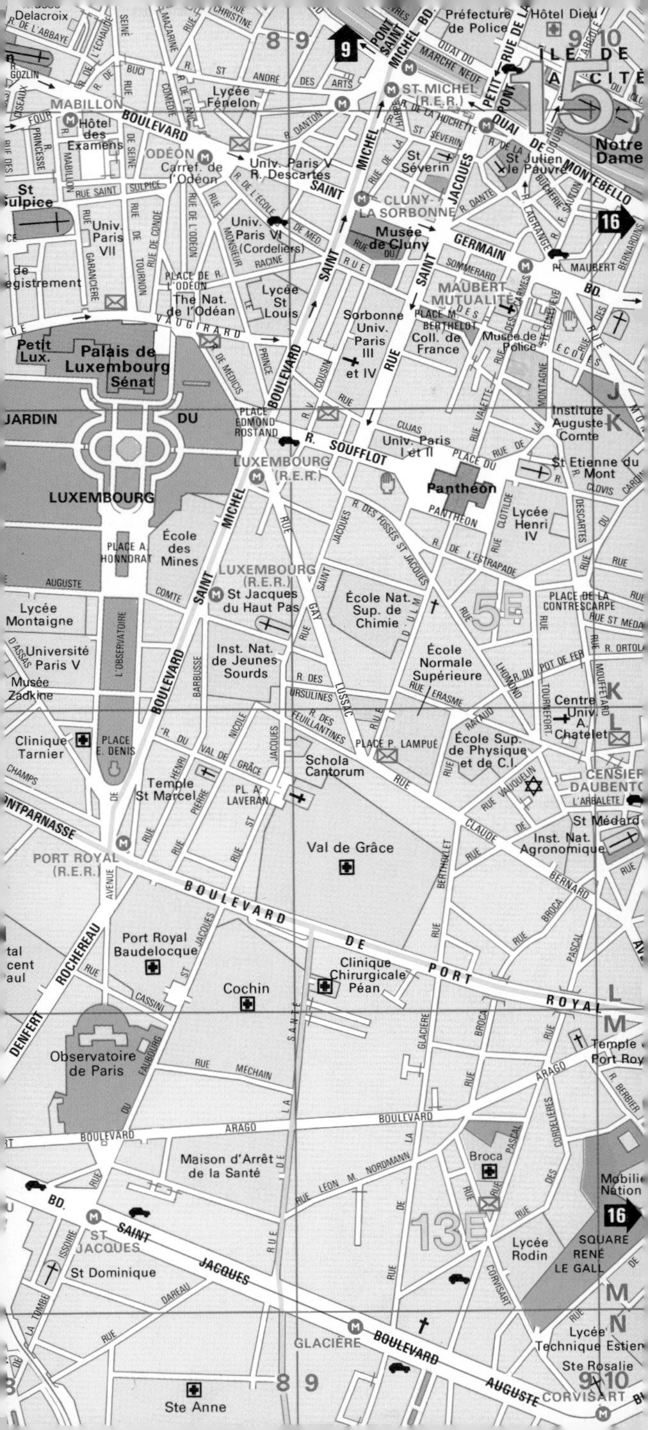

Delacroix
R. DE L'ABBAYE
GOZLIN
MABILLON
Hôtel des Examens
BOULEVARD
ODÉON
Carref. de l'Odéon
Univ. Paris V R. Descartes
Lycée Fénelon
ANDRÉ DES ARTS
PONT SAINT MICHEL BD.
Préfecture de Police
Hôtel Dieu
QUAI DU MARCHÉ NEUF
ÎLE DE LA CITÉ
15
Notre Dame
PETIT PONT
QUAI DE MONTEBELLO
ST MICHEL (R.E.R.)
R. DE LA HUCHETTE
St Séverin
St Julien le Pauvre
16
CLUNY-LA SORBONNE
Musée de Cluny
SAINT GERMAIN
MAUBERT
BD.
PL. MAUBERT
MAUBERT MUTUALITÉ
St Sulpice
RUE SAINT SULPICE
Univ. Paris VII
Univ. Paris VI (Cordeliers)
PLACE DE L'ODÉON
The Nat. de l'Odéan
Lycée St Louis
Sorbonne Univ. Paris III et IV
PLACE M. BERTHELOT
Coll. de France
Musée de Police
VAUGIRARD
Petit Lux.
Palais de Luxembourg Sénat
JARDIN DU LUXEMBOURG
PLACE EDMOND ROSTAND
R. SOUFFLOT
Univ. Paris I et II
LUXEMBOURG (R.E.R.)
Panthéon
PLACE DU PANTHÉON
St Etienne du Mont
Lycée Henri IV
Institute Auguste Comte
R. DE L'ESTRAPADE
PLACE A. HONNORAT
École des Mines
St Jacques du Haut Pas
École Nat. Sup. de Chimie
5E
PLACE DE LA CONTRESCARPE
Lycée Montaigne
Université Paris V
Musée Zadkine
L'OBSERVATOIRE
Inst. Nat. de Jeunes Sourds
École Normale Supérieure
Centre Univ. A. Chatelet
Clinique Tarnier
PLACE E. DENIS
Temple St Marcel
PL. A. LAVERAN
Schola Cantorum
PLACE P. LAMPUÉ
École Sup. de Physique et de C.I.
CENSIER DAUBENTON
St Médard
Inst. Nat. Agronomique
PORT ROYAL (R.E.R.)
Val de Grâce
BOULEVARD DE PORT ROYAL
Port Royal Baudelocque
Cochin
Clinique Chirurgicale Péan
Temple Port Roy
DENFERT ROCHEREAU
Observatoire de Paris
RUE MECHAIN
BOULEVARD ARAGO
Maison d'Arrêt de la Santé
RUE LEON M. NORDMANN
Broca
Mobilier Nation
13E
Lycée Rodin
SQUARE RENÉ LE GALL
ST JACQUES
BD. SAINT JACQUES
St Dominique
GLACIÈRE
BOULEVARD AUGUSTE BLANQUI
Lycée Technique Estien
Ste Rosalie
CORVISART
Ste Anne
8 9
9 10

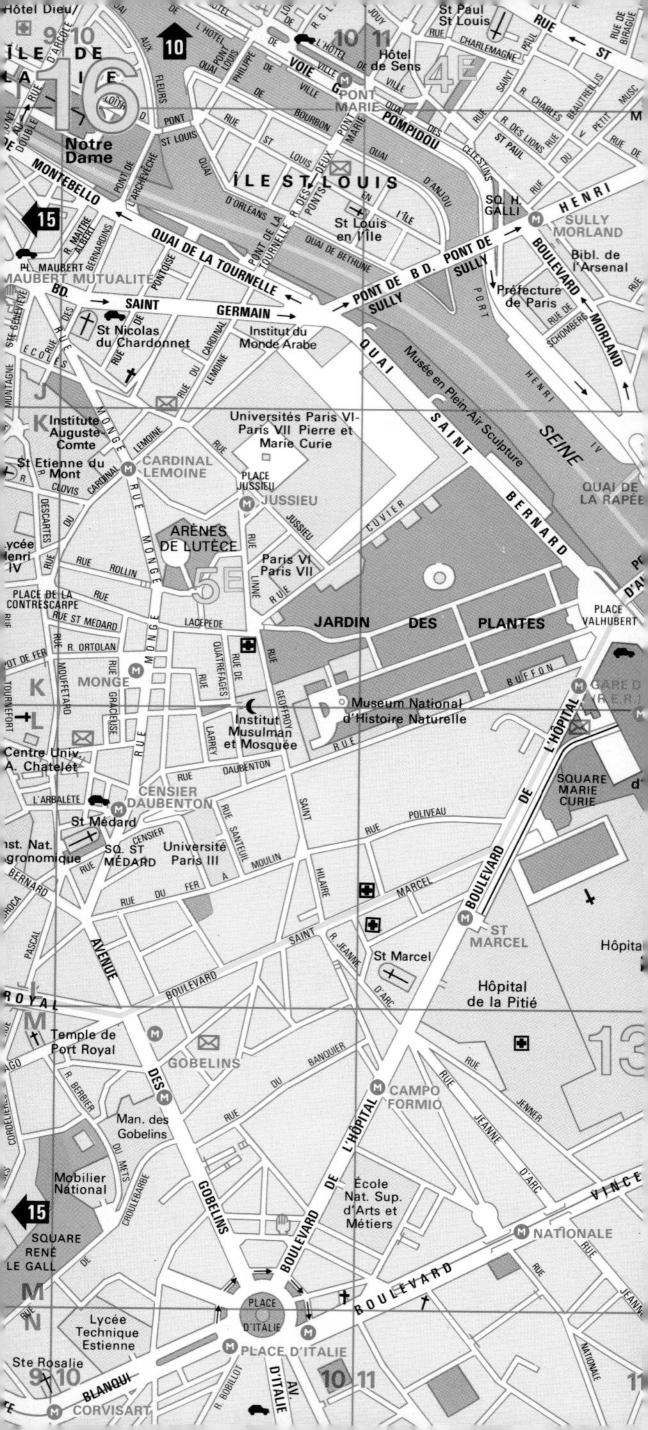
Hôtel Dieu
ÎLE DE LA CITÉ
16
10
Notre Dame
MONTEBELLO
15
PL. MAUBERT
MAUBERT MUTUALITÉ
ÎLE ST LOUIS
QUAI DE LA TOURNELLE
BD. SAINT GERMAIN
St Nicolas du Chardonnet
Institut du Monde Arabe
St Paul St Louis
Hôtel de Sens
PONT MARIE
VOIE G. POMPIDOU
4E
QUAI D'ANJOU
QUAI DE BETHUNE
St Louis en l'Île
SQ. H. GALLI
SULLY MORLAND
BOULEVARD HENRI IV
Bibl. de l'Arsenal
PONT DE SULLY
Préfecture de Paris
BOULEVARD MORLAND
QUAI SAINT BERNARD
Musée en Plein-Air Sculpture
SEINE
QUAI DE LA RAPÉE
Institute Auguste-Comte
St Etienne du Mont
CARDINAL LEMOINE
Universités Paris VI-Paris VII Pierre et Marie Curie
PLACE JUSSIEU
JUSSIEU
RUE MONGE
ARÈNES DE LUTÈCE
5E
Paris VI Paris VII
Lycée Henri IV
PLACE DE LA CONTRESCARPE
RUE ST MÉDARD
JARDIN DES PLANTES
PLACE VALHUBERT
GARE D'AUSTERLITZ
MONGE
Museum National d'Histoire Naturelle
Institut Musulman et Mosquée
Centre Univ. A. Chatelet
CENSIER DAUBENTON
St Médard
SQ. ST MÉDARD
Université Paris III
BOULEVARD DE L'HÔPITAL
SQUARE MARIE CURIE
ST MARCEL
St Marcel
Hôpital de la Pitié
BOULEVARD SAINT MARCEL
AVENUE DES GOBELINS
BOULEVARD DE PORT ROYAL
Temple de Port Royal
GOBELINS
13
CAMPO FORMIO
Man. des Gobelins
Mobilier National
École Nat. Sup. d'Arts et Métiers
NATIONALE
SQUARE RENÉ LE GALL
Lycée Technique Estienne
PLACE D'ITALIE
BOULEVARD VINCENT AURIOL
Ste Rosalie
BOULEVARD BLANQUI
CORVISART
AV. D'ITALIE
9 10
10 11

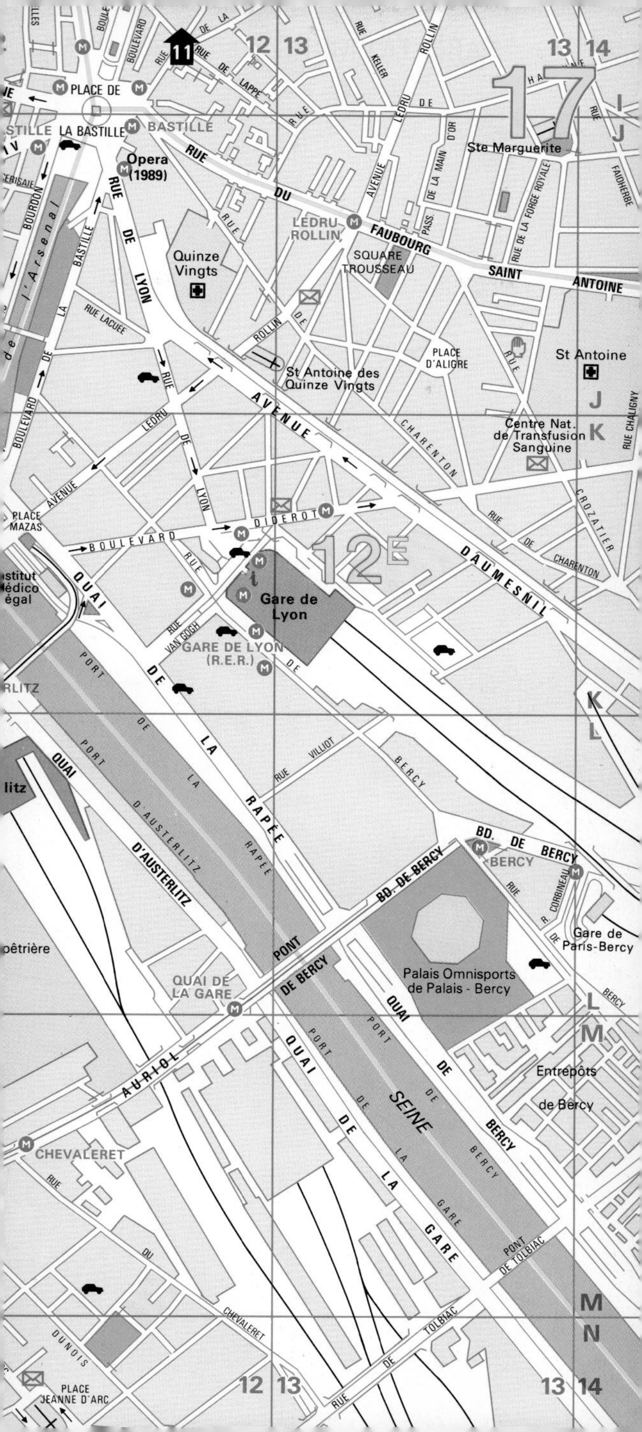

11
12 13
13 14
17
I
J
PLACE DE
LA BASTILLE
BASTILLE
Opera
(1989)
RUE DE LAPPE
RUE DU FAUBOURG SAINT ANTOINE
RUE DE LYON
BOULEVARD BOURDON
de l'Arsenal
BOULEVARD DE LA BASTILLE
RUE LACUÉE
Quinze Vingts
LEDRU ROLLIN
AVENUE LEDRU ROLLIN
RUE KELLER
RUE DE LA MAIN D'OR
PASS.
RUE DE LA FORGE ROYALE
RUE FAIDHERBE
Ste Marguerite
SQUARE TROUSSEAU
RUE ROLLIN DE
PLACE D'ALIGRE
St Antoine
St Antoine des Quinze Vingts
AVENUE LEDRU ROLLIN
AVENUE DAUMESNIL
RUE DE CHARENTON
RUE CHALIGNY
RUE CROZATIER
Centre Nat. de Transfusion Sanguine
J
K
PLACE MAZAS
BOULEVARD DIDEROT
12E
Institut Médico Légal
Gare de Lyon
RUE VAN GOGH
GARE DE LYON (R.E.R.)
QUAI DE LA RAPÉE
PORT DE LA RAPÉE
RUE DE BERCY
RUE VILLIOT
BD. DE BERCY
BERCY
RUE CORBINEAU
Gare de Paris-Bercy
K
L
QUAI D'AUSTERLITZ
PORT D'AUSTERLITZ
Austerlitz
Salpêtrière
PONT DE BERCY
Palais Omnisports de Palais - Bercy
QUAI DE LA GARE
L
M
Entrepôts de Bercy
AURIOL
QUAI DE BERCY
PORT DE BERCY
SEINE
QUAI DE LA GARE
PORT DE LA GARE
CHEVALERET
RUE DU CHEVALERET
PONT DE TOLBIAC
RUE DE TOLBIAC
RUE DUNOIS
PLACE JEANNE D'ARC
M
N
12 13
13 14

PARIS ENVIRONS

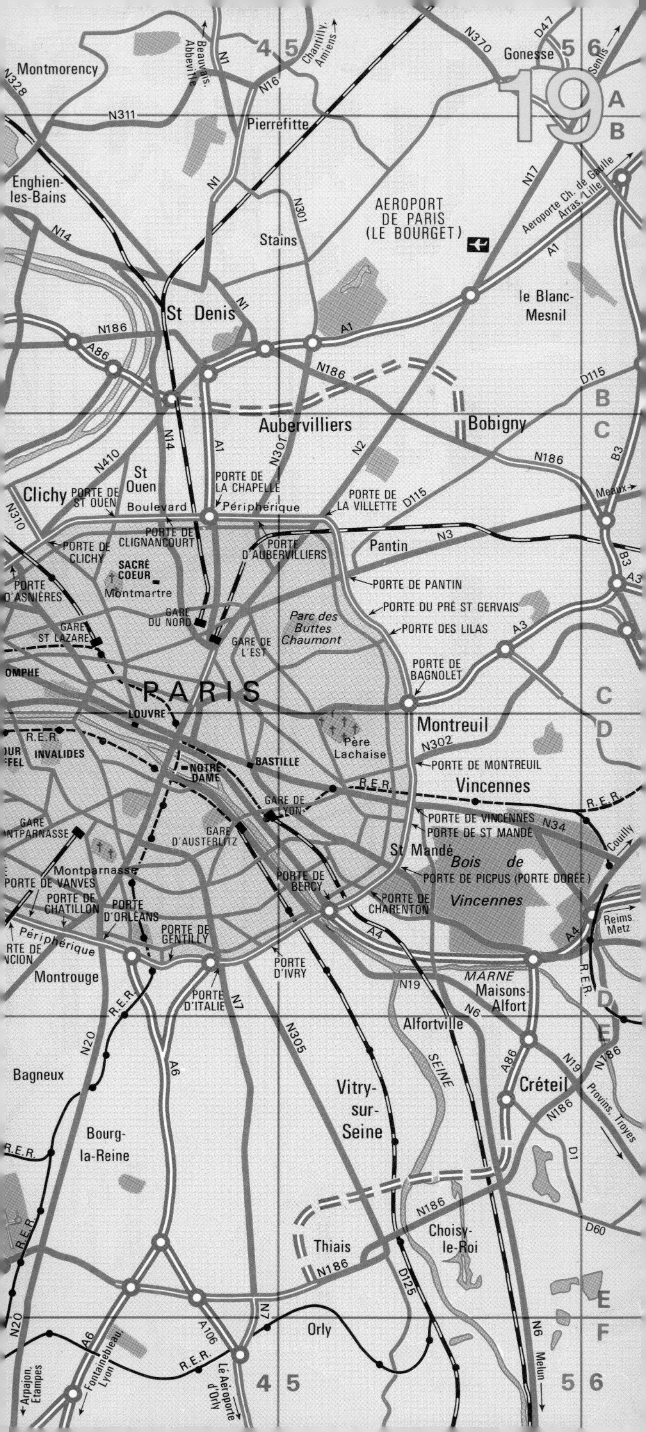
19
A
B
C
D
E
F
4 5
5 6
Montmorency
N328
N311
Beauvais, Abbeville
N1
N16
Chantilly, Amiens
N370
D47
Gonesse
Senlis
Pierrefitte
Enghien-les-Bains
N14
N301
AEROPORT DE PARIS (LE BOURGET)
Stains
N17
Aeroporte Ch. de Gaulle
Arras, Lille
A1
le Blanc-Mesnil
St Denis
N186
A86
D115
Aubervilliers
Bobigny
B3
N410
N2
St Ouen
Clichy
PORTE DE ST OUEN
Boulevard
PORTE DE LA CHAPELLE
Périphérique
PORTE DE LA VILLETTE
Meaux
N310
PORTE DE CLIGNANCOURT
PORTE DE CLICHY
PORTE D'AUBERVILLIERS
Pantin
N3
SACRÉ COEUR
Montmartre
PORTE D'ASNIÈRES
PORTE DE PANTIN
A3
PORTE DU PRÉ ST GERVAIS
GARE DU NORD
Parc des Buttes Chaumont
PORTE DES LILAS
GARE ST LAZARE
GARE DE L'EST
PORTE DE BAGNOLET
PARIS
LOUVRE
Montreuil
N302
R.E.R.
INVALIDES
Père Lachaise
NOTRE DAME
BASTILLE
PORTE DE MONTREUIL
Vincennes
GARE DE LYON
GARE MONTPARNASSE
GARE D'AUSTERLITZ
PORTE DE VINCENNES
PORTE DE ST MANDÉ
N34
Couilly
St Mandé
Bois de Vincennes
Montparnasse
PORTE DE PICPUS (PORTE DORÉE)
PORTE DE VANVES
PORTE DE BERCY
PORTE DE CHATILLON
PORTE D'ORLÉANS
PORTE DE CHARENTON
Reims, Metz
Périphérique
PORTE DE GENTILLY
A4
Montrouge
PORTE D'IVRY
MARNE
Maisons-Alfort
PORTE D'ITALIE
N7
N19
Alfortville
N6
N20
N305
A6
SEINE
A86
Créteil
Bagneux
Vitry-sur-Seine
Provins, Troyes
Bourg-la-Reine
D1
N186
Thiais
Choisy-le-Roi
D60
D125
A106
Orly
Arpajon, Etampes
Fontainebleau, Lyon
Le Aéroporte d'Orly
Melun

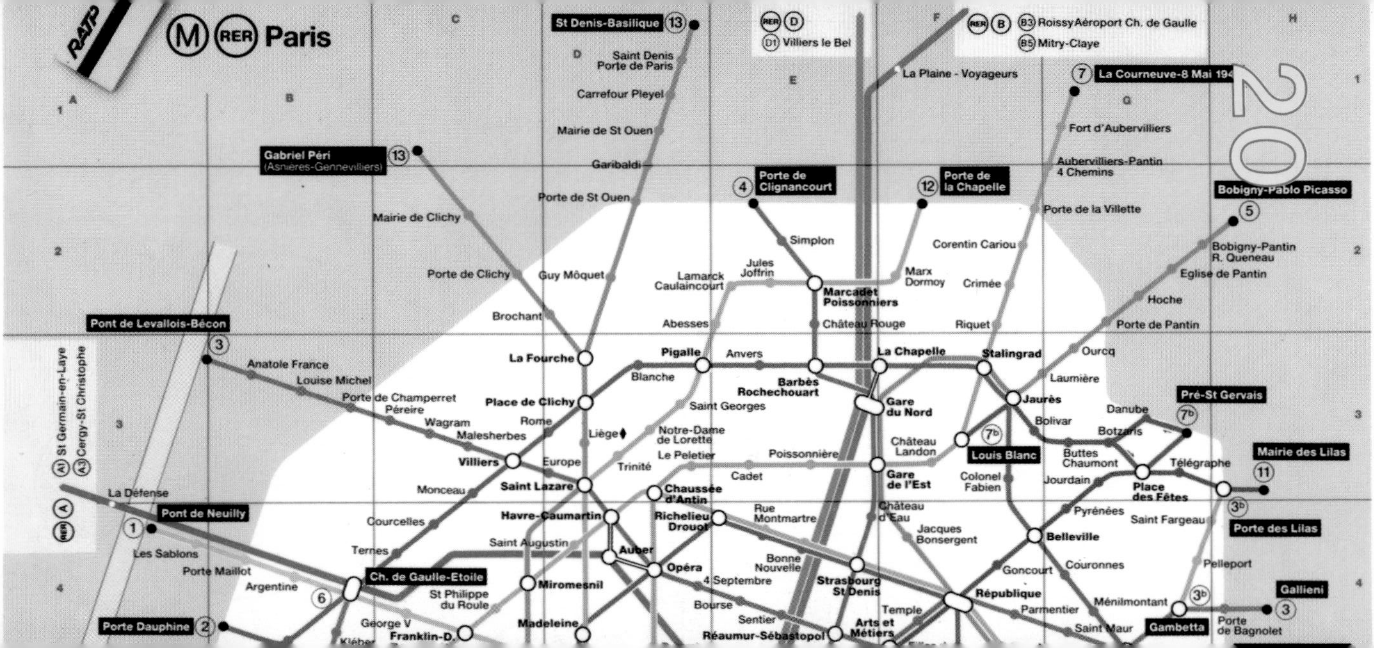
RATP
M RER Paris
20
St Denis-Basilique 13
Saint Denis Porte de Paris
Carrefour Pleyel
Mairie de St Ouen
Garibaldi
Porte de St Ouen
Gabriel Péri (Asnières-Gennevilliers) 13
Mairie de Clichy
Porte de Clichy
Guy Môquet
Brochant
La Fourche
Place de Clichy
RER D
D1 Villiers le Bel
RER B
B3 Roissy Aéroport Ch. de Gaulle
B5 Mitry-Claye
La Plaine - Voyageurs
7 La Courneuve-8 Mai 194
Fort d'Aubervilliers
Aubervilliers-Pantin 4 Chemins
Porte de la Villette
4 Porte de Clignancourt
12 Porte de la Chapelle
Bobigny-Pablo Picasso 5
Bobigny-Pantin R. Queneau
Eglise de Pantin
Hoche
Porte de Pantin
Simplon
Corentin Cariou
Jules Joffrin
Lamarck Caulaincourt
Marcadet Poissonniers
Marx Dormoy
Crimée
Abesses
Château Rouge
Riquet
Pont de Levallois-Bécon
3
Anatole France
Louise Michel
Porte de Champerret
Péreire
Wagram
Malesherbes
Villiers
Monceau
Courcelles
Ternes
Pigalle
Anvers
Blanche
Barbès Rochechouart
La Chapelle
Stalingrad
Ourcq
Laumière
Jaurès
Bolivar
Danube
Pré-St Gervais
7b
Botzaris
Buttes Chaumont
Place des Fêtes
Télégraphe
Mairie des Lilas
11
Saint Georges
Rome
Liège
Notre-Dame de Lorette
Gare du Nord
Château Landon
Louis Blanc
Colonel Fabien
Jourdain
Europe
Trinité
Le Peletier
Poissonnière
Cadet
Gare de l'Est
Saint Lazare
Chaussée d'Antin
Havre-Caumartin
Richelieu Drouot
Rue Montmartre
Château d'Eau
Jacques Bonsergent
Pyrénées
Saint Fargeau
3b
Porte des Lilas
Belleville
Saint Augustin
Auber
Opéra
Bonne Nouvelle
Goncourt
Couronnes
Pelleport
Miromesnil
4 Septembre
Strasbourg St Denis
République
Ménilmontant
Gallieni
3
Bourse
Temple
Parmentier
Gambetta
Porte de Bagnolet
Madeleine
Sentier
Arts et Métiers
Saint Maur
Réaumur-Sébastopol
A1 St Germain-en-Laye
A3 Cergy-St Christophe
RER A
La Défense
1 Pont de Neuilly
Les Sablons
Porte Maillot
Argentine
6
Ch. de Gaulle-Etoile
St Philippe du Roule
George V
Franklin-D.
Kléber
Porte Dauphine 2

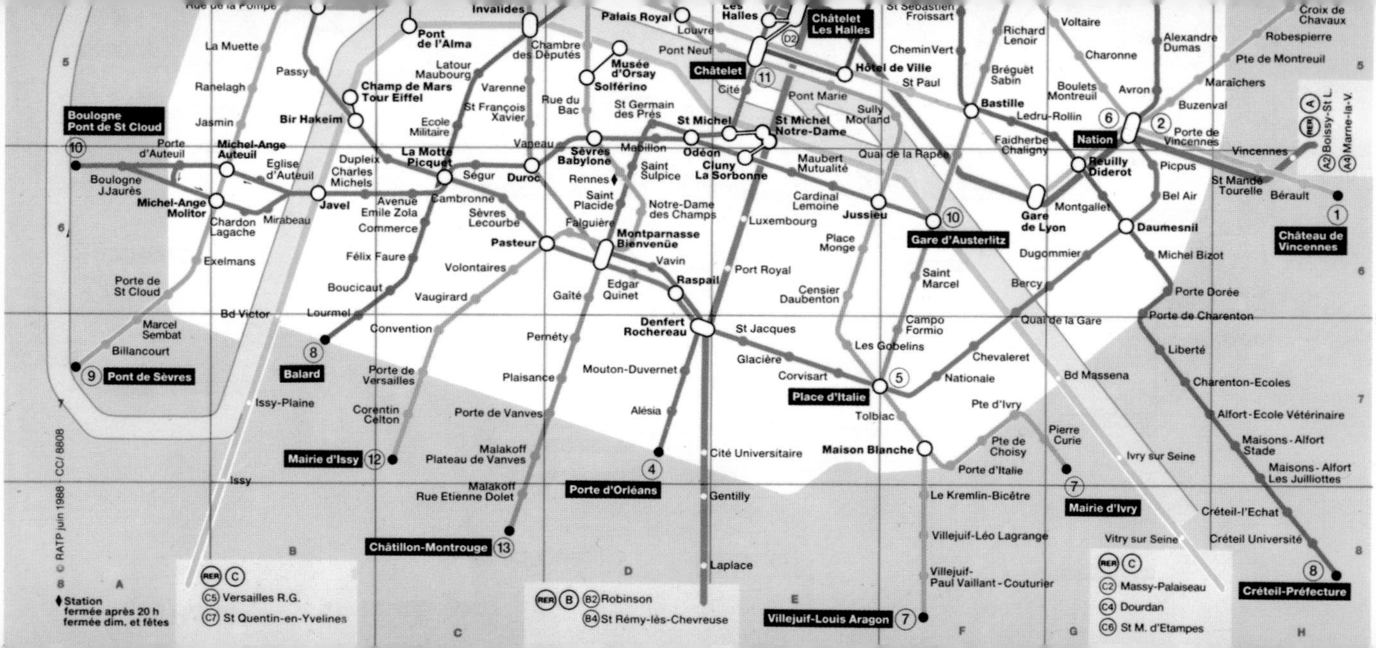

Boulogne Pont de St Cloud
Boulogne J.Jaurès
Porte d'Auteuil
Michel-Ange Auteuil
Michel-Ange Molitor
Chardon Lagache
Mirabeau
Eglise d'Auteuil
Javel
Exelmans
Porte de St Cloud
Marcel Sembat
Billancourt
Pont de Sèvres
Jasmin
Ranelagh
La Muette
Rue de la Pompe
Passy
Bir Hakeim
Champ de Mars Tour Eiffel
Pont de l'Alma
Invalides
Dupleix
Charles Michels
Avenue Emile Zola
Commerce
Félix Faure
Boucicaut
Lourmel
Balard
Bd Victor
Issy-Plaine
Issy
La Motte Picquet
Ecole Militaire
Latour Maubourg
Varenne
St François Xavier
Ségur
Cambronne
Sèvres Lecourbe
Pasteur
Volontaires
Vaugirard
Convention
Porte de Versailles
Corentin Celton
Mairie d'Issy
Chambre des Députés
Rue du Bac
Vaneau
Duroc
Sèvres Babylone
Rennes
Saint Placide
Falguière
Montparnasse Bienvenüe
Gaîté
Edgar Quinet
Vavin
Raspail
Pernéty
Plaisance
Porte de Vanves
Malakoff Plateau de Vanves
Malakoff Rue Etienne Dolet
Châtillon-Montrouge
Musée d'Orsay
Solférino
Palais Royal
Louvre
Pont Neuf
St Germain des Prés
Mabillon
Saint Sulpice
Notre-Dame des Champs
Odéon
St Michel
Cluny La Sorbonne
St Michel Notre-Dame
Les Halles
Châtelet Les Halles
Châtelet
Cité
Hôtel de Ville
Pont Marie
Sully Morland
Maubert Mutualité
Cardinal Lemoine
Luxembourg
Port Royal
Denfert Rochereau
Mouton-Duvernet
Alésia
Porte d'Orléans
Cité Universitaire
Gentilly
Laplace
St Jacques
Glacière
Corvisart
Place d'Italie
Tolbiac
Maison Blanche
Le Kremlin-Bicêtre
Villejuif-Léo Lagrange
Villejuif-Paul Vaillant-Couturier
Villejuif-Louis Aragon
Jussieu
Place Monge
Censier Daubenton
Les Gobelins
Campo Formio
Saint Marcel
Gare d'Austerlitz
Quai de la Rapée
St Sébastien Froissart
Chemin Vert
St Paul
Bastille
Richard Lenoir
Bréguet Sabin
Ledru-Rollin
Faidherbe Chaligny
Reuilly Diderot
Gare de Lyon
Montgallet
Dugommier
Bercy
Quai de la Gare
Chevaleret
Nationale
Pte d'Ivry
Pte de Choisy
Porte d'Italie
Pierre Curie
Mairie d'Ivry
Bd Massena
Ivry sur Seine
Vitry sur Seine
Voltaire
Charonne
Boulets Montreuil
Nation
Avron
Alexandre Dumas
Buzenval
Maraîchers
Pte de Montreuil
Robespierre
Croix de Chavaux
Porte de Vincennes
Vincennes
St Mandé Tourelle
Bérault
Château de Vincennes
Picpus
Bel Air
Daumesnil
Michel Bizot
Porte Dorée
Porte de Charenton
Liberté
Charenton-Ecoles
Alfort-Ecole Vétérinaire
Maisons-Alfort Stade
Maisons-Alfort Les Juilliottes
Créteil-l'Echat
Créteil Université
Créteil-Préfecture
RER A
A2 Boissy-St L.
A4 Marne-la-V.
D2
RER C
C2 Massy-Palaiseau
C4 Dourdan
C6 St M. d'Etampes
RER B
B2 Robinson
B4 St Rémy-lès-Chevreuse
C5 Versailles R.G.
C7 St Quentin-en-Yvelines
♦ Station fermée après 20 h fermée dim. et fêtes
© RATP juin 1988 CC/ 8808

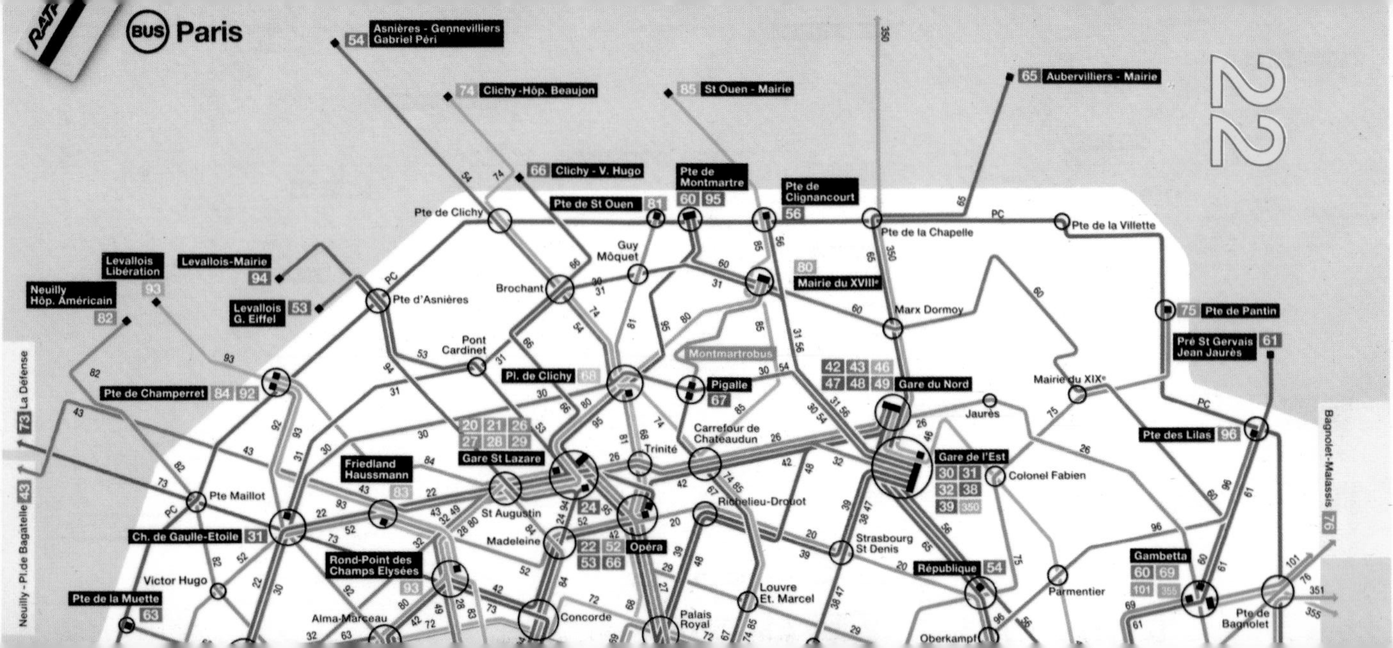

Paris
22
54 Asnières - Gennevilliers Gabriel Péri
74 Clichy-Hôp. Beaujon
85 St Ouen - Mairie
65 Aubervilliers - Mairie
66 Clichy - V. Hugo
Pte de St Ouen 81
Pte de Montmartre 60 95
Pte de Clignancourt 56
Pte de Clichy
Pte de la Chapelle
Pte de la Villette
Levallois Libération 93
Levallois-Mairie 94
Neuilly Hôp. Américain 82
Levallois G. Eiffel 53
Pte d'Asnières
Brochant
Guy Môquet
Mairie du XVIIIe 80
Marx Dormoy
75 Pte de Pantin
Pré St Gervais Jean Jaurès 61
Pont Cardinet
Pl. de Clichy 68
Montmartrobus
Pigalle 67
42 43 46 47 48 49 Gare du Nord
Mairie du XIXe
Jaurès
Pte de Champerret 84 92
73 La Défense
43 Neuilly - Pl.de Bagatelle
20 21 26 27 28 29 Gare St Lazare
Carrefour de Chateaudun
Trinité
Gare de l'Est 30 31 32 38 39 350
Colonel Fabien
Pte des Lilas 96
Friedland Haussmann 83
Pte Maillot
St Augustin
Richelieu-Drouot
24 94 95
22 52 53 66 Opéra
Madeleine
Ch. de Gaulle-Etoile 31
Strasbourg St Denis
République 54
Gambetta 60 69 101 355
Bagnolet-Malassis 76
Rond-Point des Champs Elysées 93
Victor Hugo
Pte de la Muette 63
Alma-Marceau
Concorde
Palais Royal
Louvre Et. Marcel
Parmentier
Oberkampf
Pte de Bagnolet
PC